D1736803

PATROL RESPONSE TO
CONTEMPORARY PROBLEMS

The National Tactical Officers Association

PATROL RESPONSE TO CONTEMPORARY PROBLEMS

Enhancing Performance of First Responders Through Knowledge and Experience

Edited by

CAPTAIN JOHN A. KOLMAN (Ret.), B.S., M.A.

Los Angeles County Sheriff's Department

With a Foreword by

Vice Admiral Richard H. Carmona, M.D.

United States Surgeon General

CHARLES C THOMAS • PUBLISHER, LTD.
Springfield • Illinois • U.S.A.

Published and Distributed Throughout the World by

CHARLES C THOMAS • PUBLISHER, LTD.
2600 South First Street
Springfield, Illinois 62704

© 2006 by CHARLES C THOMAS • PUBLISHER, LTD.

ISBN 0-398-07656-1   (hard)
ISBN 0-398-07657-X (paper)

Library of Congress Catalog Card Number: 2006040368

With THOMAS BOOKS *careful attention is given to all details of manufacturing
and design. It is the Publisher's desire to present books that are satisfactory as to their
physical qualities and artistic possibilities and appropriate for their particular use.*
THOMAS BOOKS *will be true to those laws of quality that assure a good name
and good will.*

Printed in the United States of America
MM-R-3

Library of Congress Cataloging-in-Publication Data

Patrol response to contemporary problems : enhancing performance of first
    responders through knowledge and experience / edited by John A.
    Kolman ; with foreword by Richard H. Camona.
        p. cm.
    At head of title: The National Tactical Officers Association.
    Includes bibliographical references.
    ISBN 0-398-07656-1 – ISBN 0-398-07657-X (pbk.)
    1. Police training–United States. 2. Police patrol–United States.
I. Kolman, John A. II. National Tactical Officers Association.

HV8142.P39 2006
363.2'32–dc22

                                                                    2006040368

This book is dedicated to the patrol officer,
whose daily efforts all too often go unrecognized.

FOREWORD

The role of the police officer continues to expand and evolve as we enter the new millennium. Historically, police officers by their mere presence usually deter crime and ensure community peace and tranquility. However, police officers today are tasked with an extraordinary and diverse set of challenges in the field requiring a variety of core competencies. During a particular shift, a patrol officer may be called upon to respond to a crime in progress, keep the peace, console a person after loss or accident, provide first aid, coordinate a SWAT response, arbitrate a domestic dispute, investigate a crime or respond to a terrorist event.

To successfully accomplish their daily missions, not only do police officers need to be technically proficient and physically fit, they also need to have an unusually broad base of knowledge in a wide variety of subjects–from law to first aid and tactics. Patrol officers are still our first line of prevention and response. Today, their jobs are unprecedented in the degree of diversity and knowledge they must possess in order to safely and professionally serve the American public on a daily basis. In short, today's patrol officer must be all things to all people. The job has immense responsibilities, and at times, the standard for our officers seems to be perfection. This is due to the fact that there are many who would *retrospectively* evaluate our officers' actions when they already know the outcome and have the benefit of all available information. The officer, however, at times has a fraction of a second to *prospectively* make a life-and-death decision with limited or incomplete information related to a given situation. Continuous training and refinement of knowledge, tactics and techniques is therefore absolutely essential for the officer to stay contemporary in thought, knowledge and action.

Each chapter in this textbook addresses important diverse and evolving skill sets that the patrol officer must possess in order to protect the public, reduce risk and maximize success during every encounter. Of particular interest are some of the new and evolving threats and responses to critical incidents that once again have broadened the scope of responsibility of the patrol officer. New threats, such as "mobile shooters" in a large geographic area and terrorists acts utilizing weapons of mass destruction, call for immediate action drills and unique patrol officer responses that only recently have become part of police academy and in-service training.

Policing is an outstanding career that requires a life-long commitment to learning and a willingness to always challenge the norm in favor of evolving and proven new tactics and techniques. The public must never forget that our police officers are simply well-trained fellow citizens with extraordinary responsibilities that they often carry out with the utmost dignity and professionalism, albeit anonymously. Let us never take for granted these everyday heroes who are willing to put themselves between good and evil, those who run toward the threat while others flee, those who sacrifice so others may live and those, the chosen few we call police officers, who exemplify service before self.

Deputy Sheriff Richard Carmona, M.D.
Pima County Sheriff's Department, Tucson, Arizona
SWAT Team Leader
(Deputy Carmona is now on active duty as Vice Admiral Carmona, the United States Surgeon General.)

PREFACE

The importance of the patrol function in preserving the peace, enforcing the law and protecting life and property is unquestioned. While all members of a law enforcement agency play an important role in fulfilling these principal responsibilities, patrol officers, as first responders, are at the forefront of attaining law enforcement objectives. However, the events of September 11, 2001, prompted law enforcement to assume additional responsibilities in their efforts to protect the members of their communities. Along with these increased responsibilities came a corresponding need for enhanced training, especially of first responders, who for the most part are patrol personnel.

Unfortunately, because of budgetary constraints, most law enforcement administrators have difficulty maintaining current training levels, let alone implementing post-9/11 training requirements. Further compounding the problem is the fact that many jurisdictions' patrol officers are not only the first to respond to an incident, they are the only officers to respond. If assistance is available at all, it may be several hours away. Aside from mandatory entry-level training, the only training received by many of these officers is on-the-job training or learning by trial and error, which can be hazardous to officers and members of the community alike. The dilemma then is how are law enforcement administrators to provide necessary and/or desirable training to their personnel if they are financially constrained?

This issue was addressed at length by the Board of Directors of the National Tactical Officers Association—one of the premier providers of law enforcement training in the United States. The board realized that an administrator's options under these circumstances may be limited to intra-agency training using in-house instructors, briefing training, etc. They also recognized that individual officers have a responsibility to enhance and maintain their knowledge, skills and abilities, regardless of their agency's ability or inability to conduct a higher level of training. Ultimately, the board decided to solicit the aid of subject-matter experts from throughout the United States to contribute to a book on contemporary topics relevant to patrol personnel. They reasoned this approach would enable both experienced and less-experienced officers to benefit from the knowledge and experience of a wide variety of subject-matter experts, while also supplementing existing agency training. Their efforts resulted in a compilation of writings directed specifically at furthering the education of patrol officers. The National Tactical Officers Association, as well as the seventeen subject-matter experts who participated in this project, are hopeful this publication will prove beneficial to those who strive to enhance their performance through knowledge and experience.

J.A.K.

ACKNOWLEDGMENTS

Preparation of this book required the efforts of many dedicated people, all of whom are worthy of recognition:

- The authors of individual chapters, who shared their experiences and expertise for the sole purpose of assisting patrol officers;
- Mary Heins, who coordinated the project and assembled manuscripts in preparation for editing;
- Janice Kolman, who was responsible for data entry of all manuscripts;
- Laurie Dau, who was instrumental in designing the cover and preparing photographs and diagrams for proper placement within the text;
- and finally the Board of Directors of the National Tactical Officers Association, without whose foresight, dedication and support this book would not have been possible:

John Gnagey, Executive Director
Brock Simon, Chairman of the Board   Phil Hansen
Bob Chabali   John Kolman, Emeritus
Keith Frakes   Ron McCarthy
Mike Foreman   Joe Martel
Bud Graves   Steve Smith
Gary Hanley   Jim Torkar

EDITOR'S NOTE

In order to avoid the distracting, repetitive use of non-specific-gender pronouns ("he/she," "him/her," "his/hers"), where it is not possible to restructure a sentence, the plural form ("they," "their," "them") will be used to refer to singular antecedents (pronouns).

Examples

Restructuring

"No officer shall use more force than *he/she* reasonably believes necessary."

"No more force than an officer reasonably believes necessary shall be used."

Plural Pronouns

"Each member will be provided with a copy, which *he/she* is expected to maintain in good order."

"Each member will be provided with a copy, which *they* are expected to maintain in good order."

To avoid sexist implications, all chapters have been edited using this widely accepted method.

Photos

All photos have been provided by the authors.

DISCLAIMER

Neither the authors, the publisher, the National Tactical Officers Association or its Board of Directors assume liability or responsibility in any manner whatsoever for any loss, damage, deaths or injuries which may occur as a result of following the information contained in this book.

CONTENTS

PATROL RESPONSE TO CONTEMPORARY PROBLEMS

Part 1

PREPARATION AND CONDITIONING

GEORGE W. RYAN

George W. Ryan has been a police officer for the Los Angeles Police Department since 1991. In that time, he has worked a variety of specialized units, including the Special Problems Unit, CRASH (gang suppression), undercover narcotics and Metropolitan Division. Since January of 1998, George has been assigned to LAPD's prestigious Special Weapons and Tactics (SWAT) team. There, he is responsible for serving high-risk arrest and search warrants, providing security and protection for V.I.P.'s visiting Los Angeles (i.e., the President of the United States, foreign heads of state, etc.), responding to terrorist activity, hostage crises, armed and dangerous barricaded suspect situations and training Department personnel.

George is also an unarmed self-defense expert and serves as an instructor for the SWAT team's "Arrest and Control" (self-defense) cadre. He holds a second-degree black belt in Tae Kwon Do and has over twenty years of experience training and teaching in the martial arts. George is a former winner of nationally and regionally rated karate tournaments and a former columnist for *Karate Illustrated* magazine. He continues to be a contributing editor for martial arts publications. George is also the advisor for the Defensive Tactics section of the National Tactical Officers Association (NTOA). In addition, he serves on the firearms cadre of the SWAT team and is a firearms and tactics instructor for the NTOA.

George currently resides with his wife and two daughters outside of Los Angeles. He would like to acknowledge his wife, Melissa, for her assistance in preparing the manuscript for this chapter and also Chapter 13, "Immediate Action/Rapid Deployment."

Chapter 1

THE INDOMITABLE MINDSET: WINNING IS EVERYTHING IN A LETHAL ENCOUNTER

GEORGE W. RYAN

INTRODUCTION

The subject of "The Will to Survive," taught in police academies around the world, is one that is taken quite seriously by all police recruits. By the time they hit the streets, recruits are raring to go—ready to fight crime and put society's worst offerings in prison. It is out on these streets, in the commission of these duties, that we law enforcement officers can expect the possibility of being involved in a struggle with a suspect or suspects for our very survival. Yet, throughout our careers, we can expect little to no in-service reinforcement training in the area of "The Will to Survive." Instead, we can expect community relations, cultural diversity and verbal judo training to frequently come our way. This human relations training is beneficial and can make us even more effective in the performance of our duties. But, keeping things in perspective, this type of training does not give us an edge during a life-and-death fight with a suspect.

To begin, it is essential to recognize that at any time and place, law enforcement officers can become involved in a situation wherein a suspect may try to cause them egregious injury or even death. This is an inescapable truth despite the fact that, statistically speaking, the odds are low that a police officer working in the United States will sometime have to fight for their life. This is also true despite the fact that these statistics are borne out by our own experiences. Nationally, law enforcement officers have written countless traffic tickets, made innumerable arrests and handled infinite numbers of radio calls with a relatively low percentage of those incidents turning into a violent confrontation. Though the numbers may be proportionally low and studies show that more harm befalls taxicab drivers and convenience store workers as a group than police officers, law enforcement personnel always face the possibility of being forced into a lethal encounter. Police work is an inherently dangerous job. Whether it is performed in the smallest of towns or the largest of cities, far too many officers have become statistics. We must also remember that statistics do not predict which officer will be involved in a fight for their life or in which circumstances this may occur.

Keeping this in mind, it is imperative that all police officers steer well clear of the complacency trap so they will avoid feeling that "IT" cannot happen to them. This may not be so easy, because we can go through our law enforcement routines day-by-day and even year-by-year without experiencing any real harm. It then becomes difficult for some officers to think that "IT" could really happen. But the potential is there. Unfortunately, any law enforcement officer who has become complacent and is then involved in a violent encounter may experience the horror of, "I can't believe this is happening!" The initial shock of being engaged in a life-or-death struggle can be paralyzing, thereby leaving the officer at the mercy of their attacker. Therefore, police agencies are doing their officers a major disservice by not providing periodic, in-service training that reminds them of these risks and provides them with strategies for cultivating not just the will to survive, but the will to prevail, *to win*, in any lethal encounter. By this, I mean that you should not just accept survival as your goal. You should not let a violent suspect injure you or anyone else in any way, and, if they do, you must fight back with the utmost conviction in order to minimize that harm. So, ultimately it becomes our individual responsibility as law enforcement officers to develop and maintain our own thorough survival training programs. If we do not, we are negligent in our duty to ourselves, our partners, families, friends and communities.

On our own, we can read the various police tactical texts that have covered the subject of "The Will to Survive." These texts, in one way or another, all encourage their readers to think of themselves involved in some type of lethal encounter and to think of themselves fighting back against the odds and surviving. This certainly is not bad advice and it also helps condition one's mind for a potential lethal encounter. But, it is my contention that this is only a start–you have to do more if you want to *win*. As law enforcement officers, we should never be content with just surviving, we must be determined to *win*.

The question now is how to develop a strategy for adopting this attitude and bringing it to fruition. How can we train ourselves to win in a life-or-death struggle? It is essential to develop the highest level of proficiency possible in proper tactics, firearms, arrest and control techniques and physical fitness. But these alone may not be enough for an officer to win in a potentially fatal battle. Instead, what keeps officers alive and ultimately allows them to win in lethal encounters is what I call, *"The Indomitable Mindset."* Simply put, this is the way a law enforcement officer can adopt the mental attitude that they may become involved in a struggle to survive and, if they do, they will win. More specifically, The Indomitable Mindset may be defined as follows:

The Indomitable Mindset is an offensive-based state of mind that is adopted and then cultivated through a positive mental attitude, visualization and intense physical and professional training.

When put into practice, this mindset endows law enforcement officers with strong willpower and an ability to harness fear in the most dire of circumstances. This mindset also promotes and seeks positive resolutions in present or pending situations, and even seeks to avert danger through readiness and a high level of awareness.

Officers who not only want to succeed at their jobs, but also want to win when they are forced to defend their lives, can train in fostering this mindset and apply it to their everyday duties. Think about it. Officers are patrolling the streets day and night, answering emergency calls for service and coming in contact with some of society's worst offenders. It is imperative that officers who haven't adopted this mindset begin, and officers who've forgotten about it, now remember. You do not have any other option, since you must see it as your duty to *win* any lethal encounter. Therefore, the information that follows is a discussion about training to achieve, develop and maintain *"The Indomitable Mindset."*

Positive Mental Attitude

"Ability is what you're capable of doing, motivation determines what you do, and attitude determines how well you do it."
Lou Holtz

To a large degree, police work is very often a reactive function. We respond when someone calls us for assistance and take action when we witness a crime in progress. Waiting for something to go wrong can foster a negative mindset in any individual. Instead, I contend that the work of the law enforcement officer should be more proactive than reactive. Law enforcement officers should be looking for criminal activity instead of only waiting for it to happen. This keeps your skills sharp and enables you to help the community before the worst can happen. Therefore, it is a much more positive approach to your law enforcement duties. Additionally, officers should view their work as do the top professionals in any field–constantly seeking to exercise and enhance their skills.

In fact, police officers should be even more than proactive–they should work from an offensive-based state of mind. I, of course, do not mean that you should be aggressive. By offensive I mean that you should be decisive, assertive and poised in both your professional duties and in your training regimen. This professional attitude gives law enforcement personnel a much-needed edge when they deal with criminal activity, or even a potentially lethal encounter, because they are prepared, confident in their abilities and certain in their choices.

For instance, this offensive mindset permitted then-Rookie Officer Leeanne Baker of the Chatham, Massachusetts, Police Department to successfully resolve an "armed intruder" call in 1999. While working alone at approximately 3 a.m., Officer Baker received an emergency radio call from a female victim who reported that shots had been fired when her armed ex-boyfriend broke into her residence. Officer Baker raced to the residence and found a seven-year-old girl with blood on her clothing standing outside the house. The little girl told Officer Baker that her "Mom" was inside and hurt. Fearing for the woman's safety, Officer Baker drew her firearm and tactically entered the residence. Immediately upon entry she was confronted with the wounded victim and her current boyfriend, who had not yet been shot. But the two were being forced to stand together in the living room while being detained by the armed suspect. Officer Baker separated the victims from the suspect and took him into custody without incident. This action prevented additional shots from being fired at the victims and likely saved their lives.

In an interview with me, Officer Baker cited her confidence in her tactics and firearms skills as the reason she was able to take immediate and decisive action in this situation. In other words, she was operating from an offensive-based state of mind. With such confidence, all police officers can cultivate what I call a Positive Mental Attitude (PMA). Working from this positive mindset can counteract the negativity that may be associated with doing police work in a purely reactive mode. Furthermore, this PMA can propel you on your journey toward achieving an indomitable mindset, because you will approach all aspects of your law enforcement career in a positive light. You will see yourself as being able to "win" in all areas of your work and training.

Officer Baker received the Medal of Valor because her decisive actions saved the lives of two people being held at gunpoint by an armed intruder.

So, right now, solidify in your mind that any situation you encounter during the course of your law enforcement duties–whether it's a domestic dispute, traffic stop, SWAT mission, whatever–you will win! Not only is it your right to win, it is also your duty, because it is your partner's, department's, friends' and loved ones' right as well. Think about this for a moment: what would your mindset be if you were fighting on your back, in some urine-saturated alley, struggling over possession of your gun with some strung-out ex-con? Your immediate and automatic response to this question should be, "I would win this battle." Furthermore, you also should be thinking that you would do whatever it takes to achieve this goal. Hopefully, just envisioning this brief scenario is also prompting you to consider the consequences of losing such a battle. If you lose, there are no second-place awards!

Now, let's take a deeper look at this scenario. At some point during this struggle, depending upon your level of physical conditioning, your body may begin screaming with exhaustion. Add to this fatigue that things may not be going well for you in the fight, and you can find that negative emotions will fill your head. You may experience feelings of helplessness and pain while an enormous amount of adrenaline floods your system. At this point, you must remember that the moment you feel like you're not going to win, you won't. If you dare to feel like giving up, you will. So, no matter how bad the situation seems, you must stay positive and tell yourself that you will prevail. *(Later in this chapter, I'll discuss how to deal with such negative emotions, pain, and the effects of adrenaline.)* Instead, tell yourself that you are going to beat this "SOB" no matter what. More importantly, do so with absolute conviction. This positive attitude will kick-start your indomitable mindset and help propel you toward victory. So, think of positive mental attitude as the spark inside you waiting to ignite your will to **win**.

Though this may sound simplistic, it is essential to note two important facts: (1) PMA is just one of the interconnected factors that allow you to develop your overall indomitable mindset, and (2) real-life experience is proof of the power of PMA. Bob Allen, who was a police officer for 32 ¹/₂ years with the Boston Police Department, can attest to the incredible difference made by having a positive mental attitude. Allen is a veteran of having to defend himself in several gun battles in which he has come out on top. He mostly credits his mental attitude and training for the success he's experienced when forced to defend his life against an armed attacker.

In an interview with me, Allen explained that his attitude while working patrol was, "I'm the one that has to go home to my family at the end of the night." This attitude allowed Allen to have a long and successful career in some of the highest crime areas Boston has to offer. He further shared what he felt inside when he realized that an encounter with an armed suspect had devolved to the point where the use of his firearm was his only option. He explained that once he understood he was involved in a fight for his life, "a calming feeling came over me, I didn't feel panicked. I just did what I was trained to do." Allen went on to elaborate that confidence in his skills and his past training and experiences allowed him to maintain the mental attitude that saw him through the toughest of experiences. Mostly, this positive mental attitude enabled him to stay calm and focused. As a consequence, Allen noted that when his encounters with an armed suspect necessitated the use of firearms, his attackers

Officer Bob Allen credits his mental attitude and training for the success he's experienced when forced to defend his life against an armed attacker.

appeared more like a blank target to him. This was not a surprise to Allen due to the fact that his police academy instructors told him this could happen. So, for Officer Allen, faith in his training, experience and mindset translated into having the proper attitude for winning a gun battle.

Visualization

"Whatever the mind of man can conceive he can achieve."
Geoff Thompson

For years, Olympians and elite athletes who have wanted to improve their athletic performances, as well as enhance their level of readiness for competition, have used visualization techniques. In their mind's eye they see themselves, in meticulous detail, overcoming adverse circumstances and performing to the best of their abilities. These athletes also will, over and over, envision imaginary performances in which their skills are perfect and they triumph.

Fortunately, these techniques are not the exclusive domain of athletes, nor does their basic implementation require any special knowledge or skills. In fact, many law enforcement officers already make a point of practicing some degree of visualization as a means of improving their work performance. Many officers have used a modified form of this mental exercise countless times without ever realizing they were utilizing visualization skills. For instance, when responding to a "crime in progress" radio call, partners will discuss how they're going to handle the pending situation. They'll discuss possible scenarios and *"what ifs"* en route to the crime location. This type of discussion prompts the officers to visualize their responses to a variety of circumstances they may encounter when they arrive at the scene. For example, officers will ask themselves and their partners about options and responses to such possibilities as, "What if the suspect runs?" or, "What if there is a get-away car waiting for the suspect?" While at the scene, officers will then be armed with their mentally rehearsed game plan. This can significantly reduce lag time and hesitation, thereby permitting the officers to take immediate action if it is warranted.

Sergeant Glenn Dietrich, an 21-year veteran of the Clarkstown, New York, Police Department and a 15-year member of their tactical team (SERT), says this about visualization:

> I don't believe there is a single police officer in this country that has not thought about a potential lethal encounter numerous times during their

"Visualization is a powerful training tool, so long as you are visualizing yourself doing the proper tactics." Sergeant Glenn Dietrich.

career. Whether you are a rookie officer or a seasoned veteran, these thoughts cross your mind as you are responding to a specific type of scenario, and one that is usually high-risk in nature. Just thinking about a lethal encounter, no matter what the scenario is, prepares you for that incident. Visualization is a powerful training tool, so long as you are visualizing yourself doing the proper tactics. Many times I have found myself visualizing a specific scenario on the way to a call, and playing that scenario over in my head many times before I arrive on scene. Whether the call is for a bank alarm, a domestic situation, an emotionally disturbed person, or a shooting, thinking about what you are going to have to possibly do puts you in the right frame of mind to handle the call safely and tactically correct.

This effective and necessary use of visualization can be augmented and made part of your overall indomitable mindset training program. Its importance cannot be underscored enough, since seconds count and split-second decisions can mean the difference between life and death for police officers involved in crisis situations. Whether you're involved in a high-speed vehicle pursuit, a building search or a pedestrian stop on a possible armed suspect, you have to make the right move the first time. Proper tactical training and real-world experience are the building blocks of the skills that law enforcement officers need to do their jobs safely. But, like elite athletes, you can use visualization to assist you in refining these skills. This is particularly beneficial, since most law enforcement officers are allowed only minimal dedicated training time to help them refine their professional techniques.

In fact, you can gain a tremendous boost in your mental and physical readiness by dedicating just ten minutes, several times a week, to the following visualization exercise. To begin, find a quiet place in your home where you can sit down and be free of any disturbances. Close your eyes, take several deep breaths and allow your body to relax into your sitting position. In your mind's eye, envision yourself working your designated assignment, whether it's on patrol, undercover narcotics, etc. Imagine the setting exactly the way it would look and sound. For example, hear the sounds of traffic, smell the aromas of the local deli and see people interacting with one another on the street. The more of your senses you involve in your visualization practice, the more realistic and effective your mental exercise will be. Once the scene is set in detail, visualize a scenario which will require you to use particular skills or tactics to successfully resolve the incident. Whether it's a vehicle pursuit, SWAT mission, felony vehicle stop or an immediate action/rapid deployment scenario, picture the performance that you want to achieve. Visualize every action and reaction, moment by moment, from the beginning of the event through its conclusion. During the scenario, you should also see yourself making positive decisions, taking action and, finally, successfully resolving the incident. Depending on the scenario, you can change that same incident to unfold several different ways in which you ultimately make the right decisions for coming out on top.

Such a visualization exercise is not designed to replace your training. Instead, it is meant to assist you by improving your level of readiness in a stressful situation. Since visualization allows you to play a scenario over and over in your mind's eye while you use the proper tactics and achieve the desired resolution, its repetition will help you perfect your techniques. These techniques will also help sharpen your responses in the event that you have to take action. Numerous studies have confirmed that athletes who have used visualization techniques have significantly improved their athletic performances. Furthermore, psychologists have concluded that visualization works because a person's subconscious mind doesn't distinguish between what they have imagined and what they have actually experienced. Therefore, when law enforcement officers visualize their winning performances, they're preparing themselves for success in mind and body.

Physical Training

"A pint of sweat will save a gallon of blood."
General George S. Patton

Physical training, such as weight training and running, is a great way to stay in shape. But more importantly, it is the means by which law enforcement officers may gain the necessary strength and stamina needed to meet both the physical and mental demands of the job. Believe it or not, physical

training not only helps build muscle, it also helps build the confidence necessary to achieve an "indomitable mindset" in officers who consistently task their bodies and minds with its demands. Officers who push their bodies past their physical limits are conditioning themselves physically as well as mentally to go the extra mile–not just in the gym, but out on the streets as well.

Rigorous physical training also helps to feed one's willpower, thereby preparing a person for success in a potential lethal encounter. That is why it is no secret that elite military units, such as the Navy SEALs, Delta Force, and the top domestic SWAT teams place such a high emphasis on physical fitness standards. Members of these units recognize that a high level of physical fitness helps their performance in both training and real-life missions. They understand that by pushing their bodies, they also are exercising their positive mental attitude and willpower. In this way, strength and endurance training helps build the mental toughness and stamina that is paramount to winning in any type of situation. Consequently, no matter their assignment, law enforcement officers need to have confidence in their physical condition if they are going to achieve the mental condition that can see them through all aspects of their work. So, when officers are called upon to use physical force in order to take suspects into custody or, even worse, to defend their own lives against attacks by those suspects, they will be both physically and mentally ready.

For these reasons, police officer Mike Odle is a staunch advocate of rigorous physical training for law enforcement officers. He is a 26-year veteran of the Los Angeles Police Department and has been assigned to the Department's Special Weapons and Tactics (SWAT) team for over 20 years. Officer Odle believes that physical exercises like weight training, running and calisthenics are all essential elements in the overall training of police officers. It is his conviction that physical fitness helps law enforcement officers maintain mental focus during crisis situations, thereby saving lives. Consequently, Officer Odle wrote the following statement regarding physical fitness training for law enforcement officers:

"As a SWAT officer, physically and psychologically demanding activities have been part

"Physical and mental fitness requires conditioning. Conditioning takes time. There is no 'finish line' with fitness. It is a way of life, and life goes beyond our law enforcement careers." Officer Mike Odle.

unusual to wear that equipment for hours on end, therefore, it is imperative that the focus be directed to the crisis at hand and **not** how tired you are. By maintaining proper focus, officers are able to maximize the quality of their end product.

"Physical and mental fitness requires conditioning. Conditioning takes time. There is no 'finish line' with fitness. It is a way of life, and life goes beyond our law enforcement careers. You owe it to yourself and your loved ones to maintain fitness so you can enjoy years of well-deserved retirement benefits. Furthermore, you cannot rely on youth or prior conditioning long since gone to save your life in a potentially lethal confrontation.

"For example, as a young police officer, I worked patrol in the south central area of Los Angeles in the early 1980s. During that time, I was involved in an incident where I apprehended a fleeing burglary suspect. After I caught the suspect, we hit the ground and the fight was on. That was the first occasion that I actually experienced an altercation that elevated itself to a 'fight-for-my-life' scenario. The suspect was recently paroled from prison and outweighed my meager frame by 20 pounds. As we rolled around on the ground, he tried numerous times to remove my sidearm from its holster. I remember thinking that I was starting to tire and tire quickly. Fortunately, I was able to render the suspect unconscious and bring his resistance to an end.

"As I lay on my back, with the suspect on top of me, I did what I could to catch my breath. I certainly was not going to let him go. Shortly thereafter, a patrol sergeant arrived on scene and assisted with handcuffing the suspect. While escorting the suspect to my patrol car, I noticed that both he and I were shaking. Without warning, the suspect vomited and dropped down to a knee. It was then that I realized how 'big' this guy was, and at that moment I committed myself to becoming stronger and more physically fit. As a result of that commitment, I am stronger and more physically fit now than at age twenty-five. My

of my duties. In order to cope with those duties, I have maintained a consistent and disciplined physical fitness regimen. That regimen consists of weight training, calisthenics and cardio conditioning 4–5 times per week, respectively. I run 15–20 miles per week for my cardiovascular conditioning, which also provides me the endurance to maintain lengthy workouts in the gym.

"Weight training produces the leg, back and abdomen strength that assists with the ability to run sprints or long distance. Strength is required to don the 40–50 pounds of gear that a SWAT officer must wear to perform duties in high-risk environments. It is not

Mike Odle on the obstacle course at a national SWAT competition.

commitment to fitness continues to this day.

"In summary, physical and mental fitness has to be an integral part of every law enforcement officer's life. Fitness will allow officers to perform their duties by minimizing the occurrence of physical altercations, assisting with the swift resolution of unavoidable altercations, maximizing quality work product and improving the overall quality of life."

So, if you're a law enforcement officer who is not currently on a physical training program, consider beginning one after you consult with a licensed medical doctor and receive a physical checkup. As is evidenced by the personal experiences of police officers such as Mike Odle, those officers who have the confidence that they've pushed their bodies and

minds in physical training also are conditioned to go the distance in all aspects of their jobs. Additionally, physical training not only improves a person's physical and mental condition, it also helps reduce the negative effects of stress, which is so prevalent and detrimental in the law enforcement profession. Furthermore, to build up and maintain a physical fitness regimen, you must pay careful attention to your diet and allow yourself adequate amounts of rest. As both of these are often difficult to achieve in police work, dedication to physical training can provide the impetus for improving your overall health.

Therefore, consider starting off with a doctor-approved training program that consists of some light to moderate levels of weight training, calisthenics, and cardiovascular conditioning. Most importantly, listen to your body and then gradually increase the intensity of your exercises every couple of weeks or when you deem it fit. If you are already working out, take careful stock of your physical fitness program and decide if it is permitting you to maximize your potential. Also, make an honest evaluation of your dedication to that physical training program. Consider trying new exercises or new routines, always with the permission of a licensed physician, if you find your workout practice lacking in any area. Then, as you demand more of your body, and therefore of your physical and mental stamina, remind yourself that you're training to achieve an "indomitable" mindset.

Professional Training

"Victorious warriors win first and then go to war, while defeated warriors go to war first and then seek to win."
Sun Tzu

For the law enforcement officer, professional training needs to be of the highest quality. To achieve this, training must be realistic, consistent, and effective. Furthermore, it must regularly cover the spectrum of skills necessary for officers to succeed in their jobs–tactics, firearms, defensive tactics, scenario-based training, etc. Such training is so essential to police work that law enforcement officers not provided training by their own departments must seek to properly train and educate themselves in the timeliest techniques. In addition, all officers must enhance any on-duty training provided them with professional training on their own time. For optimal performance at work, you should be devoting time to such off-duty training measures as dry practice, going to the firearms range and the study of proper tactics. As demanding as this may sound, the time and energy put into seeking out and participating in quality training can literally make the difference between life and death for a law enforcement officer who must combat a suspect. An integral part of possessing an indomitable mindset is having the confidence that you are proficient and confident in the proper tactics and techniques of the law enforcement community.

Time and time again, law enforcement officers discover that during a crisis situation they revert back to the way they have been trained. Therefore, it's imperative that officers are educated about proper tactics and have trained consistently and professionally in mastering these techniques. This consistency will condition officers to respond in "real-life" situations the way they have been taught to respond in training. So, it is absolutely imperative that any training an officer receives be of the highest caliber. As with so much in life, a quantity of superficial or ineffective training can never be a substitute for quality training. Today, there are plenty of training resources to draw from, such as books, magazines and videos. In addition, hands-on training provided by competent instructors can give officers the proper knowledge they need to not only succeed in their duties, but also to win. Yet, it cannot be emphasized enough that training provided by such resources be sound. The tactics taught must be proper; that is, they are sound, comprehensive, timely and, more importantly, effective. Training in tactics that are outdated or have the appearance of being "sexy," yet, when more closely examined, prove to be ineffectual or even downright dangerous, is simply a disaster waiting to happen.

To avert such disaster, seek out training as though your very life depended upon it—since it very well may. Remember first that, like any other business, there are plenty of tactical training companies and resources which teach tactics that are not up to standard because the training offered is unrealistic and ineffective. Instead, try to locate training

companies that only employ instructors with solid, verifiable backgrounds who have the operational experience that allows them to attest to the properness of the tactics they share. Also, demand of your training that it be reality based, hands on and, above all, safe. Perfect practice not only makes perfect, but, in the professional training of law enforcement officers, it can mean the difference between life and death.

This doesn't mean that you cannot enjoy your training, but do take it seriously and try to perfect your skills. Just perform to the best of your ability when it's your time to train. Furthermore, make careful, critical self-evaluation an integral part of your training process. Conduct intensive and honest debriefs of every real-life mission and training exercise in which you participate. Do so remembering that you are always training to win—to attain an indomitable mindset. So make certain that this attitude carries over and influences your performance during all aspects of the training process—from selecting proper training through participation in, and evaluation of, the training. Therefore, whether it's physical fitness, tactics or firearms training, train as though your life or your partner's life depends upon your performance.

LAPD SWAT team member Rick Massa understands the importance of such proper tactical and firearms training. He is a 33-year veteran of the Los Angeles Police Department and has served 23 of those years in SWAT. On February 28, 1997, Rick Massa was one of the officers involved in the infamous North Hollywood Bank Shootout. After that fierce and much-televised gun battle, he ultimately took the last suspect into custody, along with LAPD SWAT team members Donnie Anderson and Steve Gomez. Massa credits the proper tactical and firearms training he continuously receives in LAPD SWAT as the factor that enabled him and his partners to come out on top that day. In an interview with me, Massa explained that he and his partners reverted back to their training, and that their actions were the result of a properly conditioned response. Further reflecting on the incident, Massa added, "I never had a thought that we wouldn't make it through." Massa further noted that in training, "you're taught to always make it through, whether it's a stress course (timed firearms course/competi-

Officers Steve Gomez, Donnie Anderson, and Rick Massa are awarded the Los Angeles Police Department's "Medal of Valor" for their heroic efforts during the North Hollywood Bank shootout incident.

tion) or a PFQ (physical fitness qualification.)" Most importantly, he emphasized that, "In our business, you never stop and you never quit."

Furthermore, when discussing the North Hollywood incident, Massa is able to correlate his success in that gun battle with specific types of training he regularly receives as a LAPD SWAT team member. When interviewed, he recalled arriving on scene with Officers Anderson and Gomez intending to perform a citizen rescue because of the information they had received. But when they drove closer

and realized they were approaching the second heavily armed suspect from the bank robbery instead, their intentions had to change in an instant. Yet, despite the intensity of this entire situation, Massa recalled, "I was never stressed and we were doing what we were trained to do." He explained that Officer Anderson immediately turned the vehicle at an angle in order to give the officers cover to exit the vehicle. This also allowed the front passenger, Officer Gomez, to immediately engage the heavily armed suspect. As a consequence of Officer

Gomez's aggressive action, the suspect was forced away from their police vehicle. Massa stated that the vehicle ambush training he and his partners received, and also taught numerous times, was crucial in this vehicle deployment. As Massa elaborated, "Donnie (Officer Anderson) properly utilized their police vehicle as a tool that helped them in successfully engaging the suspect."

Proper firearms training also enabled Officers Massa, Anderson and Gomez to prevail on that day. Beyond the obvious success of their marksmanship skills and ability to perform under incredible pressure, training in clearing a weapon malfunction became integral to their success. During the gun battle, Officer Anderson experienced a malfunction with his M-16 rifle. He communicated his dilemma to Massa who immediately covered Anderson's position, just as in training. Then, also aided by training, Anderson quickly cleared his weapon malfunction and got back into the fight. Massa recalled that during both weapon malfunction training and

instances where officers experience a malfunction on the firearms range, he and his fellow officers are always taught to work through it! This advice and training aided Officers Massa, Anderson and Gomez to win that struggle for survival. Consequently, Massa concluded his interview by noting that there is nothing wrong with having a good time at training, "But," he added, "when it is your turn to step up to the line for firearms training, or if you're doing movement training, do it as though it's for real."

A Strong Will

"Strength does not come from physical capacity. It comes from an indomitable will."
Mahatma Gandhi

Traditionally, law enforcement officers are taught to remind themselves about the things in their lives that mean the most to them in order to enhance

Proper firearms training is a critical element of an officer's professional training regimen.

their willpower during trying circumstances. By recalling those things that are sacred to them, such as family members, loved ones, friends, etc., officers are motivated to fight that much harder if they become involved in a lethal encounter. Officers and other individuals caught in a struggle for survival often have reported that thoughts of loved ones drove them to fight back with absolute determination in order to live.

Yet, the will to survive cannot always be created or miraculously summoned during a life-and-death situation simply by conjuring up these important and affirming thoughts. In truth, we will never know the thoughts of those unfortunate officers who did not survive a lethal encounter. Instead, it is essential to recognize that a police officer's willpower also is grounded in their faith in past training, experience and self-confidence. More importantly, an individual's level of willpower stems from that person's psychological makeup. This is evident when a crisis situation absolutely shocks one officer but may seem very manageable to another.

Having chosen a law enforcement career, you probably already possess a strong will. But shock has a way of testing anyone's willpower, especially during an incident where you may have to fight for your life. Law enforcement officers have "frozen" during crisis situations because of circumstances they perceived to be overwhelming. So, it is crucial that you do not wait until the moment that you must summon all your willpower in order to survive to see if you truly possess enough will to make the difference. First, you must acknowledge and accept that the moment may come when you have no choice but to defend your life, the life of your partner or the life of an innocent person. Then, to help minimize the shock of dealing with such a possible lethal encounter, you must have the utmost confidence in your professional tactics and firearms skills, physical conditioning and mental attitude. In other words, training in the development and achievement of an indomitable mindset exercises and, therefore, strengthens an officer's willpower.

Specifically, there are three exercises whereby you can further utilize all the facets of your indomitable mindset training to assess, exercise and augment your own personal level of willpower. To help build or increase your willpower for any

potential lethal encounter, law enforcement officers can integrate these exercises into their training. Note that these drills are not designed to replace any part of your professional and physical training. Instead, I am offering them to you as examples of ways you can test and strengthen your willpower. In fact, you may find yourself developing exercises of your own that you find most beneficial. The important thing is that you think about and work on your will to survive. My suggestions are as follows:

Willpower Exercise #1: This first exercise is an act of mental conditioning. Simply tell yourself that "IT" will happen to you—you will have to combat a suspect or suspects in a life-and-death struggle. Seriously consider what this means, and, most importantly, genuinely accept the possibility. This may be something that you need to do only this once or it may be something you choose to do periodically. Whatever you choose, know that you have just taken a tremendous step toward minimizing the shock of being involved in a real-life lethal encounter. This mindset helps ensure that an officer won't be blindsided by the shock of, "I can't believe this is happening!" The paralysis caused by disbelief in a moment of crisis, even if just momentary, can cause an officer to hesitate before taking action. This lag time can prove very costly—even deadly. But officers who have already accepted that someone, someday, may try to gravely injure or even kill them will be able to say to themselves, "I knew this would happen and I'm ready!" if such a crisis arises. This attitude will certainly cut down on lag time and allow you to respond immediately, without being delayed by the paralyzing effects of denial and shock.

In doing this acceptance exercise, it is essential to note that I am not asking you to be paranoid. You're simply accepting the reality that in the law enforcement profession you can be called upon to defend your life or someone else's life at a moment's notice. Some may view this thought process as pessimistic, but think of your alternative. It's better to be prepared and never to have used your skills than to be unprepared and to have to learn this skill at the moment a suspect is trying to take your life.

Willpower Exercise #2: This second exercise asks you to enhance your visualization training so it includes a scenario in which you must utilize your willpower. To begin, find a quiet place where you won't be disturbed, then sit down and close your eyes. Relax your body by taking several deep breaths and settle yourself into a comfortable position. Now imagine responding to an emergency call or conducting a traffic stop. You can pick any type of scenario you like. Using your mind's eye, see your entire setting–notice the weather conditions, hear the different sounds emitting from your background, etc. The more of your senses you involve in your visualization practice, the more realistic your mental exercise will be. Next, imagine a dirty ex-con dressed in baggy clothing emerging unexpectedly from this scene, pouncing on you without notice and trying to take you out. Imagine him attacking you with a knife, a gun or with his hands and feet. Feel the tremendous impact of being stabbed, shot, or beaten. What are you thinking? What are you feeling? Experience the pain that would be associated with such a blow and know that pain, no matter how excruciating, is only temporary. Furthermore, understand that pain is not an indicator of how much you are injured. In fact, the pain of breaking your little finger can feel much more unbearable than that caused by more traumatic injuries. So tell yourself that it is just pain, push it aside and feel yourself becoming angry. Then tell yourself that it's your turn to take control. Remind yourself that no matter how bad things are, you can tap into your endless reserve of willpower, turn the tables, and fight on. Finally, envision yourself fighting back with absolute conviction–and winning.

This type of mental exercise is designed to help you cope with the shock that naturally accompanies being attacked and injured. Since you will already have dealt successfully and decisively with similar scenarios in your mind, you will be better able to work through shock and take action if you are ever forced to defend yourself in a lethal encounter. By practicing this form of visualization, you're armed with a game plan and the attitude that you will fight back until you win, no matter how dire the circumstances. While I don't recommend that you spend a lot of time envisioning suspects getting the drop on you, you must take it into consideration. I don't like the thought of such an act any more than you, but mental preparation for this worst-case scenario may

make all the difference in a real-life struggle for survival.

Now try to integrate this type of mental training into your weekly routine. It only takes a couple of minutes and the scenarios are only limited to your imagination. Also, be absolutely certain you are visualizing yourself employing the proper tactics and techniques–ones you have trained in and have confidence applying–as you successfully resolve the scenario. In this way, visualization, though it cannot and should not replace your tactical and physical training, can assist you in improving your level of readiness should you be forced to defend your life.

Willpower Exercise #3: This last exercise invites you to test and strengthen your willpower as you push yourself in your physical training. It can be conducted as you proceed through your workout or you can save it for the end of your physical training regimen. The exercise is applicable to both a weight-training workout and a session of cardiovascular exercise, especially running. Again, this exercise is my suggestion and it can be modified to suit your needs. You may even create a workout-willpower exercise of your own. The important thing is that you take some opportunity to strengthen your willpower, and a workout is the perfect venue for doing so. Besides helping your mind and body to cope with the physical manifestations of fear and shock, rigorous physical training also is an excellent way to test and tax your willpower.

Please note that I am well aware that the following form of exercise is unconventional, to say the least, so I strongly recommend that it be performed only by individuals who are athletic and in good physical condition. I also urge you to conduct this form of exercise only once a week or just when you feel it would provide you with the greatest benefit. Consequently, be sure to consult with a licensed and certified medical doctor to receive a medical checkup before beginning any exercise program. Then, be certain to listen to your body and stop the exercise if you don't feel well.

To begin, you may choose to conduct this willpower exercise while running. Go for a run at your usual training pace and distance. Be sure you receive a good workout and your body is somewhat fatigued–but not exhausted. Then, at the very end of your run, sprint up a steep hill if one is nearby, or to a landmark that's about 1/10th of a mile away. Depending on your physical condition, you can perform an all-out sprint or you can perform a modified sprint at a slower pace. But, during this sprint you should experience your body working close to maximum effort, your legs should begin to burn and your respiratory rate should increase heavily.

At this moment, think of a scenario that would test your willpower. Imagine a confrontation such as a deranged suspect fighting with you and trying to get your gun from your holster. As you're sprinting ahead, think about how you would pin and cap the suspect's hand to your holster to prevent your gun from coming out. Now, imagine striking the suspect with all you've got and using the appropriate tactics and techniques to ward off his attack. Envision yourself successfully utilizing these techniques so that you come out on top and, finally, take the suspect into custody. At this point, complete your sprint and be sure to walk for a couple of minutes so that you allow your body–and your mind–to cool down appropriately. Base the number of repetitions you perform of this exercise on your level of physical conditioning.

Now you have not only taxed your body. You have also tested and strengthened your will as you have completed a drill that has exercised your ability to THINK about how you would respond appropriately to such an attack while your body is working in an overload capacity. Some people may find it hard to think clearly while their bodies are working close to maximum effort during this exercise. At this point, try to comprehend how hard it's going to be to think clearly while you're really fighting for your life. Know, also, that performing this type of exercise is mentally preparing you for such an ordeal.

You can also integrate this mental exercise into weight, calisthenics, martial arts or boxing training. For example, complete your weight-training workout for your chest and take a brief rest. Now, attempt to do as many push-ups as you can while your chest, shoulders and triceps muscles are already fatigued. As your muscles begin to burn and your strength wanes, imagine a scenario that would test your willpower and would force you to work through pain. Envision grappling with a violent suspect and having to push him off of you. See yourself

continuing to fight until you have successfully taken the suspect into custody.

Then, for officers who enjoy working out on a heavy bag, there are also willpower exercises that you can create and employ. For instance, complete a decent heavy bag workout and immediately work the bag with a flurry of non-stop, hard punches for a full 30 seconds. Take just a 30-second rest and start the drill again. While you're engaging the heavy bag with your punching combinations, envision yourself fighting with a wild and violent suspect who's attacking you. As always, you can imagine any scenario you want, but conduct the drill only for the amount of time that is commensurate with your physical condition. Just take the opportunity to tax yourself, mind and body, so that it is your willpower successfully propelling you through pain, fatigue and overwhelming circumstances.

These drills are unique and not for the faint of heart. By conducting these drills, you are mentally and physically preparing yourself to go the extra mile in a violent encounter. You're taking the initiative to program your mind to respond appropriately and decisively in the face of aggressive, deadly behavior. Your body and mind will now be inoculated against the pain and fatigue you may experience if you are forced to combat with a violent suspect. Even more critically, you will be experienced in maintaining your focus and ability to think positively about your plan of action while your body is pushed to its limits. These drills, combined with your dedication to your professional and physical training, will assist you in developing the willpower that you need to fortify your indomitable mindset.

Fear Management

"Courage is resistance to fear, mastery of fear, not absence of fear."
Mark Twain

In the law enforcement arena, the subject of fear is one that is seldom taught–or even discussed for that matter. In fact, fear often is considered a taboo This occurs despite the fact that the very nature of police work frequently thrusts officers into situations that invoke fear in any rational human being. But, there exists a false perception that when an officer admits to feeling fear and its varied effects, they are actually admitting to inadequacy or weakness. The bottom line is everyone feels fear, and it is a topic that needs to be addressed, because an inability to understand and manage fear can prove fatal. It's how an officer perceives the fear that is essential. By training in and possessing an indomitable mindset, you've begun your journey to master the mental skills and attitude necessary for surviving a potentially lethal confrontation. You have also begun a journey to learn to harness your fear. Cultivating a winning mindset does not mean eliminating the feelings of fear. Instead, it will enable you to utilize your mental focus, positive attitude and the confidence you feel in your professional and physical skills to cope with the effects of this normal, and powerful, human phenomenon. In this way, law enforcement officers can make fear their ally.

Understanding how fear works is also crucial if you want to make it your ally. When people perceive or anticipate danger, their bodies produce adrenaline and other chemicals in anticipation of having to fight or run away for survival, i.e., *fight or flight.* The more dangerous the situation is perceived, the more adrenaline will be released into the body. Some of the symptoms of this adrenaline release are increased heart rate, body shakes, tunnel vision, nausea, anxiety and self-doubt. Many times, people will feel these potent changes in their bodies and actually mistake adrenaline as fear. This can cause people to panic. If police officers panic, they could freeze, and the results could be fatal.

To avoid this, police officers must understand that the physical manifestations of these chemicals surging throughout their bodies are not only normal, but also very beneficial. To this end, I consulted with former Los Angeles Police Department staff police psychologist Doctor Kris Mohandie and asked him for his perspective about this phenomenon. Assisted by Doctor Michael J. Craw, Doctor Mohandie wrote that, "The release of adrenaline and other chemicals during crisis situations causes many psychophysiological changes to help prepare the officer for survival. Heart rate and blood pressure increase, sugar is released to increase energy, acid flows into the stomach to get nutrients out, blood clotting enzymes flow into [the] system to minimize wound damage, and critical brain activity increases." In sum, feeling fear actually gives police officers a mental and physical edge in situations that require heightened responsiveness from the mind and body.

Similarly, it is useful to know that you may experience anger as another symptom during a crisis or stressful situation. As professionals, police officers are expected to, and they expect themselves to, keep their emotions and personal feelings within check. Understand, however, that it's an innate human response to feel angry if an adversary attacks you. In fact, acknowledging, disciplining and controlling this normal anger (not to be confused with rage) can be useful during a lethal encounter because it can help you defend yourself with even more fervor.

Finally, there is one last by-product of the effect of fear that is critical for law enforcement officers to understand. This is the probability that some form of time distortion may occur in officers' perceptual fields as they encounter and cope with a critical and/or lethal event. Numerous officers have reported that when they have been involved in a crisis situation, the events, and their responses to them, seem to unfold as if in slow motion. When I asked Doctor Mohandie about this phenomenon, he and Doctor Craw prepared the explanation that, "Perceptual distortions like slow motion–which occurs in nearly half of officers in critical incidents–may be partly a function of the fact that our thoughts are speeding faster than normal, making time seem to pass more slowly." They further added that, "For other officers–20 percent in one study–time speeds up, and often the officer perceives everything faster than usual, including their own actions. Differences in these kinds of experiences may occur as a consequence of the unique aspects of the incident and what is required to survive, training and [the] variabilities between officers in terms of their normal stress response tendencies and baseline level of arousal (more or less anxious)." Thus, police officers should recognize that time distortions are a normal function of fear. They allow police officers to make split-second decisions and take all necessary action under dire extremes of stress.

Given this knowledge, you can now recognize that when you experience fear and the effects of the adrenaline coursing through your body, you are now prepared for action. With blood pumping into your major muscle groups, you are more ready to defend yourself. With adrenaline and other chemicals altering your physiology, emotions and perceptions, your response levels are heightened well beyond the norm. Beyond understanding these complex processes, you also can practice properly managing your fear. This may enable you to have even more strength, a more acute sense of awareness, and even quicker reactions, thereby augmenting your ability to defend yourself with absolute conviction while being less susceptible to pain.

To harness fear and make it your ally, consider the following fear management techniques:

1. In order to manage fear, begin by **welcoming the adrenaline into your body**. Think of the explosion that you feel in your stomach as an instantaneous power surge waiting to propel you to victory. Your body is naturally preparing to defend itself, thereby preparing you for success. An analogy I like to use is to think of the adrenaline that's running through your body as a giant ocean wave and you're riding it. You must now stay on top, moving with the wave while not allowing it to swallow you up. Ride the wave of adrenaline all the way through until you, your partners and the people that you're protecting are safe.

2. Next, keep a clear head by **replacing any negative thoughts with positive ones**. During any scenario, if you hear your inner voice suggesting, "I can't deal with this situation," consciously replace that thought with, "I can deal with this situation." It may sound simple, but as you read in the visualization section, the power of the mind is limitless. So, repeat the positive thought to yourself again. There is no room for negative thoughts while conducting your duties–especially in crisis situations.

3. To maximize the power of thought as a tool for managing the effects of fear, develop a **Positive Repetitive Mantra** (PRM). Choose a simple saying, such as "I can deal with this," that is most effective for you and you can utilize consistently. You can use any PRM you like as long as it's positive and, more importantly, so long as it works for you. Use it in your daily life whenever you want to block

out any negative emotions or to keep these thoughts from surfacing in the first place. Regular use of your PRM will eventually make it second nature to you. It will become an automatic, effective response when you find yourself faced with a challenge. During a crisis situation, then, you've already prepared yourself to head off any potential negative emotions or thoughts just by silently repeating, "I can deal with this, I can deal with this." These PRM will assist you in keeping a positive mental attitude during a stressful, even lethal, situation.

4. Use **deep-breathing** techniques in order to control fear. By taking several slow, deep breaths, you'll be controlling your breathing and helping to lower your heart rate and blood pressure. During stressful situations, most people will breathe quickly and use only the "upper" portion of their lungs. This type of breathing will increase stress symptoms, such as anxiety, and it will cause physical tension. It could also cause a person to hyperventilate. To prevent this from happening, you can try the following breathing exercise:
Begin by breathing deeply in through your nose for a count of four. Start by filling the lower portion of your lungs with air first, followed by the middle, and finally ending with the top portion of your lungs. Now hold your breath for a count of four. Next, exhale the air through your mouth for a count of four, letting the air from the top portion of your lungs exit first, followed by the middle section and finally ending with the lower portion of your lungs. Some people prefer to use a count of six for this exhalation part of the breathing exercise. Next, hold your breath for another count of four and begin the process again. Do this exercise several times to promote relaxation in your body. As you learn the exercise, you may find that modifying the counts will help to suit your individual needs. With practice, you can make this type of breathing an automatic response to stress. For instance, police officers have found this exercise to be especially beneficial while responding to high-priority calls, since it allows them to be more

calm and focused when they arrive on scene.

For further understanding of how deep breathing can assist police officers in dealing with crisis situations and controlling the effects of the "fight or flight syndrome," I once again consulted with Doctor Kris Mohandie. Assisted by Doctor Michael J. Craw, Doctor Mohandie provided me with the following explanation:

Deep-breathing and other relaxation techniques target a reduction in sympathetic nervous system [SNS] activity. This is desirable because the SNS prepares for reactive responses (fight, flight, freeze) to an imminent threat, but can interfere with the planful responses demanded in many orchestrated tactical maneuvers. In reality, there will probably be some level of SNS arousal in many orchestrated responses, but these [breathing] techniques keep it in the window of just enough arousal for performance enhancement. Deep breathing is helpful because it puts an officer into a psychophysiological zone associated with enhanced performance and counteracts the potential negative effects of excess SNS arousal. This zone—which consists of specific brain wave activity and reduced sympathetic (fight or flight) responses—results in improved planning, coordination and control.

Consequently, law enforcement officers can utilize deep-breathing exercises to relax their minds and bodies to a degree where they can actively harness the effects of fear and use them to their advantage.

This ability to understand how fear works and how to properly manage its symptoms is crucial to any law enforcement officer's performance in any scenario. Armed with these fear management techniques and an appreciation for the fact that fear is your ally, you've added a dynamic element to the indomitable mindset. So, integrate fear management skills into your indomitable mindset training. Picture yourself feeling a surge of adrenaline and welcoming its effects while practicing visualization. Apply the fear management techniques as a tool for enhancing your performance during scenario-based training and while out on the streets. Allow the powerful effects of deep-breathing exercises to help catapult your mind and body to the next level during your physical training. In this way, you will be prepared at every possible level and you will have

fine-tuned your indomitable mindset so that you will win if you are forced to defend yourself in a lethal confrontation.

Awareness Skills

"Problems cannot be solved at the same level of awareness that created them."
Albert Einstein

Perhaps one of the most positive effects of your indomitable mindset training will be an intensification of your awareness skills. Possessing a positive mental attitude, a strong will and an ability to manage fear allows you to free your mind from extraneous negative thoughts. This will enable you to bring a keen clarity of focus to your daily work. Then, your precise attention to detail in your visualization, professional and physical training will translate into a similar detail-oriented mindset as you conduct your professional duties. This is so important because, as I am sure you already know, the benefits of proper awareness skills cannot be overestimated. That is why from the early days of your respective law enforcement academies it was probably preached that, when you're working in the field, and even when you're off duty, you must always "Be aware of your surroundings!"

But what does "Be aware of your surroundings" really mean? Without proper explanation, the true meaning of this statement could be lost or misunderstood. Let's face it, law enforcement officers, for the most part, feel they are cognizant of their surroundings. While on patrol, your overall safety completely depends upon your ability to properly assess your surroundings and identify telltale danger signs. Think about it. By possessing good observation and awareness skills, you can spot the potential trouble or a crime in progress and take the necessary steps to thwart that situation. But, as personal safety and police tactical experts know, there's a lot more to this critical subject than simply looking at what is going on in the world around you.

For instance, world-renowned firearms instructor Jeff Cooper years ago recognized that awareness skills were an integral part of personal safety, not only for police officers and security specialists, but for civilians as well. Therefore, Cooper introduced an awareness chart that used the colors white, yellow, orange, and red to represent different levels of awareness. White represented an utter lack of awareness, while yellow was used to describe people being aware of their surroundings. Climbing up the awareness chart, orange meant that a person was alert to the possibility of an impending volatile situation. Finally, red signified that a person, having already identified a threat, responded *(fight or flight)* to the imminent danger.

Furthermore, Cooper understood that a person's level of awareness fluctuates throughout the day, and day to day, since awareness depends upon a person's activities, moods, exhaustion levels, etc. To understand this, simply ask yourself what your level of awareness would be while working a crime suppression assignment in a gang-infested neighborhood after dark, versus what it would be if you were playing ball with your friends at the local park on a Sunday afternoon? By thus recognizing that human nature dictates that your awareness level is not a constant, Cooper and other experts have added essential knowledge to the mental aspects of tactical preparedness and self-defense. As this knowledge is so utterly crucial to your safety (both on duty and off duty), I, too, have devised a system whereby you can integrate proper awareness skills into your arsenal of tactical skills. In this way, law enforcement officers can both fortify and exercise their indomitable mindset.

The Awareness Spectrum

I call my system of understanding the different levels of awareness "The Awareness Spectrum." I have organized it in order to help people understand the different levels of awareness and their principles. Instead of using colors, however, to define a person's awareness level, a simple word or phrase is utilized as a title for each of my four awareness levels. These levels are *Unaware, Relaxed Awareness, Intent Awareness* and *Immediate Awareness.* It is my intention that you will be reminded immediately of what awareness level you should be at, and what that entails, by recalling the word or phrase. I hope, too, that this spectrum will assist you in becoming more cognizant of your immediate environment in both your professional and private lives.

Unaware: This title speaks for itself. At this level of awareness, a person could best be described as being in a daydream-like state. "Walking around with your head in the clouds" is the common cliché that most aptly describes this state of awareness. Try at all costs to avoid this state, of course, while working your designated assignment, but also while off duty when you are outside the safety of your home (granted that you've taken the necessary precautionary measures to make your home safe and secure). This is so essential because studies have revealed that assailants select their would-be victims (whether civilian or law enforcement officers) based upon factors such as lack of command presence and a person's overall lack of awareness.

Relaxed Awareness: This is the level of awareness you are at when you're in a relaxed state but still tending to your field assignments or patrolling your designated area. In this state of awareness, you're cognizant of your whole environment, including any potential dangers. More importantly, this is the level of awareness you routinely ***should*** be operating at unless you are in the securest of environments. To achieve this, it helps to think of your environment as an ever-changing, active "stage." As the setting changes and people come and go, be mindful of ***all*** the changes that are taking place. But do ***not*** be in a paranoid state, snapping and turning your head toward anything that moves. Any officer would suffer mental burnout in a short period of time by practicing these habits. Simply put, be aware of who or what has entered your stage and take note of their actions. By practicing this level of awareness, you can relax, successfully perform your duties and permit your instincts to inform you of potential danger.

This state of **Relaxed Awareness** allows law enforcement officers to have conversations with their partners while still taking in all the activity unfolding outside their patrol cars. While completely mindful of your surroundings, you will not become mentally fatigued during your tour of duty. At the same time, this type of mindset allows you to quickly react to crimes in progress because you will never be caught off guard by being completely unaware. Furthermore, you will be able to make the critical observations and decisions that keep the public and your fellow officers free from danger.

Intent Awareness: Think of this level of awareness as a transitional phase. In it, you recognize that a potential threat exists and you make an assessment of the situation. After identifying the possible threat or potentially volatile situation, your awareness is now focused and intent on the possibility of danger. Trust your instincts, then, without hesitation, plan your probable response. But if the situation turns to a worst-case scenario where you have to take immediate action, do so decisively. If you are absolutely positive that the possible threat was a false alarm, then and only then, go back to your regular functioning level of *Relaxed Awareness*. But, if the threat escalates, you must shift your awareness to the last level.

At this point, it is important to note that it is absolutely crucial for you to have been in a *Relaxed Awareness* state prior to identifying any potential threat. Making the transition from being *Unaware* to a level of *Intent Awareness* may require a lag time that could prove fatal. By making a habit of regularly attending to your duties while in a state of *Relaxed Awareness*, you will allow for a smoother transition to the highest level of awareness. In this way, you can eliminate being caught off guard.

Immediate Awareness: This is the final level of the Awareness Spectrum. The threat has been identified, it's *immediate*, and you are forced to take immediate action for your safety or someone else's (fight or flight syndrome). While taking action, rely on your training, experience and indomitable mindset to see you through to a successful resolution of the crisis situation. More importantly, be decisive and assertive while employing the reasonable and necessary force needed to protect the safety of yourself, your partner and the public.

So, read "The Awareness Spectrum" and evaluate what state of awareness you're in during your patrol assignment or during your daily activities, like driving to work, walking to the market or going for a jog. Then, give yourself an honest assessment of your overall awareness skills and attention to detail. Finally, try the following two awareness exercises the next time you're in a large public place, like a park or a shopping area. They will help you incorporate your awareness skills into your daily routine.

Awareness Exercises

Exercise #1: The next time you're at a park or other public place, take a look around, identify and count how many people actually appear mindful of their surroundings. You'll notice people walking with piles of shopping bags while talking on their cell phones, as well as other people staring off into space, walking aimlessly. This doesn't make them bad people, just unmindful of their surrounds. You'll probably observe more people who appear unaware of their environment than there will be people who seem aware.

Exercise #2: Conduct the exercise we just did and now ask who a criminal would look at as a potential robbery victim. Who would he pick? After you've made your mental selection, ask yourself why. Did the person's lack of awareness or their body language have anything to do with your selection? If so, you've now educated yourself on how NOT to act in public.

Relaxation for Your Mind and Body

"Meditation brings wisdom; lack of meditation leaves ignorance. Know well what leads you forward and what holds you back, and choose the path that leads to wisdom."
Buddha

As you've discovered by reading this chapter, the development of your indomitable mindset is crucial if you're going to be successful in any type of potentially lethal confrontation. This mindset can only be fostered through a lot of hard work, dedication and mental discipline–above and beyond all the exacting demands of police work. Consequently, a law enforcement officer must have the ability to relax mentally and physically in order to promote a healthy lifestyle and maintain a positive outlook on life. Many officers take up hobbies, play sports and engage in other physical activities to have a positive outlet and combat the effects of stress associated with the law enforcement profession.

But there is another simple and effective method of achieving relaxation you may want to try. At the risk of being viewed as a new-age philosopher, I offer the following breathing meditation to assist you with relaxing your mind and body. Numerous studies have proven that the benefits of meditation include relaxation, reduction in stress-related symptoms, the lowering of blood pressure, improvement in concentration and mental clarity and the promotion of a more positive outlook on life. Furthermore, people of many cultures have been using some form of meditation since ancient times. The longevity of the practice attests to the effectiveness of meditation. In fact, Samurai warriors would devote time each morning to their meditation.

The following exercise is one of those meditations that has been in use for thousands of years. It is called the "breathing meditation." I recommend it because it is simple and effective, does not involve anything like chanting and is not grounded in mysticism or religion. This breathing meditation is purely a method for achieving relaxation for your mind and body, and its benefits can be unparalleled. Your goal in its practice simply should be to quiet your mind. Hopefully, you'll be able to let go of some of the constant stimulus, some of it negative, which constantly bombards law enforcement officers. Then, as you practice this breathing meditation more and more, you should gain the ability to focus your mind more thoroughly and more efficiently–a skill that is indispensable in police work.

To begin the meditation exercise, find a quiet and comfortable place where you can sit down without being disturbed. Make sure your environment is free of any excessive noise or distractions. Sit down and close your eyes. Place your hands on your lap and let your body settle into a comfortable position. Now turn your attention to your breathing. Simply notice your breathing as you inhale and exhale in a completely natural way. Do not try to influence your breathing in any way, though you may notice that the rhythm of your breathing may slow down naturally during your meditation. Continue to monitor your breathing and don't influence any of the changes that may be occurring.

When you first begin to employ the breathing meditation, your mind may wander and different thoughts will surface from various directions. This is very common, even for people who have meditated for years. Simply allow these thoughts to pass and continue to focus on your breathing. After a few minutes, you'll find your body and mind beginning to relax even more. If you find that your mind begins to wander, just bring your attention back to your breathing. It's that simple.

When you first begin the breathing meditation, attempt to practice the exercise twice a day for ten minutes each time. In time, you'll be able to increase the duration of your sessions up to twenty or even thirty minutes. The best time to practice your meditation is early in the morning after you've awakened and then again in the evening when you've returned home from work. Also, it's preferable to conduct your meditation exercise before eating any meals. But if you don't have time to meditate before eating, allow sufficient time for your meal to digest so that the meditation will not slow down the workings of your digestive system. However, since police officers lead very busy lives and often have irregular schedules, any time dedicated to the exercise is better than no time at all. So, just give it a try for ten minutes, twice a day, and experience the results for yourself. You may find that the breathing meditation is one of the simplest, yet most effective methods by which you can achieve the relaxation that you so well deserve and need.

CONCLUSION

I know I have asked a lot when explaining how to cultivate and adopt this indomitable mindset. But it is nothing more than I ask of myself. As a former bouncer and competitive martial artist and a 14-year veteran of the Los Angeles Police Department, the last seven years of which I have been assigned to SWAT, I can attest to the fact that this mindset works. If you are serious about your law enforcement profession and doing your job as safely as possible so your odds of always coming home to your family are better, you will adopt these principles. Thoroughly invest yourself in indomitable mindset training, practicing and modifying the aforementioned exercises so you make them your own. The payoff can prove to be immeasurable, since law enforcement officers with this type of indomitable mindset work from a state of perpetual readiness.

They can anticipate, prepare for and expect to win in any challenge their work or lives may present.

Know also that the most consummate professionals I have worked and trained with in any arena all share this same mindset. My observations and experiences have proven to me that success has never been achieved by deeds alone. Instead, people who win at what they do are people who are always striving to improve their skills and add to their knowledge base—in other words, to enhance the power of their minds. For countless ages, philosophers, athletes, warriors and many, many people interested in self-motivation and self-improvement have all understood this truth. It was even written in the ancient Buddhist text, *The Pali Canon,* that, ***"All that is comes from the mind; it is based on the mind, it is fashioned by the mind."***

REFERENCES AND SUGGESTIONS FOR FURTHER READING

Blum, Lawrence N., Ph.D. *Force Under Pressure: How Cops Live and Why They Die.* New York: Lantern Books, 2000, pp. 151–166.*

Musashi, Miyamoto. *The Book of Five Rings.* Trans. Thomas Cleary. New York: Barnes and Noble Books, 1997.

Remsberg, Charles. *The Tactical Edge: Surviving High-Risk Patrol.* Northbrook, Illinois: Calibre Press, Inc., 1986, pp. 13–52.*

Thompson, Geoff. *Fear: The Friend of Exceptional People.* United Kingdom: Summersdale Publishers, 1995, pp. 51–57.*

Wilson, Paul. *The Calm Technique: Meditation Without Magic or Mysticism.* United States of America: Barnes and Noble Books, 1999, pp. 39–70.*

---

*Although only the pages noted above were consulted in the preparation of this chapter, the entire texts are valuable resources for anyone interested in this subject matter.

JOHN MCCARTHY

John McCarthy has been a police officer with the Los Angeles Police Department for 20 years. He is currently assigned to the Defensive Tactics Training Section at the LAPD Davis Training Facility. John has worked a variety of assignments throughout his 20 years, including patrol, vice, narcotics and gangs.

John has been the head referee for the Ultimate Fighting Championship (UFC) since March of 1994. He has been active in the sport of mixed martial arts and instrumental in the growth and acceptance of the sport with major athletic commissions, states and countries throughout the world.

Chapter 2

A FIGHT FOR YOUR LIFE

JOHN MCCARTHY

INTRODUCTION

You are working your sixth straight night of morning watch and are finally halfway through your shift. You travel down to your favorite patrol spot looking for that one arrest that is going to get you out of the cold weather for the rest of the night, your shift and this long, tiring week of work. Just then you see a Mustang GT coming down the street toward your location. You notice the rear window is broken out and the driver, who appears to be the lone occupant of the vehicle, seems startled and nervous. As you run the license number of the vehicle and the radio crackles in the cool night air, you hear the voice on the other end telling you that the license comes back to a stolen vehicle taken earlier in the day. You hurriedly swing a ragged U-turn as you see the Mustang quickly accelerate away from you. Your heart starts racing as fast as the Crown Victoria you're driving. The suspect takes a right turn and your vehicle is lined up perfectly for the same right-hand turn. You are driving smooth and quick, and you're closing in fast. You quickly pick up the microphone hooked on your dash and broadcast your unit designation, location and that you are in pursuit of a GTA suspect.

As the suspect takes a left turn, you see he has entered the turn with too much speed and his vehicle begins to float toward the curb and the vehicles parked alongside it. There is a sudden impact that brings the Mustang to an instant halt. You step hard on the brakes, hoping to stop before you become

part of the accident. As you bring your vehicle to a stop, you see the suspect exiting his vehicle and the adrenaline really starts to flow as he takes off running between the houses. You take off after him, grabbing at your hand-held radio so you can broadcast your location and advise everyone you are now in foot pursuit of the suspect. The race is on, but you feel confident in your ability to run the suspect down. You have been working out for the past seven months and have worked yourself up to as much as five miles on your daily runs. Now your training is going to benefit you. The suspect runs through the first backyard, over the fence and then down the alley. As your feet hit the alley, you are only 30 to 40 feet behind the suspect. He runs down four or five houses and you are closing fast. In a last-ditch effort, the suspect turns and launches himself over another fence and you follow, now only several feet behind. As you hit the ground in another backyard, you suddenly realize the suspect has stopped running away from you and is now actively attempting to separate your head from your body.

The suspect grabs at you, pulling you in close to his body. You instinctively try to push yourself away to gain some space and distance. This does not work, and now you try hitting at the suspect to get him off you. Suddenly, you feel your feet leaving the ground as the suspect lifts you into the air and then brings you back down to the ground with a body-jolting slam. As the searing pain from your head bouncing off the cold, hard earth starts to clear, you realize the suspect is mounted on top of your chest and is beginning to punch at your face and head as you frantically attempt to protect yourself. The night had started off so slow, and now everything is moving so fast. You are fighting for your life with a suspect who is actively attempting to take it, and there is nobody there to help you. Are you prepared to save your own life? Are you capable of stopping the suspect's ability to hurt you? Have you prepared yourself physically and mentally for this moment? Will you survive this fight for your life?

The Need For Training

There are officers who have worked in patrol, driving a marked police cruiser for close to 30 years, who have never been in a fight-for-your-life situation. But there are also new police officers who have been out of the police academy for less than a year who have been placed in this same situation. You never know when, where or if it is going to happen. You can only start work every day knowing that the possibility exists, so you have a choice. You can do something to deal with the possibility by training yourself in some type of self-defense system to enhance your physical and mental skills. By placing yourself in a bad situation in practice, time after time, and working through it, you will enhance your chances of making it through that real-world encounter when it happens.

Or, you can be the officer who knows they are lacking in their ability to not only protect themselves but also anyone else. You can go to work hoping and praying the day never comes that someone actually places you in a position where you will have to defend yourself, because deep down you know this is an area where you are totally lacking, deficient or even inept. Even worse is the officer who falsely believes they can physically account for themselves in any given situation. I have a saying that I live by and it has served me well. "I will never underestimate the abilities of my opponent, while conversely, I will never overestimate my own abilities." Too many people in the law enforcement community have a false impression of their ability. This has been clearly seen with the introduction of the video camera to police work. Forget about citizens or news crews, we have opened a panoramic view of our officers' deficiencies by installing, and then monitoring, the tapes from our very own cameras.

I can remember the first time I saw a law enforcement officer killed on videotape. The whole incident troubled me deeply. The tape was of a Nacogdoches County sheriff's deputy, Darrell Lunsford. Darrell was a large man, standing 6'5" and weighing 275 lbs. Darrell had stopped several suspects traveling in a vehicle. Two of the three suspects seen in the video were much smaller than Darrell. At approximately 5'6" and 140 lbs. each, the suspects successfully attacked Darrell, brought him to the ground and ended his life on that dark, cold night in Texas. I knew after watching the tape there were many lessons to be learned from the incident. It was obvious to me that Darrell never felt threatened by the suspects until they were attacking him. There were many suspicious signs or signals that something was happening: the suspects were evasive in answering questions, moved around when told to stand in a certain location, and even removed articles of clothing (a hat) in preparing themselves for their attack. None of these signals or signs seemed to matter or were even noticed by Darrell. At the time, he was too intent on gathering his probable cause and showing it with the use of the very camera and microphone that eventually captured his murder. Darrell never brought a strong command presence into play, because at no time during his stop did he feel threatened by the suspects. Darrell was very kind and cordial to the suspects during the stop.

Intimidation is a very effective tool used by many people both in and out of the law enforcement community. Many people are limited by their own mindset. Once your mind tells you "you can't win," trust me, you can't. How many of you have looked at an individual who was very large in size and stature and said to yourself, *"Man, I wouldn't ever want to mess with that guy."* I cannot say with any authority that Darrell was treated this way much of his life, but I would bet a week's pay many confrontations with Darrell were avoided simply because of his size. People just didn't want to mess with him. As Darrell was attempting to gain probable cause to arrest the occupants of the vehicle, the passenger grabbed hold of him in a manner similar to a wrestler's double-leg takedown. With the help of his friend, the suspect was able to take Darrell down to the ground. As he was first being attacked, Darrell was holding the driver's license of the first suspect in one hand and his flashlight in the other. Darrell never let go of either of these items as he was being attacked, and failed to use the flashlight as a possible weapon to defend himself during the struggle.

You have to ask yourself, why? Why would you hold onto a driver's license while two men are attacking you, bringing you to the ground and kicking you in the head and body while simultaneously attempting to disarm you? The answer is actually simple, even though we don't like to talk about it. As police officers, we don't like to talk about the deaths of other officers out of respect for them and their families. We stay away from pointing out mistakes or errors because we don't want to cause more pain to friends and family. I mean no disrespect to Darrell, his family, friends or brother officers, but there are many things we can learn from this tragedy. Darrell obviously worked at being the best police officer he could be. He went to work with a reverence for the law and respect for the people who lived in the community he served. Unfortunately, Darrell, like many other police officers, was not physically or mentally prepared to deal with certain realities or possibilities related to field police work.

Many officers falsely claim they have personally been in fights with suspects, when in reality what they were involved in was a use of force with someone who was resisting by not freely succumbing to arrest. The suspects do not want to be handcuffed, so they keep their hands in front of their bodies, resisting the officer's attempt to place their hands behind their back. Officers use a myriad of techniques they were shown at some time in the academy, like wrist locks, twist locks, pressure points and distraction strikes, to gain the suspect's compliance. This is definitely a type of confrontation, but not a fight. The officers were involved with utilizing some type of compliance technique on a suspect, while the suspect only attempted to resist so they could prevent or delay their apprehension. The suspect never actually attempted to harm the officer and

had no serious intent to inflict damage or possibly even death. There is a serious difference between the two situations.

Officers have to be brutally honest with themselves. Sometimes this is not an easy thing to do. If you were to go to work today, come in contact with an individual on the street and suddenly were attacked, how would you respond? The answer is usually easily addressed with words, but when put into actual practice, the results are frequently more different than we would care to admit. If you have never been placed in a bad position regarding a physical confrontation, how can you honestly say or know how you will respond? If you have never been punched in the middle of your face and felt the effects of such a blow, how can you say you would know how you would respond in any fashion? The simple facts are, you *can't!* There is only one way to know. It doesn't come easy, and you are likely going to end up with more bumps, bruises and headaches than you'll care to talk about, along with a healthy respect for the inventor of Motrin™. However, you will also be well on your way to achieving a physical and mental knowledge base that will help you survive a life-and-death fight.

One question that is repeatedly asked of me is, "What is the best martial art for self-defense?" This is not an easily answered question. All arts or forms have their advantages and disadvantages. You can spend a great deal of time looking at the different fighting arts and see there is a lot of good in all of them, but there is no one perfect system. They all have holes that can be exploited by the right person. If you break down the different aspects of a fight, you can find an art that properly trains you for that scenario. So, while there are many styles for you to learn from, here are the ones I believe you need to consider when looking at the three different ranges of fighting.

Western Boxing

If you want to stand and throw punches with someone, there are plenty of systems or styles that emphasize strikes with the hands. When looking at which art is best at striking with the hands, there is no better art than Western Boxing. Boxers by far have the best hands. They throw punches from a variety of angles with power, balance and speed. Although many other arts utilize striking techniques with the hands, there is no art that utilizes striking with the hands more effectively than Western Boxing.

Muay Thai

Kicks can be a very effective technique if used properly during a fight; a good kick can keep your opponent off balance and quickly end the fight. If done incorrectly or at the wrong time, a kick can put you at a great disadvantage, leaving you open to counterattacks, due to your balance being placed on one leg. Leg kicks may not be as flashy as Jean Claude Van Damme's spinning crescent kick to the head, but they can be just as effective. Again, many arts utilize kicks, but the art that uses kicks not as flash but as an effective setup and strike is the art of Muay Thai. Leg kicks can keep your opponent off balance and impede their ability to fight against you. Muay Thai teaches striking from a variety of angles through the use of various body parts. Hands, elbows, knees and feet are all used with extreme efficiency, power and precision.

Freestyle/Greco Roman Wrestling

If anything has been learned during the last decade by martial artists, law enforcement officers and even the average citizen, it is that ground fighting is a supremely effective form of fighting, especially if your opponent is lacking in experience or knowledge in that specific area. Although not flashy, ground fighting is a form of fighting that allows a person of smaller size, stature, strength and speed the ability to not only survive but actually defeat a superior opponent. Through the use of body position, joint locks and chokes, Jiujitsu stylists have proved how truly effective their style can be. However, if you want to be a ground fighter, you must first get your opponent down before you can utilize these skills.

Takedowns are a large part of any ground fighter's arsenal. The ability to take your opponent to the ground usually involves more than just a schoolyard tackle. Freestyle and Greco Roman wrestling have been part of the martial arts for centuries.

They have grown from the gladiatorial days of ancient Greece and Rome to the sport we now see in our modern-day Olympic Games. These athletes use extreme speed, agility and strength, along with a knowledge and feel for angles and leverage, to position their opponents onto the ground or, conversely, to keep themselves from being placed onto the ground. If one person could acquire all of these skills, they would be the start of what I would consider the perfect fighter, or possibly your worst nightmare!

With that being said, it really doesn't matter what it takes to make you into the perfect fighter if you don't like what you are doing. First, you have to enjoy it. No one art is made for everyone. You must like what you are doing or, simply put, you're not going to do it. You have to find an art or style that you enjoy learning about, working out to and maybe even competing in. Second, you need to be realistic about your physical capabilities. Just because the Sensei or instructor of a school can do a certain technique doesn't necessarily mean you are going to be able to do the same thing. Third, realize that you can't learn to fight and be spiritually inspired at the same time. Many martial artists will explain that they do martial arts for the philosophical and spiritual aspects of the arts. This generally is not the case. Most people don't step into a martial arts school to become spiritual. They go there because they want to learn how to protect themselves, and that is the real purpose of all these schools.

So, if you are going to learn how to protect yourself, realize early on that you cannot truly learn how to fight without actually getting into some type of fight. Katas do not make you a fighter. A kata is nothing more than a choreographed dance. That is not to say that katas don't have their place in training, because they do; but a fight is not a dance and is anything but choreographed or static. A fight is dynamic and hostile. One of the practices that take place in many schools is what I call "tag" fighting. Students are told by their instructors that certain techniques they are taught are lethal and could possibly kill their training partner if the technique is executed with full contact. Therefore, they are told to only touch their opponent, not hit them. However, playing tag is not fighting and does not teach you how to accept a real blow. If you never accept a real blow in training, it may be difficult to handle one when it comes your way in the real world. Nobody wants to get punched in the face, because there are a number of serious drawbacks. First off, it hurts like hell. Secondly, it can stay with you for many days after the initial contact. But if you have experienced this in the past, you realize that not only are you going to live through the experience but you can actually fight back. This is an experience that can pay you back tenfold in the future.

Physical Conditioning

The last, and possibly most important, area that needs to be confronted is your physical conditioning. Many people feel they are in shape because they can go out and run three miles in the morning and bench press 300 pounds in the evening. To them I say, yes, you are in shape for your yearly physical, feeling good about yourself, keeping your weight under control and even for keeping your strength at a very respectable level, but don't fool yourself by thinking you are in fighting shape. Vince Lombardi, the Hall of Fame football coach of the Green Bay Packers, once said, "Fatigue makes cowards out of all men." There is no truer statement. Once someone is fatigued, they may start to quit. They reach a point where their minds tell them they must stop, and they do. How many of you have been in this same situation? Whether it was during a sporting competition or some other event, there comes a time when our bodies start to shut down from sustained high-energy output. Everyone's shut-down point comes at different times, and those times are usually based upon the individual's degree of physical conditioning. Your physical conditioning can be the most important thing you do on a daily basis. If you are not in good cardiovascular condition, you will not be able to continue on in any fight that lasts longer than perhaps half a minute. You may have an incredible amount of knowledge in the fighting arts and be physically adept at using that knowledge, but if you are not in shape and run into someone who is and has a little bit of knowledge, you are in for one terribly miserable day. If you don't have the condi-

tioning to go along with the skill, the skill will become useless very quickly when you become fatigued.

Frank Shamrock is one of the world's greatest freestyle fighters, and openly states that his greatest asset or tool is his conditioning. He is what I call a "Cardiovascular Monster." He can maintain an incredible pace for long, sustained durations of time. When fighting, he pushes the pace of the fight, so his opponent is never able to back off and relax. This pushes them into an area where, if they have failed to properly train their cardiovascular system, they soon start to break down and are unable to keep pace. At the precise time he starts to see his opponent faltering, Frank steps up his pace at least one more notch to push his opponent mentally and physically, so they start to succumb to fatigue.

It is important that you realize who your possible opponent may be. Your opponent may have been confined at the state penitentiary for five to ten years honing their skills. Confined in a 6-by-6-foot cell, they may have nothing to do but many multiple push-ups, sit-ups and burpees. This type of physical conditioning is exactly the type of training needed for a sustained output in a physical confrontation. An opponent with this level of muscular endurance, strength and sustained cardiovascular ability will far exceed that of a man who simply goes out and runs. You must be ready for this type of opponent, because I guarantee he is ready for you. He is waiting for the opportunity to launch his assault against you and begin stomping your head into the pavement. This is his goal in life. You are the enemy, and if you have not prepared yourself at least as well or better, they are likely to defeat you.

Mental Preparation

The human brain is an incredibly complex organ I can scarcely begin to properly describe or decipher. However, I have learned a great deal about the ability of the human mind to overcome many of the body's inadequacies. The body will readily go where your mind has already been. This statement has incredible meaning in the many facets associated with the physical requirements of a police officer. The toughness of your mind can be, and usually is, the most important quality you possess. It will work to keep you scratching, clawing, biting and fighting against an opponent that is physically stronger, younger and more skilled.

For example, presume a man walks into a bar, gets into an argument and punches another man in the face with his right hand, knocking the man to the floor and into a state of submission. The next bar this man walks into, the same thing happens. He gets into an argument and punches his foe in the face, knocking him to the ground and into a state of submission. He does this time and again, over and over, until he reaches a point where he knows that if he hits someone with his right hand, it's over. Now, why were these fights over after our friend hit these people with that awesome right hand? Some of them can be attributed to the fact that our friend does deliver a solid blow with his right hand and effectively knocked out a portion of those men in the bars. Some can be attributed to the fact that some of the men punched by our friend did not want to continue and gave up after being punched. Nevertheless, our friend is now a firm believer in the power of his right hand. He has it firmly in his mind that people just don't stand up after being hit by his right hand. Now let's say you run into this man as he steps into the next bar and picks you as his next victim. He begins to argue and suddenly throws a right hand that hits you squarely along the left side of your face, knocking you to the ground. You are stunned and hurt, but this is not the first time you have been hit. During your weekly workouts and training, you have been taking and giving punches for the better part of a year. You instinctively stand up and come back at your attacker, placing your hands into a defensive position by the sides of your head and balancing your body. Now your opponent, who has been involved in many previous fights, is starting to question what is happening. The normal scenario has not occurred. Doubt has now set in for the first time. Even though he has experience on his side, and has already hit you (with you receiving some damage while he has received nothing), he is beginning to lose simply because his mind has started to doubt. Any time you believe something is going to happen a certain way and then suddenly it doesn't, you start to question why.

You must never quit! You must never stop! You must continue to fight, scratch, claw, bite, gouge and anything else it takes for you to survive.

There is no such thing as a fair fight. A fight is not a sporting event, not a competition. It is a hostile act that usually is won by the most hostile, violent and most prepared participant. I have had the honor and privilege of being involved with the Ultimate Fighting Championship (UFC) since its inception in 1993. The first UFC was marketed as "No Holds Barred." The marketing slogans that were used stated, "There are no rules," and "Two men enter, one man leaves." These marketing slogans were put into print to grab the attention of casual observers and make them pay attention to what was going to happen. Although there were very few rules in the first UFC, there were still rules. No biting, no eye gouging and no groin strikes. This was never a street fight, even though it was marketed in a way that would represent it as such.

A street fight has no rules. There are no referees to stop the fight if one of the combatants is receiving too much abuse. A street fight can end only by the goodwill of the person winning the fight or some outside influence coming to intercede. That means if you are not in a position to properly protect yourself, you will probably be depending upon the goodwill and compassion of the man who is presently trying to rip your head off. As you can see, this is definitely not a good position in which to find yourself.

When you became a police officer, you made a decision to take a job that could have a variety of situations or circumstances come up at any given moment. It is part of the excitement of being a police officer. We go to work every day realizing that we could become involved in a lengthy and boring investigation or report, or we could be going 100 mph in pursuit of robbery suspects. You never really know, and that is one of the best parts of being a police officer. You never know for sure how the day or night is going to turn out. As a police officer, you have placed yourself in a position of sometimes being asked to do things the average person wouldn't think of doing. You are asked to be the protector of the people you serve.

According to Charles Webb, Ph.D., "There is no nice way to arrest a potentially dangerous, combative suspect. The police are our bodyguards, our hired fists, batons and guns. We pay them to do the dirty work of protecting us, the work we're too afraid, too unskilled or too civilized to do ourselves. We expect them to keep the bad guys out of our businesses, cars and houses, out of our face! We want them to 'take care of the problem.' We just don't want to see how it is done."

CONCLUSION

When you took the job of a police officer, you became a professional, no different than a doctor, lawyer or pro athlete. You are expected to perform at an extremely high level, day in and day out, without making mistakes. People expect many things out of you—some of them are reasonable expectations and some are quite unreasonable. You are expected to be an expert in criminal and civil law, communications, human relations, vehicle operations, use of firearms, tactics and last, but certainly not least, self-defense! Is this fair? I can't tell you that it is completely fair or reasonable, but it is what most people expect of you, if they don't already believe it is so.

I believe you have to take a good look at yourself and assess the areas in which you are strong and those in which you are weak. You must be completely honest with yourself and set clear and specific goals. With a little hard work and dedication, you can become stronger.

My foremost desire is that you take the time to make a truthful analysis of your ability to not only survive but also win a life-and-death physical altercation. I hope that by making this analysis, you decide to either start or increase your physical conditioning to a level that will better enable you to come out on top if you ever find yourself in a fighting situation. At the very least, it will enable you to be healthier and live a better life. Lastly, I want you to know that it is never too late! Whether you are 28 or 58, you can always start learning something today that is going to make you better tomorrow.

Being able to defend yourself is a skill. It is no different than any other skill you have learned during your life. Skills are perishable, so you must constantly train to keep them at a high level. The skills of a fighter are no different than the skills of a race car driver, football player, or marksman. Without constant training, they will not be able to compete at their optimum or peak level of performance. You will not be able to either unless you constantly challenge yourself to learn and improve. So make the decision now to start doing something. You can start today or tomorrow. Some training is better than none at all. The time will be well spent for you, your department, members of the community you protect and serve, and most importantly, for your family, who needs, wants and requires you to come home to them at the end of your shift.

STACY LIM

Officer Stacy Lim began her law enforcement career in 1988 with the Los Angeles Police Department. Since graduating from the Academy, she has worked assignments at Southwest Division (patrol and gangs), Northeast Division (patrol), Southeast Division (patrol), Elysian Park Academy as a tactics instructor for recruits, reserves and in-service personnel and tactics instructor for recruits and reserves at the Davis Training Center. She currently works at the Elysian Park Academy as a tactics instructor for in-service officers.

Chapter 3

KILL OR BE KILLED: A STORY OF SURVIVAL

Stacy Lim

INTRODUCTION

I have known Stacy Lim for more than a decade. Her story is both truthful and compelling. Stacy is a young woman of average height and weight, and she received the same training as thousands of Los Angeles Police Department officers.

Recently, I attended a gathering of several hundred police officers, and Stacy Lim recounted her experience in her typically modest fashion. During her presentation she said, "You must prepare your mind for where your body takes it." These words should remain in the minds of every officer who reads this story.

Over the course of the last 12 years, Stacy Lim has been a tactics instructor for the Los Angeles Police Department Training Academy. One of the factors officers look for in an instructor, advisor or training officer is experience: Have you been there, done that?

Stacy's experience gives her a unique stage upon which to aid other officers in preparing to be good cops and survive on the street. She does not baby her students. She teaches them that they can't talk their way out of every conflict, nor can they anticipate every threat. She reminds them that there are suspects who will kill them for no logical reason and without provocation.

Stacy prepares her students by reinforcing the fact that suspects don't care if you beg, cry or if you have a family and children at home. Some suspects are predators who look for whomever they perceive to be the weakest, easiest, most unsuspecting target and try to take what they want.

Thank you, Stacy, for your story and, more importantly, your courage.

Ron McCarthy, Sergeant (Ret.) LAPD

The Incident

Some days just stick in your mind. Like June 9, 1990, the day my life changed. It was a night like most in the life of a police officer who drives home exhausted. The kind of night when you feel like you are on auto-pilot. I was so tired that I did not notice I was being followed by five gang members in a car. They saw my rims and decided this was the car they wanted to steal.

I pulled in front of my house like any other night. As I got ready to get out of my car, I grabbed my gun and opened the door. I put my gun under my arm, as usual, intending to get out and walk up the driveway. As I stepped out of my car, I turned to see the barrel of a revolver pointed at me. This is when my automatic reactions came into play. I am a firm believer in muscle memory–what you practice is what you do. As I saw the suspect's gun, I raised my gun and started to say, "Police, drop the gun!"

Lesson one: When a gun is pointed at you, the time for talking has passed. Time to get busy. I got the word "police" out when he shot me—one round, just left of center into my chest. The bullet tore through my chest like a hot javelin. My first reaction was anger. I was brought up to respect the police, and when the police tell you to do something, you obey.

Lesson two: Bad guys don't listen. After he fired, I saw him start to turn and run, so I fired at him. He ran toward the back of my car. Now my mental attitude was, "You're not going to shoot me and run away!" I went after him. As I got near the rear of my car, I slowed down. I know I didn't think. I just moved automatically. I slowed and started to "slice the pie" on the back of my car. ("Slice the pie" is a tactic of positioning away from a blind corner where a suspect could be concealed and incrementally moving to observe the suspect. Because the officer has distance, the angle allows the officer to see a suspect before the suspect, who is pressed against the corner, can see the officer.)

Sure enough, the suspect was there. He fired his additional five rounds at me. All missed. I fired three rounds at him and he went down. When he went down, I realized three things: I didn't know where he had come from. I didn't know if there were any more suspects. And man, my chest hurt! I needed to get some help.

The bullet turned out to be a .357 Magnum round. It fragmented upon entering my chest and hit my diaphragm, small and large intestines, stomach and liver. It shattered my spleen, put a hole in the base of my heart and cracked a rib on the way out of my back. It left a tennis ball-sized hole in my back.

I got back to the front of my car and stopped to see if anyone was near it. It was clear, so I started up my driveway. I felt like I was going to pass out. I grabbed my chest and fell to my knees. I remember feeling my own blood and thinking, "This is a weird feeling, really warm." I fell on my back and everything faded to black.

Thankfully, my roommate heard what she thought were firecrackers and went outside. She saw me bleeding out on the driveway and ran into the house to call 9-1-1. When the paramedics arrived, they put the MAST suit on my legs and inflated it. The intent was to get the blood to my chest so I wouldn't die. They lost my pulse and had to defibrillate me. They got a pulse back and rushed me to the hospital.

At the hospital, I had two great doctors. One of them was a trauma specialist who had served in Vietnam. Both doctors worked really hard to sew up all that was damaged. When they found the hole in my heart, a specialist was called to repair it. When I was finally sent to recovery, the doctors had a meeting with my family. I was on approximately 75-percent life support. About an hour into recovery, it was discovered that I was losing blood and something may have been missed. One of the doctors came into my room and grabbed my hand. With all the tubes in me, the only way I could communicate was by squeezing his hand. He said that if I knew he was there to squeeze his hand—I did. He told me I was losing a lot of blood and would have to undergo another surgery. He asked if I understood, and I squeezed his hand. He added that because I had only been in recovery a short time, I could not go under anesthesia again. Did I understand? I squeezed his hand. I was then taken to the operating room for a second surgery. As soon as they opened me the second time, my heart went into full arrest. A thoraxcodomy was performed, meaning they had to crack my chest open and grab my heart. They did so and gave me a 45-minute heart massage. My heart finally started beating again, and they found an artery along my ribs that had been missed. It was repaired, and I was put on 100-percent life support.

Now the tough part. My family was told I had only two hours to live and that machines were keeping me alive. They had to decide whether to keep me on the machines or shut them off. I made the decision for them. After about one hour, I started fighting back. Within five days, I was off life support. After seven days, I was out of the intensive care unit and in my own room. Then, 15 days after my shooting, I walked out of the hospital on my own. I did my own therapy, and after eight months went back to work, full duty.

Returning to Work

This was a little weird for me at first not because of the job, but because of the people. Everyone in the department knew about the shooting and they all had questions. That was the easy part. The hard part was believing in myself–believing that I could still do the job. I came on the department because I wanted to make a difference. I wanted and needed to prove to myself that I could still do the job I was hired to do. When Chief Daryl Gates asked me where I would like to work, I told him, "South Central." I knew the south end was the busiest high-crime area, and if I could make it there, I would be just fine. Southeast Division is "Watts," California. This division has a heavy workload. I asked to be transferred there and to work morning watch. So, after about a month, I was transferred to Southeast. I had a great time, but it was different.

Everyone treated me differently. It was either that I was fragile, or I was a hero. People either wanted to work with me, or they thought I was somehow damaged. I was neither of those two definitions. I did not feel any differently than before I was shot. Certainly, I didn't think I was a "super cop." Most of the time I could go about doing the police work I was trained to do. Then someone would see my nameplate or recognize me and say, "Are you the *one?*" I would say, "Yes," and smile. I mean, really, what can you say? It was such a weird feeling. People would come up to me and just want to touch me. They seemed to think something special would rub off. Others would say that touching me made them feel closer to God. I didn't quite understand it, but I did finally realize that everyone needs a role model. For a lot of people, that was me. I think that made me more uncomfortable than anything else. I am just me, no special gifts or talents. I am blessed by God with grace and some great support from both family and friends. The attention put great pressure on me to try to be perfect. We all know in police work there are no absolutes and certainly no perfects. I did the best I could and that seemed to be enough.

Everyone was really considerate and supportive. There is a tremendous support system built into our department, and this was a great help to me. I was honored to receive the Medal of Valor from our department. This is the highest honor an officer can receive. Additionally, I was voted into the police Hall of Fame as "Officer of the Year." That was also a great honor for our department and me.

Surviving the Applause

Now, you would think all this acknowledgment and recognition would go right to my head. Well, I think it did, a little bit. This is when your true friends can help you out. Not the ones who like you for what you did or the ones who are there to get a little rubbed-off glory. Your real friends, the ones who really know you. My true friends kept me grounded. I realized, after a lot of good talks, that people need to see good in others. We all need a role model. Not every police officer will get into a gunfight. But all of us wish and believe that if we encounter a life-threatening situation, we will do what needs to be done. I am no different. I always believed that I had what it takes, but until I was tested, I did not know for sure. I am so grateful for all of those people who taught me what police work is all about. It was because of them that I passed when my time to be tested came. A good friend once told me, "We have no independent thoughts. We are all products of what we are taught." I definitely agree.

What is it that keeps a police officer in the real world when they have had a life-threatening encounter? For me, it was realizing that there are other officers who have done far more heroic things than me and never got credit. We all do this job because it is what is in our hearts to do, not because of the awards we might receive. In police work, the rewards are making the community safe for the people we serve and our fellow officers. If you can save one life or make one officer *think* of survival, then you have received your reward. It may sound corny, but it is the truth. At least it is for me.

DUKE SPEED

Duke Speed is a Principal for Recon Training Concepts. He is a 20-year veteran (retired) of the U.S. Marine Force Recon community and has served as a U.S. Federal Air Marshal Instructor, U.S. Navy Anti-Terrorism Instructor, and a consultant for many organizations involved in the global war against terrorism. Duke is a certified Reconnaissance Marine, Freefall Parachutist, Combatant Diver, Mountain Leader, and FLETC-certified Federal Firearms Instructor with a Distinguished Expert rating. Recently, he returned from Iraq, where he operated as a U.S. Department of State protective security detachment (PSD) member. Duke has a Bachelor of Science degree (Magna cum Laude) in Criminal Justice and has served as the technical advisor for Tully Entertainment. He can be contacted at reconfit@comporium.net or by visiting www.ReconTraining.com.

Chapter 4

FITNESS FOR THE MODERN-DAY
LAW ENFORCEMENT OFFICER

Duke Speed

INTRODUCTION

The law enforcement officer of today is faced with a myriad of complex and multi-dimensional threats from criminal and terrorist elements. Peace officers must be multi-tasked, forward thinking, and able to accomplish a variety of mentally and physically demanding feats, all in a day's work.

Regardless of age, gender, assignment, or specialty, police officers must be capable of accomplishing a variety of physically demanding tasks, which may include the following:

- Sitting, standing, or lying prone for extended periods of time.
- Walking or hiking for extended periods of time.
- Rapidly changing direction while on foot (forward, rearward, and laterally).
- Running and sprinting for varied distances.
- High-speed driving.
- Changing elevations, either by ascending or descending various types of terrain.
- Jumping, negotiating or climbing obstacles in urban and rural environments.
- Wearing and carrying heavy and cumbersome body armor and equipment.
- Fighting, grappling, and restraining suspects.
- Operating technical and tactical equipment.
- Swimming.
- Lifting objects.
- Manipulating less-lethal weapons and firearms.

Because of the high-risk nature of police work, most physical tasks are performed during periods of extreme emotional and physical stress, oftentimes compounded by inclement weather conditions, low visibility or darkness, and several other factors that add to the physical and emotional demands of the operator's body. These demands require every officer to be physically, mentally, emotionally and morally fit. Physical fitness is essential to the day-to-day effectiveness and readiness of every law enforcement organization, as well as every law enforcement officer. This chapter will discuss the importance of a sound physical training program and program options that will assist officers in meeting the physical challenges of law enforcement work.

Physical fitness is essential to the day-to-day effectiveness of law enforcement officers.

Training Objectives

When developing an organizational physical conditioning program, the overall program focus should be on mission effectiveness, health, fitness, and unit cohesion, rather than preparation exclusively for an annual or semi-annual physical fitness test (PFT). The training program should include the following objectives:

- To contribute to the health and well being of every unit member through regular exercise, fitness testing, and health education.
- To develop officers who are physically capable of performing their duties under all potential environments (weather, darkness, urban, rural, etc.).
- To instill within officers a level of physical fitness and endurance that will enhance their probability of mission success and survival in a life-threatening situation.
- To provide a medium for the development of an officer's self-confidence and desire to excel, thereby enhancing the organization's overall discipline, morale, esprit de corps and mission readiness.

Components of a Physical Conditioning Program

Although the definition of physical fitness is subjective, it is safe to state that a law enforcement definition of physical fitness is *the ability of an officer to meet the physical demands of any duty situation and environment without undue fatigue.* In order to achieve this desired state of physical fitness, a physical conditioning program should incorporate the following components and principles:

Strength

Muscular strength refers to the ability of the muscular system to move the body through resistance. Many organizations associate strength training with progressive resistance exercises using weights and machines. However, the ability of an officer to handle their own body weight should be a prerequisite before integrating strength training with machines

into their program. This can be accomplished through calisthenics and other methodologies that will be discussed later in this chapter.

General Strength Training

This type of training strengthens the muscular system by focusing on a full-body workout for strength and size. With this type of training, the major muscle groups are exercised without a specific task or function goal in mind. This type of strength conditioning contributes to overall health.

Specific Strength Training

This type of strength training is task specific. An example would be hiking with weighted rucksacks or body armor to strengthen the lower back and legs.

Endurance

Two types of endurance conditioning are required to meet the demands of law enforcement duties, aerobic and anaerobic.

Aerobic Endurance

Aerobic activity, meaning "in the presence of oxygen," is categorized by physical demands that are sub-maximal (not an all-out effort) and involve activity that is continuous in nature (lasting more than 3–5 minutes). Examples include road marching or long-distance running.

Anaerobic Endurance

Anaerobic activity, meaning "without oxygen," is categorized by physical demands that are high intensity and of shorter (less than 3–5 minutes) duration. Examples include climbing a fence or lifting a heavy object.

Mobility

Mobility conditioning is geared toward improving quality of movement. Quality of movement depends on the following:

- Posture
- Balance and stability
- Agility
- Coordination
- Power
- Speed
- Flexibility

Principles of Physical Conditioning

There are several principles to consider in the development of a physical conditioning program.

Progression

Conditioning programs must incorporate a systematic means to increase training load.

Regularity

To realize a conditioning effect, training programs must be conducted consistently and on a regular basis, ideally 3–5 times per week.

Overload

Only when the various physiological systems of the body are overloaded will they become able to handle a greater load.

Variety

Varying a program from time to time maintains interest of the participants and prevents staleness and boredom.

Recovery

This principle is essential for allowing the systems that were overloaded during conditioning to adapt and become stronger.

Balance

Balanced conditioning programs ensure that all components of physical fitness conditioning (strength, endurance, mobility) are properly addressed.

Specificity

Conditioning that is specific in nature yield specific gains. For example, the pull-ups exercise is ideal for developing strength within officers to grasp and climb a fence or window ledge.

Identification of Tasks, Conditions, and Standards (TCSs)

When selecting the type of training program, one must "begin with the end in mind." It is impossible to navigate a course without knowing a final destination. A pilot is not going to fire up his aircraft without knowing exactly where he is heading. It is not only a waste of time, money, and resources, but it is foolhardy and dangerous as well. A physical training program (or any type of training program) is no different. Clearly defined goals need to be identified before navigating a course of action. Goals and milestone dates must be predetermined to ensure there is a logical plan and course of action in place to meet training objectives.

When beginning with the end in mind, the end result and/or goal(s) is first identified so that, by utilizing a reverse planning sequence, intermediate goals and milestones can be accomplished along the way. In order to determine the appropriate type of training program, one must ponder the question, "What physical capability do we want to possess?" Possible answers are infinite but may include the following examples:

- Chase, catch, control, and apprehend a fleeing suspect.
- Climb over a 15-foot-high vertical obstacle while chasing a fleeing suspect.
- Stand for 6 hours while wearing/carrying 35 pounds of equipment.

Based on the answer to the question, "What physical capability do we want to possess?," a list of tasks, conditions and standards (TCSs) can be developed.

Stephen Covey's text, *Seven Habits of Highly Effective People,* is an excellent map for navigating a physical training program.

TCSs are a simple tool that can be utilized in not

only physical training program management but in all areas of officer training. TCSs will address:

- The actual job to be performed (task).
- The environment in which it is to be performed (conditions).
- The criteria for completing the task properly (standard).

Listed are some examples of TCSs:

Task: Climb over the top of a 15-foot-high chain link fence and safely land on the other side.
Conditions: While armed and wearing full tactical equipment as per unit SOP during periods of daylight, reduced visibility/darkness, and inclement weather.
Standard: Maximum time limit of 20 seconds, without discarding or losing firearm or any tactical equipment.

Task: Hike a distance of three miles.
Conditions: While armed and carrying a 50-pound rucksack during daylight conditions.
Standard: Maximum time limit of 1.5 hours, without discarding or losing firearm or any tactical equipment.

Task: Swim a distance of 500 meters utilizing any combination of the crawl stroke, side stroke, or breast stroke.
Conditions: In a 25-meter pool while wearing BDU blouse and trousers.
Standard: No resting or touching the sides of the pool and maximum time limit of 14 minutes.

Task: Conduct 3 repetitions of bench press with 75 percent of your body weight.
Conditions: In a fitness center while wearing gym attire.
Standard: Participant will lift weight off of bar and complete 3 repetitions by extending arms, locking at the elbows briefly, and briefly touching the chest with the bar. Repetitions must be completed without any assistance from spotter.

Determining Fitness Training Goals

As discussed previously, it is imperative to know a final destination when navigating a course of action. Before embarking on a fitness-training regimen, officers must know what they are attempting to accomplish. The following chronological steps will assist officers or organizations in determining their individual physical conditioning goals in order to determine the appropriate physical training program.

- Identify mission-specific tasks, conditions, and standards.
- Prioritize TCSs. Based on the importance of each TCS, determine which is the most critical and prioritize in descending order.
- Based on the prioritization of TCSs, determine milestones (milestones are simply completion dates for when you'd like TCSs completed).
  Example: June 1, 2005–While wearing uniform and carrying patrol equipment, run 440 yards (.25 mile) in a time limit of 3 minutes.
- Implement the physical training program that facilitates accomplishment of TCSs and milestones.

Conduct of the Physical Conditioning Program

Once TCSs and milestones are identified, a physical conditioning program can be implemented and managed by utilizing the concept of reverse planning. Reverse planning is simply looking at the end result and establishing intermediate goals in order to facilitate accomplishment of the end result. We'll utilize the previous example to illustrate this point.

Task: Run 440 yards (.25 mile).
Conditions: While wearing uniform and carrying patrol equipment.
Standard: In a time limit of 3 minutes.

The goal is to run a quarter of a mile while wearing everyday patrol equipment within a time limit of three minutes. Utilizing the principles of physical conditioning, a plan can be implemented that will lead to the officers being able to achieve this goal.

An example of a 4-week plan might be:

Activity Day	Week 1	Week 2	Week 3	Week 4
Mon-Wed-Fri	Athletic attire	Athletic attire	Athletic attire and body armor	Patrol attire and all patrol equipment
	Warm-up stretching (weeks 1–4)			
	Jog 1 x 800 yds	Jog 1 x 880 yds	Jog 1 x 880 yds	Jog 1 x 880 yds
	Run 2 x 880 yds	Run 3 x 880 yds	Run 4 x 880 yds	Run 3 x 880 yds
	Run 3 x 660 yds	Run 4 x 660 yds	Run 5 x 660 yds	Run 4 x 660 yds
	Run 4 x 440 yds	Run 5 x 440 yds	Run 6 x 440 yds	Run 5 x 440 yds
	Cool-down stretching (weeks 1–4)			
Tue-Thu	Athletic attire	Athletic attire	Athletic attire	Athletic attire
	Core strength training	Core strength training	Core strength training	Core strength training
	Resistance training	Resistance training	Resistance training	Resistance training
Sat-Sun	REST	REST	REST	REST

As you can see from the above example, all of the principles of physical conditioning are utilized in order to facilitate accomplishment of the TCSs.

Progression: The 4-week program is progressive, in that running distances increase each week. Additionally, equipment requirements increase as the weeks progress.

Regularity: The program is conducted on a consistent, regular basis of 5 days per week with two built-in rest days.

Overload: The stress on the participant's body is increased gradually, which aids in the development of strength and endurance.

Variety: The program incorporates a variety of activities, including core training, resistance training and running utilizing variations of uniform and equipment requirements.

Recovery: Every other training day is a different type of activity, which aids in helping the body to recover. Additionally, two rest days are designed into the program for this reason.

Balance: The training program includes all of the desired components, including strength, endurance and mobility.

Specificity: The activities are specific to the TCSs, which is a running- and endurance-improving activity.

Warm-up and Cool-down Conditioning Programs

All fitness training programs, regardless of the specific goals, should include warm-up exercises, conditioning exercises and cool-down exercises. Warm-up exercises facilitate gradual distribution of blood flow to the muscles, preparing both the cardiovascular and musculoskeletal systems for the exercise session by effectively targeting both the

Assault climbers need a good balance of upper and lower body strength.

upper and lower body. The increased blood flow to the muscles produces a warming effect, increasing the elasticity of the muscles and connective tissue, which is believed to reduce the potential for injury. Conditioning exercises are those that form the bulk of the workout and are conducted following the warm-up exercises. Cool-down exercises are conducted at the end of the physical conditioning routine in order to allow the body to gradually return to the pre-exercise state and return the heart rate to its resting state.

Warm-up Program

Like all training programs, there are an infinite number of options that will serve to gradually warm up the muscles, increase blood flow and essentially prepare the body for more rigorous physical activity. A warm-up program will typically consist of flexibility stretching exercises. All of the major body parts should be warmed up utilizing a systematic approach. Ideally, it's best to work from head to toe or vice versa. Listed below is a good example of a warm-up program:

• Neck flexion and extension stretch (15–20 seconds times 3 repetitions)
• Neck lateral stretch (15–20 seconds times 3 repetitions)
• Upper back stretch (15–20 seconds times 3 repetitions)
• Shoulder stretch (15–20 seconds times 3 repetitions)
• Lower back stretch (15–20 seconds times 3 repetitions)
• Trunk rotations (10–15 repetitions)
• Groin stretch (15–20 seconds times 3 repetitions)
• Quadriceps stretch (15–20 seconds times 3 repetitions)

- Modified hurdler stretch (15–20 seconds times 3 repetitions)
- Calf stretch (15–20 seconds times 3 repetitions)

Cool-down Program

The cool-down program can mirror image the warm-up program, except it is conducted after the conditioning program and is the final event of the physical conditioning routine. Its primary purpose is to bring the heart rate back to its resting pre-exercise state. It is also believed by many experts that a cool-down program will decrease lactic acid build-up in the muscles, thereby reducing muscle soreness associated with rigorous physical activity.

Conditioning Programs

There are many options when selecting conditioning activities. Options will depend on fitness goals, facilities, equipment, time available, and several other considerations. One must weigh the desired end result with the other factors in order to determine the best possible course of action. Of course, variety is a key principle within all physical conditioning programs, so a number of different conditioning options can play a role in the overall program.

Resistance Training (Anaerobic) with Calisthenics

Calisthenics are conditioning exercises that are performed by utilizing the participant's own body weight to provide resistance. Unlike weight resistance training, no equipment is necessary for a calisthenics program. Calisthenics have been utilized by military organizations for many years, and are still in use today. Calisthenics programs have many benefits and advantages, including:

- Can be utilized for individual or group conditioning programs.
- Requires no equipment.
- Can be done virtually anywhere.
- Full body workout.
- Flexibility, mobility, resistance, and cardio-

vascular benefits.
- Program can be custom tailored for all fitness levels, gender, or age.
- Can be utilized for sport- or task-specific training.

Resistance Training (Anaerobic with Weights)

Resistance training with weights is a great option for physical conditioning programs. Weight training will provide all of the benefits of calisthenics programs, but the program has inherent limitations that are specified by available equipment and facility space.

Cardiovascular (Aerobic) Conditioning

Cardiovascular conditioning is designed to improve cardiovascular (lungs and heart) endurance and may include several types of activities. It is generally agreed by medical and fitness experts that a cardiovascular training program session be conducted for a minimum of 20–30 minutes in order to sustain the participant's target exercise heart rate. Types of cardiovascular conditioning activities include:

- Running/jogging.
- Hiking, trekking, and forced marches.
- Swimming.
- Bicycling (road or mountain bike).
- Cross-country skiing.
- Snowshoeing.
- Treadmill training.
- Stairmaster training.
- Rowing or paddling.
- Rollerblading or in-line skating.
- Aerobics.
- Martial arts sparring and/or grappling.

Water-Related Conditioning Activities

A solid physical conditioning program can be conducted in a swimming pool or open water environment and may include activities such as water aerobics, sprint swimming, running in water, finning (swimming with dive fins), and incorporating run-swim-run events, or combining poolside calisthenics with swimming pool fitness activities. The options are only limited by imagination. As always, safety should be at the top of the list of considerations.

Circuit and Obstacle Course Activities

Circuit training is best described as a specific training routine in which a variety of fitness disciplines or topics are addressed. It can accommodate a single participant or a large group. It requires little supervision, provides a great deal of variety and challenges with its progressive programming, and allows participants to progress at their own rate. The goal of circuit course training is to develop strength and endurance through a systematic and progressive conditioning program that involves stations where specific exercises are performed. These exercises are performed vigorously for a short period of time before moving to a follow-on station. The vigorous activity in short periods of time provides a near-maximal-quality training session, assuring progressive overload in an organized manner. The exercise selected for each station and the arrangement and sequence of the stations is determined by the training objectives.

Incorporating Mission-Specific Tasks in Fitness Training Programs

As discussed previously, physical conditioning programs should gel with mission-specific or real-world tasks that the law enforcement officer will face on the job. Mission-specific activities can be duplicated in the training environment and will add realism, variety, camaraderie and enjoyment into the physical training program, all while improving the fitness level of each participant. Activities can be introduced into competitive relays, drills or circuit/obstacle courses. Examples of activities include:

- Conducting a 50-meter buddy drag to a covered position.
- Conducting a fireman's carry of a "casualty."
- Pushing a police cruiser or any motor vehicle.
- Mechanically breaching an obstacle (door, wall, etc.).
- Constructing a two-man litter and carrying a casualty.
- Carrying mission-essential firearms and equipment.
- Exercising with body armor and/or weighted rucksacks.
- Exercising while wearing a nuclear, biological, chemical (NBC) mask.
- Negotiating vertical (both up and down) obstacles (hills, stairs, ladders, fences, ropes, cables, etc.)
- Striking and/or kicking a heavy bag or an assailant wearing Red Man™ protective gear.
- Grappling with an assailant.
- Sprinting a distance and field stripping a firearm or tactical equipment.
- Stress drills with live fire or Simunitions.

CONCLUSION

The law enforcement officer in today's world needs to possess an infinite number of skills in order to stay a step ahead of their adversaries. One simply needs to observe a terrorist training video or watch the evening news to see that modern-day terrorists and criminals of the world are sophisticated and determined to achieve their goals. Physical conditioning is a vital step in developing and maintaining the patrol officer's ability to effectively respond to these threats.

Part 2

TRAINING AND EQUIPMENT

STEVE RODRIGUEZ

Steve Rodriguez retired from the Albuquerque, New Mexico, Police Department in 2000, where he served with Field Services, K-9 Unit, Special Investigations, and the SWAT team. Steve has been very involved in training police officers, civilians, military personnel, and federal protection forces in the areas of weapons, tactics, supervision and critical incident management. He currently assists U.S. government agencies in the training of persons responsible for the protection of vital assets.

Chapter 5

PRINCIPLES OF COMBAT SHOOTING

STEVE RODRIGUEZ

INTRODUCTION

When asked to write a chapter that would address my observations and experiences involving life-threatening situations, I at first declined. I wasn't sure if I had anything to offer that hadn't already been said by professional writers. I had no desire to be involved in another 9mm vs. .45 ACP debate that only filled blank pages with ink. My hope in writing this piece is that the professional law enforcement officers reading it are able to use some of the information and not just be entertained. A word of caution. When you have completed reading this chapter, you will not be any better able to survive a deadly encounter than if you had read a book about swimming and then jumped into a lake. The purpose of this chapter is to get you to think, and then act, on saving your life or the life of another. How would you answer the following questions? What is my ability to handle a deadly encounter? What have I done to prepare myself physically, emotionally and intellectually? What is a realistic assessment of my skills and professional education? How do I respond during day-to-day situations?

Everyone can name a person who, if you were in trouble, you would want to have by your side. Would anyone name you as the person they would want with them if they were in trouble? Certain traits are present in all the people I've met that I consider to be true warriors. These people have repeatedly shown uncommon valor and intelligence in the protection of others, and are looked upon for leadership during moments of crisis. My goal is to assist you to be more like them. If skill at arms was all that was necessary in combat shooting, you would only have to practice presenting your weapon, aligning your sights and pressing the trigger. All you would have to do next is continue to repeat as required. If that's what you believe, you should move on to the next chapter. If, however, you realize there is more to preparing yourself for combat than just shooting, please read on.

Never forget that shooting is what we are forced to do when all else fails. The only way you should ever accept shooting another human being is if you know there is no other practical option available, and if you did not act, an innocent person would be seriously injured or die. That innocent person may be you.

In sports, the difference between amateurs and professionals is often the speed of the game and the ability to see the whole field. As you read the following sections, realize that when confronted with a deadly threat you need to see all possible options available, otherwise stated as the ability to see the whole field. Although you'll want to slow things down, the bad guy will normally determine the speed of events. The better prepared you are, the less this will affect you.

My police background is that of a working officer

who retired from the Albuquerque Police Department as a sergeant with the SWAT team. While I was fortunate to spend many hours training other police officers and working investigations, my duties normally revolved around what I call "Suspect Contact" jobs. By this I mean I spent most of my time in units that allowed me to be face to face with bad guys rather than just reading about them in reports (although I did some of that too). During my time as a police officer, I was at the scene of many police use-of-force events, ranging from the use of chemical agents to officer-involved shootings. At most of these scenes, I was able to participate as a police officer during the event, but I also had the advantage of distance during quite a few incidents. The distance I am talking about is as a supervisor directing responses, and from 300 to 1,000 feet above the scene in my role of a part-time member of the police aviation section. From this venue, I was able to see the overall scene and watch officers respond to the actions of offenders. My experiences include being personally involved in using both deadly and physical force, being a supervisor on-scene when use of force was necessary and assisting in the investigation of use-of-force incidents. These experiences have allowed me to form opinions regarding what does or does not work. You must learn from your experiences and the experiences of others, because out in the streets you rarely get a second chance to do the right thing. Currently, I work for a national laboratory and was recently a program manager involved in the training of police officers from foreign countries. These police officers come to the United States, where we teach them some of the tactics and techniques used by American law enforcement so they may better protect their own citizens and U.S. interests abroad.

A career in law enforcement is filled with many different and necessary disciplines. These disciplines range from parking enforcement, SWAT teams and investigations to forensics, patrol division, school resource officers and administrators. Many of us have held several of these positions within our career and, during these assignments, I'm sure each of us felt we were contributing to the overall mission of law enforcement. Law enforcement also has many different sizes and types of departments, with varying populations to protect,

each with its own special flavor and needs. These variables may contribute to the frequency and level of risk to which you may be subjected. However, let there be no misunderstanding. Whether you work on a 5-person department or a 5,000-person department, *a fight is a fight.* The methods you use to prepare and deal with dangerous encounters remain the same, regardless of where you work.

I'd like to note here that the following pages are not just about surviving gunfights. This information is my recommendation for surviving a *police career.* The possibility of you being involved in a life-or-death situation will vary greatly, depending on your geographical location, assignment, duty hours and level of preparation. While I hope you'll never be involved in a police shooting, I can promise that you will be faced with the less-spectacular everyday stresses associated with being in law enforcement. The very nature of your job will cause you to be placed in situations where the weak are abused by the brutal. You will be forced to respond to accidents, where people have been killed and injured, and you will be involved in situations that cause you to be subjected to some degree of force. You must realize an offender's willingness to use force against you will require that you use a degree of force in return. Whether you are personally involved in a deadly force situation or not, you *will* be subjected to situations that cause similar stresses. I hope the following information and advice will assist you in dealing with those situations encountered while performing your duties. I can think of no greater career than protecting those who cannot protect themselves.

Regardless of how good your initial academy training was, never forget it was *basic training.* You should strive to receive a minimum of 40 to 80 hours of additional training every year. I feel this should be in addition to any in-service training you may receive at your agency. This is not meant to belittle the training provided by your agency. What I want is for you to be better trained than your agency's average officer. One way to extend beyond being average is to attend training provided by other agencies and at private institutions. I know many police officers who have college degrees who never use their degree in police work. Yet, many of these officers never attended training within their chosen career field. Training is never a waste of time, and you should balance the courses you attend between your current duties and future plans.

Another police officer once told me that deadly force encounters occur in several different arenas: Preparation, Combat and Aftermath. When we discuss training, incident reviews and the constant "What Ifs?" we should do so from the perspective of these arenas.

Arena One–Preparation

Mental Preparation

When you review past violent experiences you may have been involved in, or if you have reviewed the experiences of others, you realize the types of life-threatening encounters for which we are preparing will normally be over in *seconds*. If we can agree on that, shouldn't we agree that once a life-threatening incident begins there is no time to *learn* the skills necessary to survive? This section may appear to be a little long for some people who would rather read about calibres, bullet designs and different weapons. Think of the shootings you have been involved in, witnessed, or had information about relayed to you. In all the shootings law enforcement officers have been involved in, how many were decided by calibre, bullet design, weapon type or required extraordinary marksmanship skills? I would submit that, by far, the largest deciding factor in any gunfight is the knowledge of what needs to be done, the mental ability to not panic, and the physical ability to carry out your decisions. During a defensive fight, I do not believe the marksmanship skills you'll be required to perform will be difficult. If it's true that most police shootings are at relatively close range, why do so many shots miss their target? I believe it's because the officers are desperately trying to stay alive and may be on the verge of panic. (Technical skills will be discussed in a later section.)

I used to say there is no such thing as luck. I felt we were in control of our destiny, and I didn't like to think otherwise. As I grew older and more experienced, I realized that there is an element of luck (both good and bad) in all things. Now I believe that luck is what fills the possible void between *preparation* and *need*. If I can keep my preparation high enough, I will rarely need to count on good fortune to get me through a difficult situation. Also, if my preparation level is high enough, I have a better chance of surviving if something happens to go wrong or I make an initial mistake. I fully realize that every day police officers survive deadly encounters, even though they may not be as well prepared as they should be. The question remains, how much of our safety and the safety of others are we willing to leave to chance, and how much responsibility are we willing to take in an effort to affect the outcome of an incident?

I never liked working with people who believed if your time is up, your time is up. That may be fine for them, but is that the way they feel about my safety or the safety of others? When you join a law enforcement agency, it's not the same as other jobs. The day you received your credentials you were asked to take an oath. Think about that for just a moment. *You swore to protect the innocent.* Protecting people is what law enforcement is all about. What we are doing here is establishing how much effort we are willing to put forth in fulfilling that oath. Ask yourself, what have I done to prepare myself for the events I know will occur, and what else is needed to get ready?

Many people believe this first arena of preparation begins at the police academy. I am not one of those people. We all had a lifetime of experiences before we ever put on a cadet uniform and shined our leather for the first time. Our family life and background has a tremendous effect on our perceptions of other people and how we interact with them. This is critical in law enforcement, where perceptions influence decisions that are made quickly and often based upon limited information. When we interject the possibility of physical danger to ourselves or others, it becomes extremely important that we recognize how we make decisions. Our ability to make quick and reasonable decisions during routine situations is what provides the basis to make reasonable decisions during life-threatening encounters. Personally, I have never seen an officer who displayed weak decision-making abilities on a daily basis suddenly rise to the occasion when the pressure is really on. However, I have observed officers who were respected by their peers for their day-to-day conduct who, when faced with a difficult situation, performed very well. The manner in which we operate during the routine calls will be the greatest indicator of how we will conduct ourselves during the important calls. Ask any investigator who has performed background checks, and they will tell you that past behavior is the best indicator of future behavior.

Perceptions (The First Impression)

As you arrive on the scene, you will have entered the first level of the use-of-force continuum with "presence." I have to stress that when dispatched to a call for service, listen to all of the information provided by dispatch. If time permits, ask questions and begin forming plans with other officers while en route. By doing this, you may reduce the amount of information you will have to process upon your arrival. The effort here is to reduce sensory overload and free your mind for decision making, rather than processing information you could have already dealt with. Once you have arrived at a high-stress call, first impressions will be very important. Think about how we form those impressions and how they will influence our decision making during the first critical moments of a police response. The way we perceive ourselves and others around us will influence what we consider to be fair and appropriate when dealing with people. I feel the word "fair" is a dirty, four-letter word small children use against their parents. Life is not always fair, it's more of a constant series of decisions based upon circumstances. That being said, as law enforcement officers, we must strive to be just in our dealing with the public. We must strive to avoid overreacting to situations while understanding that an underreaction may allow a situation to escalate. No one said this was an easy job.

Here are a few social filter questions. What was the income level of your family when you were living at home? What was the ethnic make-up of your community? What type of schools did you attend: public, private or parochial? Did you play sports in school? What type of car(s) did your parents drive? Did a car repair or flat tire have a large effect on your household, forcing you to choose which bills

to pay or wait on? When you or a family member became ill, what type of medical treatment did you receive? How long did your parents wait before they took you to a doctor or dentist? Did you go to dances, and with whom did you dance? How do we react when we hear a dispatch to a particular area of town? When responding to a call for service, do you have any preconceived ideas when you drive to a house that has several broken-down cars in the driveway and a house in disrepair? Would you have a different perception if you responded to the same type of call at an expensive house with expensive cars in the driveway?

The question should not be are you forming perceptions based upon your observations. *Of course you will make assumptions based upon what you perceive.* That's what we call experience and training. The question should be, are your perceptions correct, and how will they affect your decisions? Have you ever been in a situation where you are trying to explain to a third party how you knew someone was a crook? Very often I'd hear a police officer say, "Well, I could just tell." If you cannot explain what reasonable suspicion or probable cause is during a routine call, then what on earth makes you think you will give the best statement of your life after you've been involved in a police shooting? Once you realize you must make decisions based upon your observations, you must also realize what values you place on those observations. I do not think anyone's opinion is in and of itself wrong. I believe it is how we react to those opinions that matter. What's just as important is, can we explain to the courts how we processed the information we had in our possession at the time of an event? My experience is that most police officers involved in a use-of-force situation believe they were correct at the moment they used force. Where we run into trouble is when we need to explain to someone else all of the facts present at the time of the event. You will be asked to explain what you observed, how your life experiences and training have taught you to interpret those facts, and what responses were available to you at the time. I'm not trying to scare you into questioning every thought you have while responding to a possible crime scene. I want you to understand that you are processing information and to be more attuned to those things around you. Next, are you reacting correctly to those cues, or at least reacting in a reasonable fashion? Can you remember watching a police video of a scene that went bad? With the benefit of safety and distance, were you able to see when things started to go bad for the officer? What I am trying to get you to consider is, if we can increase your ability to quickly recognize cues and to place values on them, you may be able to *avoid* some dangerous situations. If you cannot avoid the danger, you'll at least be better able to respond quickly and correctly.

In a two-second gunfight, the person who can gain the first half-second has a definite advantage. If we can process information quickly and correctly, we may be able to reduce the lag time required to respond or react to a given situation. One definition for lag is "the interval between two related events." For the purpose of our discussion, it is used in the context of a cue being given and you reacting properly to it. Many trainers agree that the average person takes between .5 and 1.5 seconds to react to a given situation. If, through training, an officer can reduce and refine the information which must be processed at the moment a reaction is needed, that officer will have a better chance of reducing lag time. If the officer has a practiced series of responses that can be used if necessary, we again reduce the amount of lag time before we may have a positive effect upon the outcome of the event. Always remember that lag time works both ways. If you perceive that events are going to require an action on your part, don't wait until things are out of control before you act. Make the offender's lag time work for you. Before we leave the topic of lag time, I'd like you to consider that lag time does not only occur at the beginning of an event. It occurs every time new information is received that must be reacted to.

This is the tricky part. A common problem officers deal with is when they push or hit an offender one time more than some bystander or supervisor thought was necessary. I submit that often that last punch is thrown before an officer has time to react to the offender's lack of resistance. Occasionally, I will read where an officer fires several shots at an offender even after the offender was down and no

longer a threat. Based upon all the training I have conducted with police officers, military personnel and private citizens, I have formed the opinion that many people experience considerable lag time when reacting to a target which is no longer a threat. Often, this lag time is at least as long as the time necessary to respond to the original threat. Once a person is involved in a high-stress situation, there is a very good possibility that extra rounds may be fired due to lag time. By realizing this may occur, trainers should structure courses that will allow people to gain experience and learn about how to STOP a response, and not just how to start one. Outside of a required qualification course, I don't always tell my students how many rounds will be fired in order to have a reactive target "face away or fall." When I can, I want them to react to the change in threat.

We sometimes fail to remember that it is necessary to explain to civilians perceptions we as police officers take for granted. My first hope is to make you aware of why you feel or act certain ways during situations, and then prepare your training to match what may be required. I need to remind you that if you are involved in a use-of-force situation, eventually, you will need to explain your actions to the courts and your agency. If you have confidence in the way you perceive cues, if you understand the law, and your Standard Operating Procedures (SOP), you will have the confidence to quickly make decisions that will influence the outcome of a deadly force encounter. Later, you'll be better able to paint an accurate picture in someone else's mind as to what you experienced and why you reacted the way you did. It takes a great deal of practice to properly explain all the information present at a given moment in time. If it's true (and I think it is) that around 80 percent of communication is non-verbal, you should be aware when you write a police report or give a verbal statement there is the possibility others may miss a tremendous amount of information you are trying to send them. Once you have the ability to explain what you were aware of, your thoughts and decisions, you will be amazed at how many things you can notice during an encounter.

Rules Involving Police Use of Force

The reason I prefer to use the civil rights standard is because I feel it is more specific to the issues I am concerned with. I've seen many cases where a criminal grand jury found the officer's actions justified, but a civil jury found against the officer and department. Much of this may be due to the rules of evidence and other factors, but if we can meet the civil standard, we will be fine with the criminal standard.

At the time of this writing, the "objective reasonableness test," which is used to judge all federal civil rights use-of-force cases, is *Graham v. Conner*, 490 U.S. 386 (1989). You should contact your agency's attorney and get a copy of this case, or a more recent ruling if there is one. Read it carefully and understand the boundaries of the law. I am not an attorney, but based on my reading of *Graham v. Conner*, I believe the major points are:

1. What was the severity of the crime at issue?
2. Did the suspect pose an imminent threat to the safety of the officers or others?
3. Did the suspect actively resist arrest or attempt to evade arrest by flight?
4. Were you able to give warning prior to using force?
5. These points must be judged from the perspective of a reasonable officer at the scene and not from the perspective of hindsight.
6. Focus on what you knew at the time of the incident and not what you have learned since that time.

Of course, there is much more to civil rights rulings that involve use of force than this short section. For example, you should give warning if possible, if it would not endanger your life or the life of another. I recommend you contact your agency's attorneys and obtain all the best information possible. Then, if you are forced to act, you'll do so from a position of knowledge and confidence.

In addition to learning about federal civil rights rulings involving use of force, you should review your department's policies and procedures. It's not unusual for a department's orders to be stricter than federal civil rights law. Talk to a supervisor about

any questions you may have, and don't be afraid to speak with as many people as necessary to understand what is or is not allowed. On the topic of what is or is not allowed, keep in mind how your local community/judges enforce their control over policing. I want to emphasize again that you will not have time to "learn" anything once the fight begins.

As mentioned earlier, eventually you'll be asked to make a statement to explain what you observed, what happened, and what actions you took. When that time comes, you'll need to paint an accurate picture in several other people's minds. You will need to be sure to use terms and reference points that cannot be misconstrued by anyone who hears or reads your words. Police officers, by the nature of their work, become rather matter-of-fact and lack emotion when giving a report. Remember, people will be listening to more than just your words. You'll need to lower your guard a bit to allow others to know if you were really scared of being murdered, or that someone else was in danger of being murdered. I'm not saying that you should cry or put on an act. What you need to be is honest and not a robot.

Because we're discussing a mindset and what goes into it, here is something to consider. When the shooting is over, you'll be asked to give a statement to assist in the criminal, civil, and internal investigations. My advice is for you to talk to a good attorney first and wait at least 24 hours before giving a *formal statement.* I say this because you just had someone try to murder you or someone else, and you may still be a bit unsettled. *I do want you to give __tactical information__ that will let other officers know if there are any outstanding criminals, where pieces of evidence may be found, along with any other information that will allow the crime scene to be deemed safe and processed.* But after that, I think you should slow down and talk to an attorney prior to giving a formal statement. I suggest to all my friends that they ask their attorney to be called to the scene so that they may be available to assist the officer and suggest additional pieces of evidence to be documented. If you don't have an attorney, find one. Ask around, and meet with the person you may have to call out at 3:00 in the morning because you've just been involved in a deadly force situation, may have had your Miranda Rights read to you, and are waiting to talk to the shooting team.

Here are some of the techniques I have used when giving statements to shooting teams after an event. They are provided so you might consider these topics as you read the rest of the chapter.

1. Remember, these individuals may not have the same life experiences and training as you. That's not good or bad, it's just a fact.
2. They may not understand your professional jargon, so don't use it. Every occupation or lifestyle has jargon. Never assume the person with whom you are speaking, or the person who in six months will read your words, knows what you meant to say. My experience is that most people will just smile and nod, even if they don't understand a thing you said. What is even worse is if the person to whom you are speaking thinks they know what you meant, and interject their own meaning. Speak in clear text only.
3. Start at the very beginning of your encounter and work in chronological order (step by step) starting from the moments just before you received the radio call or sighted the situation, explaining every observation and perception you made. Because you are going to talk to your attorney *before* you give a formal statement, I would suggest your attorney make up a basic outline of your statement to be sure you cover all the important points. The investigators may ask to see your notes if you take them into the interview.
4. Speak slightly slower than you normally would. This will allow you time to choose the best words to describe your thoughts and allow the others time to understand your intended meaning.
5. If you have nothing to say, or you are thinking, shut your mouth and don't ramble.
6. If you are asked to draw a sketch or diagram of the scene, do so with care. Make sure you note that your sketch is not to scale, and I'd suggest you indicate the position of persons and objects with a circle rather than an X. It's a small point, but a circle represents an area rather than an exact location.
7. Don't ever assume you are smarter than the

person you are talking to. And never believe you're as good as you think you are. You have to prove yourself every time you open your mouth and on every call you handle. You can go from hero to zero in less than .25 seconds.

One last thought on perceptions. First impressions work both ways. As soon as a suspect saw you, he began to form an opinion as to your abilities and limitations. Command presence is not the same as an intimidating presence. I've had criminals notice my police car, the equipment on my duty belt and the weapons I was armed with. I'll bet you've had criminals do the same to you, even if they didn't tell you. ***Look and act sharp***.

Speaking and Listening Ability

Efforts to use verbal skills indicate you are in the second level of the use-of-force continuum. When I say speaking ability, I don't mean public speaking in the classical sense. It doesn't really matter if you can give a speech or present a toast at a banquet. Can you communicate with people? Can you communicate to people who may be under a great deal of stress? Do you have the ability to calm others during periods of excitement, or do you get excited right along with them? Can you understand what someone is telling you, or do you just hear their words? Taking into account that a large part of communication is nonverbal, do you notice a person's body language? Can you describe your interpretation of that body language? On which do you place greater value, a person's words, or their inflection and body language?

I'm sure you've seen at least one or two officers who, when they arrived at your scene, if you weren't in a fight when they got there, you soon would be. Some people just have a terrible time not making everyone around them mad. Hopefully, these types are corrected or fired quickly. I once told an officer never to back me up, I'd ask for someone else. Other people could work with this officer, but I couldn't. I felt there was a much better chance of talking someone into going to jail if a different officer showed up to assist me.

Most agencies have some type of training available to their officers to develop active listening skills. Most of these courses revolve around some type of investigative or negotiations training. Patrol officers need this training, too. If your agency does not have this training in-house, then find it somewhere else. Contact your state training academy and surrounding departments and see what they have available. This type of training should be mandatory for all police officers, especially those officers who tend to work high-crime areas. Some of the best courses I ever took involved dealing with emotionally disturbed or suicidal persons. If you can listen and speak effectively to someone who appears to be emotionally or psychologically disturbed, you can speak to anyone.

I mentioned that the true professionals I have known had certain traits. One of those traits was that they were all great listeners and talkers. When dealing with offenders, if time permits, (a) ask them, (b) order them, and if you must, (c) make them. This is not meant to appear that you only ask the offender once, but if time allows, you should pass through each phase. You want to be able to show an escalation and that you gave the offender a lawful order.

While the use-of-force continuum may be broken down into many sub-levels, the major areas will include: Presence, Verbal Contact, Chemical Agents, Impact Weapons, and Deadly Force.

Never be afraid to call for additional officers. If we can increase presence and thereby cause the offender to submit to our requirements without force, that's a win. If the offender fails to submit to additional presence, it may be necessary to proceed to the next level in the use-of-force continuum. Time permitting, some things you should consider are: Is there time to bring additional resources to the scene? What is the seriousness of the crime? Is the offender attempting to flee, resist or evade? What are the consequences of acting or retreating? Yes, some crimes are not serious enough to use force. In *Graham v. Conner,* one of the issues was "severity of the crime." Will the use of force required to stop a criminal act be proportionate to the severity of the crime? There are plenty of times when police are sent to a scene and there is either not enough criminal activity to warrant a police response, or it was strictly a civil scene and police have very few options. In the military, it's called "mission creep." You are tasked with one thing and

get drawn farther into other areas outside of your responsibility or the original call. Avoid this situation, because if you are involved in a use of force, you will have to explain all of your actions leading up to the event. Never push a bad scene.

Less-Lethal Force Options

Chemical Agents

The use of chemical agents signals that you have entered the third level of the use-of-force continuum. While attending initial training, you were exposed to some type of chemical agent normally carried by officers on their duty belt. Are you still carrying your Mace or "OC" spray? Are the officers working with you carrying theirs? Do you know the full capabilities and limitations of your chemical agent? What are the agents you are carrying, OC, CS, CN or a combination of agents? What is the concentration level of your agent? Does it deploy as a stream or a mist? What is the effective range for deployment, and are there issues involving cross-contamination to fellow officers? Have you ever noticed that chemical agents seem to work best against other police officers? If you were involved in a use-of-force situation and did not have your chemical agent available, do you think an issue could be raised that you failed to exercise all options? Have you ever seen or heard of chemical agents failing to work as designed? What were the circumstances where chemical agents failed? What are the first aid and reporting procedures if you use your chemical agent? Technology has vastly improved the equipment and tactics available to law enforcement. Know what options you have available, along with the capabilities and limitations of your equipment. If you are involved in a shooting, you'll need to explain why all lesser means were not practical.

Impact Weapons

The use of impact weapons means you have entered the fourth level of the use-of-force continuum. Strikes using your hands, knees, feet and other body parts are included with tools, such as batons, extended-range kinetic energy impact weapons (beanbag or baton rounds), "Air Taser," and police service dogs. Here, we should ask the same questions as in the previous section. Are you aware of what might be considered a disparity of force? Are you carrying your baton, and do you have access to a weapon, such as a beanbag gun or Taser? If you requested a piece of equipment, such as a police service dog, how long would it take to arrive? Have you seen or heard of one of these tools failing to produce a desired effect? Have you taken any training beyond the police academy to increase your level of expertise? What are the first aid and reporting procedures if an impact weapon is used?

This is the last level of force where the offender is expected to have a full recovery from any injuries he may experience. While serious injury could happen at this or a lower level of force, it is never the intended consequence. When we move to the next level of force, we intend for the offender to receive, at a minimum, serious bodily harm and perhaps death. There should be no doubt about this matter.

Deadly Force Options

If you have been forced by the offender's action to resort to this last level of the use-of-force continuum, you are in a situation that is so serious you can no longer be concerned that the offender may die. This is because a failure to act on your part will result in serious bodily harm or death to you or another innocent person. Now that you have reached the decision to use deadly force, you must act with speed and efficiency. You must stop the offender's action no matter if the offender is maimed or dies in the process. The reason I have taken the time to discuss these areas to such a degree prior to talking about combat shooting is because you must be resolute in winning a deadly force encounter. There must be no doubt that you are doing the right thing, based upon the offender's actions and the options available. Once the decision to use deadly force has been made, the only thing that should stop you is the offender making an overt act of surrender, or no longer being physically able to continue their murderous assault. There is no time for you to continue with a question as to what the law allows, what the SOPs say or what your moral beliefs are. Those areas should have been

reviewed before you went to work and had to use any level of force. Now you're in a fight for your life, and that's the way you need to think when you are training. As my friend Clint Smith, of Thunder Ranch Inc., once said, "Some people just need to be shot." If you need to use your weapon because nothing else will work, then use it.

Physical Fitness

While it's not necessary for you to be in the same physical condition as an Olympic athlete, you should be in above-average physical condition. The type of physical training you should consider needs to match the conditioning you will need if you are in a fight, and not just to lose weight, be healthy and look good. The ability to be healthy on a day-to-day basis is certainly a benefit of physical conditioning, but you also need to structure your training to provide for what may be a once-in-a-lifetime maximum effort toward staying alive. Earlier, we mentioned that first impressions work both ways, and that the suspects you come in contact with will begin to size you up as soon as they see you. What will they think if you are 15 pounds overweight? Do you believe being in better shape will contribute to your ability to handle stress better? Have you ever been involved in a foot pursuit that turned into a fight or a shooting? If you had to run several blocks at full speed, stop and make the shot of your life, do you think your physical conditioning might make a difference?

I'll leave the area of designing a physical conditioning program to a better-qualified person, such as a trainer at your local gym. What I would suggest you do is find a trainer and describe your normal schedule and explain what it's like to be in a fight for your life while wearing body armor and your duty equipment. This fight may begin with the stress of high-speed driving, or it may start from a relaxed standing position when you were expecting someone to hand you their driver's license. Your fight may involve one person who is bigger and stronger than you, or it may also involve two or three and/or their friends. Halfway through the fight, one of your opponents may pull a knife or a gun, at which time you'll need to break contact and try to draw your gun. If you're still on your feet, you may need to be concerned about accuracy, because your fight may have started in a grocery store with innocent people standing around watching, and you are afraid of hitting them. Please let your trainer know that you have no idea when this will happen, so you can't just peak for a short period of time. You may want to explain that under no circumstances can you lose this fight. Enough said.

Equipment Selection

Many agencies dictate what equipment can be used by its members, and there is very little, if any, room for officers selecting something different. Fine; learn to use what was issued to its maximum effectiveness. When possible, make suggestions on how equipment can be improved or changed and try to push those changes through your system. Remember, often the people you are trying to convince do not use these items themselves. You'll have to provide documentation as to why your suggestions are better than what is currently being used, cost estimates and a training regimen.

If your agency allows you some latitude in selecting individual equipment, you will have the ability to pick those items that better fit your duties, body size and confidence level. Regardless of what equipment is issued or you are able to purchase, you must train with it. When it comes to your duty belt, the location of tools and the way they are carried is very important. There is no excuse for fumbling for equipment.

Firearms

Your firearms must function as close to 100 percent as possible. Most people think this is obvious, but unfortunately, this is not the case. I've seen officers who routinely had their weapons malfunction during qualifications and they'd make the comment, "It always does that." Often this was due to poor maintenance, damaged equipment, such as magazines or speed-loaders, and bad ammunition. If you are using an issued firearm that is malfunctioning, take it to the armorer and have it fixed or replaced. Most of the problems I have seen involving handguns occurred when an officer had his pistol "tuned" or "accurized." I'd ask the officer how

it shot before someone worked on it. I found normally the pistol worked fine and was more than accurate enough for its intended purpose. The officer had it worked on because he read, or heard, that it was necessary to make the gun more accurate or reliable.

Handguns are like cars. You have to decide what you need, what you can afford and what you want. Try never to confuse need with want. The average handgun loaded with factory ammunition is capable of landing all of its shots within a 4-inch circle at 25 yards. Can you keep all your shots within that 4-inch circle? If your groups are larger than the 4-inch circle, what's more likely, that it's the gun or you? I'll help you. You are the weak link in this system. You can train hard, but you cannot buy skill and experience. If you decide to change weapons systems, the reasons should be because you will hit your target more often, have fewer manipulations to perform when operating it, and have greater confidence walking into a dangerous situation. The first two reasons may be objective; you alone have to determine your confidence level.

If you have the ability to choose the handgun you may use to defend your life or the life of another, plan on spending at least three times as much as the cost of the weapon alone. You'll need to purchase a good holster, magazine pouches, ten magazines, practice ammunition, duty ammunition, targets, quality instruction and range time. If you are not willing to invest that much time and money, you should consider staying with whatever your department issued you. Then we'll at least know you can perform to a minimum standard in case of a deadly threat. If that sounds a bit harsh, it was intentional. Crossing over from one weapons system to another is a big decision that may have great consequences and should never be taken lightly. If you have decided to proceed with learning to use a new handgun, buy two. If your primary gun breaks, you'll have a backup until it's repaired.

Handgun Action Types

Since the 1980s, there has been a tremendous increase in the number of handgun action types available to the law enforcement community. All of the handgun styles I will discuss are from major manufacturers and have proven to be reliable systems. Space limitation precludes me from mentioning every handgun made. I would avoid a handgun I cannot have repaired locally. I don't care how much you pay for it, if you shoot it enough, one day it will break. That's why I told you to get a backup.

Semi-auto pistols will be discussed first, followed by revolvers.

Single Action (Browning): The John Browning design can be found in many modern pistols. This system would include Colts, Kimbers, Springfield Armory and several other companies. The classic Colt .45 is one of the older designs and is still regarded as an excellent system by many. This reputation is based upon both the bullet it fires and the fact that it has a narrow grip surface area and short, light, constant trigger pull. Ammunition capacity is normally about eight rounds. A neglected option in this system is that it can be found in several different calibres, not just .45 ACP. If you choose this system, make sure you get an ambidextrous safety installed.

Single Action (Glock, Sigma): Glock's safe action pistol is now carried by many law enforcement officers. Glock-style pistols have a consistent trigger pull and can be found in many different configurations and calibres. Ammunition capacity ranges between 8 and 18 rounds.

Double Action/Single Action: Smith & Wesson, Sig Sauer, and Beretta are the pistols most often seen with this action type. The first round is fired in similar fashion to a revolver, meaning the hammer is cocked by the trigger until it releases and fires the cartridge. Thereafter, the hammer is cocked by the slide, with trigger pressure needed to fire the weapon reduced by about 50 percent. Ammunition capacity ranges between 8 and 16 rounds.

Revolvers: A revolver will fire double action for every shot unless the operator chooses to cock the hammer manually. Revolvers can be found in a number of calibres and are still used by many agencies, especially as backup weapons. Ammunition capacity is usually six rounds.

You may have noticed that I didn't list what I felt were the positives and negatives of all these action types. Yes, I've heard that a 9mm was just a .45 on stun. But I wouldn't want to be hit with either a 9mm or a .38 Special. To be honest, they all have their own advantages and disadvantages, and all would be suitable for use as a duty firearm. What will work for you may be different than what would work for someone else. What I think should be asked is, "What system fits my personal needs best?" Reliability is the most important factor you should look for when choosing a weapon. After reliability, I would look for a firearm that is not too big for my hand size, in the largest calibre I could shoot well. I've watched police officers who normally passed their department qualification course in the 90 percent range switch to a different handgun and barely pass the next training course. When asked why they were carrying a different weapon, they would try to explain why the new gun was so much better. They just wouldn't admit they spent a lot of money on a gun and couldn't shoot it well. I have no problem if someone wants to switch to a system that initially may be harder for them to shoot well. BUT, they should not begin carrying that system on duty until they shoot it at least as well as the model they are already carrying. I have argued with people many times when they wanted to buy a handgun in 10mm or .45 calibre with a double-column magazine, and their hand was too small to reach the trigger. People like this feel that the foot-pounds of energy and magazine capacity will make up for poor hits, poor manipulation skills, or lack of training. I cannot stress enough that you are not just carrying a weapon to protect yourself, you may have to protect someone else.

Long Guns

The issue of pistol-calibre carbines, shotguns and rifles is simple. If you are going to a potential gunfight, take something with a stock on it. I'd rather have a 9mm carbine than only a .45-calibre handgun. The increased sight radius, ammunition capacity, etc., will increase my ability to hit the offender, if necessary. If I can have a *real rifle*, all the better. It's a gunfight, not a fair fight. All I want is for the offender to not threaten anyone with serious bodily harm or death. If the offender fails to stop, then I want the best weapon I can operate well. *Handguns are strictly for surviving an unexpected attack, or to use when your rifle malfunctions/breaks!* I realize that we in the United States do not want to live in a country where all police have to carry a rifle. That's a good thing. I work with countries where lots of folks walk around with submachine guns. You don't want to live there. If you have access to a long gun, practice with it the same as your handgun. But you should always work with your handgun, because it is the one weapon you should always have available.

Once, when I was talking to a group of police countersnipers, I stated, "I often find the more a person talks about ballistic coefficient, muzzle velocity and foot-pounds energy, the less they know about shooting." *That made a few folks mad.* All these concerns were decided when the initial selection of equipment was made, so I quit thinking about it. After that point, there are more important issues that revolve around the individual's skill level with the equipment on hand, and that's where we need to spend our time. If your department only allows one type of handgun, then learn to operate it. I, along with most of the other gray-haired types, carried revolvers when we became cops, and I think we got plenty of police work done. Work to upgrade your equipment. But keep in mind it's not the gun that makes the difference, it's the person carrying it.

Get the best tools you can for your profession. When you're off duty, you can take whatever risks you'd like. If you want to skydive, ride motorcycles or fly airplanes, I say more power to you. But you have no right to place your fellow officers or citizens at risk because you lack the maturity to properly equip and train yourself. I mentioned earlier that in a defensive shooting, the foot-pounds energy you have and the marksmanship skill that will be necessary are normally not extraordinary.

The biggest factors in surviving a close-range deadly force encounter will be: was your reaction fast enough, did you present your weapon without fumbling and did you hit your opponent until they were no longer a threat? You must not panic! The foot-pounds of energy, magazine capacity and fancy finish on your guns mean nothing if you fail to have the mental conditioning to notice the cues that will be present before the fight begins, and the presence of mind to keep yourself under control.

Firearms Training

Every firearms and tactics instructor has had at least one student make the following statement after a poor showing during an exercise: ***"If it had been real life, I would have done better."*** *That's a bunch of crap!* I hope we all realize that if it had been real life, you would have done much *worse*. If I were chief, I would try to have everyone on the department watch their fellow officers during training, to include firearms qualifications. This would allow for a degree of peer pressure and some rivalry. Officers would also have the opportunity to see the skill level of their backup officers. With many people, few things are more important than to avoid embarrassment. The idea of possibly saving their own life, or the life of someone else, is not an easy concept for them to imagine. The knowledge that your friends will see how well, or how poorly, you perform during training may provide the incentive needed by some people. Many agencies have a special pay clause allowing money awards based upon performance in certain areas, or they may have badges or medals. Whatever works in your department is fine. The object of these efforts is to find ways to motivate law enforcement officers to practice those skills that will allow them to do their jobs better.

As a supervisor, I placed a value upon the way officers conducted themselves at qualifications and training. This is not to say that the highest shooter or most physically fit person was the best police officer. Likewise, the person chosen for a particular job, such as countersniper, need not be the best shot on the team. Other factors may be far more desirable than shooting skill alone. The best supervisors always place judgment, maturity, discipline and courage above other learned skills. I need a person with a good heart and mind. I can teach almost anybody the other things. How well an officer performs during a controlled training course is important, but it is only a part of the puzzle. As mentioned previously, observed past behavior will always be the best indicator of future behavior. This brings us back to the officer who is a total package. Among the traits possessed by the best officers is the fact that they are well rounded. They are accomplished practitioners at *every level of the use-of-force continuum.* These exemplary officers are not just good shots, they are good at everything. They are respected officers within their departments and within the law enforcement community. Sure, they are better at some things than others, but they are good at everything because they work at it and take things seriously. Another trait you should strive for during training is *consistency*. I've seen many officers shoot through a course and never miss a shot, then shoot a similar course on a different day and repeatedly fail to do well. I need consistency from officers, so I know where they can work efficiently in the system and where I need to help them improve. On a SWAT operation where I had the luxury of time to pick a team for entry, I always looked for those officers who were consistent. The last thing I needed was to be unsure of the performance level of a team member and whether they were having a good day or a bad day.

Before I get too deep into training issues, I would like to suggest you make every effort to attend any training conducted by your agency, surrounding departments, and state academies. It never hurts to become a state-certified instructor, so you can learn by teaching others. Any training you can get from the government will be at a reduced cost to you, and you may even get work time to attend. I would also *strongly suggest* you attend private schools that offer instruction in your areas of interest. I work part-time for a private shooting school, and while it's not designed for the police or military, we normally have a few in each of the courses. Without exception, the training they receive can be beneficial to their careers. There is no way for you to learn the skills necessary to effectively protect yourself and others without personal instruction from a qualified instructor.

Firearms Safety Rules

- **All guns are always loaded.**
  People get shot with supposedly empty guns all the time.
- **Never let the muzzle cover anything you are not willing to destroy.**
  That means parts of you, parts of me and anything you can't afford.
- **Keep your finger off the trigger until you are ready to shoot.**
  Your finger is fast, sometimes TOO fast; keep it straight until you need it.

- **Be sure of your target, what's in front and behind it.**
  You are responsible for every round you fire. Think about errant rounds.

The main rule here is DON'T SHOOT YOUR-SELF. I wish we had data on officers who accidentally shoot themselves. Think about how often you've heard of this happening within law enforcement. Personally, I think the person most likely to shoot you is you. If I didn't believe that, I wouldn't push safety so hard. And if safety is important during the controlled atmosphere of a training range, it's even more important during a gunfight. Practice these rules at all times. You *should* get a fellow officer to assist you when you go to the range.

Presentation (Drawing Your Weapon)

If you get to the point where you're drawing your gun, you'd better have practiced it earlier under all conditions (holster snapped, winter jacket, gloves, plain clothes, standing, lying down, etc.). If you don't own an electronic timer, buy or borrow one. You'll need it for practice sessions, both dry- and live-fire. The nice thing about electronic timers is that they don't lie. Set the timer and keep a log of your times and hits. It doesn't do any good to be the first one to miss in a gunfight.

Since this book is designed for police officers who have completed their initial training, I won't spend time discussing how to stand and draw your pistol. Something that does affect your presentation, however, is your holster and how you wear it. More than likely, your holster was designed to keep the pistol secure while sitting in a car or standing. It will also be designed for you to be able to use your dominant (strong) hand to obtain the weapon while dressed in summer-type clothes. That's fine as long as your dominant hand is always available, you never wear a jacket, gloves, and never do anything but stand when you shoot. Unfortunately, most training is geared toward teaching police officers how to pass qualification courses, not toward fighting. Recently, I watched several videos of officer-involved shootings. In none of these videos did I see a police officer shooting a handgun in the same classic stance used at the range during qualification. There is no guarantee you will have access to your dominant hand, and there is every chance you may not be standing still when you have to present your weapon.

Holster manufacturers balance comfort, security, accessibility, and price when making their holsters. You'll need to balance those same issues when you select the holster that will be used to hold the instrument that may save your life or the life of another. Any holster I decide to purchase allows me the option to draw my pistol with *either* hand.

Practice drawing your handgun (unloaded) from a variety of positions, to include standing, kneeling, sitting, lying down, moving toward cover, etc. This is where a coach is beneficial, because they can ensure that you do not commit unsafe acts, such as covering yourself with your muzzle. Practice slowly, working on technique until you feel comfortable and your coach approves of your technique. Then, load up and begin very slowly to practice shooting live rounds.

Suggested Shooting Drills

Once you've decided on a holster, you need to practice presenting your pistol and hitting a target at various ranges. If you're going to the range, be sure to take someone with you. As stated earlier, it's a good idea to have someone else around for safety reasons, and also operating the timer and camera. I'd suggest you practice at ranges from 1 foot out to at least 200 feet. The idea here is to know what your capabilities and limitations are before you get into a fight. To understand what these ranges mean in the real world, consider the following: 1 to 3 feet, you're within arm's distance, 20 feet is about a car length and 150 feet is a bank parking lot.

If you're like most people (myself included), you'll head off to the range and shoot at a large silhouette-type target while standing. In the beginning, that's fine. But, as soon as practical, you should start placing some type of covering over most of the silhouette (paper will do) to represent the target being behind cover. You should also practice moving to, and firing from behind, your own cover, as mentioned above. It is my belief that if cover is available, I'd like to get behind it. As for covering up different portions of the silhouette, I rarely plan on bad guys presenting their entire body

to me. I believe they'll head for cover too. Shooting center mass means shooting at center mass of *the available target*. That available target may be a foot, elbow or other small body part that's exposed. *Don't wait for the perfect torso shot; hit what you can as long as you can.* There's a chance the bad guy may quit after taking a couple of hits, and if not, they may move around and present a better target.

Once you have your range routine in place, you'll need to practice the same drills using your non-dominant hand. As police officers, we spend a lot of time thinking and practicing "shipping lead" and very little time on the problem of "receiving lead." Panic is often the absence of a plan. Just because you're injured doesn't mean you've lost. Should your dominant hand or arm become injured, have a plan to use the other hand. I realize you may not be as fast or as accurate with your non-dominant hand, but at least you'll have the option of doing something. While I'm on the topic of injury drills, if you have received an injury that stops you from being useful within the kill zone, *LEAVE!* I would rather have you clear the area and be a good witness than for you to think you should stay. Leaving the area and briefing other responders coming to the scene may be more helpful.

Also, with reference to using your non-dominate hand, I chose not to elaborate on the sequence of events necessary to safely draw and manipulate a pistol with your support hand because I believe it will be safer for you to locate a professional firearms instructor and have them provide this instruction.

Manipulation Drills

I presume your department has taught you to load, unload, speed reload, perform a tactical reload, and a series of malfunction clearances. Now what you need to do is practice them regularly from behind cover, moving to cover, and any other way you can think of. I do not allow my students to exchange magazines while the pistol is in the holster unless they are behind the firing line. I don't want them to miss the opportunity to practice a reload.

Make sure you practice these drills religiously. Just because your weapon malfunctions or "runs dry" doesn't mean you're losing. It just means you need to clear it or reload. As stated before, you should be able to reload and clear malfunctions using only one hand–either hand. It's a handgun, not a *handsgun*. It will take a qualified firearms instructor to teach you how to do this safely.

Varied Practice Sessions

Once you have these *basic drills* practiced with both hands, you'll need to leave the standard, lighted police-type range. For ideas, I would suggest you attend a civilian shooting club that has competitions, such as the United States Practical Shooting Confederation (USPSC), the International Defensive Pistol Association (IDPA), or others. An advantage of attending these types of civilian competitions is that they have rules, by-laws and a structure to them. While this is not police training, it does give you the opportunity to shoot a new course under pressure and practice your *police techniques*. I only see one major flaw in police officers attending this type of training; cops want to win. If you attend these matches, I'd hope you would wear your duty equipment and continue to practice responsible techniques, like reloading behind cover. Don't let the *game* suck you in. If you're there to practice for your police duties, then practice those techniques that will keep you alive, not the ones that reward you with a trophy. I'd prefer that you first attend a professional firearms academy, but these club events are cheaper and a reasonable option.

After you've seen these types of shooting drills, start setting up similar drills in low- and no-light settings. As you continue to progress in your shooting skills, there are certain areas that *MUST* be covered in training. These are shooting in low light, shooting at decisional targets (good guy/bad guy), shooting at moving targets, and shooting in a terrain that simulates your work environment (around cars, in buildings, etc.). Get away from the idea that a training course must be designed around using 50 or 60 rounds. Use your imagination and be sure to document your training. If it wasn't recorded, it didn't happen. Check with your training staff to see if some of this training will be accepted by your department.

This concludes my discussion of some of the preparation you should address on a routine basis. It only took a couple of hours to write, but it takes a lifetime to practice. I sincerely hope you'll never have to use deadly force. Hopefully, if you practice enough, are trained well enough and stay alert, you will *reduce* the possibility of being involved in a deadly force fight. But there are no guarantees. The nature of your job indicates that from time to time you will be ordered to go to violent places and deal with violent people. Odds are you'll be able to resolve these violent situations by using tools and training other than deadly force. But again, there are no guarantees.

Arena Two–The Fight

Toward the end of the movie *Saving Private Ryan*, there's a hand-to-hand fight scene between an American soldier and a German soldier in a bombed-out apartment. The American loses. Buy the movie, and watch the scene several times, because it's one of the best fight scenes I have seen. There is no glory in it, nothing fancy; it's a fight for survival. *Saving Private Ryan* is just a movie, so try watching it and reading interviews of people who have survived or witnessed violent attacks.

You cannot lose a deadly force fight. You must decide right now that there is nothing you won't do to stay alive. Once a fight elevates to the point of using deadly force, it's deadly force by any means. If you have a firearm, use it. If it malfunctions, clear it. If it runs empty, reload it. If you run out of ammo and you're close enough to beat 'em with your weapon, do it. You have to be ready to kick, punch, bite, scratch, or anything else necessary to stay alive or protect an innocent person from being killed. There's nothing pretty or fancy about it. It's not a game, and there is no tomorrow if you lose. Your family and the people you are protecting expect you to win.

Earlier, I said that luck is what fills the void between preparation and need. If you get into a deadly force fight, you'll need all the preparation you can handle.

Arena Three–Aftermath

You've survived. That's good; now you have to deal with the rest of your life. First things first: is the scene safe? Other officers and civilians are coming to the scene. Is there anything you can do to make sure they're not in danger? Do you need to tell them about additional offenders not yet in custody? Can you assist in setting up a perimeter and protecting the crime scene? You need to be prepared to continue to function as a police officer until relieved by other officers. Just stay busy until another officer lets you know things are under control.

Criminal Investigation

Now that the scene has stabilized, the investigation will be starting. Many departments have a "Buddy Officer" program, where an officer not involved in the incident arrives and assists in taking care of your personal needs. This officer is not involved in the investigation and does not have a privileged position in regards to statements you may make. The Buddy Officer's role is to support the humanitarian needs of only the principal officer. It's normal to be excited after being involved in a deadly force encounter. The Buddy Officer can help calm you down, make sure you contact your family to let them know you're okay, get you something to drink, eat, a jacket, or anything else needed to look out for your welfare.

Note: You should phone your family members when you can to let them know you're okay. They're going to see it on the news or be called by a friend who heard about it. Keep the call short and confined to matters involving personal issues, and avoid talking about the incident itself. After you hang up, look at your watch and call them back in about thirty minutes. That will give them time to digest what you told them, and when you call them back, they can really be reassured that you're okay.

I mentioned earlier that you need to provide investigators with enough information to begin processing the scene, but as I said before, I would suggest you talk to an attorney and rest before giving a formal statement. The investigation will take hours, and there is no telling how long you've been awake. Talk to your attorney, make some decisions about when you can reasonably sit down for a statement and answer questions. Your statements, both at the scene and in a formal setting, will be your best opportunities to put on record your impressions of what happened.

What follows was addressed earlier in this chapter because I wanted you to think of how it related to training. Although repetitious, I will now ask you to read it again to see how it relates to post-shooting procedures.

1. What was the severity of the crime at issue?
2. Did the suspect pose an imminent threat to the safety of the officers or others?
3. Did the suspect actively resist arrest or attempt to evade arrest by flight?
4. Were you able to give warning prior to using force?
5. These points must be judged from the perspective of a reasonable officer at the scene, and not from the perspective of hindsight.
6. Focus on what you knew at the time of the incident, and not what you have learned since that time.

Here are some of the techniques I have used when giving statements to shooting teams after an event.

1. Remember, these individuals may not have the same life experiences and training as you. That's not good or bad, it's just a fact.
2. They may not understand your professional jargon, so don't use it. Every occupation or lifestyle has jargon. Never assume the person with whom you are speaking, or the person who in six months will read your words, knows what you meant to say. My experience is that most people will just smile and nod, even if they don't understand a thing you said. What is even worse is if the person to whom you are speaking thinks they know what you meant, and interject their own meaning. Speak in clear text only.
3. Start at the very beginning of your encounter and work in chronological order (step by step), starting from the moments just before you received the radio call or sighted the situation, explaining every observation and perception you made. Because you are going to talk to your attorney *before* you give a formal statement, I would suggest your attorney make up a basic outline of your statement to be sure you cover all the important points.

The investigators may ask to see your notes if you take them into the interview (I would).

4. Speak slightly slower than you normally would. This will allow you time to choose the best words to describe your thoughts, and allow the others time to understand your intended meaning.

5. If you have nothing to say, or you are thinking, shut your mouth and don't ramble.

6. If you are asked to draw a sketch or diagram of the scene, do so with care. Make sure you note that your sketch is not to scale, and I'd suggest you indicate the position of persons and objects with a circle, rather than an X. It's a small point, but a circle represents an area rather than an exact location.

7. Don't ever assume you are smarter than the person you are talking to. Never believe you're as good as you think you are. You have to prove yourself every time you open your mouth and on every call you handle. You can go from hero to zero in less than .25 seconds.

The Media

I'm one of those people who believe the Founding Fathers of our country listed the Bill of Rights in what they perceived to be the order of importance. The media has a very important role in our country, and I'm glad we have freedom of speech. Having said that, I also believe some members of the media often embellish, taint, report incomplete stories and otherwise misrepresent what actually occurs. You need to prepare yourself, your family and your friends for the possibility that horrible things may be said about you, while in the same story, the offender may be pictured as a choirboy who was turning his life around. My observations have been that, as a general rule, if you are perceived as protecting an innocent person, such as a child, you may be shown in a positive light. If, however, you are defending yourself or another law enforcement officer, there's no telling how a story may be written. This, too, is not good or bad, it's just the way it happens sometimes. Talk to those closest to you and realize this is a part of police work we all have to deal with.

Department Review

Law enforcement has an obligation to investigate all situations where a crime has occurred or may have occurred. Your department also has an obligation to police itself and ensure its employees are operating within established rules. This type of investigation is outside of the criminal investigation, and the best preparation is to know your department's rules and stay within them. When giving your formal statement, be sure to mention the areas you know will be reviewed by the department. Talk to your attorney and see if they have any advice.

Civil Litigation

Are you going to be involved in a lawsuit? Probably. That's why we talked about it in the section on preparation. You knew your department's guidelines, the law and your training revolved around them. You talked to an attorney before and during your statement. You're ready for court. Just because you're sued doesn't mean you did anything wrong. I believe people sue for a great many reasons, and that we as law enforcement officers should be prepared to explain to any court why we *reacted to the offender* in the manner we did. If we trained correctly, and made reasonable decisions, we can withstand this test. And, while I realize in most cases there are dollar figures attached to the outcome of the civil case, I truly feel that what we as law enforcement officers are in court fighting for is our **Personal Honor**. We want the courts to tell everyone that, *"We did the right thing based upon the circumstances we were given."*

CONCLUSION

I loved being a police officer. It didn't really matter what assignment I held or what hours I worked. Looking back as I sit here in front of a computer, I think about placing tourniquets on the legs of a young man who was involved in a terrible traffic accident and having him live to walk another day. I think about helping with an investigation where we apprehended a suspect who was burning clinics, and all the other calls I worked on with others to protect my city. I used to take new team members to a high point above the city and tell them they were responsible for everyone as far as they could see. I still feel that way about everyone in law enforcement. You took an oath to protect your citizens and each other. I hope I did my part, and I hope you'll spend the time, money and effort to take care of yourself.

Please work on all three of the arenas discussed while you have the time. But, never forget that most folks are good people, just like you and your family. They may have a different income, different skin, or live in a different part of town, but they all need your protection. Keep track of the good things you see as you go through your shift. I always tried to thank people at an accident scene for assisting with first aid until the emergency crews showed up. Normally these were just regular people helping other people in need. Notice them and it'll help keep you balanced in your perceptions of the people you work for.

Enough said. Stay safe.

ROBERT W. PARKER

Robert Parker served the Omaha, Nebraska, Police Department for 30 years before retiring in 2001. He served as the Commander of the Omaha Police, Emergency Response Unit, was the Bomb Response Team Commander and chaired the Contingency Committee. Lieutenant Parker was involved in the planning and implementation of hundreds of tactical operations, including high-risk warrant service, hostage barricade incidents, dignitary protection, and the training of patrol and tactical officers in the philosophy and deployment of the police tactical rifle. Lieutenant Parker also developed and wrote the tactical rifle policy and established the tactical rifle training program for the Omaha Police Department. He is the lead instructor for NTOA's Patrol Rifle and Patrol Response to Active Shooter courses, and is a certified submachine gun instructor. Bob has written the "Countermeasures" column for *The Tactical Edge* for the past 19 years.

He currently serves as the NTOA Patrol Tactics Section Chairperson. In this capacity, he is responsible for implementing training for the Patrol Response to Active Shooter, Patrol Rifle, Patrol Counterambush, and Critical Response courses.

Chapter 6

THE INTERMEDIATE RIFLE AND PATROL

Robert W. Parker

"People sleep peaceably in their beds at night only because
rough men stand ready to do violence on their behalf."
George Orwell

INTRODUCTION

Over the years, a public image of the western peace officer became intermingled with a greatly distorted image of the gunfighter. Without doubt, the frontier produced men quite proficient with firearms, but the now-classic duel decided by speed of the draw leaped from the imaginations of later writers. *Lawmen and outlaws alike knew the dangers and limitations of the revolvers they sometimes carried but rarely displayed. Shooting would be avoided whenever possible, and when demanded it would often be done from cover and concealment. A rifle or shotgun offered clear advantages and several nearby friends produced still more favorable odds.* The fantasy picture is that of killers, good and bad, facing one another on deserted streets or in crowded saloons. Real battles normally occurred in the course of crimes or simple arrests, just as they do in every modern American community, with appalling regularity. (Frank Prassel, *The Western Peace Officer,* 248)

Mr. Prassel's use of the term "with appalling regularity," took on new emphasis in the 1990s. Serious bad guys armed with semi-auto and full-auto rifles and covered in body armor became the norm. Most lawmen were limited to the revolver or semi-auto pistols they carried on their hip for self-defense.

The western peace officer fully understood the limitations of a handgun, cover and concealment and ad hoc team tactics. Then, in the late nineteenth and early twentieth centuries, with the taming of the Wild West, the nation became more urbane. Having their law enforcement officers observed on patrol with their shoulder weapons didn't suit the sophisticated image most communities wanted to present. It offended the senses. The advantage of concealment overruled the benefits of the larger shoulder weapon. Instead of recognizing the rifle as the primary weapon in the lawman's arsenal, the rifle was marginalized and relegated to an ancillary role. In many late twentieth century American law enforcement agencies, the rifle was considered overkill and outside of tactical circles, not considered a viable or necessary patrol tool.

Law enforcement now seems to have come full circle. But that took time and some painful mistakes to accomplish. The 1960s were a decade of major social change in America. It was also a time of change in American law enforcement. One watershed event, the Texas Tower shootings on August 1,

1966, is notable for two reasons. Charles Whitman, the killer, was our first notorious active shooter. The problem was solved by two street cops, but training patrol officers to respond to active shooters and other high-risk incidents (at least until SWAT arrived) wasn't recognized as a good idea for another 30 years. Certainly, no one gave serious consideration to actually training patrol cops in the use of a tactical rifle. Secondly, the tragedy at Austin in 1966 also provided impetus for the formation of Special Weapons and Tactics (SWAT) teams around the country—a sound idea whose time had come.

This was also the start of a trend toward more specialization in police work. Agencies with tactical teams made it policy that patrol units would call SWAT for incidents involving heavily armed felons or barricade situations, regardless of whether or not the killing was ongoing. Over the ensuing years, patrol officers became so marginalized that the mantra of contain, control and call SWAT became an automatic response, even to situations that could and should have been resolved by patrol. This emasculation continued into the 1990s.

Finally, the pendulum began to swing back when the heavily armed criminal element became more prevalent and media coverage began to focus on the problem. Serious criminals armed with serious firepower require serious countermeasures. North Hollywood, Columbine and September 11, 2001, are but a few examples of the omnipresence of high-risk dangers that became increasingly common in the streets. We should never find ourselves in a fair fight. We should always have the edge. We finally learned the hard lesson that patrol officers must be prepared to handle these high-profile, high-risk encounters. They have to be prepared to fight and win. And in order to do so, they must be properly equipped and trained.

The Patrol Rifle

The western peace officer favored the Winchester Carbine as the long-arm of choice. It proved to be a handy, lightweight and reliable utilitarian weapon for both hunting and self-defense. Fortunately, today's patrol officers have many more options than did their predecessors. Many manufacturers, makes, models and configurations are

available, some better than others. In this chapter, a variety of rifles will be critiqued and reviewed. However, there is one primary characteristic upon which you should base your decision. The rifle you select had better work—the first time and every time. Add all the whistles and bells you want, but if the rifle doesn't launch the bullet down range every time you want, you've only succeeded in making the weapon heavier.

The Bank of America shootout in North Hollywood, California, on February 28, 1997, demonstrated for the uninitiated the horror of patrol officers being outgunned by thugs. As a result, the administrations of many concerned law enforcement agencies are taking a hard look at arming their patrol units with weapons that will counter the arms and armor of the violent criminals they may encounter. This requires a weapon that has long range and accuracy beyond that of a handgun and enough high-velocity energy to punch through body armor. A rifle, most likely chambered for the .223 Remington (5.56 x 45mm NATO) cartridge, will satisfy these requirements.

I don't recommend any of the several carbines chambered for a pistol cartridge that are sometimes touted as a remedy. Yes, a shoulder weapon is a more accurate weapon, but a pistol round is a pistol round, no matter what delivery system is employed. A pistol round won't defeat most commonly available soft body armor. The simple truth is handgun bullets just don't work when you need to incapacitate a suspect immediately. The argument that a pistol/carbine is easier to handle for some officers is weak at best. The .223 Remington round is a mild recoil intermediate cartridge, and chambered in a quality police rifle/carbine is quite manageable by most officers qualified for street duty. A 12-gauge shotgun fitted with ghost-ring sights and loaded with rifled slugs is a step in the right direction, but with limitations. The counter-strike capabilities of a fighting shotgun fall far short of those of a rifle. The accuracy of a .70-caliber slug is anything but precise, and a limited magazine capacity (a 12-gauge is slow to reload, no matter what gimmick or device is utilized) limits suppressive fire.

So how do we counter the Kalashnikov or SKS in the hands of criminals? There are at least four .223 rifles currently found in the inventories of law enforcement. Some can be purchased by individual officers and others can only be purchased by agencies.

AR-15/M-16 Series

In the late 1950s, Eugene Stoner designed the Armalite AR-15. Armalite sold the manufacturing rights to Colt, and in 1962, U.S. Army Rangers were the first to field the AR-15 in Vietnam. Over forty years later, the AR-15/M-16, with some changes in appearance and modifications, is still with us, more ubiquitous than ever. In addition to deployment in jungles and deserts around the world, the same Stoner system is found in the patrol vehicles of U.S. law enforcement. This gas-operated rifle has the best sighting system and fire-selector switch of any of the high-capacity semi-automatic rifles I have evaluated. The AR-15 utilizes a detachable aluminum box magazine of 20- or 30-round capacity.

Although a very accurate weapon, the trigger is only adequate. Ergonomics are good and were improved upon with the four-position retractable buttstock of the AR-15A3 Tactical Carbine. This model has two intermediate positions to accommodate shooters with shorter arms. Colt AR-15 carbines are a compact 35 inches in overall length. Collapse the stock and it shortens to 32 inches (with a 16" barrel). Weight is about six pounds for the Government Carbine and seven pounds for the Tactical Carbine with a heavy barrel. Remove the carry handle on this rifle and you can low-mount optics on the integral Picatinny rail. These weapons are compact enough to carry in and deploy out of a patrol car, yet do not suffer any loss of accuracy when compared to the full-stock AR-15A2 with a 20-inch barrel. Officers of any build or stature should be able to master this rifle with proper training. These weapons are readily available with the three above-mentioned configurations for sale to both individual officers with proper command approval and to agencies.

Armalite M15A4 Carbine

One entrant in this series of patrol carbines is the Armalite M15A4 carbine. Just like Colt, Bushmaster and the other quality clones on the market, the M15 is a straightforward AR-15/M-16. It's a gas-operated (direct gas impingement) semi-automatic, lightweight, magazine-fed carbine chambered for the .223 Remington cartridge. Practically every other aspect of the weapon is a traditional Stoner system. Both upper and lower receivers are forged aircraft aluminum. Finish is a matte phosphate. The fire-selector lever (safe-fire) is located on the left side of the lower receiver. The ejection port with dust cover is on the right. Just to the rear of the port is a brass deflector and behind this is the forward assist device. None of these features appeared on the original AR-15/M-16 of the 1960s. Just beneath the ejection port on the right side of the lower receiver is the magazine-release button. It is protected on three sides by a raised ridge to prevent accidental activation and release of the magazine. Although rarely used, the spring-loaded pushpin at the front of the trigger guard can be depressed to lower the guard to accommodate a heavily gloved trigger finger.

The Armalite model M15A4 comes without iron sights. It's a straight-out flattop. Picatinny rails on the forged flattop upper receiver and the gas block, where the front sight tower belongs, permit the attachment of iron sights. The A2 version iron sights on all modern AR-15/M-16 weapons function exceedingly well when used with a quality weapon. The weapon I tested was devoid of a flash suppressor. In its place was a muzzle device called a recoil check. The recoil check, with three diagonal oval-shaped ports on each side, will, in theory, dampen the muzzle jump and minimize recoil. As the .223 Remington cartridge generates little recoil, I was unable to evaluate the effectiveness of the device. However, what the recoil check will do is up the decibel count. Don't be standing close to the muzzle when this weapon is fired. The weapon was fitted with green (olive drab) furniture (buttstock, pistol grip and fore-end). The fore-end on the 16-inch barrel is eight inches in length, as opposed to the six-inch fore-end commonly found on other AR-15-type carbines. The barrel and chamber are chrome lined, and the rifling twist of the barrel is 1:9 inches. Overall length of the weapon with fixed stock is 35.6 inches. Weight without the magazine is seven pounds.

For a weapon that will be carried in harm's way,

the primary consideration must be reliability. Will it work every time the operator presses the trigger? Another concern, and a close second, is accuracy. Then, is the weapon user friendly? Ergonomically sound? Well, we already know this weapons system is uncommonly user friendly and well-engineered. Form follows function after over 40 years of field testing throughout the world.

Since the weapon I tested came with a platform for optics, the M15 was tested with a quality Leupold scope and EOTech holographic diffraction sight. Ammunition of various manufacturers and bullet weights was used in field testing the M15A4 carbine.

Fit and finish of the Armalite is without a flaw. No discernible defects or imperfections inside or out. No real visible machining marks. No burrs. A slight wobble in the fore-end, but not enough to be of concern. Trigger break was between six and seven pounds. Crisp enough, but still a military-type trigger.

Breaking in the barrel was done with an assortment of 55- and 60-grain practice fodder. Approximately 400 rounds were fired in combat/tactical shooting drills. A lot of rapid-fire, multiple-target exercises were included in this process. No stoppages of any sort occurred. No failures to extract, eject or feed were encountered, and none of the bullet configurations (ball, hollow-point or soft-point) caused any problems.

The EOTech HDS 551 was mounted directly to the integral Picatinny rail, and as expected made a decided difference in picking up multiple targets at varying distances (3 to 75 yards) and angles. The holographic sight with standard reticle is quick to acquire targets, while the operator keeps both eyes open and maintains peripheral vision. The lack of magnification isn't a deterrent to combat range accuracy and eliminates any potential problems with parallax, therefore allowing the operator to look through the sight at different angles and not change the bullet's point of impact. A full-sized butt-stock on a 16-inch carbine isn't a bad combination. The full-length stock offers a more stable shooting platform and is more accommodating for shooters with longer arms.

The Armalite M15A4 was fired for accuracy from a sandbag rest at a distance of 100 yards. The carbine was topped with a Leupold 3.5x10 tactical scope. Again, ammunition of different manufacturers and a variety of bullet weights were included in the testing. The rounds used were Hornady TAP 55-grain, Black Hills 60-grain soft-point, Black Hills 68-grain match hollow-point and Remington 55-grain soft-point. Armalite's own literature rates this weapon at 1.5 to 2 inches at 100 yards (1.5 to 2.0 MOA). Black Hills 68-grain match hollow-point, averaging 2,705 fps muzzle velocity, bested this prediction by a bit. Five three-shot groups were fired with each brand of ammo. The Black Hills match rounds averaged 1.27 inches. All of the other ammunition came in within the parameters set by Armalite.

There's really nothing novel about the results of the test and evaluation of the Armalite M15A4. More noteworthy for readers not familiar with this company is that there is nothing to complain about. You get a good, reliable and accurate weapon for your money. If you're looking for a patrol rifle, the Armalite is a good contender. The M15 is available in law enforcement-only configuration (flash suppressor, bayonet lug, etc.) and fully adjustable A2 sights. Because your electronic sight or scope may fail you when Murphy rears his ugly head, you will retain your tactical edge with backup iron sights.

The M15A4, one of the most preferred weapons for tactical and patrol officers.

Armalite M15A4 Technical Specifications

Caliber:	.223 Remington
Method of Operation:	Semi-automatic, direct gas impingement
Feeding Device:	20- or 30-round, double column, staggered-feed, detachable box

	magazine
Upper Receiver:	Forged flattop (aircraft aluminum)
Finish:	Mil spec matte phosphate
Furniture:	Green synthetic
Barrel:	16-inch (chrome lined)
Rifling Twist:	1 turn in 9 inches
Front Sight:	Gas block Picatinny rail
Muzzle Device:	Recoil check
Overall Length:	35.6 inches
Weight:	7 pounds
Models:	Also available to law enforcement in standard configuration with flash suppressor, etc.

The M15A4 is a totally reliable weapon with as few gadgets as possible, and will see you through most high-risk encounters.

Bushmaster Patrolman's Carbine

The Patrolman's Carbine is the most recent of the Bushmaster XM15E2S line of tactical rifles for law enforcement. Its genesis can be traced straight to the original Stoner AR-15 rifle, circa 1963. Nothing new or novel here. Most prominent is the extreme reliability of this weapon.

The Bushmaster Patrolman's Carbine has all the features of an M4A3-type carbine, less the capability of full-auto fire. It is semi-auto only. The 16-inch chrome-lined barrel has a one in nine twist. A one in nine twist will fully stabilize any of the heavier available .223 tactical and law enforcement bullets. A barrel step-down permits the attachment of an M203-type grenade/gas launcher, and a birdcage flash suppressor is standard. The four-position, telescoping buttstock accommodates shooters of varying stature. The A3-type removable carry handle contains the standard M-16A2 rear sights. With the carry handle dismounted, scopes, red-dot-type optics, lights and night-vision devices can be mounted on the Picatinny rail. Both upper and lower receivers are forged from aircraft-quality aluminum and finished in a non-reflective mil spec

hard anodize. Bushmaster lower receivers utilize the M-16-type captive front pushpin, which facilitates a quick and easy takedown of the weapon for cleaning and maintenance. A mil spec manganese phosphate outer coating on the barrel and other exposed steel parts protects the weapon from corrosion.

When Bushmaster's director of law enforcement sales, Israel Anzaldua, sent the Patrolman's Carbine to me for test and evaluation, he asked that I give it an extreme test in the field. Bushmaster rifles undergo a series of certification tests conducted by H.P. White Laboratory. This series of assessments includes function/dispersion and resistance tests, a safety drop test, temperature extreme tests, proof pressure test, 2,500-round reliability test, and drop, jar-off and rotation tests. But nothing puts a weapon to the test like an end-user operator on the range for several days. Building a mil spec weapon is one thing. Making it "cop-proof" is taking it to the next level. So for two weeks, during rifle certification classes, the Patrolman's Carbine was put through some dusty, dirty field testing in the hands of both experienced and novice shooters involved in the Omaha PD's tactical rifle program.

The weapon was first zeroed at 25 meters. Bushmaster ships zeroing instructions and target with each rifle. This is particularly helpful for trainees and first-time users. Zeroing of the carbine is explained step-by-step, and the accompanying target is sectioned into squares calibrated to the proper sight adjustments at 25 meters. A very simple, user-friendly piece of information. The test piece was fired for accuracy (it will easily shoot one-minute groups in the hands of a skilled shooter) and combat shooting that included sustained fire drills from the prone position, rollover-prone, off-hand, barricade positions, etc. The Patrolman's Carbine was also used by several different students of assorted skill levels during the two weeks of field testing.

A wide assortment of ammunition was used in the Bushmaster during testing. Imported Russian and Chinese 55-grain full metal jacket (FMJ) and soft-point (SP) ammo functioned well in the carbine, as did FMJ and SP from Winchester (64 grains), Federal, Remington, Black Hills (60 grains) and Ultra-Max remanufactured rounds. Depending on its origin, all the ammunition performed to projected accuracy potential. Bushmaster, Colt and military contract magazines of both 20- and 30-round capacity were used in the Patrolman's Carbine during the test cycle. No problems occurred.

More than 3,000 rounds were fired through the test piece, and there were no stoppages of any kind. No double-feeds, no failures to eject or extract, no bolt-over-base problems and no short-stroke troubles. No degradation in accuracy was noted. The rifle was lubricated twice, but never cleaned during the test and evaluation. Nothing was wiped down, no bore or chamber cleaning (after it was cleaned, oiled and function checked out of the box upon receipt). Carbon and dust covered every part of the weapon and not *one* malfunction occurred.

The TV cliché, "Kids, don't try this at home," applies here. It's not sound doctrine to abuse and neglect a firearm that your life may depend on. However, a weapon that will consistently function well when it's full of crud will instill a sense of confidence in the operator that the carbine will perform when lives are at stake.

The Bushmaster carbine was shipped with accessories worthy of note. The Triple Mount is a three-sided aluminum Picatinny-type rail system. It is 2 ½ inches long and mounts on the barrel at the front sight tower. Lights, bipods and other accessories can be mounted on either side or bottom of this lightweight attaching device.

In dim light or total darkness, a rifle shooter faces two problems not encountered in daylight; position disclosure and degradation of night vision due to the muzzle flash. The Phantom flash suppressor, an accessory offered by Bushmaster, resolves both concerns. In our night shoot during certification week, the Phantom performed as advertised. Muzzle flash was either reduced to negligible or was non-existent. A variety of ammunition was used in the night shoot. Even Norinco, 55-grain FMJ, with its notorious muzzle flash, was reduced to a pin-point of light.

The Bushmaster Patrolman's Carbine is a rugged performer, suited for patrol or tactical applications. Nothing novel, just a well-made, robust weapon backed up by good customer support via e-mail, phone or Bushmaster's informational Web site.

The Bushmaster Patrolman's Carbine.

Bushmaster XM15E2S Patrolman's Carbine Specifications

Caliber:	.223 Remington
Method of Operation:	Gas, semi-automatic
Method of Feed:	20- or 30-round detachable box magazine (M-16- type)
Overall Length:	34.75 inches
Length with Stock Retracted:	31.75 inches
Buttstock:	4-position retractable
Sights:	M-16A2 Type (A3-type detachable carry handle)
Barrel Length:	16 inches, button-rifled. Bore and chamber chrome plated
Rifling Twist:	1 turn in 9 inches
Weight:	6.8 pounds
Upper and Lower Receiver Construction:	Forged 7075T6 aircraft-grade aluminum
Test and Evaluation Summary:	Excellent performer. Robust, mil spec, and extremely reliable under field conditions. Available to agencies and individual officers.
Manufacturer:	Bushmaster Firearms, Inc./

Quality Parts Co.
999 Roosevelt
Trail, Windham,
Maine 04062
Phone:
1-800-998-SWAT

Ruger Mini-14

Of all the competitors in the police patrol rifle market, one domestic entry in this sweepstakes seems to be consistently overlooked. For over thirty-two years (1973), Sturm, Ruger and Co. Inc. of Southport, Connecticut, has been manufacturing the Mini-14 rifle. The Mini-14 is a gas-operated, semi-automatic rifle, chambered for the .223 Remington round. Either a 20- or 30-round detachable box magazine feeds it. These are the salient features we look for in a police rifle. But law enforcement agencies, in the main, seem to be purchasing Colt, Bushmaster and HK rifles in overwhelming numbers. While this may be true to an extent, there are more Sturm, Ruger rifles in service with law enforcement and corrections agencies than I'd previously thought. I also know many individual officers who have purchased a Mini-14 with private funds for duty use. A legitimate law enforcement agency can purchase, on official letterhead, both foreign and domestically manufactured semi-automatic "assault weapons." Individual officers are generally limited to U.S.-manufactured weapons. This pretty much narrows the field to the AR-15 weapons systems (Bushmaster, Colt and a few others) and the Ruger Mini-14.

Although the Mini-14 borrows features from both the M1 Garand and M-14/M1A rifles, the internal working parts are, for the most part, of proprietary design and not interchangeable. The 18¹/₂-inch barrel has six grooves, right-hand twist and one turn in nine inches. The standard stock is of either wood or a black polymer, with standard sling swivels front and rear. The rifle I tested was fitted with an original folding stock. The black fiberglass handguard atop the barrel does an adequate job of protecting the off-hand from the heat generated during rapid fire. The working parts of the Mini-14 mechanism are heat-treated chrome moly and stainless steel alloys. Also available in standard blue, the

matte-finished stainless steel model was used in testing.

As noted, the Ruger carbine is gas-operated. It employs a fixed piston/moving cylinder system in conjunction with a modified Garand-type rotating bolt. A Garand-style reciprocating slide handle is used for retracting the bolt to the rear to chamber a round. A portion of the high-pressure gases driving the bullet down the barrel are bled off through the gas port in the barrel; this in turn drives back the cylinder/piston assembly which operates the action, extracting and ejecting the empty casing with a common claw-type extractor and bump-type ejector. The action is then returned forward by the recoil spring, stripping a fresh round from the magazine and chambering it. After the last round is fired, a projection on the magazine follower will activate the bolt lock mechanism and hold it open. The bolt hold-open (lock) device can be manually employed by pulling the bolt to the rear and depressing the bolt locking plunger on the top-left side of the receiver.

The Mini-14 employs a Garand-type safety located in the front of the trigger guard and is applied by pushing it to the rear. The forward position is the firing mode. It blocks both a hammer and sear. The action can be cycled with the safety on. While some consider it a safety problem to put the trigger finger inside the trigger guard to off the safety, it is an excellent piece of engineering and, as with any firearm, requires the shooter to use caution when disengaging it. Internally, the firing pin is retracted mechanically as the bolt starts to unlock, ensuring that the weapon will fire only when the action is completely closed.

To load the rifle, a magazine is placed in the magazine well and rocked to the rear to seat it. The technique is similar to inserting a magazine in a Kalashnikov (AK)–more manipulation than is required for an AR-15/M-16 or HK rifle. I don't like this feature. The adrenaline dump you get in a firefight will erode fine motor skills, and the precise manipulation required to introduce a new magazine into the rifle is something we can do without. Too much room for operator error. The magazine well configuration of the AR-15 system is better suited for tactical reloading. The flapper-type magazine release is simple and efficient, and similar to that used on AKs and HK rifles.

The black aluminum alloy rear sight is adjustable for both windage and elevation. The adjustments are somewhat basic when contrasted with the AR-15/M-16A2 sighting system. Both elevation and windage can be adjusted in quarter-turn increments, moving the point of impact one inch at 100 yards. The front sight is not adjustable and not protected by wings on the civilian model that was tested.

The two critical elements in testing any tactical firearm are reliability and accuracy. In these areas, the Ruger Mini-14 acquits itself well. In the field testing, several hundred rounds of three different manufacturers were fired with no stoppages. Even as the weapon became fouled, ejection of fired cases was still crisp, usually straight up and to the right. For a left-handed shooter (such as myself), the empty casings can be a distraction, but don't pose any real hazard to the shooter (always wear your shooting glasses). Because the gases that are bled off through the port in the barrel act directly on the cylinder/piston assembly, rather than a direct gas impingement system like the AR-15/M-16 series, the action and working parts remain relatively clean.

The standard shoulder stock of the Mini-14 is a better choice than the folding metal stock (usually found on the Ruger AC556, selective fire rifle). The folder is just not as stable, more difficult to mount to the shoulder and has a slick, narrow metal butt. The combination of the rear sight aperture and the somewhat thick front sight blade makes it difficult to rapidly acquire a sight picture. This sight blade can become problematic at extended ranges, as it can obscure a target. The rifle is relatively lightweight (6 pounds), handy and well-balanced.

The Mini-14 used in testing displayed no real preference for any of the three types of ammunition used. Remington 55-grain soft-point, Hornady 55-grain TAP and Black Hills 60-grain hollow-point ammunition all averaged 3-inch groups at 100 yards, with acceptable accuracy that could likely be improved upon with a better sighting system. The stainless steel construction of the weapon that was tested can be a real plus in combating the effects of salt and humidity.

While its accuracy is not phenomenal, it is within acceptable parameters. This rifle has been found in patrol cars for many years, and will for years to come, in most parts of the country. For considerable quality at a very reasonable price, the Ruger Mini-14 is worth more than a passing glance. The Ruger Mini-14 is available to law enforcement in the Government Model configuration, which moves the front sight back on the barrel and protects it with wings. The muzzle on this model is fitted with a flash suppressor.

Often overlooked, the Ruger Mini-14 is an excellent patrol rifle.

Ruger Mini-14 Specifications

Caliber:	.223 Remington
Method of Operation:	Gas, semi-automatic
Feeding Device:	20- or 30-round, detachable box magazine
Locking System:	Rotating bolt
Weight:	$6^{3}/_{4}$ pounds
Overall Length:	Standard stock – $37^{1}/_{8}$ inches
Folding Stock:	37 inches/$27^{3}/_{4}$ inches folded
Barrel:	$18^{1}/_{2}$ inches, 6 grooves, right-hand twist, 1 turn in 9 inches
Finish:	Blue or stainless steel
Manufacturer:	Sturm, Ruger & Company Lacey Place Southport, CT 06490 Phone: 203-256-3860

The Steyr AUG

The Steyr AUG is unique and imported. Therefore, it is available to agencies only. It is of a bull-pup configuration (the receiver is to the rear of

The Steyr AUG, a reliable and robust weapon.

the trigger group). This design places the ejection port right under the operator's face. Therefore, a left-side-ejecting bolt is needed for a left-hander to safely operate the AUG. The stock, trigger group and 30-round magazines are all manufactured from fiberglass-reinforced Zeytel. The standard sighting system is a 1.5 power optical sight with a ring reticle that is a great aid in dim light for target acquisition. Once the shooter learns to position the ring on the target at varying distances, the 1.5 power scope is surprisingly precise in shot placement. At closer combat ranges, it's equally impressive. The shooter keeps both eyes open for a wide field of view. Located on top of the scope is a crude set of iron sights. The AUG is accurate in spite of the spongy, mushy, heavy trigger pull. Compact, the weapon, with a 20-inch barrel (1-in-9 twist), is but 31 inches in overall length. Empty weight is a deceptive 7.9 pounds. The weapon seems much lighter because the majority of the weight is to the rear. Despite the generous use of plastics, the AUG can withstand a lot of abuse and lack of maintenance. The AUG has a very unorthodox appearance, but when it comes to conventional reliability, it performs ahead of the curve.

After-Market Accessories

During the past decade, progressive law enforcement agencies have adopted the intermediate rifle to counter the threat from seriously armed criminal elements of America. With the implementation of these weapons (in large numbers), has come an explosion of after-market accessories and tools. These are primarily designed for and directed at the users of the AR-15/M-16 series. Even before this proliferation began, there were more add-ons, both factory and after-market, for the AR-15/M-16s than you could count. Some of these gadgets and tools

are practical and extremely useful to operators and those charged with maintaining agency weapons. Others range in value from semi-useless and unnecessary to absurd. And they will only increase the weight of your weapon. How practical is a 120-round drum magazine? Does any AR-15 really need a left-handed upper receiver? I'm 100 percent left-handed and can't imagine how this total rework of a major component would make manipulation of the weapon any easier. Why would anyone need a ten-dollar mag-loading device for an AR? If you need help loading an AR magazine, you're in the wrong business. One has to wonder if a shoulder holster for the M4 is in the works.

Patrol work often requires hands-on contact with suspects. A proper sling setup is necessary for this situation, as well as to bring the weapon up on target quickly when it's hanging. A sling is to a rifle as a proper holster is to a handgun. So what tactical sling and attachments do we use? During the past decade, the three-point tactical sling has become popular for carbines and subguns. The three-point can be adjusted to allow the weapon to hang at a level close to the operator's hands. It's right there, in position when it needs to come up quickly. Pushed aside, the weapon is out of the way when the shooter needs two hands for other tasks. On the down side, this sling can make the weapon tougher to maneuver when going prone, shooting from some non-primary positions and corner shooting. To overcome some of these problems, it may be necessary for officers to remove themselves from the sling.

The single-point sling attachment is one solution

The Bushmaster single-point sling. Also shown is the SureFire 500 light.

to the problem. On the M4 carbine and other similar weapons, the single-point sling adapter is attached to the weapon by removing the stock and receiver extension and replacing the receiver end plate with the adapter. The Bushmaster adapter comes with ambidextrous attachments—two on the left, two on the right. The slot on either side will fit a standard sling. Holes are designed to fit a lobster-claw-type hook, similar to the hook-type attachment found on HK slings. Using the hook makes the weapon quickly detachable if the need should arise. The weapon is at the correct level when hanging, and is simply pushed out of the way to go hands-on. Regardless of which shoulder the sling is on, the shooter can switch from right to left, etc., without removing the sling. The single-point sling takes that step out of the process for corner shooting. The single-point adapter attachment points are positioned low enough so as not to interfere with the manipulation of the charging handle and forward assist.

The last item for consideration comes under the heading of, "Now why didn't I think of that?" You know, those seemingly simple things that make life easier, but took years for someone to come up with a solution. With the exception of installing a barrel, I can practically build an AR-15 rifle from parts. I can disassemble one down to the bare receivers. But, I would rather have a root canal than have to take off and install the handguards on one of these rifles. That has changed with the introduction of the Handguard Removal Tool (HRT) (Global Tactical Supplies in North Kansas City, MO), which will work on all AR-15/M-16 models with the exception of those with floating handguards. Now all you have to do is insert the lug on the end of the HRT into the mag-well and the long metal handles on either side of the delta ring, squeeze the handles, push downward on the ring and simply remove the upper and lower handguard. This chore is no longer a two-person job resulting in cuts, abrasions and cursing. Easy on, easy off. This handy little device will also result in the entire upper being inspected, cleaned and lubed more thoroughly.

There are a lot more products on the market that can increase your tactical edge, but just as many superfluous gadgets that are overvalued at any price. Caveat Emptor.

Resources

Bushmaster
999 Roosevelt Trail
P.O. Box 1479
Windham, ME 04062
800-998-7928
Global Tactical Supplies, LLC
2001 Clay Street
North Kansas City, MO 64116
866-455-5842

Optics and Lights

Again, there are many choices here. Several companies make good quality pieces that are robust, reliable and tactically sound in design, function and maintenance. Others are merely glass, aluminum and red-dots that have no place on a serious working rifle. EOTech, Aimpoint and other name-brand optics lead the way. But, no matter your choice, if you opt to mount a sight on your weapon, always, always have a set of backup iron sights that can be brought into play quickly when Murphy's Law is set in motion and your mechanical sight fails you. Whether you work the day shift or patrol on midnights, you need to identify your target. Lights mounted to the weapon are a must. You shoot what you can see, not what you think you can see. Tactical incidents will most likely occur in dim light, indoors or out. Even in the middle of the day, a high-risk warrant service can take you into the darkened environs of a crack house or meth lab, where suspects never seem to have enough time or money to buy light bulbs. Recently, we have witnessed an increase in the use of the .223 carbine as an entry weapon, and it is now more commonly seen on patrol with line officers. This augmentation of the

An M4 shown with Aimpoint optics and a vertical foregrip.

intermediate rifle in patrol work has placed new emphasis on development of a good weapon-mounted lighting system

The Millennium model M500A, manufactured by SureFire, was sent to the NTOA for testing and evaluation. The Millennium M500A light is part of a dedicated housing that replaces the factory upper and lower handguards. No tools are required for installation. Just pull back the handguard slip ring, remove the factory handguards and replace with the M500A unit. No more exposed cables or loose pressure pads. The light module itself is mounted at the 1:30 position on the handguard. There is no obstruction to the operator's field of view. Nor are the front sight or optics obscured by the light. The Millennium handguards replicate those found on the M-16/M-4 carbine with its dual heatshield construction. The handguards and the entire housing of the Millennium M500A are fabricated from polyamide composite, impact- and thermal-modified plastic with glass fiber. The inserts are made of anodized aircraft-grade aluminum. The light module is sealed with a waterproof O-ring. The weight of the M500A, including the three DL123A Lithium batteries that power the unit, is 13 ounces. The shock-isolated head of the light measures 1.62 inches in diameter.

The high-pressure Xenon lamp assembly is supplied by SureFire in two configurations. The MN10, 125 lumens assembly (identified by an orange collar) has a battery run time of around 60 minutes. Replace it with the MN11, 200 lumens lamp (pink collar), and it will deplete the three Lithium batteries in 20 minutes. The MN11 lamp is called for when a very bright light is mandated by the mission requirements. Continuous running of this lamp for more than a few minutes will generate enough heat to trigger a protective thermal circuit breaker built into the batteries, which shuts down the system. It will automatically reset after a cool-down period. Utilizing the system no more than two or three minutes at a time or briefly illuminating a target or area a few seconds at a time will usually eliminate thermal shutdown. (SureFire rates its tactical lights in lumens rather than the more familiar candlepower, as lumens measure the total light output.)

My HK MP5 is fitted with the SureFire Model 628. When the weapon is stored in its case in the trunk of my car, care must be taken that no weight is placed on the pressure switch of the unit. Otherwise, you'll find the switch has been activated in the case and the batteries drained. Located at the rear of the M500A is an enable/disable switch. The unit cannot be turned on with the pressure switch (to the right side on the handguard) without the enable switch being turned clockwise to the on position. This feature totally eliminates unintentional activation of the light unit when the weapon is stored. If the operator is searching a dim-light environment and position disclosure is not a concern, or needs to use the off-hand for communication or control, the constant on switch on the left side of the upper handguard can be put to use.

In total darkness, the SureFire Millennium M500A utilizing the 125 lumens (MN10) lamp assembly can illuminate and help identify adversaries at 100 yards. A great many lights will illuminate at that distance. But actually lighting up a target for good visual identification is even more critical. This light is as good as your eyes. It acquires and identifies the target, backlights the sights and illuminates your immediate environment. From the gun-ready position, the operator can scan the area and splash the light off the deck to illuminate targets and innocents without directing the muzzle of the rifle directly at them. In dim light, the eyesight of your adversary has adjusted to the environment. The Millennium light, with either lamp assembly, will cause a devastating disruption of both sight and awareness, and the 200 lumens light will almost singe eyebrows at close distances. Even after the operator fires, switches off the light, moves away from the point of the muzzle flash and light source, the bad guy, if he's still up, is still seeing that blue dot, similar to the effect of a flash bulb.

The SureFire M500B is the super-charged version of the Millennium series. You can really light and heat them up with the 250 or 500 lumens Xenon lamp assemblies. Both the A and B series are also available for the full-length AR-15/M-16 with round handguards or the older series AR-15/M-16 with triangular handguards.

SureFire, in an advertising blurb, refers to the Millennium light as a serious lighting tool. More than that, it's a serious fighting tool. There is no more important accessory for the patrol rifle than a quality tactical light. SureFire's Colt Millennium Tactical Lights are well thought out, user friendly, mil spec and now self-contained with no exposed cables or pressure pads to fray or fall off.

SureFire Colt Millennium Tactical Light Model M500A Specifications

Light Output:	200 lumens
	125 lumens
Lamp Assembly:	High-pressure Xenon
Weight:	13 ounces
Switching:	Constant on/momentary/disable
Construction:	Housing C polyamide composite, impact- and thermal-modified plastic with glass fiber Inserts B anodized air craft-grade aluminum
Thermal Dissipation:	Dual heatshield radiation
Sealing:	O-ring
Head:	1.62" diameter
Manufacturer:	SureFire Dept. TE 18300 Mt. Baldy Circle Fountain Valley, CA 92708 Phone: 714-545-9444

"Don't fear the night. . . . Fear what hunts at night," read the T-shirt I saw recently. Ever since man began hunting two- or four-legged animals, he has been at a disadvantage in darkness, especially with four-legged predators which have better night vision, sense of smell and hearing. We have to rely on our higher intelligence and technology to pursue them at night. In law enforcement, we must likewise use intelligence and technology to go after the felonious life forms we encounter in the dark. Some criminals seem to possess a primal cunning, particularly after sundown. More often than not, the patrol officer will encounter them on the night shift, with a pistol as the primary weapon.

A pistol equipped with tritium night sights will assist the operator in aligning the sights, but do nothing to provide target discrimination or identification. So, we rely on more technology to enhance our visual acuity in the darkness and light up our environment. There are a number of good hand-held flashlights available to patrol and tactical officers to use with their pistols. There are also several proven handgun/flashlight techniques (Harries, Chapman, FBI, etc.) that the shooter can employ when the lights go out. But they all require two hands, one to hold and fire the pistol, the second to grip and activate the light. If you need to use your off-hand, you must put away one of your tools. With a weapon-mounted fighting light, two hands may still be required to activate and shoot, but the off-hand can then be used to communicate, cuff or complete another task while still having both weapon and light at the ready.

Insight Technology now markets a mil spec, compact weapon-mounted tactical light for the Glock series of pistols. The Insight Technology M3 Tactical Illuminator mounts on the accessory rail on the underside of the frame of the new model Glocks. The M3 has an overall length of 3.4 inches. Mounted, it protrudes but 3 inches past the muzzle. It has a height of 1.52 inches and width of 1.57 inches. Total weight is 3.3 ounces. Construction is of chemical-resistant, lightweight polymer. Two 3-volt Lithium batteries power it. The tungsten-halogen lamp puts out 80-90 lumens, and the beam is adjustable from spot to flood lighting. Run time is

The SureFire M3 tactical light can also be mounted on AR15/M16 family rifles.

rated at 30 minutes minimum of continuous operation. The M3 Tactical Illuminator readily snaps onto the pistol. On the Glock 21 (or any of the newer Glocks with the accessory rail), align the grooves of the M3 with the grooves on the mounting rail of the pistol and slide it straight back until the latch on the light engages the slot on the rail. This procedure takes about two seconds. It can be deployed as a simple flashlight or a weapon light if the situation takes a wrong turn. Ambidextrous momentary and steady-on switches make the M3 user friendly for both right- and left-handers. On the right side, up is momentary, down steady-on. On the left side, reverse the procedure. Although the polymer body of the M3 is chemical resistant, it takes only a second to press down on the latch to remove the light from the weapon when cleaning the pistol or to deploy the M3 as a conventional light.

Mounted on a Glock 21, .45 ACP, the weight of the M3 Tactical Illuminator is insignificant and weapon balance is not affected. In total darkness, the light will easily illuminate the area and clearly define targets out to 100 feet. When employing a light like the M3, it will backlight the sights. The tritium night sights become a non-factor. This isn't to say the night sights aren't an excellent accessory. When your opponent fires at you in almost total darkness and his muzzle signature gives him up, you can make use of your self-luminous sights rather than your light and avoid position disclosure yourself.

Mounted on your pistol, the M3 has no exposed wires to fray or snag. There is no adhesive-backed pressure pad to come loose. Its usefulness is enhanced by its adaptability. Quickly dismounted, the M3 becomes an orthodox flashlight to light up a potential target or areas you don't want to cover with the muzzle of a loaded weapon. Patrol officers should find this compact, versatile and robust light useful in a variety of duties at night. And if a Glock 21, with 14 rounds of Federal Tactical 230-grain, jacketed hollow-points, matched with an Insight Technology M3 Tactical Illuminator can't help you solve your problem, you can at least use the M3 to show you the way back to the tactical rifle you should have brought in the first place.

Insight Technology also has available the M4 Tactical Illuminator, designed for mounting on the Smith & Wesson Sigma series pistols with finger grooves. Specifications are the same as the M3. Both are available directly from the manufacturer or most law enforcement distributors.

Insight Technology M3 Tactical Illuminator Specifications

Length:	3.4 inches
Width:	1.57 inches
Height:	1.52 inches
Lamp Type:	Tungsten halogen, 80–90 lumens
Beam:	Adjustable from spot to flood
Run Time:	Minimum of 30 minutes continuous on
Power Source:	Two 3-volt Lithium batteries
Body:	Chemical-resistant, lightweight polymer
Switch:	Ambidextrous, momentary and steady-on

Ammunition

There are a seemingly endless number of choices when it comes to ammunition to feed your weapon. And again, the main issue should be reliability. Does your weapon function with the ammunition you have chosen? Rifle ammunition, like handgun and shotgun rounds, must be standardized. Ammunition makers have been paying attention to law enforcement's move toward patrol rifles. There are a lot of configurations and loadings on the market that warrant our attention. Frangible, full-metal jacket, and other special-purpose rounds all have their place. Then, there is the anecdotal evidence presented (both pro and con) regarding the field performance of different types of ammunition. None of the studies or their databases I've seen have ever been comprehensive or broad enough to convince me one way or the other as to a bullet's success or failure.

If perfect, a bullet would always penetrate deep enough (but not over-penetrate) to cause instant incapacitation of an adversary. It would always expand as large as possible, and always perform consistently, shot after shot. To date, we haven't found the perfect ammunition, and it's not likely to be discovered soon. You'll have to rely on valid ballistic testing, such as the studies done by the Federal Bureau of Investigation Firearms Training Unit, and look at the field performance of actual incidents. But, bear in mind the narrow scope of the data we have available to us. No two shootings, even using the same weapon and an identical round, will produce identical results. There are too many variables at work. Find a round that launches consistently from your weapon and gather as much input as possible. Geography, population density and prescribed duties will also help determine the round(s) selected for street duty. However, as reported in this chapter, full-metal jacket and soft-point ammunition from Winchester (64 grains), Remington and Black Hills (60 grains) performed well in the rifles tested.

Patrol Rifle Policy and Deadly Force

Patrol rifle policy need not be a complicated issue. Every agency should already have a policy pertaining to the use of the officer's sidearm, and each is governed by state statute and agency policy regarding the use of deadly force. Policy for the carrying and use of any type of firearm should dictate that the officer be certified and qualified. A rifle is no different in this respect than the handgun. A patrol rifle policy shouldn't paint the officer into a corner with unnecessary restrictions. The decision to deploy a rifle must be left to the discretion of the individual operator, just as with any other weapon in the force continuum at the officer's disposal.

It has been a number of years since law enforcement turned to the patrol rifle in order to level the playing field when engaging heavily armed criminals. In that time, countless agencies have adopted the intermediate rifle for patrol. It has supplanted, and in some cases replaced, an American law enforcement mainstay–the 12-gauge shotgun. And in the more progressive tactical units, the rifle is replacing the ubiquitous HK MP5 as an entry weapon. This is not to say that these changes have come about without debate. There are still issues that are of concern to both administrators and street cops. Policies on deployment, types of weapons, ammunition and ancillary equipment are but a few points of contention.

What follows are some of the patrol rifle policy concerns that have been brought to my attention by students in NTOA courses, e-mails and the NTOA Tac Net. They should prove of assistance in developing or refining patrol rifle policy.

A handgun, shotgun, subgun or rifles all equate to deadly force when deployed by law enforcement personnel, but some agencies place predetermined restrictions on officers deploying a rifle, even though the rifle is a more accurate and effective weapon. No such parameters are in place to encumber the use of the officer's sidearm or shotgun. If the standard deadly force and department policies are deemed adequate for pistols and shotguns, then why shouldn't they apply to rifles? Contrary to what some would have us believe, overpenetration is not a more serious concern with the patrol rifle. Policies that require personnel to get supervisory permission to deploy rifles and document that deployment, even if it's merely removing it from the patrol car, are unnecessary and dangerous. Dangerous to the health and well-being of the officer. A rifle policy should be the same as the practical philosophy taught in the NTOA's Patrol Response to Active Shooter course, i.e., the individual officer on the scene, on the ground, makes the life-or-death decisions, not a supervisor en route to the scene or a policy writer who will never be there.

Another agency's policy limits the number of officers who are allowed to certify with the rifle. This particular program calls for the officer to bear all the expenses (weapon and ammunition). Other than budgetary constraints, why would an agency want to put a cap on the number of officers that are allowed to certify with the rifle? Will we start restricting the number of personnel armed with pistols and shotguns or allow some to defend themselves and others with a safer, more effective weapon while other sworn personnel cannot? What is the rationale behind a policy statement that states the patrol rifle will be used only as a defensive or containment weapon and not as an ad hoc countersniper rifle or offensive weapon? The best weapon at your disposal when encountering an active shooter is the patrol rifle. Going after the active shooter, closing and making contact to stop the killing, is an offensive action. Would this policy statement preclude the officers of that particular department from utilizing their patrol rifles in a contact team mode and pursuing the active shooter?

A patrol rifle policy should work hand-in-hand with an agency's deadly force policy. There should be no specific operational directives for patrol rifles in deadly force circumstances. Yes, there are many patrol situations where the deployment of a rifle would be inappropriate. Likewise, it would generally not be appropriate to unholster a pistol or take the shotgun out of the rack when responding to a noise disturbance or report call. Sound judgment and quality training are more effective than unnecessarily restrictive policies. Rather than cloud the minds of officers in a high-stress situation with unnecessary parameters, there should be sound guidelines for rifle programs that spell out specifics as to weapons, ammunition, training and certification, and then leave the issue of when to deploy the weapon to the personnel on the street following use-of-force guidelines.

In summary, a patrol rifle policy should be in place and understood by all before personnel are assigned weapons. Questions which must be addressed in policy include: Who will carry these weapons and when will their use be authorized? Will there be a deviation from the standard agency deadly force policy? Will the criteria and conditions for using a patrol rifle be different than those for using a sidearm? Whether there are departures from standard policy or it remains unchanged, personnel assigned a patrol rifle have to know the policy. There should be no doubts. A line from one large police department's rules and regulations pertaining to the use of force and firearms is an excellent example of necessary flexibility: ***"An officer will not needlessly endanger themselves to conform with the contents of this order."*** Someone with street experience was involved in formulating this policy.

Patrol Rifle vs. Shotgun and Submachine Gun

Adoption of a patrol rifle program often prompts the question of whether to retire the venerable 12-gauge shotgun. The 12-gauge combat shotgun is a relatively short-range weapon. Beyond 15 to 18 yards, "00" buck pellets become non-discriminating and are not a tool for precision shooting. The pattern spread of "00" buck relegates it to tactical environments where there are no innocents immediately present. It is difficult to master and can be physically challenging for personnel who are small of stature. Transitioning from buckshot to slugs in a hot tactical scenario isn't usually practical, and over-penetration of slugs is a greater risk than that of the frangible .223-caliber round. Also, a police shotgun has a limited magazine capacity. However, a 12-gauge shotgun loaded with slugs will take down a runaway 1,200-pound steer more efficiently than a .223 carbine, and is usually quite effective against other animals, especially those that are moving quickly. But, I've really never bought into the theory that the racking of a shotgun slide has a big psychological effect on the bad guys. In a deadly force scenario, my intent isn't to scare my opponent to death. Besides, I can't rack a slide on my Benelli Super 90 Entry model. So, on balance it would seem that the police shotgun could well fall by the wayside. But that won't happen until all law enforcement adopts the intermediate rifle, and that's in the future. By then, we'll probably reconsider, reinvent the wheel, and the fighting shotgun will again find favor.

Another question prompted by the adoption of a patrol rifle relates to the submachine gun and its role as an entry weapon. Again, a strong case can be made for replacing the submachine gun with a .223-caliber patrol rifle or carbine. By now, most knowledgeable decision-makers in law enforcement are aware that concerns of overpenetration by .223-caliber bullets have been greatly exaggerated. Not only do frangible .223-caliber bullets penetrate less at close range in a human target when they fragment and expand, but they also penetrate less through walls and other barriers when the target is missed. On the other hand, hollow-point pistol bullets fired from submachine guns tend to plug up with wood, drywall or other debris they pass through, and as a result penetrate farther and deeper than the frangible intermediate rifle rounds.

A submachine gun won't defeat body armor, but a carbine will. The M4 carbine is somewhat longer than the HK MP5, but not enough to matter in a close-quarters environment. The noise signature of a rifle-caliber carbine is thunderous inside a structure. But from my personal experience and that of others with whom I've discussed this issue, it is no more damaging or incapacitating than the decibel level of a submachine gun being discharged in an indoor firefight. I have frequently experienced more hearing discomfort from a pistol being fired close to my ear than I have from rifle fire. To further validate the carbine vs. subgun issue, I know of at least two full-time, West Coast SWAT teams that have transitioned to the M4-type carbine as an entry weapon.

The patrol rifle is most likely destined to eventually replace the shotgun as the primary shoulder weapon of street officers, and it's beginning to make a statement as an efficient, safe entry weapon. But the 12-gauge fighting shotgun and the submachine gun have both been scheduled for obsolescence before and somehow survived.

Training

A patrol rifle training program should place emphasis not only on the understanding and operation of the weapon, but also the discretionary and decision-making aspects. Critical thinking needs to be addressed in all phases of dynamic training. From three yards to over 100 yards, quick decisions have to be made by the officer. First, operators should be taught the concept of avoidance. In other words, how to avoid using the rifle to terminate a problem or a life, if at all possible. Shoot/don't shoot, reload, transition, immediate action, scan, look for additional threats (plus one rule) and stand down, all of these and other considerations must be covered. Training must be dynamic. Long gone are the days of static line shooting as a sole and adequate form of training. Shooting, moving, communicating and working as a team should all be included in training patrol officers to win deadly encounters.

Because many agencies are now equipping their personnel with level "C" chemical protective suits, protective gloves and air-purifying respirators (APR), training must include operating and shooting while wearing life-saving personal protective equipment (PPE). Even the more advanced level "C" suits can make movement more awkward, and wearing them, particularly in warm climates, limits the time an officer can remain in a chemical, bio-

logical, radiological, nuclear or explosive (CBRNE) environment. Heat exhaustion or heat stroke become a consideration. Also, two layers of protective gloves will make the manipulation of a weapon and equipment a challenge. The mask adds to the heat factor and limits vision, particularly peripheral. Making accurate shots with a shoulder weapon can be a real test. The sights are more difficult to acquire and line up on target, and proper cheek weld is more complex. The APR also decreases peripheral vision, increasing the danger of not seeing a threat or pulling the trigger just as a teammate enters your line of fire. Agencies which do not have APRs yet should train more regularly with chemical agent protective masks. Speed, surprise and violence are going to be necessary to overcome an encounter with terrorists whose intent is to deploy a WMD. Quick and accurate shots will be required to terminate an adversary with a device. Therefore, shots can't be delayed by struggling to line up your sights. Strong consideration should be given to having patrol rifles fitted with a red-dot-type sighting device, such as the EOTech 550 HDS series. The critical advantage of this sight is the ability of the shooter to acquire the target without concern for a cheek weld. Nor is the issue of alignment of the shooter's eye, the reticle and the target a problem with the EOTech sight. The operator can move their head about in a fluid environment and the reticle remains on target. This non-parallax feature facilitates both-eyes-open shooting and increases the shooter's peripheral vision in a fast-changing close-quarters setting.

Training should include making head shots at close-quarters distances and beyond. A terrorist may be wearing a suicide vest laden with explosives, and the only option may be a brain shot. The bio/chem agent could be in a container on the terrorist's body or in his hands, so if a shot is taken, it must be precise. Training with the APR will also get the officer accustomed to limited vision, and to scanning more in the close-quarters WMD scenario, where everything is evolving rapidly and their weapon must be brought to bear quickly, with accuracy and regard for their fellow officers' safety. Manipulating a weapon and equipment takes on a different feel when wearing two pairs of protective gloves. Fingers suddenly feel much thicker, and the familiar eyes-closed, hands-find-hands sense is diminished. It might help to unhinge the bottom of the trigger guard on the M4. Yes, it drops down. Just push the pin. For high-speed magazine changes, commercially available mag-pull devices are available, or they can be made to help reduce fumbling with the grip on the magazine body.

Training hours are precious to us all, but we have to prepare for WMD scenarios in this century, just as we learned to adapt and change our tactics in response to active shooters. Overcoming or mitigating the disadvantages of wearing personal protective equipment can only be achieved by addressing them during dynamic, realistic training.

Establishing a patrol rifle program for a law enforcement agency requires much more than merely selecting a weapon. It requires a total commitment on the part of the administration to establishing a successful program. It requires a commitment to establishing sound doctrine and policy, as well as quality training time, both initial and recertification. When the Omaha Police Department's tactical training cadre first suggested a minimum four-day patrol rifle training program, the administration immediately committed to it, understanding the need for its total support of quality training and equipment. There was no half-stepping here. We decided to do it right. And taking line personnel away from their primary assignments for a week, and doing this every month with another class required logistical shuffling of personnel on a large scale. Large or small, law enforcement agencies are always short of people, but a commitment to a patrol rifle program by your administration is the first step in finding the time.

Justifying the Patrol Rifle Program

Overcoming resistance may be the most difficult and critical aspect of justifying a patrol rifle program. Therefore, it is important that you have gathered all available supportive information and contacted other agencies in the area which have implemented similar programs. Their experience could prove to be extremely helpful in determining the most effective approach to take. Whatever approach is decided upon should emphasize that the purpose for implementing the program is to enhance the patrol officer's ability to save lives–the lives of police officers and members of the community. It should also place emphasis on the superiority of a patrol rifle over a handgun or shotgun, both in terms of ballistics, as well as long-range accuracy. Other points that can be made include the following: Heavily armed, vicious criminals roam the streets in every part of the country, armed with high-capacity, semiautomatic and automatic weapons. They wear body armor and don't play by any rules. Two heavily armed suspects held the trump card in the North Hollywood Bank of America shootout with patrol officers. This should not be allowed to happen again. While armed criminals are shooting members of the community and police officers (1,100 rounds were fired by the suspects in North Hollywood), patrol officers shouldn't have to rely upon the neighborhood gun shop to acquire reciprocating weapons. For the past several years, the National Tactical Officers Association has promoted the value and advantages of the patrol rifle in engaging serious armed criminals, including those involved in "active shooter" scenarios. However, law enforcement now faces an additional challenge. Even before 9/11, but more of a reality since, American police must now contend with terrorism and the threat of weapons of mass destruction (WMD). The patrol rifle will play a critical role in countering the threat of suicide bombers, as well as the terrorist WMD danger, because it will mitigate the problem more accurately and expeditiously than a handgun.

Whomever is given the responsibility for presenting the patrol rifle proposal to the agency head must not only be well versed in the proposal's content, but prepared to answer anticipated and unanticipated questions. Questions related to cost of the program, the amount of training required and the type of rifle proposed are obvious. Perhaps less obvious are the following:

- Isn't it true that rifle bullets are more likely to overpenetrate, thus endangering members of the community? The response to this question should include information reflecting that the patrol rifle is a more accurate and efficient weapon than a handgun or shotgun and more precise than either. This translates into a safer weapon. A frangible .223 Remington round will usually expend its energy in soft tissue and reduce the hazard of overpenetration and injury to innocents. This frangible round will also fail to penetrate common building materials to the extent of some handgun rounds.

• The department can't afford to purchase rifles for every patrol officer. Is there another alternative? The answer, of course, is yes. Qualified officers could be allowed to purchase a designated patrol rifle and a specified amount of ammunition for the training program on an individual basis. Another approach could be to allow officers to purchase designated patrol rifles from the department utilizing a payroll deduction plan.

Programs that involve individual officer purchase are a win-win situation for both the agency and street officers. As with any piece of personal equipment, officers are more likely to maintain their own rifle than a department-issued weapon.

CONCLUSION

The patrol rifle concept has proven itself to be more than a passing fad. Contrary to the prediction of some that the police use of the patrol rifle was a knee-jerk reaction to the North Hollywood Bank of America firefight (mentioned previously), and we in law enforcement would soon realize the error of our ways, the patrol rifle is here to stay. In fact, more and more agencies have been convinced by their own hard-learned lessons. Over the past decade, the patrol rifle has become an icon as well as a life-saving tool–symbolic of a shift in the mindset of American law enforcement. Most of us now recognize that no longer can patrol/first responders be marginalized, but must be equipped and trained to handle violence on a major scale, and be prepared to do battle until specialized tactical intervention arrives.

The patrol rifle enables the patrol officer to engage a deadly threat in both close-quarter scenarios and long-range distances. Its high-capacity magazine permits the officer to engage multiple adversaries and, with a long sight radius, the patrol rifle allows for more precise shooting. The patrol officer's rifle will defeat most commonly available body armor and the intermediate rifle round (.223 Remington) poses less overpenetration danger to innocents and fellow officers. Without a doubt, terminal ballistics of the rifle are superior to the handgun, shotgun and submachine gun. The Bank of America experience was no anomaly of the 1990s, and there are many more serious and heavily armed criminals (both foreign and domestic) to be dealt with in the new century. By arming and training patrol officers with appropriate rifles and protective equipment, agencies will not only increase their effectiveness in dealing with conventional incidents, but also enhance first response capabilities to terrorist acts.

DON WHITSON

Don Whitson is a sergeant with the Fort Collins, Colorado, Police Services. He has 20 years of law enforcement experience and has been with the Fort Collins SWAT team since 1990, where he is currently a team leader. Sergeant Whitson is an explosive breaching specialist and instructs for the National Tactical Officers Association in SWAT tactics. He is the co-author of the NTOA Less-Lethal Instructor Course and the NTOA Response to Civil Disorder Course. Sergeant Whitson is certified as a less-lethal instructor for the FBI as well as Defensive Technologies/Federal Laboratories. He is also a certified instructor for Pepperball Technologies, FN303, TASER and Simunitions. Sergeant Whitson can be reached at dwhitson@fcgov.com or 970-221-6543.

Chapter 7

LESS-LETHAL FORCE OPTIONS: SPECIALTY IMPACT SYSTEMS

Don Whitson

INTRODUCTION

As police departments continue to develop strategies and standards for the use of less-lethal weapons, they often get stalled by the seemingly overwhelming options available on the market today. When considering the use of less-lethal devices, a clear mission and value statement must be established. The National Tactical Officers Association Less-Lethal Instructor Course emphasizes force philosophy and tactical decision-making principles over the selection of any one munition type. Although specific munitions are mentioned or pictured in this section, this should not be considered an endorsement or criticism of any manufacturer's product.

If your agency had to select just one less-lethal weapon, what would it be? That would be like asking the question, "If you had to choose only one tool to keep in your garage, what would it be?" Would the tool be used for woodworking, car repair or plumbing? It would be necessary to narrow down the intended uses of the tool before deciding on just one. Similarly, a thorough understanding of tactical principles and decision-making skills, along with anticipating the most common need of the less-lethal system, will help direct an agency to the proper selection of less-lethal options. Police agencies might find they need more than one less-lethal tool

in their inventory. Generally speaking, discussions about less-lethal systems are often in the area of specialty impact munitions. The use of chemical agents, flash/sound diversionary devices, personal impact weapons, police canines and others, are also less-lethal options, but they all rely on similar sound tactical doctrines for them to be used safely and effectively.

Less-Lethal Force Philosophy

When considering less-lethal options for an individual agency, the overall philosophy of the department must be considered. Less-lethal devices must be placed into the force paradigm so officers can measure the application of less-lethal force appropriately. The force paradigm does not change with the introduction of less-lethal devices. Too often, use-of-force principles are neglected when analyzing less-lethal force options. Sound tactical principles should apply to all levels of force.

Less-lethal systems require a philosophical understanding by the agency, as well as the mission for which the systems are to be used. *The selection, training and application of the devices, rather than the simple purchase of a less-lethal weapon, more appropriately define less-lethal systems.*

The less-lethal force philosophy emphasizes five primary sections:

1. Defining the mission
2. Training
3. Selection criteria
4. Tactical planning and less-lethal decision-making
5. Force application considerations

Defining the Mission

First, a mission-based philosophy of less-lethal systems must be clearly defined. The agency must identify the type of system that will provide appropriate force, based on the need. Some systems provide a variety of applications, while others are very narrow in scope. Some systems, for example, provide specialized munitions for crowd control that may not be suitable for direct impact on individuals. For some agencies, more than one system may be the best choice when selecting less-lethal options. The intended purpose of the system will direct the agency to the proper selection of the weapon. Some administrators take a cursory look at use and selection of a less-lethal weapon that does not meet the needs of the agency. For example, many agencies utilize the 12-gauge flexible impact projectile (beanbag). Agencies report different degrees of success with these munitions. When administrators are asked why they selected this particular less-lethal option, almost every response related to cost. The relative low cost and availability of the beanbag was the driving force for the selection of the device, with little or no consideration to effectiveness, injury potential or associated issues. The selection of the 12-gauge beanbag was not mission-based, rather, it was cost-based. Cost is a factor, but it should not be the only factor for consideration. Unfortunately, cost is too often the primary consideration when researching which option is best for the agency. Defining the mission for potential use and deployment should be the starting point for the selection of less-lethal systems.

When evaluating less-lethal systems, there must be a clear and objective statement of purpose; a *combination of trained personnel, proper selection of munitions and appropriate deployment of force, with less potential for causing death or serious bodily injury than conventional force options.* It is important to be cognizant that police officers are not in control of the suspect's actions, only their own. Proper selection and application of less-lethal systems will reduce jeopardy and increase the potential for a successful outcome.

Training

Training is often the most neglected aspect when considering less-lethal options for an agency. Often, there is no difference in cost between training munitions and service munitions, causing the cost per application to be very high. The selection of any system should consider the total operational cost of training. Many of the less-lethal systems are user friendly, but require ongoing training for proficiency and competence. While there is no absolute standard for training in less-lethal systems, training should be consistent with the contemporary standards of the industry.

Zero % – Industry standard for training – 100 % training   training

Training must include aspects that are specific to the selected system, and be reality-based, with live or similar munitions. End users must constantly be challenged with reality-based scenarios. For systems that don't allow direct impacts on human targets, realistic targets should be used. Many impact weapons, for example, require a select target zone. Using a paper silhouette target with no appendages does not allow for targeting those zones.

Training in less-lethal systems must be consistent with organizational values. Policies, standard operational orders and directives must place the less-lethal system on a par with the entire agency; *training and operational philosophy dedicated toward reducing unnecessary and/or avoidable confrontations with suspects, while recognizing that many situations appropriately require higher levels of force.*

Selection Criteria

There is no less-lethal system that works every time for every situation. When selecting a less-lethal system, there are several areas that should be considered:

Accuracy: Accuracy is of the utmost importance. If the system cannot deliver force accurately, the effectiveness of the system is of diminished value.

Flexibility: The system can be used with a variety of munitions for more than one application.

Low Lethality: Many less-lethal systems can, and have, caused unintended death or serious bodily injury. The selection of the system that has a low likelihood of both is desirable.

Cost: Understandably, cost plays an important role in the selection of a less-lethal system, but it should not be the driving force. The cost of ongoing training, operational maintenance and munitions replacement should be factored into the total cost of the less-lethal system.

Effectiveness: Effectiveness is usually closely connected to cost. Selecting a system for its low cost can often result in an ineffective tool. The system must deliver force adequate to gain compliance, with low potential for serious bodily injury or death.

Tactical Planning and Less-Lethal Tactical Decision Making

There are many models to describe the process of decision making. The decision to apply less-lethal force has many components. Some would argue that the application of less-lethal force requires less timely decision making than deadly force because the threat is not always imminent. However, that is not always the case. Many times, the decision to use force is driven by the opportunity, and not the imminence of a threat to the officer or third person. There are many factors that influence tactical decisions. At the core, three important tactical principles that influence less-lethal tactical decision making are:

1. Citizen jeopardy
2. Distance
3. Contingency planning

Tactical planning is essential in the decision to use less-lethal force. With few exceptions, the standard life priority schedule will dictate the mission. Following the safety of life priorities, hostage, innocent person, police officer and suspect pertain to less-lethal use of force, as well as lethal force. Tactical planning depends on many interrelated factors, including:

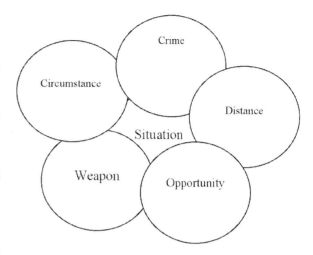

Tactical response occurs rapidly in the field. However, the planning process must begin with the training of all personnel long before the less-lethal system is deployed. *Without proper and in-depth training of the concepts of tactical planning, field operations often rely on good luck, rather than good tactics.*

Concept of Managing Officer Jeopardy

Perhaps the most important, and often most difficult, aspect of tactical planning and training is the concept of managing officer jeopardy. This is an important element of training in the use of less-lethal weapons. It is also the most violated tactical principle.

This concept has a modern reference in the case of *Quezada v. County of Bernalillo,* 944 F.2d 710 (10th Cir. 1991). The basic premise describing officer jeopardy was found in the court ruling that stated police officers should not leave a position of tactical advantage and force a deadly confrontation. Officers may be held liable under common-law negligence principles for putting themselves in a situation that requires the use of deadly force against an armed, suicidal person.

Quezada Facts: *A deputy sheriff stood in an open area of a parking lot while trying to "talk down" a suicidal woman seated in her car with a loaded gun. When the woman raised the gun and took aim at the deputy, he shot and mortally wounded her.*
Holding: The district court judge (in a bench trial) concluded that the deputy was negligent, and that his negligence was the sole cause of the woman's death. In affirming this portion of the district court's decision, the 10th Cir. Court of Appeals reasoned that the deputy, by standing in the open and disregarding his own safety, "forced the deadly confrontation" which resulted. LAAW International, Inc.

This case is referenced in many excessive use-of-force claims where officers used deadly force after relinquishing tactical advantage. These cases are highly dependent on the facts at hand, and are often related to the reasonableness of the officer's actions. Nevertheless, this case is one of the cornerstones for evaluating police response to incidents where force is used upon a person. The reason this case is so important is that it illustrates the current standards of care in situations wherein force is used.

Editor's Note: The *Quezada* case is extremely controversial, and its findings apply only within those states which comprise the 10th Circuit. There is no question that the case is used elsewhere as precedent.

The concept of officer jeopardy taught in training for the use of less-lethal weapons is essential, and cannot be understated. Failing to manage officer jeopardy can be referred to as the ***"noble cause conflict."***

The noble cause conflict is the source for many tactical decision-making errors. Good police officers want to help. They thrive on conflict management. They are driven to be in the middle of conflict. Those attributes are what make police officers our modern-day centurions for community safety. But the noble cause characteristics that push police officers to risk their lives for others are the same ones that create officer jeopardy. There is a difference between rushing into a building where an armed suspect is shooting civilians and rushing up on a single armed person threatening suicide. Both are noble causes, but only the first situation is worthy of dying.

The officer in *Quezada* was undoubtedly doing what he thought was right. He tried to negotiate the safe resolution of a suicidal woman by standing in the open in a parking lot. She pointed the gun at him, he fired his gun in self-defense and she died. Many people would say his actions were not unreasonable, yet in the opinion of the court, the actions taken by the officer forced the confrontation. It may be unpalatable, but that is the standard of care for the profession of police officer in modern society, and officers need to be trained to understand the consequences of their actions.

The use of less-lethal weapons has opened a new area of concern in tactical decision making, because officers often surrender their position of tactical advantage to use them. When this occurs, officers create jeopardy that could otherwise be avoided if the principles of distance and contingency planning are considered.

For example, a patrol officer complained that a commanding officer responded to a call of a subject threatening suicide inside his home, alone. As officers were outside the home making a plan, the commander entered the house, shot the suspect with a 12-gauge beanbag, disarming him. The dumbfounded officers were shocked at what they felt was a reckless act. It worked out, but if it had not, the commander most certainly would have faced criticism for his actions. Because the situation was resolved without deadly force, the commander was commended for his actions. In retrospect, had deadly force been utilized, one could question his actions based upon his having created officer jeopardy.

Another example involves use of the TASER. The system is very effective when used properly. However, too often the device is used after violating one basic tactical principle–***distance***. Agencies which have had success with a certain device, and claim to have lowered overall incidents of higher levels of force, seldom acknowledge unsafe and precarious deployment methods. A case in point occurred when officers confronted an armed, suicidal suspect outside his home. The officers were more than 30 feet away from the suspect, and had adequate cover and escape routes. The suspect was holding a knife in his hand and yelling at officers. When the suspect backed away, the officers rushed the suspect and deployed the TASER from a distance of three feet. The TASER did not immediately incapacitate the suspect, but fortunately he was disarmed as he fell backward. If the officers had used deadly force in this situation, their actions might well be considered to have forced the confrontation. They surrendered their position of tactical advantage in order to deploy the only less-lethal option they had, which required a closer deployment distance. So, again, the *Quezada* case could apply.

Another case worth consideration in tactical planning and training is *Allen v. Muskogee, et al.* 119 F.3d 837 (1997). This case involved three officers. They responded to a report of a man sitting in his car with a gun. It was thought that he posed a threat to a third party in her home. As officers approached, the subject fired at the officers and they returned fire, mortally wounding the suspect. The officers responded to protect a civilian. They reacted to a threat. However, the court had to consider expert testimony about the current standards of care and response to a situation such as this.

> Appellants append. III at 572. He stated if the officers were trained to respond to this kind of call by staying in the open, leaving innocent people in the open, and doing provocative things like trying to grab the gun and get into the car, the training was out of synch with the entire United States in terms of what police are being trained to do.
> Id. at 576. To my knowledge, I'm not aware of any significant debate in the law enforcement or expert witness community about the fundamental principles we're talking about here. Cover is better than no cover. Communicating from a safe distance is better than not. Getting innocent people as safely out of the way as possible is desirable. Not engaging in certain actions with mentally disturbed armed people, not getting close to them is preferable. I've never heard any knowledgeable debate or argument about any of those subjects in the 25 years I've been doing this type of work.
> Id. at 580. Referring to the training provided the officers through a state program, Dr. Kirkham states: "If the State of Oklahoma through CLEET trains their officers to not be mindful of cover, to be aggressive with mentally ill people, do all these things that are totally off the board, then the State is wrong and out of synch with the rest of the country in the police profession.

This case illustrates that there is a perceived standard of care for training, response and application of force in policing. Again, while there is no absolute value to describe the appropriate action for any specific case, agencies must constantly maintain current training techniques and professional standards of care.

It is recognized that the application of deadly force is sometimes necessary. The factual situation will dictate the appropriateness of the use of deadly force. *Training, planning and proper less-lethal deployment will reduce the necessity to use deadly force, but it will not eliminate it.*

Tactical Decision Making Elements

Less-lethal tactical decision making requires an understanding of some important concepts. These should be implemented in training through reality-based scenarios.

Opportunity

The set of circumstances or movement created by the officer or the suspect that allows for the successful deployment of a less-lethal option. Opportunity can be fleeting, and must be recognized and exploited without hesitation.

Space and Time Continuum

Space applies to the proximity of officers to suspects when sudden engagement occurs. More space, within reason, allows for more rapid neutralization of the suspect with reduced immediate danger to officers.

Time applies to the brain's ability to recognize danger and respond appropriately, before the suspect gains a tactical advantage or aggresses officers.

Use of Cover, Concealment and Barriers

The use of hard cover or concealment is important in preparation for the incident changing to a deadly force encounter. In most instances, it is not acceptable for officers to give up cover just to get the chance to deploy less-lethal options.

Crisis vs. Controlled Incidents

Some incidents are static in nature. This occurs when the incident has appropriate contingency plans in place and officers have the ability to systematically resolve the incident with less-lethal force. Other incidents are resolved while in the midst of crisis. These incidents rely heavily on previous training, as well as the immediate availability of an appropriate less-lethal system. While in crisis mode, for example, officers can make mistakes, select the wrong rounds or get too close to a suspect. With consistent and ongoing training, officers and supervisors are able to control their actions and make good decisions.

Dog Pile

Once again, training and discipline are required to discourage rushing up on a suspect following the application of less-lethal force. There are many incidents where the suspect was momentarily incapacitated, but had the ability to recover and cause injury to officers as they tried to control the suspect.

Appropriate Less-Lethal System

Not every less-lethal system is appropriate for every situation. For example, extended-range impact systems are not well-suited for close-quarter engagements. Selecting the proper less-lethal system for the incident is crucial to a successful outcome.

Adequate Lethal Cover

Crisis contacts with some people can turn unexpectedly violent. Less-lethal force is an option, provided it can be deployed safely and effectively. *Dedicated lethal-force cover should always accompany less-lethal systems.*

Response Team Movement

Whenever possible, a contact team configuration should be utilized when confronting potentially violent subjects. The contact team allows for flexible response movement, better communication among team members and immediate access to force options. The response team is composed of at least two officers, and can grow in number based on the mission. It can be configured in a variety of forms.

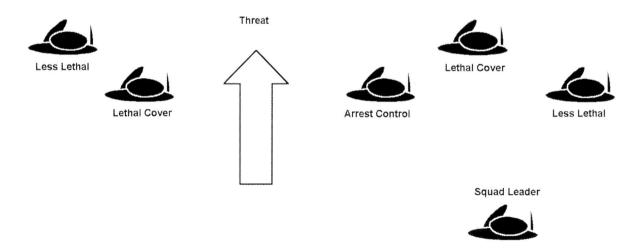

Verbalization

When practical, every use of less-lethal options should include a communication with other officers that less-lethal force is being deployed. This will reduce the likelihood of a sympathetic reaction by assisting officers.

Force Application Considerations

Accuracy

The most critical consideration for the selection of the less-lethal system is accuracy. If the system is not accurate at anticipated deployment distances, it will create unintended hazards for both the suspect and the officer. The current training model for specialty impact munitions focuses on target selection over reduced energy munitions. However, the probability of serious injury is very high with center mass body impacts. Some manufacturers of kinetic impact projectiles produce low-energy munitions, but accuracy and effectiveness must not be compromised.

Target selection is a critical component in less-lethal applications. The target selection, or aiming point, is generally defined by regions of the body and the potential for injury upon impact. When selecting a less-lethal weapon system, consideration should be given to the accuracy of the weapon and ability of the projectile to strike specific areas of the body. These zones are described as:

Zone One or Green Zone: Meaty areas of the body, or large muscle groups, i.e., buttocks, thigh, calf.

Zone Two or Yellow Zone: Skeletal and medium muscle groups, i.e., shoulder, upper arm, forearm, wrist, elbow, knees.

Zone Three or Red Zone: High-risk areas for serious bodily injury, i.e., head, throat, chest, neck, spine, groin.

Distance

While accuracy is the principle feature when considering a less-lethal impact system, it must also effectively and immediately incapacitate the suspect. It must also be accurate and effective at vari-

ous distances. Close-range engagements with high-energy projectiles may increase the likelihood of incapacitation, but may increase the unintended potential for serious trauma. Conversely, long-range engagements may result in recovery time or eroded effectiveness due to loss of kinetic energy transfer to the body.

It is a difficult balance to find a less-lethal system that will be safe and effective at various distances. Most importantly, the system must be effective at distances that allow the advantage of space and time for the officer.

Effectiveness

The effectiveness of the less-lethal system must consider immediate incapacitation through pain compliance with the potential for unintended serious bodily injury. Ultimately, the system should provide for compliance without lasting injury.

Incapacitation

The less-lethal system must have some measure of immediate success. In some cases, where chemical agents combined with kinetic energy impact are used, the incapacitation time may be dependent on the time it takes for exposure to the chemical agent.

Injury Potential

The injury potential of the less-lethal system generally considers the unintended consequences of the impact. With certain types of projectiles, some injury is almost always expected, even when the appropriate target zone is selected. Unintended injury results in more serious injury, due to the suspect's body type, for example. The injury potential should be clearly understood and defined prior to application. *Medical attention should always be provided when someone is struck by a specialty impact munition.*

Cost

Cost of the less-lethal system should extend beyond the initial purchase price. Training costs for end users, and ongoing training costs for regular recertification, should be factored into the cost evaluation. The selection of a less-lethal system that doesn't allow the use of inert or reloaded training munitions will have a higher overall cost than those that can use less-expensive training rounds.

Accessibility

Closely associated with the cost of the less-lethal system is the consideration of availability. Some agencies have elected to reduce operational expenses by only placing the less-lethal devices with supervisors or tactical teams. In many cases, the first responding officers are in a better position to tactically deploy the less-lethal option, which allows the supervisor to manage the overall incident. Less-lethal systems that are stored in the vault of police headquarters, or in the trunk of a sergeant's car, do little for the first responder. When evaluating the system, consideration should be given to the personnel most likely to need the system. In some cases SWAT, mobile field force or other special-duty personnel may have different accessibility to the munitions.

Reality-Based Training

Realistic training with scenario-based incidents is essential to the provision of legitimate less-lethal training. Human-like targets and interactive role play can not only lead to better skills for deploying less-lethal, but also reinforce operational objectives. Simunitions™ training weapons and marking cartridges will significantly enhance the reality of training scenarios. Again, this area is closely linked to overall costs for providing less-lethal options to officers.

The less-lethal system should be deployed in training to simulate realistic situations. It is unlikely that a flexible 12-gauge projectile will be deployed beyond 50 yards, or closer than two yards. Training distance should be within the expected and safe deployment range, based on the product specifications.

It is important to follow the manufacturer's recommendation for the selected specialty impact weapon. It is also imperative that officers consistently duplicate the results at the range with the selected system. The optimum operating range of the projectiles and the effects of the munition at given distances must be understood by the operator.

Other considerations that must be addressed in training are factors which influence aiming points and target selection. Clothing, physical stature, age, target picture and so on, will influence aiming points. Practice targets that simulate these variables should be included in training scenarios.

The Selection of Specialty Impact Munitions

The first step in the selection process for a less-lethal system is to identify the anticipated need of the agency. For example, an agency with a history of large-scale crowd management issues may find indirect-fired munitions more effective and used more frequently than direct-impact munitions. A historical event chart should be created to give an inference as to what the agency will most likely use. In many cases, even this might prove to be inconclusive if the agency responds to a wide variety of incidents.

A comparison to national or regional data collection sites is also a valuable tool in the preliminary stages of less-lethal selection. While not by itself absolutely conclusive, the study conducted by Ken Hubbs and David Klinger, *Impact Munitions Data Base of Use and Effects,*[1] provides some insight into the types and demographics of encounters involving the use of less-lethal force. These findings can provide the agency with a foundation and guidelines to anticipate deployment probabilities for the use of less-lethal weapons. For example, in this study of 373 encounters, more than one half (181) of the incidents involved the application of specialty impact munitions on suicidal or emotionally disturbed persons. The data also shows that nearly 90 percent of the suspect encounters involved a weapon by the suspect. Of those, 50 percent of the cases involved edged weapons. The data illustrates that the vast majority of the incidents resulted in less than four projectiles used during each encounter.

This data can serve as a general template for the selection of the less-lethal system, and training emphasis for the end user. At the time of the Hubbs/Klinger report, of the munition types used in the reported cases, 65 percent were 12-gauge bean-bag rounds, followed by 37mm plastic baton rounds.

One very important area of interest in this report

was the relative distance between the suspect and officer. Of the reported encounters, 38 percent of the deployments were between 10 and 19 feet. Another 25 percent of the deployments came at an average distance of 20–29 feet. The most common impact areas of the body were the abdomen and chest. Bruising, abrasions and lacerations were the most common injuries reported. Another important finding was the relationship between the distance of the deployment and the relative injury to the suspect. It is not surprising that more than 10 percent of the impacts produced broken bones when impacted within 10 feet of the suspect.

When examining this data, or data from other sources, it is important to note that many variables can produce different conclusions. They should serve only as a guide for the selection process of the less-lethal system best suited for the agency.

Another valuable resource in the defining process for the agency selection of a less-lethal system is the *Attribute-Based Evaluation (ABE) of Less-Than-Lethal, Extended-Range, Impact Munitions,* by Dr. John M. Kenney, et al.[2] This study was conducted to provide law enforcement and the military with an unbiased, objective comparison of available less-than-lethal munitions. The study, co-sponsored by the Los Angeles County Sheriff's Department and Penn State University, offers a comparative analysis of munitions available to police agencies. It is another reference source to assist agencies in the selection of less-lethal systems. The study provides important observations about specialty impact munition performance from a variety of manufacturers. It also provides insight into the variation and configuration of specialty impact systems, as well as a relative comparison of vendors.

Specialty Impact Systems

After careful consideration and analysis of philosophy and tactical principles, the selection of the specific munition will be the next step when considering the best less-lethal system for an agency. Again, this may result in the conclusion that there is not one sole munition or system that will provide applications for every situation.

Generally, specialty impact munitions can be categorized into classes. The three most common

classes are: 12-gauge, 37/40mm and .68 caliber. There are also subcategories for multiple launched projectiles in .60- and .32-caliber projectiles.

Within these general classes, the projectiles are further defined by flexible and non-flexible munitions. These projectiles are produced in a variety of materials, including rubber, polyurethane, Styrofoam, plastic, wood and more. Some of the projectiles are encapsulated, using a membrane of material to enclose lead shot, liquid or powder.

Depending on the intended delivery purpose of the projectiles, some are made to be direct-fired, while others are designed to be skip-fired or fired indirectly. Additionally, these projectiles have varying levels of energy and potential for injury. Direct-fired 37mm wood batons to the chest have a significant injury potential compared to other types of projectiles to the same target location.

Accuracy Potential

Regardless of the type of munition, accuracy still plays an important role in the selection of a specialty impact munition. There are basically four methods used to increase the accuracy of a launched projectile.

Spin Stabilization: Projectiles launched from a rifled-bore barrel catch raised ridges in the barrel as

it is propelled away, similar to that of a conventional bullet. As the projectile moves through the barrel, it is spun by the spiral ridge design. The projectile then stabilizes in flight by the spinning action of the projectile. The projectile must be aerodynamic in design to be affected by the spin stabilization. An oblong beanbag, for example, will have little or no in-flight spin stabilization effect, due to its non-aerodynamic shape.

Fin Stabilization: Another method to increase the accuracy of a projectile is through fin stabilization. The projectile is equipped with fins on the rear of the projectile, similar in shape to a torpedo. The opposing fin design allows for aerodynamic stabilization in flight, and enables the projectile to be launched from a smooth-bore barrel.

Drag Stabilization: Most of the newly designed flexible projectiles have a tail configuration that also assists in stabilized flight. Much like a kite, the drag-stabilized tail compensates for the air resistance in flight and provides more accuracy than the original square projectiles.

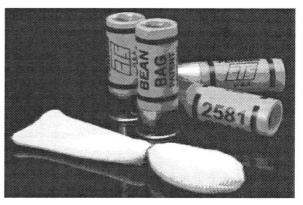

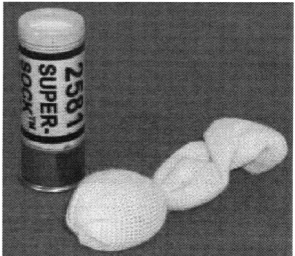

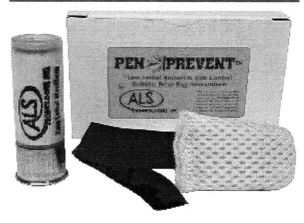

Shape Stabilization: Some projectiles do not utilize any of the three previous stabilization methods. These projectiles are generally round, and have a smooth surface. The actual shape of the projectile has reduced air resistance to in-flight disturbance, which creates increased accuracy. While the airfoil design could also be added to this shape category, there are no commercially manufactured airfoil projectiles at this time.

Intended Purpose of the Projectile

Direct-Impact Projectiles

These projectiles are intended to deliver sufficient energy to temporarily incapacitate an individual. The energy must be sufficient to render immediate incapacitation without causing unintended serious bodily injury. These projectiles are most commonly delivered one at a time at individual suspects. They require accuracy for shot placement. These projectiles can be flexible or non-flexible, depending on the specific munition used.

Indirect-Impact Projectiles

These projectiles are generally used to deliver kinetic energy upon impact, but because they usually contain multiple projectiles, they cannot be delivered with discriminating accuracy. They are usually non-flexible, high-energy configurations, and most commonly used for crowd control.

Flexible Projectiles

Flexible projectiles are intended to conform to the contour of the surface upon impact. These can be batons made of soft, pliable material, such as foam or rubber, or they can be encapsulated projectiles filled with material that will move, to allow for conformation upon impact. The most common materials for the encapsulated projectiles are silica sand, viscous aqueous solution and multiple lead shot pellets.

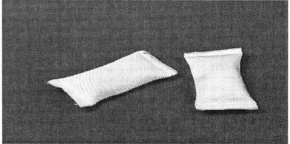

Non-Flexible Projectiles

These projectiles are formed of material that has little or no conformation upon impact. These non-flexible projectiles can be single projectiles, or used in multiple-projectile configurations.

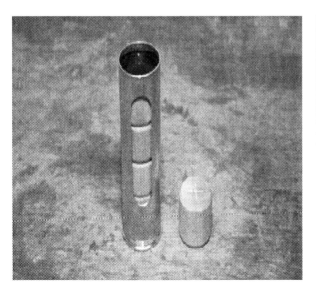

Delivery Methods

Most of the specialty impact munitions are delivered from a weapon system much like the design of a traditional firearm. The 37mm and 40mm munitions utilize powder propulsion principles. Other projectiles are launched with high-pressure air, and some can be delivered by hand from an exploding grenade.

12-Gauge Shotgun

The most common delivery platform for specialty impact weapons is the 12-gauge pump-action shotgun. The munition is projected out of the barrel at high velocity using black powder or smokeless powder propellants. The 12-gauge munition is widely used, mainly due to its ready availability, ease of operation and relatively low cost.

37mm Launcher

The 37mm launching platform is available in smooth-bore and rifled-bore configurations. The 37mm launcher can deliver a variety of payloads and munition types.

40mm Launcher

This launching system is very similar to the 37mm, and has a rifled bore.

Both the 37mm and 40mm systems can be found in single-shot and multiple-shot configurations, and each can deliver a variety of payload sizes.

Compressed Air Launchers

These launching systems use compressed air to propel the projectile from the barrel of the launcher. They use .68-caliber projectiles, similar in shape and size to a common paintball projectile.

Hand-Delivered Projectiles

These projectiles are contained in a grenade, designed to propel the munitions from the device using an explosive charge. The projectiles are indiscriminately launched away from the device in a

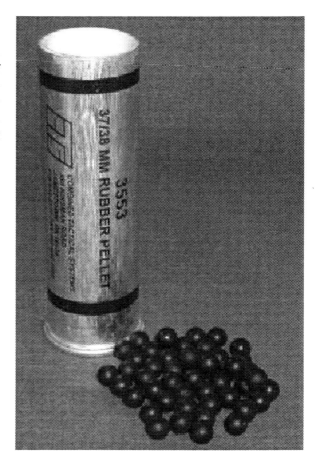

scattered pattern. The launching platform obviously depends on the type of projectile selected for the agency's use. Most manufacturers of the projectile also sell the launcher. With few exceptions, most of the projectiles can be delivered from any manufacturers launching platform, but this is not recommended.

FN 303 Launcher

. 15 "STINGER"

Evaluating the Projectile

Performance criteria can be obtained for impact projectiles by referencing the *Attribute-Based Evaluation of Less-Than-Lethal, Extended-Range Impact Munitions Study* mentioned previously. The agency should select the class of projectile, i.e., 37mm, 12-gauge, 40mm, etc., and then examine the perform-

ance of each brand of projectile in that class. For example, if the agency selects the 37mm non-flexible baton as the primary less-lethal projectile, a comparison of attributes for that munition can be determined by the agency.

Accuracy

Accuracy can be determined by referencing the product specification manual for that particular munition, and verified by the agency in field trials. There is less deviation between projectiles from the same manufacturers than in the past. Reputable manufacturers of these munitions have improved the performance and reliability of the devices, not only to meet the requirements of police, but also to maintain competitive proprietary interests.

Effectiveness

The selected projectile must also be effective at incapacitating the suspect, while providing the least amount of serious injury as possible. The product manufacturers of less-lethal projectiles are constantly challenged to provide a projectile that causes immediate incapacitation with minimal potential for serious bodily injury.

The effectiveness of the less-lethal projectile is correlated to its kinetic energy. Greater energy levels create more dramatic results. Likewise, the more kinetic energy, the greater chance for significant injury or death as a result of blunt or penetrating trauma on the body.

Kinetic Energy

Kinetic energy is the energy an object has because of its motion. Kinetic energy can be translational, like the dropping of a hammerhead onto a nail, or rotational, like that of a spinning fan blade. A thrown baseball has kinetic energy because of its forward movement. If it is spinning, it has additional kinetic energy because of its rotational motion. If an object has mass and velocity, then the magnitude of its kinetic energy is given by $K=(1/2)(m/g)v2$. If the object is rotating, like the wheels of a moving car, two other factors influence the kinetic energy–movement of inertia about its axis or rotation and its angular velocity.[3]

Generally, the kinetic energy calculations for less-lethal projectiles do not take into account the sum of both equations because the projectile is not rotating enough to significantly influence the total energy sum. So, kinetic energy can be determined by calculating the relationship between the mass and the velocity of the projectile. This total kinetic energy analysis will relate to the effectiveness of the projectile to produce pain and trauma on the human body.

Less-lethal projectiles are intended to cause incapacitation of the suspect through pain. The effects of pain can cause psychological and physiological conditions that contribute to compliance.

Psychological Effects

The impact of a specialty impact munition can have a tremendous mental effect on humans. The psychological response from the impact of a specialty impact munition can often be more effective than the physical effect. Anxiety produced by pointing a weapon directly at someone can arouse fear, and sometimes panic. It has become a practice to document the responses and effectiveness of less-lethal projectiles, even when no projectiles are fired. Very often, the ominous sight of a 37mm launcher pointed at the person can alone induce compliance.

Physiological Effects

Specialty impact weapons are used with the intent to cause pain and, at times, sufficient blunt trauma to disorient or incapacitate an individual. Therefore, some degree of injury is expected. This may be necessary to achieve compliance or a momentary degree of incapacitation.

The injury from a less-lethal projectile will be varied.

Contusion: An injury of a part without a break in the skin, with a subcutaneous hemorrhage. It is also called a bruise.

Laceration: A torn, ragged, mangled wound.

Abrasion: An area of the body surface denuded of skin or mucous membrane by some unusual or abnormal mechanical process.

Fracture: The breaking of a part, especially the bone.

Trauma: An injury, psychological or emotional damage.

Penetrating or Missile Wounds: Also called velocity wounds, they are caused by an object entering the body at high speed.

A less-lethal projectile striking the body can also cause a condition related to fluid shock. Fluid shock results from the kinetic energy transfer from a solid object to a body of fluid from the forward motion of the object. Fluid shock is energy transferred from the forward motion of an object.

Potential Risks and Injury From Specialty Impact Munitions

Blunt trauma injuries are the most common injury associated with specialty impact munitions. Unintended penetrating trauma is the most undesirable outcome of an impact munition. Penetration can be the result of many variables, including excessive kinetic energy of the projectile, body composition, distance, shot placement and so on.

Other potential injuries occur even without penetrating trauma. Blunt trauma impacts to the head, neck, groin, face, chest, abdomen and spine can result in death or serious bodily injury.

Blunt Trauma to the Body

Injuries as a result of kinetic energy impact projectiles can be unpredictable and unintentional. Blunt trauma injuries to the chest depend in most part on the depth of deformation as it relates to the speed of compression, and the internal organs' reaction to it. The chest and its protective rib cage can tolerate large compression loads if applied slowly. Under these conditions, a compression load of 40 percent may occur before critical crushing injury is noted. Likewise, a compression load of 5 percent at 100 fps can cause a fatal compression injury.

Blunt trauma to the abdomen will compress soft tissue and displace the liquid in the visceral area. The liquid does not compress, it transfers the kinetic energy in a wave-like motion, pushing and stretching the internal organs. Soft tissue injury is determined by a relationship between two factors: the speed and amount of the body deformation. The relationship between these two parameters is called the viscous criterion, which can be used to predict the severity of soft tissue injury caused by an impact.

When evaluating the selection of specialty impact munitions, these issues should be considered. The projectile should provide immediate incapacitation for compliance, with reduced potential for unintended serious bodily injury or death. As the kinetic energy increases, so does the potential for pain compliance from blunt trauma injury, but so too does the potential for serious injury. The challenge is to balance the expected injury potential with the intended compliance.

There is no definitive scale for comparing these two attributes. Common sense would direct one to the conclusion that at the lowest end of the kinetic energy scale there is little potential for serious injury, but less potential for compliance. At the same time, at the high end of the scale, the compliance expectations are greater, but so is the potential for injury.

Controlled studies on gel, modeling clay or mechanical calibration devices can measure deformation from projectiles and make inferences as to the total deformation on the human body. Generally, specialty impact projectiles on the market today range between 8 ft-lbs to 187 ft-lbs of kinetic energy. As the kinetic energy approaches 200 ft-lbs, there is sufficient energy to cause unintended serious bodily injury. That appears to be the threshold for total kinetic energy, regardless of its mass or velocity. The 37mm beanbag, for example, at 260.5 fps will generate around 153 ft-lbs of kinetic energy. If the same projectile were to be delivered at 500 fps, the lethality potential would be considered too high.

It is important to consider this kinetic energy issue carefully when selecting less-lethal systems. There should be a clear understanding of the potential and expected injury using these projectiles. Reducing the kinetic energy value may decrease the effectiveness in generating compliance.

Legal Considerations

Photographs of any injuries should be included in the case documentation to show that the force used to gain compliance was objectively reasonable and

necessary at the time for protection of the suspect, the officer or a third party. The use-of-force principle is contained in *Graham v. Connor,* 490 U.S. 386 at 384, *"The calculus of reasonableness must embody allowance that police officers are often forced to make split-second judgments in circumstances that are tense, uncertain and rapidly evolving about the force and amount of force that is necessary in a particular situation."* The need for force, and the relationship between that need and the amount of force used, will be primary issues when establishing reasonableness.

Not every situation requires less-lethal force to be applied when deadly force is required to protect another. *Plakas v. Drinski,* 811 F.Supp. 1356 (N.D. Ind. 1993) *held that there is no requirement to use less-intrusive force when deadly force is required for protection.* There are times when less-lethal means might be used to disarm a suspect with a gun, for example. If the circumstances are such that it can be done without compromising safety, it is an option, but not a requirement.

Another important case to note is *Davis v. Mason,* 922 F.2d 1473 (9th Cir. 1991), wherein the court commented that, *"You can train a monkey to run into a room and pull the pin on a fragmentation grenade. Officers must be educated and conditioned."* The case involved the consequences of inadequate training. Adequate training on the technical components of the weapon is not sufficient. Officers must also have adequate training in the Constitutional limits as well. Simply knowing that your weapon works is not enough.

When deploying less-lethal munitions, it is advisable to give warning whenever practical. The warning serves two purposes. First, it communicates to other officers that less-lethal force is going to be utilized. This may minimize sympathetic reactions by officers who think it is a lethal threat to another officer. The second issue is contained in *Deorle v. Rutherford,* No. 99–17188 (9th Cir.). The suspect was unintentionally struck in the eye with a 12-gauge beanbag. In this case, the court held that warning should be given prior to the deployment of these devices, due to their inherent danger.

There are, of course, times when a warning would not be tactically sound. It is also argued that a verbal warning prior to deployment could diminish the effectiveness of the device–assuming the suspect is capable of comprehending it.

If steps are taken to properly train officers in all aspects of the force paradigm, and they act in a reasonable manner, litigation becomes much more avoidable. Detailed documentation, adherence to policy and procedure and thoughtful after-action analysis of cases involving force must also occur to avoid litigation.

Author Recommendations

The selection of a less-lethal system for an agency should be considered carefully. There are many manufacturers with similar systems, and a wide variety of munitions from which to choose. Depending on the circumstances and needs of the department, more than one of these systems may be desirable. The general recommendations that follow are not intended to constitute an endorsement for any specific company, but rather as general guidelines for agencies interested in selecting a less-lethal system.

40mm Projectiles

The 40mm foam projectiles, such as the Combined Tactical Systems 4557, or Armor Holdings Exact Impact 1006, are high-energy rounds that deliver sufficient energy for incapacitation with lessened potential for serious injury. They are spin stabilized for increased accuracy and distance, but can also be fired at relatively close range.

37mm Non-Flexible Projectiles

The rigid projectile, such as the Sage K01 round, is a high-energy round with spin stabilization for increased accuracy. It has reload capabilities to lower training costs. The energy is sufficient to provide immediate incapacitation in many cases, but it does have the potential for serious injury.

Compressed Air Propelled Munitions

The Pepperball Technologies and the FN303 system deliver projectiles that combine kinetic energy impact with chemical agents. The projectiles burst upon impact, and powdered chemical agents are forced into the air. They are designed to impart a low level of kinetic energy, and rely on the chemical exposure for incapacitation. The projectiles have a very low probability of causing serious injury. The decontamination of the powdered chemical agents is relatively simple. Projectiles can be delivered from sufficient distances for officer safety, but also used at close range, if required.

A combination of these three systems will provide a variety of applications and flexibility.

The National Tactical Officers Association provides instructor certification for the use of less-lethal systems. In-depth discussions, product demonstrations and course instruction will provide more detailed information about all aspects of less-lethal force options. Contact the National Tactical Officers Association Training Division for more details at 800-279-9127.

CONCLUSION

There is much to consider when selecting the best less-lethal force options. It is not the less-lethal technology that provides the standard of care, but rather the training and understanding of tactical principles.

There are pros and cons to each system. Large-bore systems deliver a wider variety of munitions, but are bulky, more expensive and generally produce a higher potential for injury. An agency must select the less-lethal system that will provide the greatest degree of flexibility for a variety of incidents. There are departments which have equipped every officer with a TASER, for example. These officers are fortunate to have been supplied with the means to deal with less-lethal encounters. However, the agency must also provide officers with tools that allow for distance deployment as well. Relying on one less-lethal system that is designed for close-quarter deployment does little for other applications.

ENDNOTES

1. Kenneth Hubbs and David Klinger, Ph.D. *Impact Munitions Data Base of Use and Effects.* Grant funded by

the NIJ Under the Solicitation for Law Enforcement, Courts and Corrections Technology Development, Implementation and Evaluation

2. John M. Kenney, Ph.D., Charles S. Heal and Michael Grossman. *Attribute-Based Evaluation (ABE) of Less-Than-Lethal, Extended-Range Impact Munitions.* The Applied Research Laboratory, the Pennsylvania State University and the Los Angeles County Sheriff's Department. February 15, 2001.

3. *Macmillan Encyclopedia of Physics,* Simon and Schuster Macmillan, volume 2, 1996.

TOM LYNCH

Tom Lynch is a 21-year veteran of the Philadelphia, Pennsylvania, Police Department, where he currently serves as a Bomb Technician with their Bomb Disposal Unit. He is the Explosive/EOD Section Chairman for the National Tactical Officers Association and the recipient of the NTOA Award for Excellence. Officer Lynch also serves as a subgroup member with the Technical Support Working Group (TSWG).

Chapter 8

EXPLOSIVES RECOGNITION FOR FIRST RESPONDERS

TOM LYNCH

INTRODUCTION

Law enforcement officers are increasingly encountering explosives and explosive-related materials during the normal course of their duties. With the high threat of terrorist activity in the United States, it is important that officers in the field recognize the dangers and potential hazards associated with these items. It is also important that they recognize some of the indicators, especially those related to improvised explosive devices (IEDs) and the potential components associated with the construction and deployment of these types of terrorist weapons.

Law enforcement and military bomb disposal teams in the United States have been recovering and disposing of various types of commercial, military and improvised explosives as part of their routine duties. In most incidents, these items can pose an enormous risk to both the emergency first responder and the general public. The explosive items often recovered by emergency response units include commercial, military and improvised explosive devices. Law enforcement and other emergency responders' roles are changing as we enter a new post-9/11 era. The war on terrorism and high terrorist activity have created a need to redefine our basic level of preparedness in order to meet this current and emerging threat from both conventional and improvised explosive devices. Because

law enforcement and emergency response personnel are the front line of defense in the war on terrorism, it is important that first responding elements within state and local government understand how critical their role will be in preventing, protecting against, responding to and recovering from terrorist attacks.

This chapter is intended to acquaint law enforcement emergency response personnel with common commercial, military and improvised devices routinely recovered by bomb disposal units. It is not intended to be a render-safe manual, but rather a brief recognition and awareness guide. Explosives and improvised explosive devices present an extreme danger and should only be handled or rendered safe by qualified bomb disposal technicians.

Explosives

Explosives continue to play an important role in our society. Explosives have helped the United States achieve a standard of living matched by no other nation in the world. It is estimated that there are over five billion pounds of explosives used every year by the commercial industry. The military also uses a large amount of explosive material, which unfortunately seems to find its way into the civilian population here in the United States. With the war on terrorism expanding around the world, explosives will continue to be the weapon of choice for both domestic and international terrorist groups.

Explosives can be broken down into several categories, depending on their performance and reaction speed. These categories are often referred to as low explosives, high explosives or blasting agents. Low explosives are characterized by their low reaction speed, which is often referred to as deflagration. Examples of materials that fall into this category are black powder, smokeless powder and other energetic materials referred to as pyrotechnics. Pyrotechnics are a combination of various fuel and oxidizer mixtures used to produce a variety of visible and audio effects through the burning process. Today, pyrotechnic materials are used in a number of commercial industries and are credited with modernizing and improving safety within the aviation, automotive and entertainment industry, just to name a few. The military also produces and uses a large quantity of pyrotechnic materials, which often fall into the wrong hands.

Low explosive materials, such as black and smokeless powder, along with pyrotechnics, account for a large portion of the explosive filler found in improvised explosive devices in the United States and abroad. Individual criminals, criminal organizations, along with experimenting juveniles and terrorists both in the United States and overseas, find easy access to the materials used in improvised explosive device manufacturing. Improvised explosive devices are one of the main weapons terrorists are deploying in their operational campaign. These devices represent a serious threat to the national security of the United States and will be discussed further in this chapter.

Commercial Low Explosives

Black Powder: Black powder is a mixture of potassium nitrate or sodium nitrate, sulfur and charcoal, and is considered a low explosive. A low explosive is characterized by its slow reaction speed, which is often referred to as a deflagration. Black powder is one of the oldest and most dangerous explosives known to man. It is very sensitive to heat, shock and friction. Black powder at one time was the only energetic material available for

weapons and mining operations.

With advancements in explosive technology, the role of black powder has been dramatically reduced. Today, black powder is mainly used by the fireworks industry, black powder sport hunters and, on a limited scale, the commercial mining industry. Sporting-grade black powder is the most often used and encountered by law enforcement. Goex, Inc. is the only manufacturer in the United States. Another manufacturer of black powder is a company called Elephant, a Brazilian-based company that imports black powder to the United States.

Sporting-grade black powder granules are usually black, with irregular sizes and shapes. The designated symbol on the can that identifies sporting-grade powder is Fg, FFg, FFFg and FFFFg. The letter "F" indicates sporting grade and the small lower case "g" symbolizes graphite.

Substitute Black Powder: There are several substitute black powders available in the United States. The most popular substitutes are Pyrodex, Goex Clear Shot and Black Canyon. These powders are designed as propellants for muzzleloaders and other black powder guns. Both black powder and black powder substitutes are extremely sensitive. Law enforcement officers should use extreme caution when coming in contact with this material. Often, officers will encounter this material incorporated into an improvised explosive device.

Smokeless Powder: Smokeless powder began to replace black powder as a weapons propellant in the late 1800s. The first use of smokeless powder appears to have been by a Prussian artillery officer in 1864. Since then, smokeless powder has undergone numerous improvements and changes in order to accommodate a variety of weapons systems. Today, smokeless powder is the main energy-providing propellant used in military and law enforcement weapons systems, and is widely available to the general public for purchase.

Smokeless powder is manufactured by a number of companies both in the United States and abroad. While smokeless powder is designed to burn rapidly and is classified by the Department of Transportation as a low explosive, the material can be extremely powerful and dangerous when used in an IED. Even though smokeless powder is classified as a low explosive, the energy-producing ingredients are the same material found in high explosives, and under certain conditions can react with the same intensity. Nitrocellulose and nitroglycerin are the same ingredients found in both gelatinized dynamite and smokeless powder.

Pyrotechnics: Pyrotechnics are energetic-material items used to produce visible, thermal or audible effects through the burning chemical reaction process. Law enforcement officers regularly come in contact with pyrotechnics during the normal course of their duties. The most common types of pyrotechnics encountered by law enforcement are commercially manufactured consumer fireworks, illegally manufactured explosive devices (commonly referred to by law enforcement as forbidden/illegal explosive devices) or military simulators and smoke grenades. The energetic materials found in pyrotechnics are often used in improvised explosive devices. Individual bomb makers or terrorist groups have been known to disassemble these types of energetic materials for use in improvised explosive devices.

One of the most dangerous explosive items encountered by law enforcement is the forbidden/illegal explosive device. This item can be referred to on the street by several names. Some of the most common names may include M-80s, M-100s, Quarter Sticks or Block Busters. These items are very dangerous due to an extremely sensitive explosive mixture called photo flash powder. While there are a number of mixtures used in manufacturing photo flash powder, one of the common mixtures is potassium perchlorate, aluminum powder and sulfur. This mixture is extremely sensitive to heat, shock, friction and static electricity. Law enforcement personnel may encounter these items as part of criminal activity. Criminals and juveniles have been known to increase the destructive capability of these items by attaching additional fragmentation, such as nails, BB's, nuts and bolts, etc. Law enforcement officers coming in contact with these items should use extreme caution.

Military Pyrotechnics: The military uses a number of pyrotechnic items which often find their way into the civilian population. Law enforcement bomb squads and military EOD (explosive ordnance disposal) units are often called to remove or take custody of these items as a result of criminal activity or as souvenirs. There are a variety of different types of military pyrotechnics used for various military applications. All present a potential risk to both law enforcement and the civilian population. These pyrotechnic items are extremely dangerous in the wrong hands.

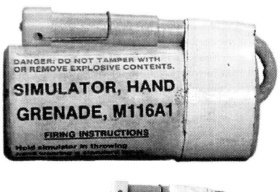

Primary High Explosives

High explosives are categorized as either primary or secondary explosives. Primary explosives are sensitive high explosives used to stimulate the

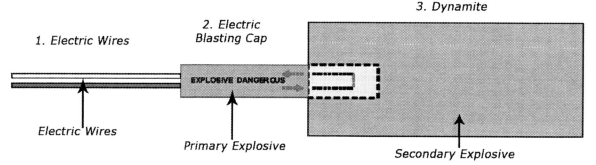

Diagram of an explosive train.

chemical reaction of a less-sensitive secondary explosive. These primary explosives are often referred to as blasting caps or detonators. When activated, the blasting cap or detonator starts the initial detonation process within the secondary high explosive. The initial reaction from the detonator/blasting cap sends a shock wave through the explosive material creating a violent chemical reaction. This violent chemical reaction is an almost instantaneous reaction followed by high temperature, violent shock waves and a loud noise. This process or reaction is often referred to as a detonation. The strength of a secondary high explosive is normally rated by its reaction speed. There is a direct relationship between the velocity of detonation (VOD) of an explosive and the amount of pressure it will produce. This is why there are so many variations of different high explosives. Each explosive is selected based on its performance and applied to a specific application.

Detonator/Blasting Cap: Commercial and military blasting caps are often encountered by civilians

and law enforcement personnel. These items may be found as a result of criminal activity, stolen from military installations or recovered from old, neglected storage sites. These primary explosives are extremely dangerous and should only be handled by trained personnel. There are several types of commercial and military blasting caps. Electric, non-electric and shock tube caps are the common types often recovered by law enforcement personnel.

Commercial High Explosives

Commercial high explosives are generally used in mining, construction and tunneling operations. In the 1990s, the commercial explosive industry in the United States used nearly five billion pounds of explosive material each year. There are numerous types and various manufacturers of commercial high explosives. While the commercial explosive industry has an excellent safety and accountability record, there are often times when explosives are discovered in a deteriorated state or fall into the wrong hands. With the threat of terrorism high on the national agenda, law enforcement officers need to be aware of the possibility of criminals or terrorists obtaining this material. This section will briefly cover some of the common commercial explosive materials often encountered by law enforcement officers.

Dynamite: Dynamite was discovered by Alfred Nobel over 130 years ago, and revolutionized the blasting industry by replacing black powder. Nitroglycerin, added to an absorbed material packaged in cylindrical cartridges, was the main energy producer. Today, dynamite is a generic term used to describe a variety of different types of cylindrical-shaped high explosives. They are manufactured in various sizes and chemical compositions.

Law enforcement personnel often come in contact with dynamites, either in a stolen or deteriorated state. In either state, this material needs to be handled with extreme caution. Only trained military EOD units or certified hazardous device technicians (bomb squads) should be used to handle this material.

Detonation Cord: Detonation cord is a high explosive used in commercial and military applications as a primer or connecting charge. Detonation cord is a round, flexible cord generally containing a center core of RDX, PETN, HMX and a sheath of various textiles, waterproofing materials or plastics. The function of the protective sheath is to prevent or minimize damage to the explosive core from abrasion or moisture. Various coloring and textile patterns are used to identify different strengths and types of detonation cord. Detonation cord has a general resemblance to safety fuse. Detonation cord is measured by the amount of explosive material per foot and is supplied in rolls or coils. Law enforcement often encounters this type of material.

Blasting Agents

The increase in blasting operations in the United States has lead to a demand for more cost-effective blasting materials. Ammonium nitrate and fuel oil (ANFO) and water-resistant explosives have been developed and are used extensively today in the commercial blasting industry. This material is often referred to as a blasting agent. A blasting agent is a material or mixture consisting of a fuel and oxidizer, which is intended for blasting operations. Technically, a blasting agent is not classified as an explosive as long as the package for the finished, shipped product cannot be detonated with a #8 blasting cap.

ANFO: ANFO was introduced into the commercial blasting industry in the early 1950s. Today, ANFO products account for nearly 80 percent of the domestic commercial explosive market. This material gained notoriety in the law enforcement community as a result of the 1995 bombing of the Alfred P. Murrah Federal Building in Oklahoma City. This material is a very powerful explosive, and is easy to manufacture. One of the main ingredients in ANFO is ammonium nitrate. Ammonium nitrate is an oxidizer used as a fertilizer in the agricultural industry. Once ammonium nitrate was found to be a useful ingredient for explosives, it revolutionized the explosive industry. Today, ammonium nitrate is a major ingredient in most commercial explosives.

Grenades

Federal, state and local law enforcement agencies throughout the United States routinely encounter various types of military hand grenades during the course of their duties. These grenades are often encountered as souvenirs in the possession of civilians or military veterans. Grenades are used by various criminal and terrorist groups operating in the United States. These items pose a high threat to law enforcement and emergency response personnel because of their ability to be used as a weapon.

US Mark-1 Fragmentation Hand Grenade: The MK-1 Fragmentation Hand Grenade was introduced in 1917 during WWI. Due to flaws in the fuse mechanism, the grenade was redesigned and put into production in 1918 as the MK-2. The explosive filler for the MK-1 was 4 oz. of TNT or Trojan Grenade Powder. This grenade is often recovered by both law enforcement and military EOD units.

US Mark-2 Fragmentation Hand Grenade: The MK-2 was designed as a replacement for the MK-1 during WWI. The original MK-2 initially used MK-1 bodies until they were redesigned. The MK-2 has endured several subtle evolutionary changes during its span of active duty. These consisted of slight changes in the body, fuse and explosive filler. The explosive filler may be TNT, Trojan Grenade Powder or EC Blankfire Powder.

US M-30 Practice Hand Grenade: The M-30 Practice Hand Grenade was used as a training grenade for the M-26 series fragmentation hand grenade. The grenade is a cast iron, lemon-shaped body that contains a M205A1 pyrotechnic delay practice cap, along with a small black powder charge. The pyrotechnic delay cap has a 4- to 5-second delay. The additional black powder charge is used to enhance the audible and visual effects of the grenade during training exercises. This grenade is classified as an obsolete training grenade by the United States military. Although considered obsolete by the U.S. military, there are still hundreds of these items in circulation throughout the civilian population. Law enforcement and emergency response personnel should use caution when encountering any type of military ordnance. These types of grenades are often activated as improvised explosive devices by adding a low explosive powder.

US Military M-69 Practice Hand Grenade: The M-69 Practice Hand Grenade simulates the M-67 series of fragmentation hand grenade. The grenade provides realistic training and familiarizes the soldier with the functioning and characteristics of the fragmentation hand grenade. Many of these items contain live explosive material. This particular grenade may contain a practice cap containing black powder. This grenade is often converted into an IED by sealing the bottom and filling it with a low explosive material.

Improvised Explosive Devices

Pipe Bombs: One of the most common improvised explosive devices found in the United States today is the pipe bomb. Pipe bombs can be manufactured in various shapes and sizes. The destructive capability will usually depend on the type of pipe, amount and type of explosive material and the method of ignition. Pipe bombs can range from simple to very sophisticated. The easy access to various types of explosives and common pipe material make the pipe bomb very appealing to juveniles, criminals and domestic and international terrorist groups. Law enforcement and emergency response personnel need to be aware of the dangers associated with these items. They are extremely dangerous and should only be handled by trained military or law enforcement bomb technicians.

CO_2 cartridge pipe bombs are small, depressurized cylinders that are filled with an explosive material (low explosive), along with a piece of hobby fuse. Nails or nuts and bolts are often added to the outside of the cartridge, which will increase the destructive capability. Matches are often wrapped around the fuse and secured in place to increase the speed of ignition. This particular device is similar to the devices used at Columbine High School. The device could be used as an improvised hand grenade, and deployed against patrol and SWAT teams engaging active shooters.

Steel pipe is the most popular material used to construct pipe bombs, because it offers a high degree of confinement, which increases the explosive reaction. Pipe bombs can be initiated by a non-electric fusing system (burning fuse) or an electrical fuse system (improvised or commercially manufactured) that can be time delayed. Added shrapnel can be attached to the inside or outside of the pipe to increase the destructive and lethal capabilities. Pipe bombs can easily be designed as a booby-trap device by simply incorporating a mechanical or timed initiating system. The initiating system can range from simple to very sophisticated electrically timed mechanisms. Emergency personnel should use extreme caution when dealing with a suspected booby-trap device.

Grenade bodies account for a large number of IEDs recovered in the United States. Many grenade bodies can be purchased as souvenirs at military surplus stores and gun shows. They react similar to the way the pipe bomb reacts when an explosive material is used. There are numerous types of inert

Steel pipe bombs using a burning fuse and another using an electric igniter with a clothes pin switch as a booby trap.

Grenade body used as an improvised explosive device.

grenade bodies and fuse assemblies recovered on a routine basis by civilian and military bomb disposal units. These items are easily converted to live grenades by filling and sealing them with an explosive material. The explosive material can range from black powder to smokeless or photo flash powder.

There are numerous publications and computer Web sites available today that describe in detail how to manufacture explosive material and improvised explosive devices. Some of this material is from declassified military manuals, which are often found by law enforcement when encountering subjects who manufacture and deploy improvised explosive devices. This material has become more prevalent with juveniles, criminals and domestic and international terrorist groups. Many international terrorist groups are currently using these manuals to manufacture materials to be used as terrorist weapons. Many of the formulas and recipes outlined in these manuals are very dangerous, and the results are often tragic.

The use of IEDs is increasing worldwide at an alarming rate. The level of sophistication in both the explosive material and firing systems continues to evolve throughout the world. The TTPs (tactics, techniques and procedures) terrorists use are constantly improving and changing in order to elude and defeat security measures. As the war on terrorism continues and the threats to the United States increase, the role of law enforcement and emergency response units will increase in order to comply with the President's Strategy for Homeland Security. Many of the methods terrorists use to prepare and execute their acts of terrorism are the same methods used by criminals in the United States and around the world.

Vehicle-Borne Improvised Explosive Device (VBIED): The VBIED is currently the most destructive weapon in the terrorist arsenal. The vehicle offers an ideal method and means to conceal and transport large amounts of explosive material to the intended target without generating much attention. This terrorist tactic of using explosive-filled vehicles as a weapon continues to plague countries throughout the world, with devastating and demoralizing effects.

The VBIED presents a serious threat to the United States, especially in heavily populated metropolitan areas, and should be a major concern for law enforcement and emergency management agencies. The VBIED should be considered a true weapon of mass destruction and a serious threat to the national security of the United States. U.S. troops in both Iraq and Afghanistan face this threat on a daily basis. In the United States, we have seen the devastating effects of two large-scale vehicle-borne improvised explosive devices, one at the World Trade Center in New York and the other at the Alfred P. Murrah Federal Building in Oklahoma. We will most likely encounter more as the war on terrorism continues. The Federal Bureau of Investigation, Department of Homeland Security and Central Intelligence Agency continue to release advisories, bulletins and threat assessment warnings of the terrorist deployment of the VBIED within the United States.

State and local government officials, as well as department administrators, must understand that the VBIED is the current weapon of mass destruction, and can cause massive casualties and major property damage with long-term economic losses. Due to their destructive capabilities, it is vital that emergency operational plans consider all areas of emergency management planning to facilitate rapid improvised explosive device disposal and render-safe procedures.

Educating the private and public sectors of the consequences of a VBIED, along with specific contingency planning, especially in metropolitan areas, will help stress the need for cooperation between the two sectors. Both private and public sectors should consider developing and coordinating their individual terrorist operational plans together in an effort to reduce confusion and unnecessary duplication during a critical, time-sensitive incident. Pre-planning and active communications between the two sectors should be a priority for government emergency planners when preparing to deal with any potential terrorist acts in order to minimize or eliminate the loss of lives and property damage.

The Suicide/Homicide Bomber

The types of devices used by the various Palestinian and Al-Qaeda terrorist groups are mostly improvised devices. The explosive devices may be delivered by vehicle, hand-carried bag, backpack and body belt, or built into the clothing. The explosive material can vary from commercial and military to improvised explosives. Improvised explosives seem to be the most popular, because of the ease in obtaining the precursors and manufacturing the material. The Israelis have been very aggressive in controlling the amount of weapons and precursor chemicals flowing into the occupied areas. This has slowed down some of the material used in the manufacturing process, but has not stopped the terrorists from extracting precursors from common items. Even before the crackdown, the improvised explosive mixtures seemed to be the most widely used, and are constantly being recovered in the Palestinian terrorist bomb factories. Examples of some of the improvised explosive mixtures most widely used by terrorist groups are:

- **Triacetone Triperoxide (TATP)** is manufactured from hydrogen peroxide, acetone and citric or sulfuric acid. This mixture is the most widely used and the most sensitive. This was the material used by Richard Reid in his attempt to blow up American Airlines Flight 63 on December 23, 2001. We are seeing an increase in the terrorist use of this material in the United States and overseas. The Israelis are being plagued with this material and finding it in mostly all the Palestinian bomb factories.

- **Hexamethylene Triperoxide Diamine (HMTD)** is manufactured from hexamine, citric acid and hydrogen peroxide. This material is very similar to TATP and just as sensitive. This is the material that was discovered along with other explosive material in December 1999, when an Algerian national and an Al-Qaeda operative (Ahmed Ressam) were arrested at the U.S./Canadian border. It was also used by terrorists on July 7, 2005, to attack London's transport system. These attacks resulted in the deaths of 56 people (including the terrorists) and the wounding of 700 others.

Firing systems used by these groups are normally an electrical system that is controlled by the suicide/homicide bomber. There have been unconfirmed reports that cellular phones have been used to fire the explosive devices. However, we do know that cell phones are used in devices that are placed. ***Palestinian Suicide/Homicide Bomber Organization Operations:*** Suicide/homicide bombing operations are well organized, and can involve up to four separate groups to carry out a successful attack.

First Group
- Recruits and trains potential suicide/homicide bombers.
- Determines the motivations of the potential martyr and if they have the mental capability to complete the mission.

Second Group
- Determines the target and the IED to be used.
- Target planning, surveillance and recon.

Third Group
- Manufactures the IED.

Fourth Group
- Delivers bomb to the suicide/homicide bomber.
- Provides last-minute instructions on the operational use of the device.
- Escorts the bomber to the target.

In order to maintain a high motivational level, the bomber is not made aware of the mission until the last possible moment. If a cellular phone is used as the initiation system, a bomber escort could have control of firing the explosive device, or it could be a secondary firing system if the suicide/homicide bomber fails to function the device.

The use of a cellular phone as an initiation system for an improvised explosive device is increasing among Middle Eastern terrorist groups. For the most part, the firing system on a suicide/homicide

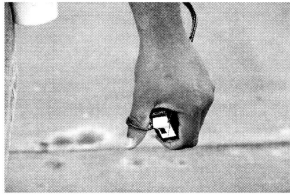

An example of a suicide/homicide bomber belt with a rocker firing switch used as a law enforcement training tool.

bomber is a simple electrical firing switch, usually a rocker- or toggle-style switch that is controlled by the bomber. The bomb builder usually installs a safety mechanism into the switch to prevent it from firing prematurely.

CONCLUSION

There should be no doubt the United States is facing a serious, long-term battle against terrorism. The emerging threat from international and transnational terrorists, gangs and organized criminal elements also threaten the security of our country. Radical terrorist and criminal groups are not only operating in other parts of the world, but some have been, and still are, operating within the borders of the United States. While the projected threat of terrorists using some type of chemical, biological or even nuclear material is also a concern, the fact is the use of firearms and explosives at the present time are the main operational tools of terrorism. Acts of terrorism have dramatically increased in many places around the world, especially in the Middle East, Southeast Asia and parts of Europe. The recent train bombings in Madrid, Spain, London, England and the terrorist activities in Iraq and Afghanistan confirm that we continue to face a dangerous worldwide situation. These and other acts of terrorism occurring around the world should be an indication of things to come, and how easy these acts can be committed in an open society. State and local agencies must have accurate threat analyses and risk assessments in order to make the most out of limited resources during this continuing high-threat environment.

While the national focus is on trying to integrate separate large federal bureaucracies under one department, state and local first responders will be tasked with assuming more responsibility. When examining the role of the first responder, a priority needs to be placed on key elements that can effectively operate within the spectrum of counter-terrorism operations. Along with complacency, time is one of the greatest enemies when dealing with terrorism. Time will play a critical role in determining key elements within the first responder's group, along with funding priorities. Clearly, the responsibility for preventing or mitigating a terrorist act falls squarely on the shoulders of the first responders.

Part 3

PATROL PROCEDURES

BRAD SMITH

Brad Smith began his law enforcement career in 1981. He is currently a canine handler and trainer for the West Covina Police Department in Southern California. Officer Smith is the Canine Chairperson for the NTOA and a subject-matter expert for the California Association of Tactical Officers. He has been a canine handler since 1986, and a SWAT dog handler since 1989.

Officer Smith has instructed thousands of canine handlers and SWAT team members during the numerous courses he has given on K-9 SWAT deployment throughout the United States, Canada, and Brazil.

Besides being a contributing editor for *Police K-9 Magazine,* Officer Smith has published articles for a variety of publications, including *The Tactical Edge, Law & Order,* and *Police Magazine.* He is a graduate of the Los Angeles County Sheriff's Department's SWAT school, as well as the California P.O.S.T. Master Instructor Development Program. Officer Smith is qualified to evaluate and certify any police dog in the states of California and Utah. Officer Smith designed and implemented the first and only P.O.S.T.-certified K-9 SWAT school in the states of California and Arizona. The acronym for this school is S.K.I.D.D.S., which stands for SWAT & K-9s Interacting During Deployment School.

Officer Smith has competed internationally in Germany, as well as regionally in numerous police canine competitions. He has won six Grand Championships, five Reserve Grand Championships, six Top Agency Awards, and over 60 other K-9 awards. Officer Smith has also been a judge in over 25 police K-9 competitions and a guest speaker at numerous K-9 and SWAT seminars in the United States, Canada, and Brazil. He may be contacted at www.skidds.com.

Chapter 9

CANINES AND PATROL OPERATIONS

Brad Smith

INTRODUCTION

Depending on when you were born, you first became aware of how devoted, trustworthy and dependable dogs could be when you saw movies like, *Lassie, Rin Tin Tin, My Dog Skip,* and my favorite, *Turner and Hooch.* Over the past several decades, police dogs have proven to be a valuable law enforcement tool. Unfortunately, many patrol personnel are not aware of a canine's capabilities in certain situations, and even worse, have received very little, if any, training with police dogs. Police dogs have proven their ability to quickly find hidden suspects, while providing greater officer safety. However, officers must remember that dogs are just another law enforcement tool. Police dogs are not perfect. They do make mistakes, and more than we like to admit, handlers can misread their dog and what the dog is trying to tell them.

According to the National Law Enforcement Officers Memorial Web site (www.nleomf.com), between 1997 and 2001, an average of 155 police officers were killed each year, nationwide, in the line of duty. This does not include the 71 police officers killed at the World Trade Center on September 11, 2001. I strongly believe this number would be greater if it were not for police dogs. On average, approximately 5 to 10 police dogs die each year, and an unknown number are injured while attempting to save the lives of police officers. This chapter will include a brief history of canine usage, basic

facts about dogs, legal decisions affecting deployment of a dog, canine deployment and other areas I consider important for patrol officers to understand.

As canine handlers, we sometimes take for granted that patrol officers know how to work and act around police dogs. Deployment methods vary from department to department, and sometimes from state to state. I hope the information contained in this chapter will help prepare you for a canine deployment in a patrol environment. After reading this chapter, I strongly recommend you talk to your handlers and discuss deployment and searching methods.

Michigan State University Canine Search Study

Most police officers would not question that the speed and reliability of a canine search is superior to one conducted by patrol officers alone. However, this belief was confirmed by a Michigan State University study conducted several years ago. This study compared police search teams, with and without dogs, and the results were impressive.

Research Method

1. Search scenarios were set up in four different

121

types of buildings, with suspects hidden inside.
2. There were five searches conducted in each of the four buildings.
3. There were 29 suspects hidden. Some of the searches involved more than one suspect.
4. Both the canine search teams and the non-canine teams consisted of 2 to 4 officers, depending on the building size.

Buildings Used

1. Uniform Store	5,445 square feet
2. Multi-Purpose Church	11,000 square feet
3. Water and Light Department	40,500 square feet
4. Warehouse	138,995 square feet

Results of Study

Search Percentages

	Officers Only	*Officers with Canines*
1. Uniform Store	83%	100%
2. Multi-Purpose Church	100%	100%
3. Water and Light Department	45%	82%
4. Warehouse	28%	100%

Average Searching Times

	Officers Only	*Officers with Canines*
1. Uniform Store	20 minutes 25 seconds	1 minute 24 seconds
2. Multi-Purpose Church	18 minutes 9 seconds	4 minutes 20 seconds
3. Water and Light Department	60 minutes 30 seconds	14 minutes 15 seconds
4. Warehouse	148 minutes 15 seconds	15 minutes 51 seconds

Officers searching without a canine found 17 of 29 suspects (a 59 percent success rate).

Officers searching with a canine found 27 of the 29 suspects (a 93 percent success rate).

Canine History

War Dogs

Dogs have been serving humans since they were tamed during prehistoric times. Relying on their prey drive, dogs were used to help hunt for food and stand guard over the camp at night (defense drive). Archeologists have found ancient Egyptian wall paintings in the pyramids that date back to 4000 B.C., showing Egyptian warriors holding leashed savage dogs, and temples in Iraq contain paintings which show huge Mastiff battle dogs wearing spiked collars. Attila the Hun used large dogs to stand guard at night so the enemy could not sneak into camp while they slept. Even the Romans used giant Mastiffs and Colossian hounds to create fear among their enemies.

During World War I, the military began using dogs to carry messages and first aid supplies to the troops at the front. World War II saw the first mass recruitment of dogs through the "Dogs for Defense" program. Donated dogs were trained for sentry, scout, messenger and mine-detection duty. After the end of World War II, the Marines built a war dog cemetery on Guam in appreciation of the role dogs had played in helping win the war. They named the cemetery, which still stands today, "The Devil Dog Cemetery." Following World War II, war dogs were returned to the United States. They were de-trained, and then returned to their civilian masters or ex-military handlers to live out the rest of their lives in peace.

During the Vietnam War, dogs again played a significant role in U.S. military operations. Once again, the military asked the civilian population to donate dogs. The "Dog Reception Center" was set up at Lackland Air Force Base in Texas, where dogs were examined and assigned to their training specialties and branches of service. While the Air Force trained their dogs at Lackland, the Army and Marine Corps trained their dogs and handlers at the

Army's 26th Infantry Scout Dog Platoon at Fort Benning, Georgia. The war dogs of Vietnam did not go home after their handlers completed their one-year tour of duty. They served in Vietnam for life, and were reassigned to new handlers as the old handlers returned home. Unbeknownst to the civilians who donated their dogs, this would be a death sentence for nearly all the dogs, even the ones who survived the war. In World War I, World War II and Korea, war dogs were treated the same as soldiers and sent home when the war was over. In the years after Korea, the war dogs were reclassified as "equipment," and were not returned to the United States, but instead turned over to the South Vietnamese Army or "abandoned in place."

There are a few documented cases of some dogs serving almost five years/tours in Vietnam. Two Army Scout Dogs, Ramo and Budda, with the 38th and 39th Scout Dog Platoons, respectively, served from 1966 through 1971. Their fates were markedly different. Ramo was returned to the United States in June of 1971, after the 38th "stood down." Budda was not as lucky. When the 39th "stood down" in late 1971, rather than turning the dog over to the South Vietnamese Army, Budda was "put to sleep." When some members of Congress heard about the dog's death sentence, they lobbied for bringing back the dogs to the United States. The military made a "token" effort by returning approximately two hundred dogs to the States. But when the commotion died down, so did any attempt to bring back any more of the dogs. It is estimated that of the 4,000 dogs that served in Vietnam, less than 200 returned to the United States, and nearly 500 were officially listed as "Killed in Action." It has been estimated that if it were not for the war dogs of Vietnam, there would be an additional 10,000 names on "The Wall" in Washington, D.C.

In October 2000, a bill was passed by the United States Congress and signed by the President requiring the military to de-train and put up for adoption military working dogs no longer needed for military duty. At this point, only experienced military or ex-military handlers can adopt one of the dogs. On February 21, 2000, a War Dogs Memorial was opened at March Air Force Base in Riverside, California. A second War Dogs Memorial was opened on October 8, 2000, at Fort Benning,

Georgia. For more information about war dogs, visit their Web site at www.war-dogs.com.

Canine Facts

In order to understand how a dog functions, it is necessary to discuss a few basic facts about canines. One must keep in mind that dogs do not think or reason like humans. No matter how much you train a dog, they cannot comprehend that a person in uniform is a "good guy," and the person in civilian clothes is the "bad guy." Whomever the dog has locked onto, or as handlers say, has "Suspect ID," that is the person the dog will go after. Now in some cases, given enough time and distance, the dog can be called off a person and redirected onto the correct suspect.

Why are dogs quicker to respond to certain situations than humans? The reason is dogs do not think or reason like we do. Dogs react out of instinct or as a result of their training. It takes approximately 1/40th of a second for a dog to see something, process it through his tiny brain and then react to it. If a dog has never been exposed to or trained how to react to a certain situation, it will react out of instinct. Unfortunately, that response may not be the reaction we are looking for. This is why it is so important that dogs be exposed to as many situations as possible in training.

Three Basic Drives of a Dog

A dog has three basic drives: play drive, defense drive and prey drive. Play drive is needed for narcotics and bomb detection dogs. Some people refer to this drive as the fetch or retrieve drive. Play drive is not needed in a patrol dog unless it is to be cross-trained for narcotics or bomb detection. The play drive is easily recognized by the eagerness of the dog to always want to play and go after objects.

The defense drive is present in every dog. Defense drive is also known as fight or flight. When there is a lot of pressure put on the dog, does the dog stay and fight, or does the dog flee? Obviously, in police work we want the dog that stays and fights, no matter how fierce the situation. Defense drive is recognized by many different expressions in the dog's body language. When defense drive kicks in, the dog can show one or many signs of defense aggression. Some of the signs a dog may show are: (1) the hair is raised on the back of the neck all the way down to the tail, (2) the dog growls and shows his teeth, (3) if the dog is barking, it is a very deep bark, (4) the dog's tail could be standing out very rigid, or in some dogs, tucked between their legs, and (5) they may turn and run away.

Prey drive is something that must be present in every patrol dog. Some trainers refer to prey drive as hunting drive. Prey drive is the willingness to go out and hunt/search for suspects. A good patrol dog should have a proper balance of prey and defense drive. Ideally, this balance should be approximately 80 percent prey and 20 percent defense. A dog with the right prey drive is easy to spot because he is all business. The dog is still searching for the suspect, even after a long, intense search. A dog that does not have enough prey drive will slow down after only a few minutes, and appear slow and lethargic, as if just going through the motions.

Three Senses of a Dog

How do dogs function in their surroundings? What makes the dog so special? How can we use a dog to make our jobs safer? These are all important questions. Properly trained police dogs function in an environment through their senses. These senses are smell, eyesight and hearing. There are many different opinions concerning the strength of a dog's sense of smell. They vary between one hundred to one million times stronger than that of a human. In certain situations, a dog can alert on a hidden suspect, before he is deployed, from over 100 feet away, and pinpoint the suspect's exact location in a matter of seconds. This is possible because of a dog's superior olfactory system and what is called the "scent cone." The scent of a suspect is blown downwind in a cone pattern. The dog instinctively follows the scent to the suspect. Dogs learn that if the scent gets weaker, they are going the wrong way, and if it gets stronger, they are getting closer to the suspect.

When a suspect is hiding in a building, the scent does different things, depending on the weather. If the room is hot, the scent will travel up toward the ceiling. The scent can even travel to the other side

of the room and settle in a corner. If a dog alerts in the corner, where the scent has dropped, the dog is correct. It will be up to you to figure out how the scent is traveling. Dogs may show their alert by barking at, or trying to jump up, the wall. When you put dry ice in water, vapors spill out over the top of the container and fall to the ground. Once on the ground, the vapors travel whichever way the wind is blowing. The same thing applies to human scent in a cool room. The scent will travel down to the ground and move with the currents. If the scent travels across the floor and over to the other side of the room, the dog should be able to follow the scent back to the suspect. Some believe the reason dogs are able to locate suspects is because they smell their "fear scent." However, this is easily disproved. When we hide from a dog in a training exercise, we are not afraid, but the dog still finds us. That is why I like to say the dog is trained to locate *human* scent.

The dog's sense of hearing is also very acute. I know from personal experience that, at certain times during a search, my dog will stop and listen. His head cants from side to side, and his ears start to rotate like radar. When my dog starts searching again, he usually goes to the area where the suspect is hiding.

Dogs do not see like humans. They have a depth-perception problem. However, dogs do pick up movement very easily. It is possible for an officer to see a suspect who is partially hidden from view, but if the scent cone is not blowing in the direction of the dog, the dog might not see the suspect at all. But once the suspect moves, or the dog gets into the scent cone, the police dog should have almost immediate "Suspect ID."

Case Law Related to the Use of Canines

For many years, attorneys have argued that the use of police service dogs constitutes deadly force. It is important to note that deadly force is defined as "that force which creates a substantial risk of causing death or serious bodily harm." In all the years that police service dogs have been used, there has been only one reported death resulting from the use of a police service dog. In that particular case, *Robinette v. Barnes,* 854 F.2d 909 (6th Cir. 1988), a police service dog was properly deployed into an auto dealership to search for a burglary suspect. When the dog found the suspect, the dog did what it was trained to do, bite the first thing with which it came into contact. In this case, the suspect was hidden under a car, and the dog bit the suspect in the neck. The suspect died before he got to the hospital.

In reviewing the *Robinette* case, the United States Court of Appeals for the 6th Circuit relied upon the United States Supreme Court case, *Tennessee v. Garner,* 471 U.S. 1, 85L Ed 2d 1, 105 S Ct. 1694 (1985) to assist them. The court held that two factors are relevant to determine whether the use of a specific law enforcement tool constitutes deadly force. These two factors are:

1. The intent of the officer.
2. The probability known to the officer that the tool being used creates a substantial risk of causing death or serious bodily harm.

Even though deadly force resulted from the use of the police dog in the *Robinette* case, the United States Court of Appeals concluded the use of a properly trained police dog to apprehend a felony suspect does not carry with it a substantial risk of causing death or serious bodily harm. They continued by saying that when a properly trained police dog is used in an appropriate manner to apprehend a felony suspect, the use of the dog does not constitute deadly force. The United States Court of Appeals went as far as to say, "the use of a police dog can make it more likely that the officer can apprehend the suspect without the risk of using his firearm, thus, frequently enhancing the safety of officers, bystanders and the suspect."

There are two other cases that support the use of a police dog, *Matthew v. Jones,* 1994 Fed. App. 327 (6th Cir. 1994), and *Fikes v. Cleghorn,* 47 F.3d 1011 (9th Cir. 1995). They state, ". . . police service dogs are not deadly force and police service dogs can often help prevent officers from having to resort to, or be subjected to, deadly force. . . ." In *Quintanilla v. Downey,* 84 F.3d 353 (9th Cir. 1996), the court looked at the evidence presented at trial and, referring to *Tennessee v. Garner,* and *Fikes v. Cleghorn,* the court ruled the use of a police dog during the arrest

of a felony suspect did not create substantial risk of causing death or serious bodily harm (the definition of deadly force).

Canine Deployment

As we all know, the person who really controls whether a canine is deployed is the suspect. Suspects are given every opportunity to surrender, but if they refuse to do so, it may be necessary to deploy a canine to assist in apprehending them. Policies for deployment of canines may vary by department. If you are unsure of your department's policy, talk to your handler or review the department's procedural manual. Even though a canine handler or field supervisor will have the final say if a police dog is deployed, it is a good idea for every patrol officer to know what justification is necessary for deployment. This will assist you in deciding whether to request a canine. It will also help you to inform the supervisor at the scene, who might not be up to date on canine deployments. Some departments only deploy their dogs on suspects who have allegedly committed dangerous and violent felony crimes. Other departments deploy on felony and certain misdemeanor crimes. Whatever your department's policy is, make sure you are familiar with it and follow its requirements.

Canine deployment is governed by *Graham v. Connor,* 490 U.S. 386 (1989). Although this case does not specifically relate to canines, its findings are used to determine what must be considered prior to deployment of a canine. Consideration must be given to the "totality of circumstances," and the information that is available at the time of the incident. The handler should also use a three-prong test to justify a canine deployment. As long as the handler can meet this test and is within department policy, a dog can be deployed. The three-prong test consists of the following:

1. The severity of the crime.
2. Whether the suspect poses an immediate threat to the safety of law enforcement officers or others.
3. Whether the suspect is actively resisting arrest or attempting to evade arrest by flight.

Felony vs. Misdemeanor Deployment

There continues to be a debate over whether to deploy police service dogs after a misdemeanor suspect. As already mentioned, some departments have a very restrictive canine policy, while others are more liberal. Two hypothetical situations illustrate both sides of the argument.

1. You make a traffic stop for a vehicle code violation. The driver pulls over, but immediately jumps out of his car and jumps over a fence.
2. You are involved in a short, slow-speed vehicle pursuit for a minor traffic violation. The driver either crashes, or pulls over and runs from the car. You are not fast enough, and the driver climbs over a fence. Can you deploy your dog on one or both of these scenarios? Some say "yes," some "no." The "no" side says maybe all you have is a driver who has no license or insurance. The "yes" side says maybe you have a driver who broke into a house down the street and killed a family inside. However, as yet, no one has reported the crime.

There are several case decisions that support using a police dog on a misdemeanant, as long as the suspect poses a threat to the officer or residents, and is actively resisting or evading arrest by fighting or hiding from the officers. One of these cases, referred to previously, is *Matthew v. Jones,* 1994 Fed. App. 327 (6th Cir. 1994). Matthew was wanted for speeding, reckless driving and fleeing from officers in a vehicle pursuit. The court looked at *Tennessee v. Garner, Robinette v. Barnes,* and *Graham v. Connor* to address the issue of felony versus misdemeanor crimes. The court concluded that a reasonable officer, under these circumstances, would have believed Matthew posed a threat to the officers' safety, as well as the safety of others. The court also basically stated that police dogs can often help prevent officers from using deadly force.

A second case, also mentioned previously, that supports police dogs being used on a misdemeanant is *Fikes v. Cleghorn,* 47 F.3d 1011 (9th Cir. 1995). Fikes was arrested and pled guilty to driving while under the influence, driving without a license and

resisting arrest. The court looked at *Graham v. Connor* and concluded the police officer used reasonable force in effecting the arrest of Fikes with the assistance of his police dog. The court also ruled the use of a police dog during the arrest of a misdemeanant did not create substantial risk of causing death or serious bodily harm.

A later case is *Vera Cruz v. City of Escondido,* 126 F.3d 1214 (9th Cir. 1997). Vera Cruz had vandalized a person's property, was intoxicated in public and challenged people to fight. The court looked at *Graham v. Connor* and determined the use of a police dog on a misdemeanant was reasonable. The court also looked at *Tennessee v. Garner* to determine if police dogs constituted deadly force. The court concluded that police dogs are not deadly force. They also added that criminals can largely control the circumstances of their crimes, and thus minimize the force that will be needed to arrest them. Other cases that support using police service dogs on misdemeanants are *Gill v. Thomas,* 83 F.3d 537 (1st Cir. 1996), and *Shannon v. Costa Mesa,* 46 F.3d 1145 (9th Cir. 1995).

However, there are two cases which do not support using a police dog on a misdemeanant who poses no threat to the officers. These cases are *Marley v. City of Allentown,* 961 F.2d 1567 (3rd Cir. 1992), and *Kerr v. City of West Palm Beach,* 875 F.2d 1546 (11th Cir. 1989).

Planning a Deployment

Planning, communication and execution are key elements to any successful patrol operation. When it is time to formulate a search plan, the canine handler should be in charge of doing so and have the final say on how the dog will be used. One of the keys is to make sure everyone involved knows their assignment. There are numerous situations that can develop on any deployment, and they need to be discussed prior to the dog being deployed. For example, before every deployment, I gather my search team together and discuss several different aspects of the search, including:

1. How many dogs will be needed for this search?
2. How will we make our approach to the loca-

tion or search area?

3. Will my dog walk point, or stay in the back of the stack?
4. Where will I give my canine announcement?
5. How are we going to search with the dog?
6. Will my dog be searching on or off leash?
7. Will I let my dog go deep, or search close?
8. What areas of responsibility will my team cover and who will cover me?
9. What will we do if the dog finds someone, but is not biting the suspect?
10. How will we approach the suspect?
11. How will we take the suspect into custody?
12. Who will give orders to the suspect?
13. Who will handcuff the suspect, and who will take the suspect out of the search area?

Announcements

Prior to deployment of a police dog, some type of canine announcement is almost always given. Whether an announcement is given will depend on your department policy and the situation at hand. Canine announcements serve two purposes: (1) they give the suspect a chance to give up peacefully, and (2) the dog knows it is time to go to work (hearing the canine announcement activates the dog's prey drive). When an announcement is given, there are many ways to independently establish it was made. It is critical that announcements be given loudly, so neighbors can hear them. Neighbors are potential witnesses, and can testify that the suspect was ordered to surrender or a dog would be used. Canine announcements can be made over the public address systems of police vehicles or helicopters. Some departments prerecord announcements and play them periodically or continuously. It is also possible for officers to "key" the mike on their radio as the canine announcement is given. By doing so, the announcement is recorded on dispatch tapes. Other officers carry a small microcassette tape recorder with them and record the announcement. If a microcassette tape is used, the date, time and location should be recorded on the tape prior to the announcement. It may also be helpful to have back-up officers identify themselves on the tape. Several announcements should be made without the dog being present. This accomplishes two things: (1) the

dog's barking doesn't "cover" the announcement and provide an opportunity for suspects to claim they didn't understand it, and (2) suspects have additional time to surrender, because the handler has to go to the canine vehicle, get the dog and return prior to deployment.

Vehicle Pursuits

During vehicle pursuits, an officer's senses can be overwhelmed. However, if the pursuit continues for some time, they tend to calm down, and are better able to think. Also, if a pursuit continues, a canine unit may join the pursuit. If possible, the canine unit should take the lead in the pursuit in case the occupants of the car run when the pursuit ends. If the canine unit is not in the lead when the pursuit ends and the suspect flees, most patrol officers, especially younger officers, will go in foot pursuit of the suspect. Depending on the situation and surroundings, this could be a great opportunity for a dog to be sent after the suspect. Unfortunately, if officers are between the dog and the suspect, the handler must hold the dog.

During a foot pursuit, if you happen to hear the handler giving a canine announcement, something like "stop or I'll send the dog," this would be a great time to immediately come to a stop, because the handler is about to release his dog. Yes, I know the suspect will most likely continue running, but the handler should not send the dog if you are still chasing the suspect. Even if you do stop, the handler should not send the dog after the fleeing suspect until the dog has "Suspect ID." If you recall, the dog's eyesight picks up movement extremely well. That's why, after you stop running and the suspect continues running, the dog should lock onto the movement of the fleeing suspect. The dog can now be released, running by the stopped officer and directly to the suspect.

Clearing Felony Vehicle Stops

Vehicle pursuits often end with the suspect running away and officers going in foot pursuit. Although each situation is different, for reasons of officer safety, consideration should be given to not chasing the suspect and letting outer perimeter units

After ordering everyone out of the vehicle, send the police dog up to clear it before you make your approach.

set up containment, so the odds are in your favor when you find and confront the suspect. Otherwise, the fleeing suspect could be armed, or, as you run past the vehicle, there might be more people hiding inside. Depending on how many people appear to be in the pursued vehicle, I would suggest the closest units respond to assist the handling officer at the end of a pursuit. After several units have arrived, the next units that arrive should set up containment in the area the suspect was last seen running. Don't be afraid to set up a large outer perimeter. You can always scale it down, but it accomplishes little to expand the perimeter thirty minutes later. Once there are enough units at the end of a pursuit, the dog can be used to clear the vehicle before officers approach. Hopefully, a door or window has been left open to the suspect's vehicle. This will allow easy access for the canine to jump inside and clear it of any suspects.

If all the doors and windows are closed to the vehicle, the dog can be used to search the outside of the vehicle. The dog will let you know if someone is hiding inside. If the dog alerts on the vehicle, there are several approaches that can be taken.

1. Handle the situation as a barricaded suspect, and request a SWAT team if it meets their criteria.
2. Use other means of getting the doors or windows open. Once a window is broken or opened, it might allow the dog entry into the vehicle so it can be safely cleared before officers approach it.
3. Leave the dog at the suspect's vehicle while you tactically approach. This will keep the suspect occupied and provide early warning should the suspect come out while you are approaching. Once close enough to the vehicle, break a window or open a door and let the dog enter to clear the vehicle.

If the doors are closed but a window is open, the dog can jump into the vehicle through an open window.

If a suspect in the vehicle refuses to come out, the dog is also an excellent motivation for them to exit. Since the dog is used to the handler's voice, the handler should be the one giving orders to the suspect. Also, some dogs will be more interested in the yelling of police officers than a passive suspect in the vehicle.

There are times when a suspect will get out of the vehicle, but not comply with orders. So officers do not have to approach the vehicle, where a second suspect may be hiding, the dog can be used to run up and safely bring the suspect back. This way the suspect is preoccupied with the dog, and officers are less likely to get injured during the arrest. There are also occasions when a suspect will exit the vehicle and be extremely hostile and violent. In this event, there are two different less-lethal options that can be used at the same time. Depending on the situation, one officer can engage the suspect with a beanbag, while the handler releases the dog after the suspect.

In both cases, it is recommended that the suspect be ordered back to the safe area of the patrol units.

Perimeters

Now that the vehicle has been cleared by the dog and everyone is safely in custody at the vehicle crime scene, attention can be directed to the second crime scene, the perimeter, where the other suspect was last seen running. In most departments, if you are the first person to arrive at the area where a suspect was last seen running, you are responsible for setting up the perimeter until you are relieved by a supervisor or a senior, ranking officer. Do not be afraid to tell people what position to take. They are looking to you for direction and guidance.

The same thing applies to a crime in progress. The first unit should go to the victim's location, so the officer can obtain and transmit as much suspect information as possible. The second patrol unit should immediately start setting up a perimeter based on the information given by the first patrol officer at the victim's location. Canine units should also assume a position on the perimeter until more units arrive. Once enough units are at the location and a good perimeter is set up, the canine unit can be relieved. When a handler and supervisor arrive at the perimeter, they will set up a command post in the area. The handler will normally develop a search plan, determine if the crime warrants a canine search and if more dogs are needed. If more dogs are needed, it is preferred to request them from your own department, because your personnel are used to their own dogs and how they search. If you call in another agency's dog, you may not always get the same caliber dog.

The handler will normally pick the officers with whom they want to search. They will look for ex-handlers and officers who have searched with the dogs before, and are comfortable with them. It is common for someone who has limited experience around police dogs, or is nervous around dogs, to watch the dog search instead of watching and covering their areas of responsibility. This could get someone hurt or killed. For this reason, I recommend patrol officers attend and participate in canine training with their handlers, so they will get used to, and understand, how the dog works. It will also show the handler you have an interest in the dogs. As a result, the handler will be more likely to pick you to help conduct the next search.

Approach and Entry

The approach to the location of building and area searches is sometimes overlooked. Because of the dog's superior olfactory system, the handler can use the dog to "walk point," and clear the danger area in front of the search team as they approach the point of entry. If the dog locates a person hiding, it will alert the search team prior to their arrival. It is also important for the search team to realize there may be times when some handlers may not have their sidearm out as they deploy the canine. This is sometimes the case because they may have too much equipment and not enough hands, i.e., long lines and flashlights. For this reason, the search team should assign a person to the canine handler

The dog should be deployed in front of the entry team, stopping at the threshold of the door.

as the backup officer. This officer goes wherever the handler may go.

Once the search team has safely reached the building to be searched, whenever possible, the best way to deploy the dog is to let the dog work out in front, stopping at the threshold of the door. By placing the dog in the threshold, you will know if someone is standing just inside the door. It also makes use of the dog's senses, and enables the dog to survey the area in front, while using his nose, eyes and ears. By leaving the dog in the threshold for approximately 30 to 45 seconds, there is ample opportunity to pick up any human scent blowing toward the point of entry. On the initial entry, the dog should be used to only clear approximately 15 to 20 feet into the building. Limiting how deep the dog goes into the building will let the search team know if there is anyone lying in wait just inside the entryway.

Handlers who lack control over their dogs keep them close during a search by using a long line to limit the distance the dog will enter into a building. The long line can be either retractable or freehand. Once the dog has searched an area, the search team should make entry into the room to do a detailed search of the area. When the search team has completed their detailed search and secured the area, the handler will decide which direction to continue the search.

Outside Searches

On any type of outside search, one of the first things a good patrol officer and canine handler will determine is the wind direction. Whenever possible, the police dog should be deployed into the wind or on a crosswind. As mentioned earlier, a suspect's scent travels with the wind in a "scent cone." By using the wind to your advantage, the suspect can be located safely and quickly. When conducting an outside area search, the handler must determine how the dog is to be deployed, and whether to release the dog into the search area on or off leash; also, if the dog will be directed to certain areas to search, or a long line used to clear the areas. Once again, before actual deployment, it is important to let the dog survey the area and use its senses.

Stay behind cover and call the suspect to you. Don't leave your point of cover unless it is necessary.

Locating a Suspect Out of Sight–No Bite

I mentioned earlier that communication is one of the keys to any successful operation. Also, that there are situations that must be discussed prior to every deployment, so there are no mistakes. One situation is deciding which arrest technique is going to be used when a suspect is located out of sight. When a suspect is located, everyone's first reaction is to rush into the search area. The problem with doing this is that there might be places that have not been cleared, or multiple suspects hiding. It is important that you take your time and move carefully. Clear those remaining unsearched rooms and open areas that lead you to where the suspect has been located.

The handler should not recall the dog until he is able to pinpoint where the suspect is hiding. If the dog is recalled before the suspect is located, the suspect may move to a different hiding spot. Should the dog again be sent inside, it will go back to where the suspect was hiding, not the new hiding spot. There are a few reasons for this. Dogs have excellent memories. They remember where the suspect was, and this is confirmed by the strong odor left behind. Also, keep in mind the dog is still correct. The dog is trained to alert on human odor, and the odor is very strong in this old hiding place, much stronger than in the new hiding place. By keeping the dog where the suspect is believed to be hiding, you assure the suspect will not leave and escape. Once you are able to see exactly where the dog is alerting, the handler will now recall the dog to your position of cover. Because the dog is used to the handler's voice, the handler should be the one who orders the suspect out from their hiding spot. Do not leave your position of cover and enter the room to arrest the suspect. There might be more than one suspect hiding in the room. Wait until the handler orders the suspect out of the room, where you can safely arrest them without exposing yourself to unknown dangers.

Many years ago, after completing a basic handler's course, I heard one of my classmates, from Idaho, had found a burglary suspect on his first night back. He released his dog to search a restaurant, and a short time later the dog started barking deep into the business. The handler followed the barking and discovered the dog in the kitchen. With gun drawn and the dog holding the suspect at bay in a far corner, the handler entered the kitchen through the double doors. The handler approached the dog, which was approximately 30 feet from the double doors, and took the suspect into custody. While turning around to walk the suspect and dog out of the kitchen, astonishingly, a second suspect was seen standing in the other corner of the kitchen with his hands up. The second suspect was hidden from view by the opening of the double doors. During later questioning, the second suspect said the dog pushed its way through the double doors and went over to the opposite side of the room, locating the first suspect. The suspect said he stayed in hiding out of fear the dog would give chase if he ran. The second suspect watched as the handler entered the kitchen and walked to the other side of the room. Luckily, the second suspect was not armed. Had he been, the handler never would have seen it coming.

Locating and Biting a Suspect

When a police dog is biting a suspect out of sight, once again, everyone wants to rush in and observe the incident. This is not a safe maneuver. As already mentioned, there could be places that have not been cleared, or multiple suspects hiding. If you decide to go deeper into the search area, you must take your time and clear the remaining unsearched rooms and open areas in front of you as you go.

If the dog has found a suspect deep in a building, and there are still many rooms to search, the handler can try two different approaches. Before moving deeper into the search area, the suspect may be ordered to the handler's secure location while the dog is still biting the suspect. Pain can be a very good motivator. This will save time and effort in clearing several rooms before you actually get to where the dog is biting the suspect. Because the dog is used to the handler's voice, the handler should be the one giving orders to the canine and the suspect.

A second approach is for the handler to command the dog to release the bite of the unseen suspect and recall the dog to their location. Once the dog has returned, the handler can order the suspect to do the same. If the suspect complies, fine. But, what if they do not? Should the dog be sent back in to search for the suspect? What if the dog bites the suspect a second time? Should the dog be released again to see what happens, or should the dog and suspect be ordered back to the handler's (and your) location? If the handler decides to call the dog and suspect back, there are several arrest techniques that can be used. One of the biggest questions is when do you take the police dog off the bite, and who is going to handcuff the suspect? Some departments require the canine to be released from a distance, before the suspect is handcuffed, and before the handler has actual physical control over the canine. Obviously this could cause problems, such as re-biting, accidental bite or the suspect fleeing.

Several years ago, a police department in Orange County, California, used this arrest technique when the dog found and bit a robbery suspect. From his position of cover, the handler ordered the dog to release his bite of the suspect. The dog complied immediately, and returned to the handler. The suspect got up from his position and ran. The handler sent his dog after the fleeing suspect. Once again, the dog caught and bit the suspect. When the handler got to where he could see the dog and suspect, the handler ordered the dog to release its bite. The dog again complied immediately, and returned to the handler. The suspect got up from his position and ran again. The handler sent his dog after the fleeing suspect once more. This happened six times before the handler left the dog on the bite until the suspect was handcuffed and in custody. The suspect was found guilty in court for his crime, but sued the police department for excessive force. Unfortunately, the suspect won the civil lawsuit and the department had to pay him several hundred thousand dollars.

To reduce this problem, some departments call the canine and suspect back to their point of cover and safety. When the search team has control of the suspect, the canine handler will take physical control of the dog and have the dog release the bite. The search team will then handcuff the suspect. Other departments have the canine handler handcuff the suspect while the dog is on the bite to ensure control of the suspect. Whatever arrest techniques your department uses, make sure the search team knows which procedure is going to be utilized before the incident.

Crawl Space and Attic Insertion

Most officers don't like getting dirty. That's because they wear clean uniforms, spend hours shining their shoes or boots and wear 20 pounds of equipment. The last thing they want to do is climb under a house or into a hot, dirty, confined attic looking for a fleeing suspect, who might be armed. Most dirty jobs go to the person who has the lowest ID number. However, when it comes to crawling into crawl spaces and attics, these jobs go to the smallest officer.

The only member of a patrol force who, after proper training, conditioning and motivation, really loves to go into these godforsaken places is a police dog. When a police dog has been properly exposed to this type of search environment, they will drag their handler to any crawl space they see. A dog can easily clear under a house or clear an attic in a matter of seconds, when it would take a patrol officer 10 to 15 minutes.

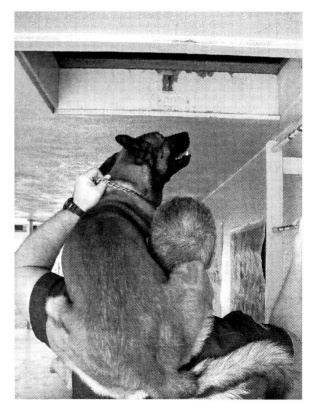

The police dog can easily be lifted into an attic.

The dog can be used to clear under a house or narrow tunnel.

There is not a great difference between an attic insertion and a search under a house. The difference is the way the dog gets into, and out of, the search area. To check the crawl space under a house, the dog is positioned in the opening to smell the air coming out of the search area. The dog should be able to tell if there is anyone hiding under the house, and the handler reads the dog's change of behavior. If the dog does find someone under the house, the safest way to take the suspect into custody is to have the dog and suspect come to the opening and crawl out from under the house.

To check an attic, an attic mirror is used prior to inserting the dog into the opening. The attic mirror allows patrol officers and the handler to survey the attic to see if there is someone close by waiting to ambush whomever comes through the opening. After clearing the opening, the handler can put the dog on their shoulder while patrol officers cover the

opening from the ground. Using a ladder, the handler then climbs up and inserts the dog into the attic. If the dog bites someone in the attic, it is handled the same way as a bite under a house (the dog and suspect are ordered to the opening). Some dogs will slowly come over to the opening and allow the handler to pull them out of the attic, or they may jump into the handler's arms. Other dogs will avoid the opening like the plague. When the handler has coaxed the dog over to the opening, it may be necessary to grab the leash and pull the dog down, being careful to catch the dog before it hits the ground. Depending on the dog's temperament and personality, the handler will muzzle the dog before attempting to do this.

Canine Officer Down

From time to time, a police dog pays the ultimate price for their handler and fellow officers. This is like losing a member of your family. It affects the handler, the handler's family and the entire department. However, the handler may be the one injured or killed during a deployment. When this occurs, how do you handle the dog? This is a situation you need to discuss with each handler, as well as how their dog will react, and what will be needed to secure the dog in the unit. Many people, including police officers, believe police dogs are vicious and unfriendly to everyone except their handlers. This belief is sometimes the result of dogs in the back of their canine units barking uncontrollably and rocking the unit from side to side. I believe that *most* dogs, once they are out of *their* patrol unit, are very approachable and extremely sociable.

I am also of the opinion that if a handler goes down and the dog is loose, just about anyone can walk the dog back to the canine unit and secure the dog. This presumes the officer who approaches the dog has the correct body language, and the dog is not showing any signs of defense. Whomever approaches the dog must show they are confident and sure of what they are doing. They should call the dog's name and speak in a very calm and serene voice. If they approach the dog in a slow, unnatural walk or body posture, the dog may sense this as a sign that they are being stalked and about to be attacked. As a result, the dog may kick into defense drive to protect itself and its handler.

For those dogs which cannot be approached, there are alternatives. If time permits, an animal control officer should be requested to respond with their equipment to take control of the dog. This may be done with either a lasso or tranquilizer gun. If it is still not possible to remove the dog from the handler, a bite sleeve from the canine vehicle's trunk can be used. Most dogs will bite the sleeve and not let go. This may enable the dog to be dragged to the patrol unit while biting the sleeve. Both rear doors of the patrol vehicle should be open. While the dog is still on the bite, the officer should get into the back seat and exit out the other side. Once the officer is out the other side and the dog is still in the unit, the sleeve can be released and the door closed. As a last resort, if the officer's life is in danger, the dog may have to be shot.

Tactical Release

It has been my experience that one of the biggest fears of patrol officers doing a search with a police dog is that the dog may bite them. Their most popular response is to shoot the dog. They are not aware that almost anyone can quickly and safely remove the dog from a bite. Having been bitten a few times over my canine career, I know what I am about to say sounds absurd, but if you are the one being bitten by a police dog, you need to remain as calm and quiet as possible. Everyone's first reaction is to yell, scream and try to shake the dog off the bite. This is the worst thing you can do. All this does is excite the dog more. It must be remembered that dogs do not think or reason like humans. This means they cannot distinguish between biting a good guy or a bad guy.

For those rare times when the handler is incapacitated and cannot take the dog off a bite, there are a few simple rules to follow. The next time you are in a briefing ask your handler to give you the dog's release command and how to take the dog off a bite. When you approach a person who is being bitten by a police dog, it is very important you stay calm. Your instinct will be to rush in and try to get the dog off. If you rush toward the dog, some dogs might have a tendency to play "keep away." They may release their bite and re-bite somewhere else,

because they know someone is going to take them off the bite. When you come within approximately 10 to 15 feet, you should be walking. Something else that sounds foolish, but is necessary, is to talk to the dog in a calm voice as you approach. Yelling will only make the dog nervous, and possibly defensive. By remaining calm, the dog will sense it is doing the right thing, and not try to play keep away. When you arrive, hopefully the person being bitten will be on their feet. If not, and it is possible to do so, have them get on their feet. It might be more difficult for an inexperienced officer to get the dog to release a bite when the person being bitten is on the ground. As you pet the dog, feel around its neck for a collar. The type of collar the dog is wearing will determine which technique to use.

There are basically two kinds of collars dogs wear. Both are similar, but have slight differences. If the dog has a traditional fur-saver collar, you want to position the collar high up on the neck behind the base of the ears, not at the base of the neck, where it rests. You then want to place your hand under the collar, palm up, and have the collar come to rest deep in the palm and web of your hand. If the dog has a pinch collar, you will probably not be able to move the collar around as easily as with the fur-saver. You will need to find the live ring of the pinch collar, which will be located on the "triangle" portion of the collar. Once you have determined the location of the live ring, place your hand deep into the triangle, palm up, and have the collar come to rest deep in the palm and web of your hand. If you grab the collar with an overhand grip, you may break your little finger. Once you have placed your hand deep under the collar, palm up, tighten the collar around the dog's neck by twisting the collar. This twisting procedure applies to both the fur-saver and pinch collar. As you twist the collar, give the dog's "out" command in a forceful tone. Your natural reaction as you twist the collar and give the "out" command will be to pull the dog off the bite and toward you. This is the worst possible thing to do, because it will cause more damage to the area that is being bitten. This is also going to sound ridiculous, but as you twist and give the "out" command, you should push the dog's mouth *into* the area where the dog is biting. By doing this, you will make the dog gag, which will cause the bite to be

When using a tactical release on the dog, it is important to stay close to the dog and suspect. Twist the collar and push the dog into the suspect.

released more quickly. If possible, you also should have the dog's front feet off the ground as you do this technique.

A third technique that may work on the dog is what I call the upward pull technique. No matter which collar the dog is wearing, find the live ring and tighten the collar by pulling the live ring upward. At the same time, push the dog's mouth into the area the dog is biting and give the "out" command. Whichever technique you use, once the dog releases the bite, take a few steps backward, away from the person being bitten, and be sure to keep the dog facing the person he was biting for a short time. Do not immediately turn the dog away. It is also extremely important you immediately undo the twisting motion around the collar and let

the dog breathe.

I have been teaching these outing techniques to my department for over 15 years, and to numerous departments throughout the United States. All the techniques have been used on the streets for years, and are proven to work. The key to all of this is education, training and communication between you and your canine handlers. Take a few minutes to talk to them about how they get their dog to release a bite. Ask them to show you how they do it, then ask if you can try it yourself. You will be astonished how easy it is.

Traffic Stops

When you back a canine handler on a traffic

stop, you must always keep in mind that the handler can deploy the dog from the patrol unit at any time. If an altercation with a suspect occurs, or a person runs during the detention, the handler may release his dog from the vehicle. The sequence of events starts when the handler pushes a remote control transmitting device they normally carry on their belt. One of two things will happen, depending on how the patrol unit is equipped. When the handler pushes the remote control transmitting device, either the rear passenger door will pop open, or the front passenger window will roll down, or both. You might even hear the handler calling for his dog to come "HERE." Now you might be saying to yourself, I already know that, why is he reminding me. The reason is I have seen a lot of patrol officers standing very close to the window or door of the canine unit. The best place for a backup officer to stand is out of the direct line of sight of the dog and handler. Depending on the situation, the backup officer might stand a good distance behind the suspect, or if tactics permit, put the suspect between you and the canine unit.

If you and the handler are in a fight with the suspect when the handler decides to release the dog from the canine unit, hopefully he will give you advance warning, or tell you to get back. This will be your clue that the dog is coming. One of the first things you should do when you move away from the fight or pile is put the handler and suspect between you and the canine unit. When the dog comes out of the canine unit, he will be in a "Prey/Pack" frame of mind. In the wild, "only the strongest survive." When the dog comes out of the canine unit and reaches the handler, the dog will go for whomever is on the bottom of the pile. That is why it is so very important the handler releases the dog when they know they are able to maintain some semblance of control over the suspect, and remain on top until the dog gets to the pile.

Post-Operation Procedures

Witnesses

Patrol officers should canvas the neighborhood for witnesses, and also thank residents for their cooperation. Inform them the suspect is in custody,

the area is safe and they may return to their homes. By notifying the public about what happened, you will gain better cooperation in the future and put them at ease that they are once again safe.

While you are talking to residents, ask them what they saw or heard. You will be amazed how cooperative most people will be when you give them a little information. Remember, not everyone sees or perceives the same situation exactly alike. Do not be surprised when people you are talking to give you similar, but not precisely the same, story. Ask them if they heard canine announcements. Did they hear anything the suspect or other officers might have said during the incident? Document the names, addresses and telephone numbers of all civilian witnesses you contacted. Place their statements in a supplemental report, whether they heard anything or not. This way, you have their story documented in case they change their minds or forget.

Evidence

Once the suspect is taken into custody, it is time to search the area where the suspect was found for fruits of the crime. When evidence is found, photograph it before you collect it. At the same time, take pictures of where the suspect was found.

A dilemma that most police departments face is the preservation of evidence for a possible civil trial years after the criminal case has been adjudicated by the courts. As the arresting officer, you may never see the suspect again until you appear for a civil lawsuit in federal or state court three or fours years after the incident. The suspect pled guilty, or made a plea-bargained agreement with the district attorney in the criminal case, and now is suing you civilly for excessive force.

This is where the dilemma begins. When the criminal case was adjudicated, the criminal court sent a letter to your department saying they no longer needed to keep the evidence. Your department gave this letter to the evidence technician, and the evidence technician destroyed the evidence. Compounding the problem is the fact that some attorneys wait until the last day to file a claim or federal lawsuit. By the time the police department is made aware that a suit has been filed against it, the criminal case is usually closed and evidence may have been destroyed. Of course, the attorney representing the plaintiff will say the evidence was destroyed because the police department had something to hide, or the evidence that was destroyed would have proved his client's claims of excessive force, violation of his constitutional rights or whatever else the plaintiff has claimed.

To preserve the evidence for a possible civil case, check your department's policy to determine if you can write on your evidence package in big, bold letters, "Do Not Destroy." Under some federal case law, suspects who are injured while being taken into custody have up to one year after completing their federal sentence to file a lawsuit. By this time, most evidence will have already been destroyed. If for some reason your policy will not allow you to do this, see if your policy can be changed. This will help preserve the evidence for any potential civil lawsuit.

Report Writing

After the incident is over and things calm down, it is now time for the patrol officer and the handler to write a report. When you write your report, make sure it is accurate and concise. The patrol officer who is handling the incident should write the original crime report, which should include the facts of the case. The handler will write about the canine deployment, search and arrest. The handler's deployment and arrest report should contain a summary of what information they received about the incident. Do not be afraid to relate your state of mind regarding the incident. It will be at least three or four years before a possible civil lawsuit goes to trial. It is unlikely you will remember your state of mind at the time of the incident unless you write it down. The courts will allow you to testify to your state of mind regarding the incident.

As the incident progressed, your dispatchers should have been keeping track of all the pertinent information during the call. When you write your report, document the arrival time of the original officers, your arrival time, the time the suspect was taken into custody, the time the suspect was taken to the hospital or jail, who transported the suspect and the time they arrived at the hospital or jail. The handler might also want to document in their report

what time medical treatment was given to the suspect, and what time photographs were taken of the suspect. This will help prove you did not leave the suspect sitting in the back of a patrol unit or in the hospital emergency room for hours without receiving medical treatment. More than likely, the handler will take the bite photographs, but as a patrol officer, if you are assigned to take photographs of the suspect's injuries, make sure the wounds are completely cleaned and not bleeding before you take the picture. Also, make sure these photographs are not placed into the normal evidence area. Keep these photographs in the department's canine notebook, so they are not later destroyed after the criminal trial is adjudicated.

When you are at the hospital, keep inappropriate comments to yourself. There are some doctors and nurses who do not like the police, so you must act as professional as possible. Several years ago, one of our handlers took a suspect to the hospital for medical treatment after the suspect was bitten in the leg. One of our reserve officers went to the hospital and asked the handler if he could see what "Cujo" did. Keep in mind the dog's name was not "Cujo." The dog had never been called this name before, and the reserve was only trying to be funny. One of the nurses overheard the reserve make this inappropriate comment, and later told the defense attorney when he came to the hospital to get his client's medical records. Approximately three years later, at a deposition for a civil lawsuit, the same attorney asked the handler if his dog had any nicknames. Since the dog had no nicknames, the handler said, "no." The attorney then asked him about the name "Cujo." The handler remembered what the reserve had said, and had to admit that what he said was wrong and inappropriate. The Department later won the lawsuit, but it was a very embarrassing moment for the Department.

CONCLUSION

Hopefully, this chapter has been informative, and stimulated you to sit down with your canine handler and ask questions about canine deployment. However, if you have any questions, please do not hesitate to give me a call or send me an email at (626) 814-8400, ext. 8998, or Topdogwck1@aol.com.

I would like to conclude with a poem a friend sent me a few years ago. Unfortunately, I do not know who wrote it. "Your dog is your friend, your partner, your defender. You are his life, his love, his leader. He will be yours, faithful and true, to the last beat of his heart. You owe it to him to be worthy of such devotion."

ROBERT D. MAGNUSON

Bob Magnuson is a sergeant and training officer with the Canfield, Ohio, Police Department. Sergeant Magnuson graduated from the Ohio Peace Officers Basic Academy in 1975, served as an Auxiliary Officer with the Youngstown Police Department, and as a Reserve Deputy in the Narcotics/Detective Division of the Mahoning County Sheriff's Department. He joined the Canfield Police Department in 1978.

Sergeant Magnuson is a Certified State Instructor in General Topics through the Ohio Peace Officers Training Council and a Specialist Defensive Tactics Instructor. Besides being a frequent guest instructor at the O.P.O.T.A., he has taught throughout the country and trained well over 10,000 officers from throughout the United States and Canada. Sergeant Magnuson has also published numerous magazine articles dealing with defensive tactics, police survival, and vehicle stops, and has appeared as a consultant and guest of the Donahue Show in New York. He received both Associate and Bachelor's degrees from Youngstown State University, and is currently enrolled there in the Master's Program in Criminal Justice.

Since 1997, Sergeant Magnuson has served on the Ohio Peace Officers Training Council's standards committee to upgrade the law enforcement curriculum for the State of Ohio under the Ohio Attorney General's office in the areas of vehicle stops, suspect approaches, and also defensive tactics. He holds numerous titles in the Martial Arts, including a 5th Degree black belt in Kwan Mu Kan Karate-Do and a 5th Degree black belt in Kenka Aiki-Jitsu. In 1999, Sergeant Magnuson was chosen as one of twelve United States police officers to travel to Gotenborg, Sweden, to attend the Volvo Security Driving Academy program.

Chapter 10

VEHICLE STOPS[1]

ROBERT D. MAGNUSON

INTRODUCTION

The purpose of this chapter is to lay the foundation for vehicle stop strategies, tactics and survival tactics related to vehicle stops. Throughout this chapter, it must be recognized that although officers acknowledge the possibility of felonious assault while engaging in vehicle stops, statistics indicate that accidental assault is an even more likely occurrence. Therefore, accidental assault should at least receive equal consideration. When effecting a traffic stop, deployment tactics are used to provide protection from injury or death by both felonious and accidental means. *All tactics must consider these two threats*. A vehicle stop is defined as any situation where an officer or officers are deployed directly from a patrol vehicle (i.e., marked cruiser, unmarked cruiser, motorcycle, bicycle, etc.) to employ direct contact with a vehicle(s) or pedestrian in the performance of their duties. Whether a violator is stopped in a vehicle on a roadway, sitting in a vehicle in a parking space, or a pedestrian is hitchhiking on the side of the road, the deployment tactics outlined in this chapter can be effectively utilized. A vehicle stop begins when an officer observes a violation or obtains other information that develops into a legal reason (probable cause or reasonable suspicion) to stop (detain) a vehicle or pedestrian. Every stop has a beginning (assessing the stop, positioning the cruiser), a middle (tactical control of the stop, contact) and an end (clearing the stop scene), with the "middle" being the area where most tactical changes occur.

Supporting Data

The following statistics related to vehicle stops were taken from and/or calculated based on information contained within the publication entitled "Law Enforcement Officers Killed & Assaulted: Uniform Crime Reports," U.S. Department of Justice, Federal Bureau of Investigation, Washington, D.C., 1997.

- Between 1988 and 1997, 89 officers were feloniously killed while on traffic pursuits/stops.
- Between 1988 and 1997, 103 officers were killed accidentally while on traffic stops, road blocks, directing traffic, or assisting motorists, etc.
- In 1997, there were 65 officers killed feloniously (all males).

1. Editor's Note: The information contained within this chapter is excerpted from a comprehensive manual on the subject (*Strategies and Tactics of Patrol Stops, Fourth Edition,* 1999) written by the author and submitted with permission by Lieutenant Robert Chabali of the Dayton, Ohio, Police Department.

- In 1997, there were 60 officers killed accidentally (seven were struck by vehicles).
- In 1997, there was a total of 49,151 officers assaulted (down 15,761 from 1994). Of the total, 5,043 officers, or 10%, were assaulted while involved in pursuits/stops.
- In 1997, there were 7 officers (just under 11%) murdered while effecting pursuits/stops.

Note: 83% of the assaults on officers occurred with personal weapons, i.e., hands, fists, feet, etc. Therefore, it is important for officers to keep their holsters snapped and their gun side back (away from a suspect). Officers must also be ready to use their hands and other tools.

- 1,996 officers were assaulted with a firearm in 1997 (4%).
- 295 of the officers assaulted with a firearm were actually hit and injured in 1997, or just under 15% of the officers shot at.
- 63, or just over 21%, of these officers died as a result of their injuries, or 3.2% of the total officers assaulted in 1997.
- Three officers, or 4.6%, were killed with their own firearm in 1997.

Survival Mindset

Statistical data indicates that there is little correlation between assaults, firearms assaults and being injured during a firearms assault. In addition, the correlation between being shot at and killed is almost non-existent. To instill a "survival mindset," officers must first accept and believe in the fact that the odds of being hit in a gun battle are almost 4 to 1, and secondly, the odds of dying from a gunshot wound are an even more remote possibility. Law enforcement officers must prepare themselves psychologically for this eventuality. Part of this preparation requires adopting a survival mindset that instills the "I will not die" philosophy.

As children, we learned to correlate the words "bang, bang" with the words "you're dead." This belief can remain long into adulthood, but the actual correlation between these two phrases is minimal when you look at the statistics. Only a little over

one-fourth of officers who were shot at died. Officers should engrain these statistics into their actual survival schema and embrace the concept.

As mentioned previously, it is incumbent on officers to keep their holsters snapped and gun side back as a starting point for weapons retention. Lastly, officers need to wear holsters that have superior retention qualities. Remember, there may be a gun at every call to which you respond. The number of officers killed with their own firearm continues to drop. However, "zero" should be our goal.

- In 1997, 47 of the officers murdered (72%) were patrol officers (the backbone of the department); 34 of the officers were assigned to one-officer vehicles, 13 of the officers were assigned to two-officer vehicles.
- Between 1988 and 1997, there were 633 officers feloniously killed by firearms. The distances between the victim officer and offenders were:

0-5 feet:	53% of officers killed
5-10 feet:	21% of officers killed
11-20 feet:	12% of officers killed
21-50 feet:	8% of officers killed
over 50 feet:	6% of officers killed

Note: Distance is your ally!

Between 1988 and 1997, 253 out of 633 officers feloniously killed by firearms (40%) were wearing body armor. It is important to note that 380 of the officers feloniously killed with firearms during this time period were not wearing body armor.

Tactical Considerations

Theoretically, if an officer remained in a patrol or traffic assignment and made only five vehicle stops per day, they would make over 32,500 traffic stops during the course of a 25-year career (counting time off for vacations, etc.). Making this many vehicle stops should result in a high level of safety and proficiency. However, this is not always the case, because repetition often causes complacency, which in turn can result in officers taking unsafe and unnecessary risks. It is important to remember that vehicle stops can be more difficult than building entries, because buildings don't move.

Control Through Voluntary Compliance

Patrol officers have a primary responsibility during their tour of duty of providing **control** (traffic, people, situation, etc.), and the best way to control is through voluntary compliance. Voluntary compliance requires the officer to verbally convince people that "going along with the program" helps them and is in their best interest (i.e., "If I have to arrest you, your vehicle will be towed, you will miss work, and you will have to post bond."). Establishing and maintaining control enhances an officer's opportunity for survival. Always remember, if it wasn't for the voluntary compliance of the vast majority of the public, we couldn't even begin to keep the "dam from breaking."

During an arrest situation (when probable cause exists) while effecting a traffic stop, officers should follow steps outlined in the "Stages of Arrest" (which follow) in sequence to afford the best survival opportunity. Officers should establish "control" (verbal and/or physical) before they "handcuff." After handcuffs are applied to maintain control, officers should conduct a thorough "search" of the person (including the groin), and then prepare the suspect for "transport." The "Stages of Arrest" in the correct tactical sequence are: control, handcuff, search and transport.

- **Control:** Attempt to gain voluntary compliance through good verbal skills, but always remember that there is a time to talk and a time for action.
- **Handcuff:** Utilize a tactical handcuffing system. Gap and double-lock the handcuffs whenever practical to do so. Always handcuff prior to searching, and use the two-officer contact/cover principle.
- **Search:** Do a thorough, systematic search of the person from head to toe, as though you are looking for a handcuff key (if you find that, you can find a gun).
- **Transport:** Check the suspect and the handcuffs. Utilize seatbelts whenever practical to do so. Continue to monitor the suspect and use verbal calming techniques. Handcuffs should be double-locked whenever practical. If the suspect complains that the handcuffs are too tight, check and/or loosen the cuffs (but don't release and replace). If transporting a suspect in a prone position, transport quickly and monitor constantly to prevent positional asphyxiation.

Contact/Cover Principle

As this commonly used combination of terms implies, contact is the physical touching and cover is the maintaining of a weapon on the suspect (i.e., to "cover him"). Contact is physical control and cover is control with a firearm (when used in this context). An important rule in weapon retention is for officers to stay a minimum of 10 feet from a suspect covered with a firearm. This safety rule is utilized to keep the suspect out of grabbing range of the weapon to prevent disarming the officer. An officer should not attempt to physically control or handcuff a suspect that they are covering with a firearm, as the results can be devastating for two reasons. First, the weapon may accidentally discharge. When an officer is applying enough physical pressure to control an individual with one hand, it is difficult for the brain and body not to tense up the other hand. This sympathetic balancing response can easily cause the discharge of a weapon that only takes seven pounds of pressure or less to activate. Secondly, as previously stated, an officer can be disarmed if they are within grabbing distance of the suspect.

Assessing a Stop

To devise a "tactical plan," three assessment categories (to be discussed shortly) can be utilized by officers to mentally evaluate or assess the potential level of a particular stop prior to initiating it. The assessment is the most crucial component of the stop. Without a proper assessment, the officer cannot choose an appropriate course of action. An officer who does not assess a vehicle stop does their job blindly and relies on luck. The assessment (evaluation) can change at any time during an actual stop (escalate or de-escalate), based on additional information and observations. While the best tactical approach would be to consider *all* stops as "high risk" in nature, this would not be a socially acceptable standard. Officers need to balance the risk of potential assault with tactics that are acceptable to the public in general, and objectively "reasonable" to other officers ("objective reasonableness standard" as defined in *Graham v. Connor,* 490 U.S. 386, 396–397 (1989). If we were viewing a scale with social considerations on one side and tactical considerations on the other, the scale would tip slightly in favor of tactical considerations. To illustrate this point, consider how the public would react if police officers always drew their weapon on every stop, no matter what the circumstances or reasons for the stop.[2] Certainly this would give the officers an almost foolproof tactical advantage, but it is not reasonable. Obviously this approach is tongue-in-cheek and very extreme, but sometimes officers seem to come on strong, believing they are using good tactics. In reality, most officers rely on luck and tricks, rather than strategies and tactics. If an officer is that lucky, why not play the lottery, win, and retire from law enforcement! Good tactics are subtle, yet effective. Most of the time, tactics can be used without the violator even realizing the officer is using them. This type of approach is sometimes called "hidden tactics."

Officers need to be familiar with the assessment categories for two reasons. First, the author recommends that officers be able to articulate (explain) why they used a particular tactic if asked by the police chief, supervisor, violator, citizen or court. They should also be able to articulate why they assessed a particular stop a certain way. Therefore, officers should be familiar with the examples outlined below and the reasons why these examples meet the criteria for the particular assessment category. Secondly, for their personal safety, officers should be familiar with the assessment categories.

The correct tactic cannot be selected until the potential risk of the situation is evaluated. Tactics must always be weighed against the risks presented.

Past assessment standards of felony vs. misdemeanor were not always definite, and relied more on information than observations. The terms are also not cognitive, or in other words, do not paint a mental picture that officers can correlate into tactics. In addition, a few misdemeanor stops may be High Risk and many non-violent felony stops may be more appropriately labeled as Unknown Risk, according to the standards set forth in this chapter. For example, who is more dangerous, the person who has a misdemeanor resisting and assault record, or the felony bad check passer?

In making and/or changing an assessment of a stop, the officer must consider many factors, including available information, time of day, type of vehicle (structural design), number of occupants, weather conditions, traffic congestion, location, movements of occupant(s), reason for the stop, availability of backup, situational surroundings and other factors.

Vehicle stops fall into three general categories, "Low Risk," "Unknown Risk," and "High Risk." Above all, there is no such thing as a "No-Risk" stop! The examples which follow include only a few of the many representing the three categories.

- **Low Risk**
  Definition: Unlikely potential felonious assault.
  Examples: - Minor traffic violation (speed, red light, etc.), daytime conditions, with few occupants who are unlikely to pose a threat of violence.

- **Unknown Risk**
  Definition: Unknown potential for felonious assault.
  Examples: - Suspicious vehicle/per-

---

2. Editor's Note: There are times when it may be reasonable and advisable for an officer to approach with their sidearm drawn and held inconspicuously alongside their leg. The weapon can be reholstered when the situation no longer warrants its presence. However, if the offender observes the officer holstering the weapon and objects, the officer need only articulate why it was unholstered initially, i.e., a high violent crime area, circumstances surrounding the stop, etc. Officers should emphasize their concern for their own safety as well as the offender's.

sons.
- Driving under the influence.
- Driving while license suspended.
- No operator's license.
- Fictitious registration (altered or not belonging to the vehicle).
- Unusual driver actions (shoulder, head and/or unusual movements, such as exiting a vehicle without officer's request, stepping out "butt first," agitated state, revving engine, turning around to visually locate the officer's expected approach, etc.).
- Unusual passenger actions (unusual head/shoulder movement, exiting vehicle without officer's request, agitated state, etc.).
- Situational surroundings (high crime areas, bars, gangs, etc.).
- High-profile violation (excessive speed, reckless operation, etc.).
- Suspicious (non-articulable circumstances).
- Unusual vehicle actions ("turn out," slow in pulling over, back lights coming on, etc.).
- Aggressive body language or aggressive verbal cues.
Note: From a tactical standpoint, the majority of all stops fall into the unknown risk category.

- **High Risk Definition:**

Likely potential for

Examples:

felonious assault.
- Known, possibly violent, felony stops.
- Suspected violent felony stops.
- Known or suspected weapons-related stops.
- Pursuits.
- Possibly some high-risk misdemeanors (i.e., assault warrant, etc.).

As can be seen from the above examples, those that are "Unknown Risk" far outnumber the "Low-Risk" and "High-Risk" categories. After observing the tactics of the average road officer, it seems apparent that many officers are under the misconception that the majority of stops are "Low Risk," as evidenced by the "Walk-Up"-type approaches they most frequently use.

Within the three assessment categories, there are also varying degrees of threat levels, "High-Risk," low-level, "High-Risk," high-level, etc.

Covert Names for the Three Assessment Categories

For tactical communications purposes, the author has assigned "covert" names for the three stop assessment categories. In this way, officers can communicate their assessment of a particular stop to other units over the radio, and then utilize the appropriate choice of tactics (by name) to coincide with their assessment. The "covert" tactical names are as follows:

Low Risk = Level-1 Stop
Unknown Risk = Level-2 Stop
High Risk = Level-3 Stop

Positioning the Cruiser/Patrol Car

There is no one right way to position a cruiser that will account for every variable an officer may possibly encounter. The following recommended cruiser/violator positions have both pros and cons, but an officer who is educated on the strengths and weaknesses of each position can utilize any position at any given time, and thus have several basic patterns and variations (options) from which to choose. First, the choice should be based on which position provides the best ***control*** based on an officer's prior assessment. Second, an officer must consider which hazard is of foremost concern (i.e., felonious or accidental assault). Third, the cruiser positioning should be compatible with the contact method the officer intends to use (i.e., don't use right offsets with left side approaches, etc.). The four basic positions are as follows:

- Offset to the left 3' and 20' back.
- Offset to the right 3' and 20' back.
- Offset to the left 3' and 3' back.
- Offset to the right 3' and 3' back.

When possible, officers should try to minimize interference with the normal flow of traffic.

The "offset" in each of the four basic positions is normally one-half the cruiser's width, or "three feet." Basically, the cruiser's front license plate would line up with the right or left side of the violator's vehicle, depending on whether a right or left offset is used. Utilizing a left offset creates a "buffer zone" from passing traffic when an officer is at the contact point with the violator. This buffer zone forces traffic out and around the officer. In the event a passing motorist attempts to feloniously assault the officer with his vehicle, this offset will force the violator to miss or severely slow down due to the angle created.

The four basic positions provide different advantages that need to be thoroughly understood by each officer so they may best judge for themselves which technique to choose for a particular stop. Above all, do not choose a position because "we've always done it this way," or because you just don't know why ("clueless in law enforcement!").

Optional Cruiser Positioning

There are several optional deployments which are based on the tactical advantage of the four basic positions. The optional positions can be utilized whenever the violator's vehicle is parked "out of position" for standard cruiser deployment, or at the officer's discretion during any given stop. Optional cruiser positions are as follows:

- **Corner Stop (3' back/left offset):** This position can be used when the violator's vehicle stops around a corner or pulls into a parking space. Although officers can use the P.A. System to have the violator pull up farther on the roadway, remember not all vehicles will be occupied.
- **Corner Stop (3' back/right offset):** This position is not used for Left Side Walk-Up Approaches.
- **Angled Left Offset to Rear:** For "daytime" only! Can be utilized from 3' or 20' back. This position is commonly used by the Ohio and California Highway Patrols, because it affords a margin of protection from oncoming traffic ("buffer zone") when officers are exiting their cruiser. The left front corner should extend farther out than the edge of the driver's side cruiser door when it is fully opened. This provides the officer with a safe and quick exit from the cruiser (like a right offset would), while also providing a buffer zone for the officer making a left side walk-up approach.
  Note: This position is not practical for nighttime stops, as the takedown lights and headlights will be aimed into the roadway directly at approaching vehicles.
- **Angled Left Offset to Front:** This position is often used to end a pursuit or discourage forward escape of suspects during high-risk, felony-type stops. Caution must be used when deploying the cruiser in this manner. If the position is used during a high-risk vehicle stop (pursuit, felony warrant, etc.), the officer should remove the ignition keys, seek cover away from the cruiser, and allow the officers who have tactically positioned behind to complete the stop. When deploying in this fashion for a low-risk (disabled vehicle, etc.) or unknown-risk stop (semi, tractor-trailer, etc.), the officer should not approach the violator, but rather have the violator exit and approach the cruiser (see below), while the officer maintains a position of cover behind the cruiser trunk.
- **Positioning of Backup Cruiser:** The backup cruiser should have the headlights in the ***"off"***

position when deployed in this position during the evening hours, but should have the parking lights, 4-way flashers, and/or over head flashers on. The backup cruiser should be far enough (20' +) to allow the primary officer to move to the rear to escape felonious action by the violator. The officer from the backup cruiser should move up to the passenger side of the first cruiser to serve as the second officer, thus creating a two-officer unit. Officers need to ensure that their cruiser doors are unlocked at all times for access by the backup officer.

Note: When stopping motorcycles, always use "walk-back" tactics. Also, when stopping vans, position the cruiser 20' behind so that both sides and the rear door(s) of the van can be viewed. Use "walk-back" tactics.

Tactical Lighting

Many officers, including the author, utilize "wig-wag" and "takedown" lighting on both daytime and nighttime stops. When positioning the cruiser during a nighttime vehicle stop, the officer will need to optimize and focus available cruiser forward lighting to impair the vision of all vehicle occupants and provide illumination of the vehicle to gain tactical advantage. If the stop is "low risk," and the officer plans a "tactical walk-up" approach, the headlights should be on *low* beam. Illumination to the sides should be avoided because it may reveal the officer's position during the approach, either directly or indirectly. This is not a problem during "unknown" and "high-risk" vehicle stops, as the officer is *not* making an approach. The "angled offset" cruiser positions present different problems at night, because the tactical cruiser lighting is shifted left. This creates three problems. First, the violator's vehicle is not lighted efficiently. Secondly, an officer using a "walk-up" tactic will be exposed in his own light. Third, approaching traffic is blinded by the cruiser lights, which may aggravate the officer's exposure to accidental approach. When making a nighttime stop, officers need to utilize their takedown lights, headlights, wig-wag lights, spotlight and flashlight to gain a maximum advantage.

Takedown lights (emitting from the light bar overhead) should be focused on the interior passenger compartment of the violator vehicle. These lights are maximized at approximately 20 feet. The driver's side spotlight should be directed into the driver's side view mirror of the violator's vehicle. Wig-wag (alternating headlights) can be utilized to further disorient the occupants of the violator's vehicle. The flashlight can be illuminated to the rear during an approach to alert traffic from that direction.

Force Considerations

The relationship between the amount of force used needed to overcome the amount of resistance offered has been defined in numerous "Force/Resistance Continua." Officers conducting vehicle stops may encounter anything from polite violators to weapon-firing assailants, and need to prepare for the worst-case scenario, as well as any other actions in between. It is good advice for the professional law enforcement officer to "treat others as you would like to be treated" under similar circumstances (the Bible's "Golden Rule"). This includes a polite introduction (when possible), such as, "Good morning (sir or madam), may I see your operator's license and registration, please?" The presence of a neatly uniformed police officer (officer presence), coupled with polite verbal commands and direction (verbal/physical commands), is enough to control *most* traffic stop situations. If more resistance (action) is encountered, the officer will need to know appropriate techniques that will bring a suspect under control with the least amount of potential injury to the offender, with greater consideration given to the safety of the officer. These physical techniques can be learned in a defensive tactics course and applied to traffic stop situations. Officers are not required to stay at the same level as the resistor. This would create a no-win situation and increase both the officer's and suspect's chances for greater injury. Officers can use slightly more force to overcome the resistance offered, and should attempt to gain control in the fastest time possible with the least amount of injury being inflicted on the suspect.

Generally, response techniques are divided into two categories, lethal and less-lethal force. While the application of any technique has the potential to result in injury or death, lethal force techniques are generally more inclined to result in death or serious injury, and less-lethal force techniques are less likely to do so. Propensity toward injury is the defining factor that differentiates these two categories.

Officers should not only use force continua as guides for street confrontations, but also as guides in report writing. It is the officer's goal not only to survive the streets, but also to survive the courts. In the present litigious society, this is a sound premise to follow.

Verbal Tactics

Ask most officers what they use for verbal tactics and they'll look at you dumbfounded. Verbal tactics? Officers have a wide array of typical responses to stupid questions posed by stopped citizens. We've all done it at one time or another. When asked by a violator, "Well, does this mean you can meet your quota?" Our typical responses are, "We don't have a quota, we can write as many tickets as we want!" or "Yes, my daily quota is one and you are it." Cops know how to get even at the end of a stop by stating, "Have a nice day," with articulation placed on just the right syllables so that the driver knows exactly what we mean. And let's not forget about the professional language that many of us have used or still use, such as, "Do you know how fast you were going?" or "Do you know why I stopped you?" This may seem like a great verbal starting point, but what if the driver replies, "No, I do not, and if you don't know, why did you stop me?" In the minds of many officers, it is about coming out ahead personally in a verbal exchange. Who won? The emphasis should be placed on the professional nature of the contact, with sound verbal tactics that build the foundation for physical tactics if needed.

Deadly Force Considerations

Many instructors and texts recommend that when confronted with a firearm, the officer's best option is to "Draw . . . Shoot . . . Move." The emphasis is on drawing the weapon and firing. There are five things that can happen when an officer is shot at:

- The suspect's bullets miss.
- The officer is hit in the body armor.
- The "hits" are non-fatal.
- The "hits" are fatal, but the officer is still temporarily in the battle.
- The officer is fatally immobilized instantly, but their weapon may still fire at that instant because the message to shoot has already been routed from the brain to the muscles.

In all five circumstances, the officer is capable of returning fire and hitting the assailant.

The same five things can happen when a suspect is shot at. In all five circumstances, the suspect is capable of returning fire and hitting the officer. "Draw, Shoot" is a no-win situation for the officer, as the suspect has all the advantages. It is the suspect who initiates the action and the officer who has to respond. The author believes there is another alternative, "Move, Draw, Shoot and Move." These actions will quickly turn the tables, and place the ***officer*** in a position of tactical advantage.

Regardless of the officer's position when a stop is upgraded from a "low-risk" to a "high-risk" category, an officer should immediately take evasive action, ready their weapon, seek cover/concealment and prepare to utilize lethal force. The officer should move, draw, take appropriate action, and move again to a position of cover. Moving should be the officer's first and foremost concern. After reaching a position of cover, the officer should remain there and follow recommended procedures for conducting a "high-risk" vehicle stop. If lethal force is used and a suspect is "down," the officer should maintain a position of cover until assistance arrives.

A suspect electing to utilize deadly force against an officer who is making a "walk-up" approach to a vehicle will be in an initial position of tactical advantage. The suspect will have the advantage of concealment, cover, stationary position, target acquisition, timing and location of the assault. On the other hand, the officer must react to the suspect's actions while moving in an open area without cover, shooting stance, weapon in hand, etc. In order to react to the suspect's actions, the officer must mentally and physically complete four different cognitive functions: perceive, evaluate, decide and act. These steps can be recalled by remembering the acronym P.E.D.A.

- Perceive (the threat)
- Evaluate (intention and available delivery system)
- Decide (choose an appropriate tactical response)
- Act (or respond to the threat)

Why "Walk-Back" Patterns are Safer than "Walk-Up Patterns"

- Walk-back patterns keep the officer from approaching a violator they know nothing about.
- During "walk-up" patterns, the violator can easily detect the officer's location (hand and equipment positions), while the officer cannot view the violator's hands until contact is made at the violator's vehicle.
- A violator who plans to assault an officer is forced to revise or abandon his plan when an officer initiates a "walk-back" pattern.
- During a "walk-back" pattern, an officer only has to deal with the driver and not the other occupants.
- The officer is stationary and in a ready position prior to the violator's exit during a "walk-back" pattern, and the officer has some degree of cover available at all times.
- During a "walk-back" pattern, the officer can view the driver (and the driver's hands) at a distance prior to the initial interview, thus providing time to observe body language.
- The officer has immediate access to their cruiser in the event the violator flees during a "walk-back" pattern.
- The officer is less vulnerable and distracted by traffic during a "walk-back" pattern.
- In the event the violator initiates felonious assault against the officer, it is the violator who will be in an exposed position, and it is the violator who will have to be concerned with traffic if an officer is using "walk-back" patterns.

- "Walk-up" patterns have been killing police officers for years. Isn't it about time we try something more tactically effective?

When Risk Factors Change

Variables that May Change a "Low-Risk" Stop to an "Unknown-Risk" Stop

- Unusual movements by the occupant(s) in the vehicle (shoulder, head turning, slight or full opening of a door, back-up lights coming on, mirror adjustment, etc.).
- Additional information provided by dispatch or observation.
- Change in surroundings, i.e., an additional head pops up in the violator's vehicle, another vehicle pulls up, etc.
- Occupant's failure to comply with the officer's request (failure to show hands, etc.).
- Exiting the vehicle by the occupant(s) without a command to do so.
  Note: It is tactically acceptable to order an occupant back into a vehicle and then request that they exit the vehicle again at the officer's command.
- Additional vehicles (non-police) deploy in the immediate vicinity of the stop.
- Movement of the vehicle.
- Unusual driver action, such as opening vehicle door, exiting vehicle in an unusual manner, i.e., "butt first," etc.

Tactical Considerations

- Regardless of the officer's position when a stop is upgraded from a "Low-Risk" to an "Unknown-Risk" category, the officer should immediately attempt to make a tactical retreat to the recommended officer position for "Unknown-Risk" stops (behind an open cruiser door with weapon holstered, but ready).
- The position should be maintained and the officer should follow the recommended guidelines for conducting "Unknown-Risk" stops.

When "Low Risk" Changes to "High Risk"

An officer's initial assessment/evaluation of a "Low-Risk" stop may prove to be incorrect. When the assessment is upgraded to a "High-Risk" stop (based on new information, observations, felonious assault initiated by the occupant[s], etc.) after the officer has begun to approach the violator vehicle, the officer must immediately take evasive action. All evasive actions should ideally take the officer immediately out of the line of fire (felonious assault) and away from traffic (accidental assault).

Variables That May Change a Low-Risk" to a "High-Risk" Stop

- Unusual "weapon"-type movement by the occupant(s) in the vehicle (shoulder movement, head turning, slight opening of the door, back-up lights coming on, etc.).
- Visible weapon/weapon fire.
- Other unusual movements that might indicate a "High-Risk" situation, i.e., dispatch radio traffic indicating "armed and dangerous," etc.
- Vehicle movement (begins to flee, felonious assault on the officer with the violator vehicle, etc.).
- Occupant(s) failure to comply with the officer's request (fail to show hands, etc.).
- Exiting the vehicle by the occupant(s) without a command to do so, in a highly aggressive posture.
- Additional vehicles (non-police) deploy in the immediate vicinity of the stop with aggressive individuals.

Additional Guidelines

- If possible, take your time prior to initiating a stop. Follow the suspect's vehicle and set the stop up. Many times officers get in a hurry and feel they must make the stop immediately. Wait for back-up prior to making the stop, if possible, and always wait for back-up prior to making contact with the suspect(s). If the suspect crashes or stops, cover the vehicle from a low-profile position behind the open cruiser door with the weapon in the high-ready position until back-up arrives.
- Communicate directly to other units to organize the stop. If possible, go to a common radio frequency that is clear for your traffic only. The minimum units needed to safely effect a high-risk stop are two cruisers and four officers. If only 1-officer units are available, have two cruisers park behind and advance to the primary cruiser, thus creating two, 2-officer units.
- Position the cruisers to create a wall between the suspects and the officers. **Stay behind the wall at all times!**
- Remain behind cover in low-profile position at all times during the duration of the stop, with weapon in the high-ready position until all suspects are in custody. **Stay behind cover at all times**. The front wheel of both cruisers can be turned to assist in protecting the officers from low incoming rounds.
- Give loud and clear verbal commands of direction to the vehicle occupant(s). Verbally control the suspect's every action. Give short, loud, concise and clear verbal commands. Make sure they are told when to respond to a particular request ("now"), and to move slowly when doing so, as it is easier to detect and react to a sudden, quick movement when a suspect is moving slowly at the start. Ensure the suspect(s) understand the possible consequences of disobeying the officer's verbal challenges.
- Each officer has a job, and must stick to their area of responsibility in order to ensure that the team's plan is safe and successful.
- Verbally control all suspects' movements (car keys, hands, eyes, etc.) until all have been directed to exit one at a time, and physically controlled (handcuffed and searched). Direct all suspects to look forward and put their hands up or out the windows. Immediately get control over the car by directing the driver to place the keys out the window and onto the roof at this time.
- The officer with the best direct view of a suspect should give verbal commands and control that suspect.
- Utilize "Contact & Cover" principles: One

officer covers the suspect with their weapon while another controls, handcuffs and searches.

• Follow the "Stages of Arrest" in tactical order: Control, Handcuff, Search, Transport.

CONCLUSION

"To attack the enemy's plan," and "to subdue the enemy without fighting is the acme of the skill." These words were written in 500 B.C. in Sun Tzu's tactical manual, "The Art of War" (*Sun Tzu: The Art of War,* by Samuel Griffith, Oxford University Press), and even today provide a sound philosophy for good law enforcement tactics. As we are all aware, traffic stops are dangerous situations, and account for approximately 20 percent of officer fatalities annually. Any vehicle may contain a "little ol' lady" or a wanted felon, with officers usually working on sketchy information at best. If an officer's initial assessment indicates no "perceived threat" and the situation is actually felonious in nature, the officer will be placed in a disadvantageous position.

The "safest way" to conduct a traffic stop would be for the officer to maintain a shotgun at the "high ready" and order all occupants out face down, whereupon a traffic citation could be issued in relative safety by the officer's partner. Socially, this is obviously an unacceptable practice, but officers can still deploy other tactically sound techniques that can be adjusted to ever-changing situations and are acceptable to society.

The reason we lose during traffic stop battles is that we deploy in an expected manner. As a result, a suspect need only attack when the officer walks into the best position for them to do so. By interrupting the suspect's plans, we may surprise and subdue them before they can take aggressive action against us. Hopefully, this chapter has presented alternative procedures which are less predictable than those presently being utilized and, in the process, enhance officer safety.

RONALD M. McCARTHY

Ron McCarthy retired from the Los Angeles Police Department as a Sergeant after 25 years of service. During 14 years with "D" Platoon (SWAT) as a Squad Leader and Senior Supervisor, he was involved in several hundred SWAT operations. Mr. McCarthy continues to lecture extensively throughout the United States and a number of foreign countries on subjects ranging from SWAT operations and crowd and riot control, to use of force and counterterrorism.

Following retirement from the Los Angeles Police Department, Mr. McCarthy became the Chief of Tactical Operations for the U.S. Department of Energy Central Training Academy in Albuquerque, New Mexico. Subsequently, he accepted an offer to become the Manager of the Center For Advancing Police Studies for the International Association of Chiefs of Police. In 1990, he was appointed to the New York City Police Department Firearms Review Committee, and in 1993 was selected to participate in the evaluation of the F.B.I. operation at the Branch Davidian Compound near Waco, Texas. He testified before the U.S. Congress regarding this operation. Mr. McCarthy now operates a consulting firm, R.M. McCarthy & Associates, with offices in California and Arizona.

Ron is the co-author of *The Management of Police Specialized Tactical Units,* and the author of numerous law enforcement articles. He is a court-qualified expert witness on use of force/deadly force, SWAT, crowd and riot control, and police/private security practice. Mr. McCarthy is the recipient of the Los Angeles Police Department Medal of Valor, the Police Star and two Unit Citations, as well as numerous commendations. He is also the recipient of the National Tactical Officers Association (N.T.O.A.) Award of Excellence, the N.T.O.A. Lifetime Achievement Award, and the "All American Hero Award."

Chapter 11

BUILDING SEARCHES

Ronald M. McCarthy

INTRODUCTION

Although law enforcement officers most often search buildings for suspects, there are circumstances where the search may be for missing persons or contraband. This chapter will address the subject of searching buildings for suspects who are, or may be, armed, and may not only be attempting to evade arrest, but may also attack the officers to avoid arrest.

Generally, officers who train and work at being proficient in building searches should have an advantage over a hidden suspect who is prepared to attack an officer if discovered. However, this advantage will only hold true if the officer prepares to be proficient.

Most of the time, suspects have left the scene, and a careful search discloses this fact. Sometimes there is a tendency to assume the suspect has left the scene, creating the potential for a less-than-careful search. As officers move through a building and the suspect is not located, complacency can result. Incrementally, room by room, the officers begin to believe the suspect has, as in previous situations, left the scene. Then, a less-than-tactically sound entry into a room that has not been searched, or the opening of a closet door without good search and cover technique, creates the opportunity for the suspect to attack. The mindset of the officers must always be, "The suspect is, in fact, hidden here."

Each year, patrol and SWAT officers are attacked and killed by suspects because the tactics, techniques, and equipment that are available are not used. "He really is not here anymore," or "Let's get this over with because I don't like it in here," are attitudes that often create a vulnerability that give a felon with a weapon the opportunity to successfully attack an officer.

Officers can hurt each other if they are not well-schooled in sound and proven building search techniques. Old concepts often sound good, but are flawed. For example, "avoid crossfire hazards," has often been mentioned in training. If officers do not know where the suspect is hiding, it may be impossible to avoid a crossfire scenario in certain situations. Therefore, the solution to crossfire hazards is accuracy and identification of the target. Some search efforts can require several officers to be in close proximity to one another in a relatively confined space, making crossfire between officers an unavoidable circumstance. This almost always occurs in drug raids by narcotics officers and SWAT officers. Control and accuracy, as well as target identification, are the key components to avoid errors and potential tragedy.

Application of K-9s

When considering the advisability of searching a building, the first question to ask is, "Could a K-9 officer and his dog do this better and more safely?" Certainly, K-9s have abilities beyond those of police officers to find hidden suspects. Therefore, it is almost always preferable to use a K-9 unit when searching for hidden suspects. K-9 officers and their dogs are usually very well trained in searching for hidden suspects, either inside or outside. Generally, the K-9 handlers will ask for support for themselves and their dogs from on-scene patrol personnel. Ideally, the dog should enter first, followed by the K-9 officer. The patrol officers follow very close behind in support of the dog and the K-9 officer.

Putting a K-9 out in front is recommended, but is not a perfect solution. Based upon a number of circumstances, such as heating and cooling systems and the air movement and drafts these systems can create, a suspect's scent can be transferred to another area of the building. Officers can also become fixated on the movement of the dog instead of concentrating their focus on those areas where the suspect could be concealed.

Regardless of the search method, outside containment by officers is critical to the success of the situation, primarily for two reasons; (1) officer safety, and (2) containment of the suspect to ensure that the suspect does not leave the area without being seen and arrested. Diagonal containment is the most prevalent outside deployment, but some agencies give up one side of the building so that officers never leave each other's line of sight. The primary factor in safe containment is to deploy in such a position as to be so close to the building that a suspect inside cannot see the officers in order to target them. The second option is to deploy away from the building in positions where officers cannot be seen and targeted. Using the high-beam lights of the police cruiser and spotlights allows officers to move and deploy behind the lights. Using lights down the side of a building is also a way of reducing the likelihood that a suspect inside will exit into the glare of the lights. The first officer at the scene can use this technique to attempt to contain until back-up arrives.

Announcements

There is no legal requirement to announce your presence before entering a building in search of a suspect who is hiding from a lawful arrest, unless you are serving a search/arrest warrant and the state you are operating in requires a "knock and announce." Burglars are not homeowners and are not entitled to the protection of "search and seizure" laws in the building in which they are committing a crime. However, it can be advantageous to announce that you have the location contained and the suspects will not be harmed if they surrender. Although the author has never personally had a hidden suspect who was wanted for a crime surrender after such an announcement, some officers have had success with this approach.

Suspects and How They Think

Suspects who are trying to hide will usually go to the farthest location from where they entered, or from the location they think officers will enter. They will hide under things, inside things or on top of things. Suspects will expect you to enter from the "front" door, or the door they came in, if they used a door. If the suspect is going to set up on a location to attack the officer, these locations will usually be his first targets. Therefore, the primary entry point should be a location other than the front door, or the suspect's entry point, if possible.

Experts tell us that the great majority of criminals, about 90 percent, are sociopaths. Also, 98 percent of all sociopathic persons are male. The sociopath can be violent, and think spontaneously and selfishly. The sociopath does not mind inflicting pain upon others, but fears pain or the threat of serious injury to himself. Psychologists and professional negotiators tell us that the sociopath, when confronted with certain harm and reality, will be most likely to surrender. However, if an officer is alone and vulnerable, and the sociopath sees a "way out," an attack on the officer is likely.

Think of all the cop killers who have murdered officers and then escaped. Many have said they would never be taken alive or go back to prison. When officers with dominating tactical positions and firepower confront them, the suspects almost always surrender. An example of this is the "Texas Seven." After escaping from a Huntsville, Texas, State Prison, they robbed and murdered a Texas police officer. When they were located in Colorado, six surrendered and one committed suicide. The lesson here is obvious. The goal is to search buildings in a way that places the suspect in a position to be harmed, and minimizes the officer's exposure to danger. Officers usually receive some training in police academies regarding building searches. However, it is doubtful they receive continuing training in this area of police tactics.

If a suspect's intention is to ambush an officer, they will set up an anticipated situation. The suspect will point the muzzle of a gun at the middle of a doorway, chest high, or down the middle of a stairwell or hallway. If a suspect is in a closet and intends to attack, the suspect will hide behind the hanging clothes with the muzzle of the gun pointed chest high. If the searching officer stands in front of the closet and opens the door in the normal manner, the suspect will in all likelihood shoot and kill the officer. Almost always, if the suspect is hiding, armed, and intends to attack the officer, they will not do so if their environment is dominated and their safety threatened by armed officers deployed properly and in position to use deadly force. Often, when a suspect surrenders from a position of concealment, a weapon is found hidden in the hiding place. Obviously, if a suspect surrenders, the location should be carefully searched for discarded weapons.

Equipment

Methods of searching for suspects can vary, but the logic of having the right equipment is obvious. The use of lights will minimize the risk to searching officers because the intelligent use of lights and mirrors can virtually destroy a suspect's ability to successfully attack officers in building search situations.

Formerly SureFire, Laser Products Company, manufacturer of "SureFire" lights and "Streamlights," provide training for SWAT and patrol officers that increase officer safety and enhance the use of lights for tactical advantage. The combination of brighter lights, smaller and more portable lights, and light-mounted weapons have increased the margin of safety for officers. SWAT teams have long been aware of the advantage of light-mounted weapons. Every agency should do their best to provide all patrol officers with light-mounted pistols.

Mirrors are essential tools in trying to clear cramped areas and for seeing around corners. Many police officers have had the experience of suspects shooting a mirror when the mirror revealed their location. If the mirror had not been used, the officer's head would probably have been there instead. The problem for most officers is first, the availability of a mirror and second, the availability of a mirror that is large enough to allow them to be able to see and identify what they are looking at. (A small pocket mirror generally does not provide enough of a view to be relied upon.) Tactical Electronics, Inc. manufactures pole-mounted cameras that can locate suspects hiding in attics and crawl spaces, and Mesa Associated, Inc. can provide tracked robotics with cameras that transmit images back to officers in safe locations. Instrument Technology, Inc. and Search Systems also provide very good tactical search systems. Obviously, this equipment can be costly. However, one or two of these units in a supervisor's police vehicle, that can be called to the scene of a search when necessary, is certainly a reasonable expectation for officers who are at risk of injury or being killed by a hidden suspect. A handmade mirror, using a painter's aluminum pole, a one-foot square piece of plastic mirror, and a podium microphone stand from Radio Shack, will serve the same purpose and cost about $50 to make.

The ability to use equipment that officers carry on a regular basis can also aid in building searches. Using a side-handle baton to wedge a door open, or hobble restraints to tie a door closed can also be helpful. Using items available in a residence or business building you are searching should not be overlooked. Pushing furniture in front of doors or hallways to block a suspect's ability to move through is also an option. *Usually, if officers go slowly enough, these ideas are thought of and utilized.*

Entry into Buildings and Rooms

There are two primary entry techniques for doorways and entry into a building or room: (1) Staging, and (2) Stacking. There are other obvious tactical deployment problems when dealing with doors that open out, attic crawl spaces, or cellar and basement entry points. These problems will be covered later in the chapter.

Staging

Staging is the deployment of two or more officers on both sides of a door that opens in. For tactical reasons, it is a better deployment decision for the particular entry point. Once it is necessary to enter, the crisscross or crossover entry technique or the buttonhook technique are appropriate. This chapter deals with searching for hidden suspects, not high-risk warrant service or hostage rescue. In building searches for hidden suspects, there is no compelling reason for officers to move fast and give up a margin of safety.

It is not advisable to enter into a dark area that can conceal a hidden suspect. Therefore, it is recommended that officers turn on lights or, if there are no available light switches, use portable lights. For many years, fire departments have used 50,000- and 60,000-candle power lanterns that have adjustable heads to direct bright beams of light. These lanterns are rechargeable, and easily positioned into a dark room by using an expandable aluminum boat hook or pole to push and position the lights. Once the lights have been placed in position to see those areas that may conceal a hidden suspect, the second, and very possibly most important, item of equipment is inserted into our search plan–a tactical mirror. If we have the money, high-tech camera systems described earlier in this chapter are introduced. There are those who argue against the use of mirrors, believing their use is clumsy and slow. Officers have been shot by suspects who were hiding that would have been discovered with the use of a mirror. Often, suspects will hide under piles of blankets, sheets and pillows, or in closets under and behind clothes. The mirror will disclose a mass of clothes or bedding. With the mirror focused on the mass, another officer should use a boat hook or pole to pull away the concealment to uncover the suspect who may be hidden there. The Los Angeles Police Department's SWAT teams have used mirrors for more than thirty years with great success, even though they have had suspects shoot at their mirrors. This begs the question, what would be the target without the mirror?

Working behind lights and using high-intensity lights to create barriers of blinding light that suspects are likely to avoid or cross, is easily taught. Obviously, it is recommended that lights and mirrors be used prior to entering a building or room, or searching closets, crawl spaces, attics, and behind basement stairways.

Stacking

Stacking at an entry point is the positioning of officers in a line on one side of the door, usually the hinged side of the door. This affords the first officer the first and usually best immediate view of a room when the door is opened. Here again, the use of a mirror and lights is recommended. Once this has been accomplished, the first officer would enter, moving quickly across the doorway and into the room. The second officer would enter immediately behind the first officer so as to cover the first officer's back. Both officers should clear the doorway and then begin to slow down and, if reasonable, stop and study the area before going farther. It is absolutely essential that both officers enter simultaneously so that both can cover each other's backs. Both officers **must** clear the deep corners to the left and right of the doorway entrance before being distracted by any other circumstances in the room. If the luxury of more officers is available, and additional officers are needed to search more safely, the additional officers should be called into play by the primary handling officer or supervisor at the scene.

There are a variety of entry techniques that can be added to the crossover or buttonhook. Again, equipment is an issue. Ballistic shields can be a great resource if they are used properly and to the best advantage of searching officers. A ballistic shield is more than a position. While cover is its primary role, it should also be considered as a moveable fighting position that gives officers using it "a place to fight from, not a place to hide behind." The ballistic shield should be used to protect more than just the officer carrying the shield. There are two distinctly different philosophies regarding the deployment of the shield: (1) the "shield officer" carries the shield and has a pistol in their weapons-side hand and is the first in and primary shooter; (2) as an alternative, the "shield officer" provides cover for the team and manipulates the shield, but with no weapons responsibility. Experienced trainers teach both options, because there are positive and negative issues to each. What is consistent with the shield is that only the "shield officer" can see forward, and the view is very limited due to the window in the shield creating tunnel vision. The remaining team members cannot see what is ahead unless they can see around the team members in front of them and around the shield.

Unless the suspect is out in front more than five or six feet, entry into a house or an apartment with small rooms can create a vision problem from the view port in the shield downward to the floor. Because of the small space, the proximity of the suspect may be too close.

The issue of the shield is critical for patrol officers, who may be provided with little or no training time and yet must manipulate the shield and a pistol at the same time. It is highly unlikely that accuracy will result when a shield is being carried in the support hand and a sight picture is being attempted through a view port. The author has never seen consistent accuracy from officers using the shield and a pistol. The goal of an officer in a life-threatening confrontation with an armed suspect is always accurate rounds fired rapidly (a pair in less than 1.5 seconds to end the threat).

Doors and Entry Points

It is important to reiterate that the suspect expects you to use the front door to enter, and will anticipate your appearing in a doorway or hallway.

Time can be, and often is, our enemy. Becoming impatient or complacent because we haven't found a suspect through most of our search is natural, and you must avoid succumbing to this natural human tendency. You should take the time required to enter a building through the "smart" entry point, as opposed to the front door. You should wait until you have appropriate back-up, even if you have to request back-up from another agency.

Once you have a partner, a brief but complete discussion of an entry plan should take place. If the owner of the building or alarm company cannot provide keys to facilitate entry, are you trained to force the door? Do you have the correct tool to

force the door? When a door is forced open, or "booted," no officer should be in front of it as it flies open. Once it is open, no entry should be made until the room is viewed from the outside by "mirroring" the room and/or "pieing" the doorway slowly with the use of well-placed high-intensity lights. If it is not possible to accomplish a good "clear" from the outside, another entry point should be considered.

Booting or kicking doors is an art, and is rarely done enough to create expertise on the part of patrol officers. Narcotics officers and SWAT officers do more of this than anyone, and they all have stories of comical and sometimes costly failures when booting doors. Injuries from officers kicking very substantial, heavy doors, as well as old or fragile doors, often occur. Getting your leg stuck in a door you have kicked a hole through can be embarrassing, painful, and life threatening.

Shooting Positions–What Works?

While searching for suspects, it is of great importance to be able to shoot accurately and rapidly when necessary. Therefore, it is important to be in a good shooting position as much as possible. When entering a room, you should move only as fast as you can shoot accurately.

Your weapon should be at a "low-ready," or about a 45-degree angle. High-ready is often used, and has an obvious weakness: officers cannot see what is right in front of them. Using this position, an officer can only see long-range threats over the sight radius of the weapon. A shoulder weapon should be maintained with the stock of the weapon in the shoulder position and the muzzle of the weapon at a 45-degree angle, or "low-ready." Officers entering the room should be in an upright, ready-to-shoot position as they go through the door.

Entering a door using the "high/low" entry is a popular alternative to the upright entry. The advantage of the "high/low" entry is that both officers enter simultaneously, as opposed to a slight half-second or so delay before the second officer enters. The disadvantage to this technique is that, (1) we rarely practice shooting from a moving, squatting body position, so we lose accuracy, and (2) the officer going low can be startled by something, and unintentionally block the "high" officer's line of fire. Unfortunately, in one case, this resulted in an officer shooting another in the back of the head.

When a minimum number of officers is available to search a building, a problem often occurs when the search reaches a hallway with three or four doorways, with doors either opened or closed. The first rule in this situation is to slow down and think. One solution to this problem may be to stop searching in this direction, holding the area already cleared with one officer, and using lights tactically positioned to deny movement into the cleared area by the suspect. Then, remaining officers should exit the building and enter through another entry point. Once the same problem area is reached, the new direction of search may provide a different tactical problem that may be easier to deal with than the original position.

Opening and closing doors and moving high-intensity lights is also a tactical option. If any officer moves into a doorway, or across a doorway that has not been in some way tactically prepared for that movement, it is a serious and potentially deadly tactical mistake.

Recently, in a southwest city, a search was conducted for a barricaded suspect. The suspect had fired shots, so there was no doubt that he was armed and dangerous. Chemical agents had been used with no effect, and the decision was made for the police to locate and arrest him. Upon entry, three officers were focused toward the area of the single-story residence where they thought the suspect was located. Two other officers moved toward another area of the house, working down a hallway where three rooms were located. Two doorways were on the left side of the hallway and one doorway was at the end of the hallway. The officers quickly entered the first two rooms, and just as quickly, cleared them by entering, scanning the room after entering, yelling, "Clear," and exiting back into the hallway, then moving toward the doorway at the end of the hallway. Unknown to the lead officer, the suspect had set up in the bedroom closet with the closet door open. He was seated or kneeling in the closet with his handgun pointed at the area he expected to see the officer appear. As the lead officer moved into the room, it was darker than it was outside. The suspect was to the extreme left of the officer as he

entered. The officer did not have a light-mounted weapon and there had been no effort to use a mirror or other device to clear the far left portion of the room. The lead officer was shot by the concealed suspect and died almost immediately. The suspect later surrendered, unhurt. Tactics that have been in place for thirty years could have prevented this incident from happening. However, the question is, "Why is it more than 90 percent of patrol officers in the United States do not have light-mounted pistols, shotguns and rifles?" There is no question that this equipment is "safety equipment," and should be provided by their agencies. Some agencies already allow their patrol officers to carry light-mounted pistols, and others are slowly following suit. There is a long-held axiom that, "high-tech equipment does not make the cop proficient." While this is true, failure to provide basic contemporary equipment can defeat a good cop. *The spouses and families of dead officers are becoming more and more aware of the fact that their husbands and loved ones have been killed because their departments have failed to provide appropriate equipment and/or training. This knowledge has and will undoubtedly continue to result in legal action.*

You Have Located the Hidden Suspect–What Now?

Let us assume that we have carefully moved, covered our movement, and have either seen or heard the suspect. We know where he is hiding. The suspect should not be verbally addressed until all officers involved in the search are notified. This should be done without alerting the suspect to the fact that he has been discovered. A good general way of accomplishing this communication is to audibly tap your hand to some part of your body three times, a hand slap to a leg or your chest that other team members are able to hear. They, in turn, should be trained that those three slaps mean stop and look at the officer signaling. Once their attention is on the officer who knows where the suspect is located, that officer extends his hand, with fingers spread and thumb up, straight out in the direction of the suspect. Now that the officers have been alerted, every officer moves to a tactical position that is away from where the suspect will appear if he intends to surrender or attack. Lights are placed to create a tactical advantage for officers and loss of visual acuity on the part of the suspect. When every officer has a solid cover or concealed position, the officer who first located the suspect should begin verbalizing with him.

Without screaming or yelling loudly, the suspect should be told that he has been located and must follow all instructions. The suspect should then be assured that, if he does what he is told, he will not be harmed. He should be told to drop all weapons and walk backward into view of the officers. This should be followed with, "Do it now!" said very loudly. The suspect should be directed to continue walking backward slowly, to a predesignated spot where, if possible, at least two officers can control him after he is proned out. Once handcuffed, the suspect should be removed from the building and the search continued, always assuming an unknown suspect is still at large in the location.

Much is made of verbalization. Verbal skills used by the right officer in the right way in the right situation will usually create the best outcome. *The key word here is* **usually**—*"will* **usually** *create the best outcome, but not, unfortunately, always."* Domination of the house, the room, and eventually the suspect, with the use of lights, quick communications (hand signals) and invisible deployment will more likely result in the suspect's surrender.

If a suspect is located, but refuses to surrender, this should be considered a barricade situation and SWAT should be called to the scene. The suspect should be contained, and no part of the controlled area given up. Once SWAT arrives, they will appreciate the fact that you kept the problem contained to the smallest area possible. Pre-positioning furniture to create a barrier the suspect must overcome to reach officers is desirable. However, there should be a clear path to officers designated as the arrest team available to the suspect. If a SWAT team is not available, the use of chemical agents is usually the best option to dislodge a resisting suspect. Officers should assume positions as far away as possible, but within the contained area. A less-lethal 37mm, 40mm or M26 TASER should be in position prior to introducing chemical agents. The suspect may "explode" from his location upon the introduction of chemical agents, hence the reason for earlier creating space between the suspect and officers. It is

virtually impossible to avoid crossfire, so only one or two designated shooters should be in place to use deadly force, if necessary. Certainly, protective masks are to be worn by officers prior to the use of chemical agents.

Worst-Case Scenario– OFFICER DOWN!

The author believes that if officers are well trained, it is highly unlikely that an officer will be shot as a result of a building search. For many years, there has been a standing rule for SWAT teams, "Thou shall never leave a fellow officer down in a field of fire." There is also a tactical rule for a downed officer in a suspect's field of fire. When an officer goes down, the closest officer yells, "Officer Down! Officer Down!," and then directs accurate gunfire at the suspect. The next closest officer moves to the downed officer and drags the downed officer to safety. This contingency plan should be rehearsed whenever officers are training to conduct building searches.

There is a very good reason why the police should always come out on top in building search situations. Officers train to search buildings, while suspects seldom train to do more than hide. Also, suspects usually do not train to establish tactical moves to defeat officers who are searching for them. They very well may train to shoot accurately, but not in how to destroy the advantage officers gain by using high-intensity lights or to avoid an eight-foot pole mirror. Officers should be tactically skilled to move, uncover, and apprehend suspects.

Deploying at Difficult Locations During Building Searches

Sub-Floors and Crawl Holes Under Houses

When a suspect is believed to have crawled into a crawl hole and under the floor of the house (mobile homes and houses in warm climates often have raised floors), the first thought should be the use of a K-9. There usually will be some physical evidence at the entry point. If no K-9 is available, or if the suspect is believed to be armed, chemical agents may be considered.

If a physical entry and search are deemed necessary, the following method has been used successfully:

1. The suspect will probably be on the opposite end from the crawl hole he entered. Place high-intensity lights at other crawl spaces away from the area the suspect entered.
2. Place a cardboard target back over the crawl hole where the suspect entered (this is where you will enter).
3. Place a blanket over the cardboard. The first officer to enter crawls under the blanket while the cardboard is in place.
4. Remove the cardboard. Now the officer can crawl in without being seen. The reason the suspect cannot hear the officer is that the low ceiling under the sub-floor literally baffles and absorbs sound. A caution here is that the officer cannot hear the suspect either. Once the first officer is in and moves away from the crawl hole, the cardboard is replaced. The second officer crawls under the blanket, the cardboard is removed, and the second officer enters the crawl hole, unseen by the suspect. This is repeated until the appropriate number of officers are under the structure in a line, ready to slowly crawl forward in search of the suspect(s).
5. The officer under the house can communicate by radio to officers outside to move lights and/or turn lights on or off when needed by shining the lights in through the crawl holes located around the base of the structure. The suspect could be hiding behind a floor furnace or a floor support, and may even dig a shallow hiding place in the dirt. Once the suspect is located, he should not be approached, but should be directed to crawl to a crawl hole where officers outside will take him into custody.

False Ceilings

Suspended ceilings that are usually found in office and business buildings offer a suspect a quick and invisible hiding place. A suspect can stand on a desk or file cabinet and lift one of the lightweight acoustical tiles that make up the ceiling. He can then locate a pipe or ledge, drop the tile back into place, and move to the preselected area. At this point, he can climb through the suspended ceiling onto the pipe or ledge, and replace the ceiling tile behind him. When searching an office or business, look for evidence of shoe prints on desktops or file cabinets, possibly indicating that a suspect may have climbed up into the false ceiling. A piece of furniture moved to an out-of-place position could indicate the same thing. Certainly a good K-9 can help find the suspect, and a pole mirror or search camera will also be of value. If this is not possible, one officer should move away from the officer who is going to look up into the false ceiling and create a distraction, such as removing a ceiling tile and shining a light through without exposing any part of their body. If the suspect is a shooter, he will focus on this distraction, enabling the search officer to "quick peek" the area.

Elevators and Elevator Shafts

One of the easier hiding places to access is an elevator or elevator shaft. The suspect can enter the elevator, use the ceiling hatch (most building codes require elevators to have a ceiling hatch), climb through the hatch and replace the cover. The suspect will often sit on the hatch cover to create the thought that it is a non-removable hatch and, therefore, no one could be hiding there. The suspect can also jump to an adjoining shaft, using the cables, and go to the bottom of the shaft by sliding down the cables. Here again, a K-9 can almost always locate the suspect.

Trash Containers and Shelves

Large trash containers usually found in businesses can create a hiding place for a suspect. Suspects can also climb to the highest shelves in business and warehouse environments and hide under and behind products and items that are stacked on the shelves.

Are Burglars Violent? YES!

Many businesses keep guns in the office area.

When a business has been burglarized and the office ransacked, it is a distinct possibility the suspect may now be armed. Many burglars go to the target armed. The old-time burglar who engaged in burglary because he did not want to commit a violent crime is virtually nonexistent today. Many officers have been attacked and killed by burglars. The author knows of six officers from his former department who were murdered by burglary suspects.

The very definition of the crime of burglary should be a warning to officers. The suspect is entering to commit theft or some other felony. That theft or other intended felony can have a variety of actions. Some of these actions are in and of themselves violent crimes, rape being but one example. Burglars are dangerous! Burglars do kill!

CONCLUSION

It is recognized that there are officers in different parts of the United States who have to search without back-up. For example, there are Alaska State Troopers whose closest back-up is more than 1,000 miles away. Therefore, lone officers are often forced to search a structure or area without assistance. Officers searching without back-up must follow the guidelines previously discussed in this chapter relating to slow movement, use of lights and mirrors, and anticipating those areas where a suspect may be hiding and from which they may attack. A lone officer may consider using private persons to assist, just as officers sometimes resource them to help lay down flare patterns when necessary at the scene of traffic accidents. *Note: There can be a problem with using private persons. Obviously, they are not trained police officers, and as a result, liability can accrue on the part of the agency should they be injured.*

It is not always possible to guarantee a perfectly safe tactical environment, but using common sense, preparation through training, and selective use of available lights and equipment, including K-9s, will reduce considerably the potential of a successful attack on an officer.

Part 4

PATROL RESPONSE TO CRITICAL INCIDENTS

MICHAEL G. WARGO

Michael G. Wargo is a 30-year veteran of law enforcement and retired from the Illinois State Police after nearly 28 years. Previously, he spent two years with the Lake County (IN) Police Department. His investigative assignments included the areas of narcotics, white-collar crime and crimes against persons. The last six years of his career were spent investigating terrorist incidents. He was a crisis negotiator for more than 19 years, and spent the last six years as the CNT team leader for the northern third of Illinois. Mr. Wargo is a past president of the Illinois Tactical Officers Association and the author of numerous articles on crisis negotiations.

Chapter 12

FIRST RESPONSE TO A HOSTAGE/ BARRICADE/SUICIDE INCIDENT

Michael G. Wargo

The first response to a hostage/barricade/suicide incident is a critical part of the overall police response. The first officer responding to the scene will set the tone for the entire police response. If the first responding officer doesn't get the job done, no one will get the chance to perform their function(s)– not the highly trained and equipped tactical team, not the negotiators who work together as a team and not the command personnel who are up to date on the latest command and control techniques.

The number one priority for the first responding officer is self-protection. The initial moments of a critical incident are filled with sensory stimuli for the officer. A million thoughts will be going through their mind. Sometimes, officer survival techniques will fall by the wayside and an officer gets hurt. That becomes a dilemma for the other responding officers, who will have the rescue of the downed officer as their number one priority. Energy and assets that could be better utilized in resolving the incident will have to be diverted to officer rescue.

Another area where officers are frequently hurt is rushing into the location in an attempt to resolve the incident quickly. This act is a function of the way some officers are trained, both at the police academy and on the job at the police department. Officers are trained and instructed to respond to their calls, get in and handle them as quickly and efficiently as possible, in order to get to the next call or back on patrol. Rushing in can be deadly for the officer. Consider the mindset of the suspect. They are in an unknown situation, don't know what is going to happen next and, as a result, may be nervous and anxious. The suspect will probably resort to instinct, the strongest of which is survival. An officer rushing in is a threat to that survival, and the suspect will act instinctively. It is far better in situations such as this to back away, contain, observe and get the resources necessary to handle the problem.

The next order of business is containment. The first responding officer needs to ensure that the situation is contained to the smallest area possible. This will enable others to bring physical and psychological pressure on the suspect. If the suspect can be contained to a point where there is no access to food, water and sanitary facilities, the police can force them to bargain for even the most basic human needs. On the other hand, if containment is not tight, there is a good chance that the suspect can escape from the area, leaving the police to look foolish laying siege to an empty building. Even if the suspect does not escape from the crisis point, the incident will last much longer, because the suspect has free rein to move wherever they want (within certain restrictions), and has access to those items which can provide comfort during the siege.

In order to accomplish the containment goal, the first responding officers should begin to set up an inner and an outer perimeter. The inner perimeter is designed to keep the situation contained. It should be as close as possible to the specific crisis point, the hostage-taker and captives. The officer should take a position of cover, and make sure that anyone who comes out of the crisis point is detained until their identity and part in the incident can be ascertained. Hopefully, more officers will arrive quickly and establish a good, tight inner perimeter as soon as possible. Invisible deployment is often best, effectively using cover so as not to give one's position away. Some situations may call for a higher profile deployment as part of the psychological side of law enforcement's response.

As if the first officer on the scene does not have enough to do, they must also advise other responding officers of the safest routes to the scene and suggested locations to set up their positions once they get there. The first responding officer is the only police officer in a position to do so, since they have "eyes on" the scene of the incident, as well as necessary information to make these decisions. The safety of other responding officers depends on the judgment and communications from the first officer. Additional information should include the fields of fire available to the suspect(s) and their weapons capabilities, if known. This will help other responding officers choose appropriate cover. All real or perceived dangers should be reported.

Once the inner perimeter is in place, responding officers must set up an outer perimeter. This is designed to keep anyone not involved in the incident out of the area. It should be done in a manner that will provide the minimal disruption possible in the area involved. The control of the area would include both vehicular and pedestrian traffic. This process is manpower-intensive, in that these incidents attract a considerable amount of attention from both the media and the public. As word of the incident spreads, curious onlookers will flock to the scene. It is incumbent upon first responding officers to keep these persons away from the scene–for their own safety, as well as the quality of the police response.

Once the perimeters are set, and before the tactical team gets into position, responding officers should begin to evacuate those who are near the scene and potentially in harm's way. All non-involved personnel must be evacuated out of the area and care taken to secure them along a safe route. Officers must also realize that they cannot order a person to leave their home. If they do come

across someone who refuses to leave their home, the officer should instruct them to remain in a part of their home farthest from the crisis point, so the home's structure will offer maximum protection from danger. The officers should document their actions, including the refusal on the part of the occupants to leave their home. Anyone choosing to remain in their home should be advised that they should not attempt to leave or interfere with police operations at the scene, and, if they do, they are subject to arrest and prosecution. Such a warning, when issued, should be enforced, or it will become meaningless in the future. In some instances, evacuations will not be practical because they may put the evacuees and officers in harm's way. Officers should seek alternate means for communicating with these people in the interest of their safety and welfare. Possible means of communication might include phone calls or using the media to advise them of their safest course of action.

Once additional officers have arrived and secured the perimeters, the situation usually stabilizes. It is at this point that the suspect often calls out, looking for someone to talk to. This may take the form of someone shouting out from inside the crisis location, or a phone call into the 911 center. Should one of the first responding officers or the 911 operator begin to engage in dialogue, or should they wait until the negotiation team arrives? The answer to this question is the answer to all questions involving crisis management. "It depends." If there is a possibility of waiting until all the parts are in place, it is best to wait until an arrest team and emergency action team have been designated and are in place prior to initial verbal contact. The suspect may decide to come out, and someone should be in place, with a plan, to receive them. On the rare occasion something goes terribly wrong at first contact (shots fired inside), there should be a team in place for an emergency response, if necessary. Sometimes there will not be a choice about communicating. Bad things may be threatened or occurring, and the best course of action will be to start communicating with the suspect(s) in hopes of keeping them occupied and diverted from harmful actions. This is a concept known as "Verbal Containment." The suspect, while engaged in conversation with the officer, is kept busy, and other options can be presented to the suspect.

Choosing the officer who will be doing the communicating is an important decision. The initial conversation with the offender is probably going to be unpleasant. Personal attacks on the officer and the officer's family (who the suspect does not know) will abound during the initial moments of dialogue due to the high level of emotions and anxiety on the part of the suspect. An officer who cannot remain cool amidst such attacks, and would likely respond in kind, should not be chosen to begin communication with the suspect. If, on the other hand, there is an officer at the scene who will not overreact to such a verbal attack, they should be the one chosen to talk to the suspect. The officer chosen should be a good communicator, with emphasis placed on the listening portion of communication. Usually, the first communicator should not be a supervisor. Although supervisors usually have more experience in dealing with people in crisis, it is the supervisor's job to oversee the operation, to "supervise."

If the initial suspect contact comes in the form of a call to the 911 center, then of course someone should talk to them. Proactive law enforcement agencies are providing crisis communications classes for their 911 operators for just such emergencies. The 911 center has the option of continuing to communicate or forwarding the call to someone at the scene.

Once the choice has been made to initiate dialogue, all officers within earshot of the crisis point should be aware of the primary rule. This rule is that only one officer will communicate with the suspect. If the suspect realizes that they can talk to multiple officers, they have gained a great deal of momentum in the communication dynamic. If the suspect doesn't like what they hear from officer number one, they can seek a better deal with officer number two. They could then conceivably go from officer to officer to obtain the most favorable deal. In doing so, the suspect plays all the officers against each other. As a result, there will be no positive agreement to come out of the negotiation process for the police. If there is a possibility of this occurring, the first responding officer should sit tight and not initiate dialogue with the suspect.

The first officer to speak to the suspect should understand their mindset and mental and emotional condition. Anxiety, the fear of the unknown, is building and this is causing an increase in the suspect's emotional level. At this point, the rationality level is very low, as a result of the high emotional level. The suspect is not problem-solving well, is not considering options and not putting whatever is troubling them in the proper context. Now is the time for logical argument on behalf of the officer.

The first order of business is to lower the emotional level of the suspect. This is often a slow and sometimes emotionally painful process for the officers. The ventilation process includes allowing the suspect to rant, rave, yell and scream. For the officer, these rantings usually come in the form of personal attacks on the officer. The response to these personal attacks is for the officer to simply take it. These are times when the suspect is highly energized, and these attacks can last for hours. It takes a great deal of discipline to withstand several hours of constant vitriolic harangues and not to respond to them. If successful, however, many good things can be realized. The lowering of the emotional level of the suspect will bring about an increase in the rationality level. At some point, the rationality level is raised to the point where problem-solving skills increase. Once this point is reached, the suspect will not only make better decisions, but begin to see there are consequences associated with their acts. A word of caution here is appropriate. Ventilation may have to be done several times, especially if negotiations are lengthy. The officer/negotiator should not relax after the initial ventilation. At various times during the process, the suspect's emotional level may again rise to the initial level. This could occur any number of times during the negotiation process. Officers who undertake the task of negotiation must realize this and not succumb to the temptation of frustration when it occurs. If the officer becomes frustrated, there is a tendency to push too hard to solve the problem, and this might cause them to lose credibility with the suspect, requiring other officers to start the process over from a diminished bargaining position.

The concept of ventilation before problem-solving is something that does not come naturally for the police. Police officers are, by nature, problem-solvers. They go into a situation, gather data, make a decision and implement the solution. The officer then moves on to their next call. Officers have been trained and encouraged to operate this way. It is alien to many officers who have not been trained in crisis negotiations techniques to buy time and stretch out an incident to allow ventilation and problem-solving on behalf of the suspect. If officers are expected to deal with these types of incidents, they must have the training to know what to expect.

Just listening to the person may pay dividends in the long run. Often, they want to tell their story. One of their problems may be that no one ever listens to them. Listening to someone tells the person you respect them as an individual, and this may help establish a working relationship. Listening will also provide all types of intelligence. You will hear their mental state, emotions, intentions and possibly what it will take to resolve the problem. Listening also allows for the passage of time. Time for officers to plan and time to research intelligence. With the passage of time, emotions may come down naturally.

Once more officers arrive at the scene, the first responding officer(s) must ascertain what type of situation they are dealing with. This is important because the three types of incidents, hostage taking, barricaded suspect and suicidal subject/suspect, will all bring a distinctively different set of skills into play.

Regardless of the type of incident the officer confronts, the first rule for an officer considering the decision to communicate is to remain calm. Everything the officer does, from voice quality to body language, should send the message of the image they wish to project. That image should be one of the officer being calm and in control. The officer and the entire police department cannot control the situation. They are in a reactive mode. The only element the officer can control is their own reaction to whatever happens. If this control is not present, there is very little hope of positive resolution through negotiation.

A hostage situation occurs when one or more persons are being held by one or more persons against their will. In these cases, the hostages are held pending the fulfillment of certain terms. In hostage takings, the authorities have something the suspect wants. It may be escape, money, transportation or some other specific item the authorities

can provide the hostage taker. Captives are held as security for these demands. The response by the police in these types of situations is a straightforward bargaining position. There is give and take. Demands are made, compromises are suggested and agreed to, and a deal is struck. Remember that all decisions must be cleared through the command post. Once this is accomplished and an agreement is reached, the only matter left to be cleared up is to implement the terms that have been agreed to by both parties. While this may not always go quickly and efficiently, there is always some hesitation at the last minute. The implementation of the agreement is usually the easiest part of the incident. Other officers at the scene can help or hurt the negotiation process. In hostage takings, officers at the scene who are handling containment duties, should utilize highly visible containment techniques to send a message to the suspect that the imminent use of force is always an option for the police. Such a posture very forcefully encourages the hostage taker to compromise and come to an agreement for their own safety.

The second group who take captives is a little more difficult to deal with. These are people who are undergoing some type of emotional crisis. To these people, the police and other authorities don't really have anything they want. Often, the first communication with the police is to tell them (police) that they are not needed there and they should just go away. Of course, the police response to such a statement is that they have been called to the location and can't go away until they are sure that everyone at the residence is not injured. The suspect often assures the police that everyone is OK and that nobody has been hurt. At that juncture, the officer is left with the ploy that they believe the suspect, but the officer's boss requires that everyone come out of the location and be seen. In most cases, the suspect will then proceed to make some negative comments about the officer's boss, but will continue the dialogue. These situations often involve the forcible detention of one or more persons against their will. In the strict sense of the term, however, this type of incident is not a hostage situation, and the captives are not hostages. In the vast majority of these incidents, the suspect and captive(s) have a relationship. It may be a spousal relationship, or at least something beyond a casual relationship. The purpose here, unlike a strict hostage situation, is not to persuade someone on the outside to do something for them, but to persuade someone on the inside to do something. This often requires the captive to do nothing more than listen to what the suspect has to say. The captives are not hostages, they are victims, or more accurately victims-to-be. Chances are that, at some point, there will be a threat to harm all or some of the captives. These are incidents that too often result in the killing of the captives and the suicide of the suspect, or the release of the captives and the suicide of the suspect. Both are losing situations from the police perspective.

What is the first responding officer(s) to do in such situations? The answer to this problem is not the bargaining tactics of hostage negotiation, but the techniques of crisis negotiation. One of the main elements of crisis negotiation is a technique known as active listening. The seven skills of active listening are as follows:

- Emotion Labeling
- Paraphrasing
- Reflecting/Mirroring
- Effective Pauses (Silence)
- Minimal Encouragers
- "I" Messages
- Open-Ended Questions

Of these skills, emotion labeling is the primary initial tactic for the first responding officer to use. In doing so, the officer/negotiator tells the person how they "seem" or how they "sound" to the officer. They do not tell the person how the person feels, because they really don't know how they feel. However, they can express the feelings from their (the officer's) perspective. This technique is very powerful and appropriate. Emotion labeling serves several purposes. One, it allows the person to ventilate excess emotions, as previously described. Two, emotion labeling allows the person to tell their story to someone who will listen to them in an uncritical way. Very often, this is the one thing they want more than anything. Sometimes, the situation will end properly after the person has had an opportunity to say whatever it is they wish to say. In con-

trast to a hostage situation, barricaded suspect incidents with people who are in crisis require a bit more finesse as far as containment is concerned. Officers on containment duty in these types of situations should practice invisible deployment at the scene, especially those officers who are assigned to the inner perimeter closest to the crisis point and the suspect. A strong and visible use of force sends the wrong message to this type of suspect. It raises the level of emotion and anxiety, and makes the situation as a whole much more volatile and dangerous for everyone involved.

The person who is suicidal also presents a group of distinct challenges. Not only do the police face an individual who is in crisis, but add to this a mindset where they do not care if they survive the incident and, in many cases, prefer not to survive it. Ambivalence is often present, with the person "sitting on a fence," unsure of which way to fall. In other types of cases, the police have the advantage in that they always have the imminent use of force at their disposal. Such is not the case with a suicidal person. They can disobey police commands or instructions with impunity. There is no fear of punishment or retribution if they disobey. Again, crisis intervention skills and active listening come into play. In addition, officers who are communicating with them need to show a considerable level of empathy. Empathy is a communications technique wherein the officer/negotiator sends the message that they understand what the person is saying, both in word and deed. It does not say or imply that the officer agrees or disagrees. Unlike sympathy, which implies pity and overcommitment, empathy sends a different message. It only says, "I understand how a person in this type of situation might feel." If this sentiment can be communicated successfully, the officer/negotiator will be successful in a vast majority of the cases they handle.

A phenomenon that appears to be on the rise is "Suicide by Cop." In these instances, a person wants to die, but does not have the courage to do the deed themselves. Instead, the person seeks to put the police in a situation where they will have to kill them, and be legally justified in doing so. There will be no indicators as to what they want to do. They won't talk about the future and will indicate that they want to "go out big," so that people will remember them. Often, these individuals will brandish weapons in some manner, so as to give the officers the legal right to defend themselves from the threat. In this way, the person gets what they want, namely to be killed, but they don't have to do it themselves. The officer who is going to take the shot is engaged in a legal act. Sometimes, after the person has expired, investigations reveal an unloaded, inoperative or toy weapon was used to threaten officers when the fatal shot was taken. Legally, of course, the officer was justified, but psychologically, the officer often pays a heavy toll. Recent studies into "Suicide by Cop" have shown a willingness on the part of some to use operable and loaded firearms in these types of incidents, and they will shoot at or assault officers to get the end result they desire, which is death. There are two "victims" in a "Suicide-by-Cop" incident, the person who wanted to commit suicide, and the officer who was used to accomplish this end. As with the barricaded suspect, officers involved with containment should take a low-key, invisible approach. Having the person see them can only serve to make a bad situation even worse.

If they wish to surrender to one of the first responding officers, a critical point has been reached. This is not the time for the officer/negotiator to relax and declare victory, even in their own mind. Hopefully, some type of surrender plan has been discussed by the arrest team and this information passed on to the officer negotiator. A good plan has safety and control as its prime considerations. A good surrender plan also has some flexibility built into it. The plan can be discussed with the suspect and modified if necessary. Sometimes they will not know how to surrender, and it will be up to the officer to suggest a plan that is safe for all. The surrender plan should be clearly understood by all parties. This is not a time for mistakes or misunderstandings. The surrender is a critical part of the resolution of the incident. It is also one of the most dangerous parts of the incident for all involved. None of the officers involved should leave their position of cover until the suspect is in a vulnerable position. Verbal commands should be kept simple. The officer/negotiator should realize that this is a very tense time for the suspect. Reassurances should be provided that they will not be shot or roughed up when

they come out. The suspect is leaving a position of safety and moving into a strange area that is potentially very dangerous for them. The officer/negotiator should take these steps very slowly, and not lose patience. Additionally, when the suspect does what the officer/negotiator instructs him to do, the officer should positively reinforce this behavior by thanking and reassuring them. The officer should realize that surrender is a major decision for the suspect, and that slow and deliberate movement is the preferred rate of action. In some cases, the suspect may want to surrender to the officer/negotiator in person. The officer should coordinate all movements with the arrest team and stay behind cover until it is safe. Part of the plan is to decide what to do with any weapon. The suspect should never be allowed to surrender with a weapon in their hand.

A note of caution should be expressed. A situation in which a suspect who is very agitated, and suddenly becomes very calm without a good reason, is not a good sign. Too often, inexperienced officers see this as a victory, and relax. In truth, it is far more likely that the suspect has decided to commit suicide. The decision to commit suicide is a horrible, agonizing experience. People sometimes go through years of indecision before they decide to take their own lives. Individuals who are threatening suicide and become very calm, with no good reason for this sudden change, have often made the decision to commit suicide. When this occurs, they become visibly relaxed and seem at peace with the world. The only task left to be done is to act on that decision. Oddly enough, the action is the easy part. The most difficult part has been done in making the decision. The officer/negotiator should not be misled by this relaxation.

If the situation is not resolved by the first responders, and some time has passed, the department-designated crisis negotiator will arrive at the scene. What happens then? If the first responding officer has made initial contact, has developed rapport with the suspect and feels comfortable with their position as a negotiator, they should be allowed to continue with the dialogue. The negotiator should coach the officer throughout the process. There is no reason to start from the beginning when there is an officer on the scene who has already successfully begun the negotiation process.

The first responding officer plays a critical role in the peaceful resolution of a hostage/barricade/suicide incident. Without the initial steps being properly taken, there is very little hope of an organized police response to the incident. The first responding officer may also find themselves in a position of police negotiator. This is not an impossible task if the officer follows a few basic rules and uses good common sense. In fact, if this is done, there is a great chance of success.

MIKE ODLE

Mike Odle has been a police officer for the City of Los Angeles since May 1979, and was assigned to Metropolitan Division SWAT in April 1985. He is currently assigned as an element leader. This assignment includes responding to a range of incidents, from barricaded suspect and hostage incidents to alleged terrorist activity with both local and international overtones. Officer Odle also provides training to SWAT team personnel. His consultant experience includes being an instructor and Firearms Chairperson for the National Tactical Officers Association, as well as an instructor for the International Association of Chiefs of Police, United States Department of Energy Central Training Academy, International Association of Law Enforcement Program, adjunct instructor for the Firearms Training Unit of the Los Angeles Police Department, and trainer and senior firearms instructor for the Special Weapons and Tactics team.

Officer Odle also developed the Immediate Action/Rapid Deployment training outline for the Los Angeles Police Department and the National Tactical Officers Association, and is a subject-matter expert responsible for developing the LAPD Training Bulletin and Training Video. He is currently the lead instructor for the Submachine gun Instructor Certification and Handgun courses.

Chapter 13

IMMEDIATE ACTION/RAPID DEPLOYMENT

Mike Odle

INTRODUCTION

On April 19, 1999, the job of the law enforcement officer changed forever. Events at Columbine High School in Littleton, Colorado, jolted the law enforcement community and the public into a new awareness. The tragedy there made us all realize that schools in upper-middle-class America are no longer immune to the violence too often experienced in the inner-city school systems. The law enforcement response at Columbine High School has been both praised and scrutinized by the media, parents of victims and members of the law enforcement community. As a member of that community, it is not my intent to criticize or pass judgment on the response. Instead, I believe we must heed the lessons of that tragic day. Reflecting on the events at Columbine, I began to realize that past "conventional" law enforcement methods needed to be reconsidered. It became apparent to me that what was required were alternative tactics to combat the changing face of crime. This set of tactics became known as "Immediate Action/Rapid Deployment."

Historical Background

In August 1998, Officer Richard Massa, a 30-year veteran of the Los Angeles Police Department, and I were working with the Botetourt County Sheriff's Special Weapons and Tactics Team in Fincastle, Virginia. Under the command of Major Gary Guilliams, we trained with their team in various SWAT-related tactics, including officer and citizen rescues. During that training, SWAT officers practiced techniques to recover downed victims in both interior and open-air environments. This was done because Major Guilliams stated to me that: *"We need to prepare our officers to deal with incidents such as the Jonesboro Schoolyard shooting where injured children may be exposed to an ongoing and dangerous situation."* The forward thinking of Major Guilliams would become a grim reality as the Columbine High School tragedy unfolded just a few months later. It would also become unequivocally clear that police officers need to develop, train, and implement tactics tailored to this type of heinous crime.

I can clearly recall the horrific and chaotic news reports that filled the airwaves while Dylan Klebold and Eric Harris brought havoc and mass murder to Columbine High School. With host support from Captain Tom Mauro of the Town of Poughkeepsie Police Department in the state of New York, LAPD SWAT officers Donnie Anderson, George Ryan and I were providing training to several jurisdictions when we heard the news. Officer Pete Tyler, of the Ithaca, New York, Police Department, who was attending the training, asked what our response would be to that type of incident. Without hesitation, we answered, "quickly gather the first few officers on scene, enter the location and stop the gunmen's behavior." That opinion was given independent of and prior to any information gleaned from news reports from Littleton, Colorado. It was simply a response based upon prior experience where immediate intervention stopped ongoing, aggressive and deadly behavior—and that intervention worked.

Upon our return to Los Angeles, Lieutenant Tom Runyen (LAPD SWAT OIC) held a meeting with the LAPD SWAT team leaders. He wanted to discuss what type of response should be expected from patrol officers confronted with a "Columbine"-type incident. The overwhelming consensus was that the first responding officers on scene—ideally four officers—should enter the location as a contact team using a diamond formation. It was determined that the main objective should be to stop the assailant's deadly behavior. It was further agreed that additional officers could be used as another contact team, if needed, or as rescue teams to help with the removal of victims who were in need of emergency medical care. This, then, became the core of what is now called "Immediate Action/Rapid Deployment."

The decision to respond to a Columbine-like incident with the diamond formation was based upon the vast operational and training experience of the officers attending that meeting. The National School Safety Center in Thousand Oaks, California, has reported that California leads the nation in schoolyard violence and deaths. The Los Angeles Unified School District alone is made up of approximately 460 schools—far too many of which are the location of violent criminal activity, and even death. Given the Los Angeles Police Department's level of experience with schoolyard violence, the team leaders felt confident in their selection of the diamond formation. It is a tactic that provides 360 degrees of coverage for officers as they move toward their objective. Furthermore, it has been successfully utilized in the rescue of wounded victims in other scenarios. Approval of these tactical decisions was given, and shortly after this meeting members of LAPD SWAT were tasked with providing training in immediate action/rapid deployment techniques to the rest of the Los Angeles Police Department.

Compounding the sense of urgency instilled in so many of us by the tragedy at Columbine, the knowledge that armed assailants do not just target schools further underscores the necessity for the development and implementation of these type of tactics. Unfortunately, workplace and public-space violence has also taken a deadly toll. Aggressive and deadly assailants, bent on creating chaos and mass murder, are not venue specific. The massacre that occurred at the McDonald's Restaurant in San Ysidro, California, on July 18, 1984, is one such example. There, James Oliver Huberty walked into the restaurant and began indiscriminately shooting patrons, who were mostly women and children. Before his killing spree was brought to an end by a police long rifleman's bullet, James Huberty had killed 21 innocent people and injured 15 others.

As with Columbine, questions regarding delayed police intervention at the San Ysidro McDonald's tragedy have been the subject of many conversations. During that incident, a police long rifleman outside McDonald's requested permission to terminate Huberty's deadly behavior. The SWAT Commander responding to the scene denied the long rifleman's request until he had arrived on scene. Needless to say, such a decision may have resulted in many unnecessary injuries, if not deaths. Clearly, law enforcement responses to these incidents must be studied, so that more innocent lives can be saved in the future.

To begin, this type of crime needs to be classified. In these cases, the assailant is: *"An armed person who has the wherewithal to use deadly physical force on other persons and aggressively continues to do so while having unrestricted access to additional victims."* Furthermore, the rampages committed by these assailants are situations that require an immediate response by the first law enforcement personnel on scene. In these cases, the potential for multiple victims is present, and delayed deployment could have catastrophic consequences. This, then, is where conventional police tactics do not apply and immediate action/rapid deployment tactics must be implemented.

If such a tragic situation occurs and a SWAT officer happens to be the first responder, their training and experience can prove a valuable resource, and should be exploited. As a member of the tactical community, I have long since accepted the fact that my duties as a SWAT officer may place my safety secondary to that of people held against their will in hostage-crisis scenarios. However, this acceptance would never lead me to make rash or irrational tactical decisions. First, this acceptance is always very mission-specific. Second, I have developed the confidence to aggressively move against a hostage-taker and prevail, because I train extensively with my team members in time-tested tactics. Finally, years of operational experience further bolster my confidence. As a consequence, I am able to fully embrace the conviction that a SWAT officer's focus must be on the recovery of the hostage, and not on self-preservation. This, I am certain, is true of the tactical community at large.

However, time may not permit waiting for sufficient numbers of SWAT team members to arrive on the scene of an immediate action/rapid deployment incident. Though tactical team members may not be the first on scene, the response to such scenarios–and the mindset of the officers involved–*must* be like that of a SWAT officer handling a hostage crisis with regard to officer safety. The reason for this is plain and simple. When dealing with this kind of assailant, aggressive intervention may be the only means by which many innocent lives can be saved. Therefore, first responders must focus on the mission at hand; that is, to make *contact* with the assailant(s) and *stop* the deadly behavior.

Traditionally, however, law enforcement officers are trained and armed with tactics that foster and preach officer safety. Starting at the police academy and continuing throughout our careers, officer safety is considered "priority number one." Without a doubt, this is good. I would not suggest for a moment that officer safety is not important. But consider this: police officers are trained to intervene and stop criminal activity. Police officers are often issued body armor, and police officers are armed with GUNS! *If we decide not to intervene against an aggressive and armed assailant, what recourse do unarmed citizens (especially school kids) have? The answer is painfully clear.*

No matter the urgency of the situation, though, I do recommend that officers who remain steadfast in their conviction that "their" safety is priority one must find alternative ways to assist with the resolution of these deadly scenarios. There will be other duties vital to the success of the mission, such as establishing incident command, perimeter containment, controlling fleeing victims, etc. For instance, a group of first responders to an active-shooter situation may collectively decide to move forward aggressively and stop the assailant. Yet, others at the scene may be adamant that they will not move against the active shooter without making continuous use of hardened cover options, such as hand-held ballistic shields. Having made such a determination, these officers would only hinder the efforts of those employing immediate action/rapid deployment tactics. Consequently, such officers must make an honest assessment of their capabilities and decide what is best for responding officers and innocent persons alike.

Here, it must be understood that I am not asking anyone to respond in a rash or irrational manner. Nor am I suggesting that officers who make the decision to aggressively pursue armed assailants are unafraid, while those who choose not to are more so. No matter what, one would be foolish to assume that there are no risks associated with this kind of intervention. In fact, honest introspection tells us the possibility exists that an officer may be injured or killed, because there are times when first responders are unavoidably exposed to danger. Yet all law enforcement officers, in any situation, should understand that feelings of anxiety and/or caution must not be interpreted as an expectation of *failure*. In fact, these feelings are normal emotional responses to danger and, therefore, should not be permitted to debilitate the decision-making process. Instead, officers must understand that normal feelings of fear can stimulate a sense of heightened awareness in them. This, then, can provide the motivation to move forward with the vigilance, determination and aggressiveness necessary for the successful resolution of an immediate action/rapid deployment situation.

In fact, many law enforcement officers have made that leap of faith and chosen to set aside their instincts for self-preservation in order to stop the deadly actions of an armed assailant. Their stories are instructive to us all. One such incident occurred on May 27, 1997. On that day, Detectives Lazzaretto and Frank, of the City of Glendale Police Department in Glendale, California, were investigating an attempted murder. Mischell Bowen reported to Glendale police that her common-law husband, Israel Gonzales, had attempted to kill her, and that she believed he might be found at his workplace. Based upon her statement, Detectives Lazzaretto and Frank proceeded to a warehouse located in the Chatsworth area of Los Angeles. The Chatsworth location was used to produce, store and distribute pornographic videos. Detectives Lazzaretto and Frank were searching a portion of the location when Gonzales opened fire on the duo. Detective Frank exited the shooting location and summoned help. Detective Lazzaretto was struck by gunfire and was not able to retreat with Detective Frank.

When Los Angeles police officers arrived on scene, they met with Detective Frank who relayed what little information he could provide. Armed with that information, the LAPD officers formulated a plan to enter the location and rescue Detective Lazzaretto, who they believed to be injured. Officer

Officer Chris Yzagurrie

Chris Yzagurrie, an eight-year veteran at the time of this incident, arrived on scene and observed numerous law enforcement resources in various modes of response. He further noted that the apparent rescue efforts lacked one critical element–organization. Consequently, Officer Yzagurrie, with the assistance of other officers, formulated a plan to rescue Detective Lazzaretto. Once underway, Officer Yzagurrie observed the downed detective in the warehouse and believed that he saw Lazzaretto move. Later, Officer Yzagurrie would realize that the movement he observed might instead have been the suspect, Gonzales, removing Detective Lazaretto's service pistol. Yet, the one thing that Officer Yzagurrie did know was that delayed recovery of Detective Lazzaretto might result in his death. Therefore, Officer Yzagurrie, putting his own safety aside, gathered additional officers and moved forward.

Their plan consisted of having two officers enter the location armed with 12-gauge shotguns to provide cover fire, while other officers entered to physically remove the fallen Lazzaretto. Once inside the location, the LAPD officers located Detective Lazzaretto and attempted the rescue. They immediately came under fire from Gonzales and two of the rescuing officers were shot. The cover officers returned fire toward the assailant, then retreated with the injured officers. Much to their tremendous disappointment, this rescue and evacuation did not include Detective Lazzaretto. Shortly thereafter, a combination of LAPD SWAT and canine officers entered the location for a second rescue attempt. After the canine team came under fire, the rescuing officers developed a third plan to rescue Lazzaretto.

As the third attempt began, Gonzales again fired at the rescue team. Two SWAT officers, armed with Colt M-16 rifles and responsible for providing cover, did not see the origin of the gunfire, yet stood their ground as other officers attempted to carry Detective Lazzaretto out to safety. When Gonzales opened fire on the rescue team again, the cover officers were able to observe the muzzle flash produced by Gonzales's weapon and immediately returned controlled and steady cover fire. This allowed the rescue team to recover Detective Lazzaretto and evacuate him to a waiting rescue ambulance. Tragically, the officers' efforts proved futile, as

Detective Lazzaretto succumbed to his wounds.

After Detective Lazzaretto had been removed from the location, LAPD SWAT officers transitioned to conventional barricaded gunman tactics. The need for immediate action and rapid deployment had passed. As this makes clear, immediate action/rapid deployment tactics do not replace conventional police tactics. Instead, they are supplementary tactics designed for very specific implementation in very specific circumstances. Consequently, the SWAT officers deployed chemical agents at this point, along with a bomb squad robot equipped with video capabilities. Approximately seven hours later, Gonzales was found dead in the warehouse from a self-inflicted gunshot wound.

Though Detective Lazzaretto lost his life despite the best efforts of the officers who chose to risk theirs, the implementation of immediate action/rapid deployment tactics can be credited with saving lives in other situations. The entry into a crisis site does not have to include stopping the active shooting of an assailant in order to be successful. Rapid entry also drives officers to find, treat and evacuate injured persons in as expeditious a manner as possible. In immediate action/rapid deployment scenarios, any indecision on the part of responding officers could allow victims to expire from blood loss. One such scenario unfolded on March 22, 2002, a little after 0800 hours. William Lockey, a veteran employee of Bertrand Products in South Bend, Indiana, entered the northwest side of the manufacturing company and began shooting members of management, who were meeting in a conference room. Disgruntled and bent on revenge, Lockey left four co-workers dead and two others injured before fleeing from the location.

On that day, at 0815:51 hours, the first of many 911 calls was received at police dispatch centers. Just two minutes later, Sergeant William Schmidt, a uniformed police officer with 28 years on the South Bend Police Department, was the first to arrive on scene. Once there, he observed employees running from all exits. Sergeant Schmidt positioned his car near a corner of the building so he could watch the front of the building and assess his deployment options. Several fleeing employees told Sergeant Schmidt that he needed to enter the location because there was an employee shooting people. Schmidt, concerned both for possible downed victims and with the gunman's continuing and deadly behavior, grabbed a first aid kit and, with pistol in hand, entered the building.

Once inside, Sergeant Schmidt located a woman who was having trouble breathing. The woman had been shot twice in the chest and was being comforted by a male co-worker. Schmidt gave this man a piece of plastic to cover the bubbling wounds of the injured woman. He then continued his search for other victims and the gunman. After entering the production area of the location, Schmidt encountered two more downed victims. He also found Corporal Lesczynski, another South Bend police officer. Corporal Lesczynski had also chosen to enter the location in order to search for the gunman. At that moment, Sergeant Schmidt observed a rifle on the floor of the production area that he believed to be abandoned by the gunman. In addition, he heard the police radio traffic of a vehicle pursuit of a suspect believed to be the fleeing gunman. Confident the gunman was no longer in the building, Sergeant Schmidt stopped his search for the shooter and continued to provide assistance to the injured.

On that day, Sergeant Schmidt chose to move forward in order to locate and assist victims. If contact with the gunman was made, Sergeant Schmidt was prepared to terminate the gunman's deadly behavior. Like Sergeant Schmidt, at least four other South Bend officers immediately chose to enter the building prior to having any knowledge that the gunman had fled. Instead, their decision to enter the location was a consolidated effort to locate and stop an active shooter. Sergeant Schmidt and the other uniformed officers made the conscious decision to set feelings of self-preservation aside, and the result was that innocent victims were rescued.

At this point, it is essential to note that Sergeant Schmidt's commitment to entering the location, armed only with a handgun, was not without thought or assessment. First, the sound of approaching police sirens caused Sergeant Schmidt to believe additional police response was imminent as he made his determination to enter the location. Second, Sergeant Schmidt based his decisions upon his training. The South Bend Police Department's

(SBPD) Special Weapons Team had received training on immediate action/rapid deployment tactics from LAPD SWAT Officers George Ryan, Richard Massa and me. The SBPD SWAT team then took the initiative to immediately put together their own training program. They trained several specialty units, school resource officers and their drug unit in immediate action/rapid deployment tactics. Less than 90 days before the shooting at the Bertrand Products workplace, Sergeant Schmidt and the other SBPD officers who made entry into the building had received this training. I feel privileged to have been a part of the process.

As the incidents in Chatsworth, California, and South Bend, Indiana, make clear, immediate action/rapid deployment situations are all unique and extremely fluid. Because no two situations are ever going to be the same, no two responses can ever be exactly the same. Yet, the results of making the decision to enter quickly and aggressively pursue an armed assailant can be the same. Utilization of immediate action/rapid deployment tactics can help contain the breadth and scope of an already tragic situation. This fact is epitomized by an event that occurred in Monroe, Louisiana. There, patrol officers Larry Matthews and Mickey Tucker, from the Monroe Police Department (MPD), responded to a "shots fired" call at an Alternative Center School. As luck would have it, the MPD officers were nearby, and arrived on scene only moments after the call for help was received.

While responding to the location, MPD officers communicated via police radio and began forming a contact team while en route. As the first officers to arrive, Matthews and Tucker were quickly informed that the youthful assailant, who had already fired several rounds from his handgun, was still inside the school gymnasium. The officers assessed the situation and concluded that waiting for an additional unit to arrive on scene might prove harmful, even deadly, to the students at the school. Consequently, Officers Matthews and Tucker chose to move for-

Sergeant Larry Matthews and Officer Mickey Tucker of the Monroe, LA, Police Department.

ward and stage next to the doorway leading to the gymnasium. It was there that the officers heard what they thought to be the gunman manipulating a firearm. This belief caused Officers Matthews and Tucker to make entry into the gymnasium. Once inside, they found the 14-year-old gunman on the gymnasium stage attempting to clear a jammed handgun. The youthful assailant was taken into custody without incident and, most fortunately, before he was able to cause physical harm to anyone.

If Officers Matthews and Tucker had opted to follow conventional tactics and stay by their police vehicle while waiting for additional resources, they would not have detected the activity that caused them to move forward and take action against the gunman. That intervention most likely averted the assailant's ability to clear his weapon and continue his rampage. The officers' decision to make entry was admittedly motivated by training they had received in immediate action/rapid deployment tactics. Prior to this training, officers from the Monroe Police Department would have handled this event with conventional police tactics, such as "contain and wait." If so, the outcome may have proven to be immeasurably more tragic. Coincidentally, Captain Tom Torregrossa of the Monroe Police Department had attended immediate action/rapid deployment training I had provided in Dallas, Texas, just months after the Columbine massacre. After that training session, Captain Torregrossa took the tactics he had learned and trained MPD officers in these techniques. As a consequence of Captain Torregrossa's perseverance and determination, the officers responding to the active shooter at the Alternative Center School had the "go-ahead" to move forward and resolve the crisis with the new tactics they had learned. As a point of interest, Officers Matthews and Tucker received their immediate action/rapid deployment training the *day prior* to the aforementioned incident.

So, as with SWAT officers, once first responders determine that their *focus must be on stopping the deadly behavior, and not on self-preservation,* the key to their success lies in the correct implementation of the proper tactics. To begin, during such a crisis situation, either a supervisor on scene or an officer designated as the Contact Team Leader will make the decision for first responders to enter the crisis site.

This decision should only be made if a reasonable expectation of success exists prior to the officers entering the structure. Then, the tactics that are employed by the first responding officers should be those that will lessen the likelihood of serious bodily injury or death during intervention. These tactics are intended to *minimize* exposure time. At their most basic, and if possible and time permits, these tactics ask that you respond with additional officers, arm yourself with a shoulder-fired weapon and exploit available cover, while continuing to move aggressively toward the assailant. With proper training and implementation, these tactics can better prepare officers to handle these types of scenarios. They will also help to minimize the risk of personal injury when responding to an active shooting in progress. A more detailed explanation of these tactics follows.

Immediate Action/Rapid Deployment Defined

"The swift and immediate deployment of law enforcement resources to ongoing, life-threatening situations where delayed deployment could otherwise result in death or serious bodily injury to innocent persons."

General Characteristics of Assailants and Their Aggressive, Deadly Behavior

The following list of characteristics commonly associated with an assailant engaged in aggressive, deadly behavior was compiled from commonalities amongst descriptions of past assailants, and is not meant to be all-inclusive. Each crisis situation is unique.

- Assailants usually focus on assaulting persons with whom they have had prior contact. Their intention is usually an expression of hatred or rage, rather than the commission of a crime. Numerous post-interviews with assailants of schoolyard shootings have rendered information indicating that the assailant was bullied or made fun of at school.

- The assailants are likely to engage more than one target, and may be intent on killing a number of people as quickly as possible.
- The assailants often go to locations where there are numerous potential victims, such as schools, theaters, concert locations or shopping malls. They may even strike at their victims from a distance—much like a sniper—from a location with which they have at least some degree of familiarity. The infamous tragedy, often referred to as the "Texas Tower Incident," that occurred in Austin, Texas, on August 1, 1966, is one such example. There, Charles Whitman killed 15 people and wounded 31. It was not until law enforcement personnel intervened with direct contact with Whitman that his deadly rampage was brought to an end.
- Tactics such as containment and negotiation, normally associated with standoff incidents, may not be adequate in these types of events. Assailants typically continue their attack, despite the arrival of emergency responders.
- Assailants are often better armed than the police, sometimes making use of explosives, booby traps and body armor. They may also employ some type of diversion.
- Assailants may have planned their attack and prepared themselves for a sustained confrontation with the police. Historically, these assailants have not attempted to hide their identities or conceal the commission of their attacks. Escape from the police is usually not their priority.
- Assailants may be suicidal; they decide to die in the course of their actions, either at the hand of others or by a self-inflicted wound.
- These events are dynamic, and assailants may go in and out of an active status. A static incident may turn aggressive, then go inactive, because it turns into a barricaded situation—with or without access to victims. *Note: If the incident does become a barricaded suspect situation, officers should transition to the use of conventional police tactics.*

General First Responder Duties

Upon arrival at the scene where aggressive, deadly behavior is ongoing, first responders must prioritize their response. Their first priority is to form a contact team, the objective of which is to locate the assailant(s) and ***STOP*** the aggressive, deadly behavior. Responding personnel must keep in mind that their primary role is to protect children and other innocent persons who are at risk.

Although four officers are considered an adequate number to form a contact team, exigent circumstances may necessitate fewer than the desired amount of responders to proceed (i.e., two officers with a supervisor, a School Resource Officer, or a DARE Officer, etc.). Each scenario is situation-driven and requires the first officers on scene to rely upon prior training and good judgment when forming a contact team with less than four officers. In such a case, a patrol supervisor or detective may deploy as a contact team member. The necessity for a supervisor to deploy as a contact team member may outweigh the need to immediately establish incident command. The contact team will communicate their observations on the run. This will assist responding units and the incident commander (IC) once incident command has been established. Therefore, the role of incident commander should be established as soon as is practical. The incident commander is responsible for:

- Facilitating the communication process.
- Establishing a central location where information is collected.
- Systematically disseminating this information to the appropriate responding resources.

This is generally the responsibility of the senior officer on scene, but later can be assumed by a supervisor or other command staff person. Additionally, as soon as the initial contact team collects pertinent information, they must communicate that information to the incident commander, thereby starting the flow and dissemination of vital information.

General Response Guidelines

Tactical Missions

- Assess situation
- Broadcast a situation estimate (prioritize)
  - Location and number of suspects (if known)
  - Type(s) of weapons involved
  - Estimated size of the crowd
  - Number of injuries and deaths (if known)
  - Additional assistance needed (fire, medical, etc.)
  - Location of staging area
  - Ingress/egress routes for emergency vehicles
  - Incident Command Post location (if possible)
- Request Additional Resources
  - Urban Police Rifle (UPR)
  - Additional patrol units
  - SWAT and K-9
  - Bomb Squad
  - Fire Department and Paramedics
- Assemble Contact (Rescue) Teams
- Establish command and control

Note: Since these incidents contain many variables, the effective handling of this type of situation can never be completely reduced to specific procedures. Additionally, these procedures are not meant to exclude the role of conventional police tactics that may be employed, when appropriate, throughout the dynamic situation.

Entering the Stronghold

Beyond the obvious problems associated with deploying into large structures, the fact that the suspect often is not readily identifiable further compounds the tactical complexity of entering the stronghold. Added to this are the natural advantage a suspect has when lying in wait, and the inherent disadvantage first responders have in searching for and apprehending such a suspect.

These issues are exacerbated by the fact that schools, workplaces and other public spaces can be populated by anywhere from just a few, to even thousands of innocent victims, all of whom are potential targets and/or hostages. Additionally,

depending on the size of the facility, there can be a large number of entrances and exits to be secured, watched or breached.

The decision to enter the structure will be based upon reasonable assessments of the information that has been gathered. Upon arrival at the crisis site, intelligence may be sparse and fragmented. But first responders can make their assessments based upon such sources of information as statements from fleeing witnesses, seeing spent casings on the ground, observing damage from fired rounds and hearing reports from Communications Division. Also, such things as broken windows make excellent indicators for locating where violent acts have occurred or are occurring.

After critical intelligence has been gathered, additional intelligence may be obtained on the run. This information may include: Who is the assailant? What does the assailant look like? Where was the assailant, exactly, at the time of the assault? What weapon(s) does the assailant possess? Additional information may include: What level of training or experience does the assailant have? What is the assailant's agenda or motive? Bottom line, if you observe or hear activity consistent with an assailant actively involved in killing, use *that information* and start moving.

What to Expect Upon Entry

There will be many distractions while making entry. I can say with conviction that senseless acts of violence, such as sexual abuse, torture and the murder of children, are very disturbing and will put to task anyone's ability to remain focused. Yet, when you enter an arena that is scattered with innocent victims–especially children–you must focus on the living, and aggressively seek out the assailant whose crime spree may be ongoing. This is essential, because the longer intervention with the assailant is delayed, the greater the chance there will be additional victims. FOCUS and move forward. STOP the behavior.

Beyond the horror of the carnage that may be present in one of these crisis situations, innumerable other sources of distraction may also be present. These include, but are not limited to:

- Noise from fire alarms, school bells, people screaming, etc.
- Fire sprinklers spraying water.
- Confusion from fleeing and frightened victims. Those hiding may not respond to police directions.
- Victims may become physically aggressive and cling to rescuers.
- Explosive devices.
- If the crisis occurs at a school, there may be a lockdown situation. Teachers will lock the classroom door and have students sit on the floor until they receive police or school official instructions.

Formation and Mission of Contact and Rescue Teams

Establishing a contact team will organize and provide structure to an otherwise chaotic effort to locate and stop the assailant. Establishing rescue teams will facilitate the recovery process for potential and/or present victims. The contact and rescue teams are most effective with a minimum of four officers. Both contact and rescue teams are structured as follows:

1. **Team Leader (TL)**–This officer delegates team member responsibilities and formulates and directs the plan. They also provide cover to a flank position during movement. The team leader is not necessarily the senior officer on scene. When timely decisiveness is critical, someone must be in a command position to make decisions that will make things happen. So, someone must assume the team leader role.
2. **Assistant Team Leader (ATL)**–This officer maintains communication with the incident commander and other units during deployment. They assume the rear guard position and provide cover to the rear of the team. If you do not assign someone as the communicator, this essential job may go undone.
3. **Designated Cover Officer (DCO)**–This officer deploys a shotgun (slug ammunition, if qualified and available) or an Urban Police Rifle (UPR of .223 caliber). They take the

point position during the search, and provide cover forward of the team. If deployed with a shotgun loaded with 12-gauge, "00" buckshot, the DCO must remember the limitations of the load at extended distances.
4. **General-Purpose Officer (GPO)**–This officer provides cover to a flank position during movement and acts as a rescue or contact officer.

Contact Team Missions

- Locate the assailant.
- Limit the assailant's movement.
- Prevent the assailant's escape.
- Stop the assailant's deadly behavior.
- Communicate progress to the incident commander and other officers.
- Direct victims out of the location through secure areas to the staging area.
- Communicate the location of downed victims to the incident commander and responding rescue teams.

The primary missions of the contact team are to locate and stop the assailant's deadly behavior and prevent the assailant's escape. The secondary mission is to direct victims out of the crisis site through secured areas to the staging area. The contact team's goal is to save lives by stopping or containing the assailant. This denies the assailant mobility, thereby ensuring that no one else can become a victim. It also allows for the safe and orderly evacuation of innocent persons. Throughout this process, communication must be maintained with the incident commander and other officers, so that the contact team's progress will be known.

Rescue Team Missions

- Enter site to locate victims.
- Extract victims to a safe area.
- Transport wounded victims to medical personnel for treatment.
- Establish a triage area within the crisis site, if necessary.
- Report suspect's location, if known.
- Notify the incident commander of progress.

- Notify the incident commander where to send additional rescue teams, if they are needed.

Note: Additional officers can be added to a rescue team, or extra teams can be activated when multiple victims are present.

A rescue team should never become so focused with the recovery effort of victims that they disregard the possibility of contacting an armed assailant. The rescue team can become a contact team if they physically encounter the assailant or hear activity nearby that is consistent with the assailant's behavior. In that case, the rescue team should transition into a contact team and make contact with the assailant.

The primary missions of the rescue team are to locate and evacuate victims who need to be treated by medical personnel. The rescue team can follow the contact team. Once the rescue team reaches the victim, the point officer (DCO) maintains forward security, the team leader provides rearward cover, and the additional officers carry the victim out to safety. The technique for recovering a downed victim is as follows:

- The first officer will place the victim into a supine position and stand next to the victim's head.
- The second officer will take a position next to the victim's feet.
- The first officer will reach under the victim's shoulders and lift the victim into a seated position.
- The second officer may assist by placing the victim's hands toward their waistline.
- The first officer will reach under the victim's arms and grasp the victim's wrists. The officer will then cross the victim's wrists and pull them toward the victim's chest and prepare to lift.
- Using the legs to lift, the officer will stand with the victim.
- The second officer will face away from the first officer and grasp the victim's ankles or pant legs, then lift.
- Both officers will communicate when they are ready and, under the direction of the team leader, will exit the location with the victim.

In this way, the victim is carried out of the crisis site as expeditiously as possible. During this process, the responsibility for providing cover will vary and necessitate officer flexibility. In general, the point officer and rear guard officer exchange duties as the team moves out. If other officers have posted in positions of cover, the last cover officer will sound off, "LAST MAN," as the rear covering officer passes their position. The cover officer assumes the role as rear cover and continues the evacuation. This collapse of responsibility will continue, depending on the number of cover officers in place. Then, after evacuating the building, the victim is taken to the medical triage staging area for treatment.

Note: *There may be occasions when it is deemed appropriate to hold ground after the victim has been located. It may not be appropriate to proceed with the victim into a volatile area, or if the victim is deceased, or the victim is in need of minimal medical care. The decision to hold will be left to the discretion of the team leader.*

The Diamond Formation

When entering the crisis site in a contact or rescue team configuration, the officers move in a Diamond Formation (Diagram #1). The point officer (DCO) takes a position in the front of the diamond. This officer generally carries a shotgun, UPR, or slug-loaded shotgun. The team leader will assume a position to the left or right flank of the diamond, while the general-purpose officer assumes a position opposite the team leader's flank. The assistant team leader will assume the rear guard position to the rear of the diamond. This allows for 360-degree coverage to be maintained while the team is moving.

Note: *The rear guard does not necessarily walk backward while the team aggressively moves toward the activity. It is acceptable for the rear guard to go forward with the team, moving straight ahead, while looking backward every three or four steps in order to check the rear.*

When the contact and rescue teams travel in the diamond formation, their movement is fluid. The officers move in a manner that is aggressive, controlled and precise. Furthermore, each officer must remain flexible, as individual responsibilities can vary in an ever-changing and unpredictable environment. In addition, communication is critical. Never assume that what you see, everyone else sees. When you see a threat or activity (muzzle flash, gun smoke, etc.), **communicate** your observations and verify that all team members are aware of what you have observed.

Note: *When moving through some wide corridors or intersections, the team may find it preferable to adjust the diamond formation so it resembles a "T" configuration (Diagram #1a). The diamond formation is designed to be fluid and flexible in this way so it can accommodate all situations. It is possible, for example, that as a team moves toward known activity, they will encounter wide hallways or intersections. Once there, the team may find they must travel past areas and open doors that have not been physically cleared. By making the transition from a diamond to a "T" formation, the DCO and the flanking officers are able to provide instantaneous cover for each other while moving forward. For this reason, the "T" configuration can prove advantageous in these circumstances.*

Other Tactical Considerations

Use of Deadly Force

Law enforcement officers are authorized to employ deadly force when it reasonably appears necessary to: (1) protect themselves or others from an immediate threat of death or serious bodily injury, (2) prevent a crime where the suspect's actions place persons in jeopardy of death or serious bodily injury, or (3) apprehend a fleeing felon for a crime involving serious bodily injury, or the use of deadly force where there is substantial risk that the person whose arrest is sought will cause death or serious bodily injury to others if apprehension is delayed. Simply put, when a suspect's behavior presents an immediate-defense-of-life (IDOL) scenario against an officer or other persons, and other options have been exhausted or deemed unreasonable, it is appropriate to use deadly force to stop the individual's deadly behavior. It is, therefore, reasonable for an officer to use deadly force

against an assailant whose activity has resulted in serious bodily injury or death and who is attempting to flee while armed.

Use of Cover Fire

Cover fire is defined as "controlled and deliberate fire, directed at a life-endangering threat (target-specific), or where an officer reasonably believes the threat to be located (threat area)." It can be utilized when officers are exposed to an immediate life-endangering threat, such as an active shooting, or it may be used to suppress an assailant's ability to shoot. Support officers can utilize controlled cover fire to distract an assailant from shooting officers who are moving to either gain a tactical advantage or conduct an officer/victim rescue operation.

The decision to utilize cover fire should be commensurate with the level of the threat. Cover fire should always be considered deadly force. The use of cover fire should not place citizens at greater risk than the activities of the assailant. Background is a consideration when firing against an aggressor, however, background is secondary to an *immediate-defense-of-life* scenario. In rescue scenarios, cover fire is often a planned event. When cover fire is a planned event, all concerned personnel must be alerted that cover fire will be employed prior to its use.

Lag Time

It is also critical to consider what is commonly referred to as "lag time." Lag time is the time frame between an "action" that has been observed and the time it takes to "react or respond" to that action. Studies have shown that reaction time varies from one person to another. However, it is certainly safe to say that reaction time is generally around 25/100ths to 75/100ths of a second. Few police officers will be able to react to most scenarios within 25/100ths of a second. Most will respond within the 50-75/100ths of a second time frame. Police officers are also encumbered by the tremendous responsibility of having to assess whether or not a person is a threat prior to responding to that threat. Many variables (low light, distance, positioning, etc.) could further hinder the decision-making process and increase response time.

Make no mistake, lag time is ***not*** commensurate with the time it takes to perform a task. For example, after a person *starts* firing a handgun, that person could conceivably fire up to four rounds within a one-second time frame. It is just as conceivable that an officer could be shot multiple times before they can even react. Therefore, if an armed gunman is in close proximity to potential victims, mere presence alone can constitute imminent danger to those persons. This imminent danger can be described as an action pending. Given the opportunity, the gunman could inflict serious injury or death if the officers wait to react to the assailant's pending action. An officer's warning to "drop the gun!" may give an assailant the unhindered ability to commit at least one last act of irreversible violence.

Encountering Explosive Devices

If contact or rescue teams encounter something that appears to be an explosive device, officers should make a quick visual inspection of the suspicious items. Officers should never move or touch the device, but need to visually inspect it in order to look for potential detonation mechanisms, such as timing devices, trip wires, a lit fuse, etc. Once this is done, officers should mark the location of the suspicious items. DO NOT ASSUME that your fellow officers have seen the device. VERBALIZE the location of the device! Then, if possible, officers can verbally report the location of the device to the incident commander. However, it is important to limit the use of radios, cellular phones or Mobile Digital Terminals (MDTs) around the device. So, in order to inform others of the device's location via radio, you should: (1) distance yourself from the device, (2) exploit the cover afforded by any hardened barriers, then (3) radio the device's location. Finally, move *past* the device when you are part of a contact or rescue team. Additional officers can be sent to control the area surrounding the device as soon as possible.

Fire Department and Tactical EMS Considerations

Due to the size or complexity of the crisis site, it may be appropriate to establish a triage within the crisis site. If reasonable and necessary, the definitions and guidelines which follow will assist with that endeavor.

- **Hot Area**
  - Unsecured area.
  - Contact teams still pursuing the assailant(s).
- **Warm Area**
  - Area that is clear of assailants but has the potential for a change in condition.
  - Area that rescue teams are sent for victim evacuation.
  - Area that police personnel establish as a safety corridor for escorting firefighters and paramedics to a Safe Zone for triaging/treating victims.
  - Rescue team can become contact team, depending on the assailant's actions.
- **Cold Area**
  - Area where there is little or no threat from the assailant, i.e., location of command post, staging of personnel, etc.
- **Safe Zone**
  - Zone within the Warm Area that is secured by police personnel for firefighters and paramedics to triage/treat victims.
  - Once established, police personnel do not leave the Safe Zone unprotected.
- **Safety Corridor**
  - Path that police officers take firefighters and paramedics along to move them from the Cold Area through the Warm Area to the Safe Zone.
  - Path that police officers take firefighters, paramedics, and victims along to move them from the Safe Zone through the Warm Area to the Cold Area.

Fire Department or Tactical EMS Rapid Deployment Procedures

Firefighters and paramedics normally only enter a Warm Area when they are accompanied by police officers unless there are mitigating circumstances that will then require approval by the incident commander (police-IC) with the concurrent consent of the fire department.

Firefighters and paramedics will proceed through the Safety Corridor to the Safe Zone and remain there under police protection. Rescue team officers who accompany firefighters and/or paramedics will *remain* with them as security until the danger is mitigated. Other rescue teams that are not assigned to firefighters and/or paramedics, and who have the responsibility for bringing victims to the Safe Zone, have no such restrictions.

Firefighters and paramedics who are taken to the Safe Zone are there for the purpose of triaging and treating victims.

- Firefighters and paramedics assigned to the Safe Zone will follow the tactical direction of police personnel assigned to that Safe Zone.
- Firefighters and paramedics assigned to the Safe Zone will follow the medical direction of the IC and fire department representatives.

The ultimate goal is for victims to be transported to the hospital. Treatment in the Safe Zone is limited. Therefore, firefighters and paramedics will determine the severity of the victims' injuries and decide which victims must be immediately evacuated. To this end, police officers are tasked with making the tactical decisions that will ensure the safety of victims, firefighters and paramedics. *Deviation from the procedures listed above requires approval from the IC and fire department personnel.*

Basic Considerations and Decisions Related To Immediate Action/ Rapid Deployment

Make no mistake. The decision to make entry into a structure looking for an aggressive and deadly assailant is a worst-case scenario. When conventional tactics are appropriate, conventional tactics

should be used; i.e., containment, waiting for additional back-up, waiting for SWAT, etc. However, a crisis involving aggressive and deadly assailants bent on inflicting mass casualties is not a time for restricting law enforcement to just the use of conventional tactics. It is the time for implementation of immediate action/rapid deployment tactics.

Pace of Entry

The core of immediate action/rapid deployment is the maintenance of fluid momentum while officers search hallways, rooms and other areas. Therefore, you should not move faster than you can make reasonable decisions or, when necessary, shoot accurately. Furthermore, when the assailant's activity is detectable, the contact team's pace will be aggressive and driven toward that activity. Then, if the assailant's activity is no longer detectable, the pace should decelerate and include slow, systematic room-clearing techniques. This pace will continue until such time as the assailant's activity is detectable or contact with the assailant is made.

Need for Flexibility

Beyond adjusting the pace as the situation dictates, each officer must also remain tactically and mentally flexible when moving through the crisis site. For example, forward cover or flanking responsibilities may shift quickly. Additionally, the assailant may appear without warning. Yet, such an appearance of an assailant should never come as a surprise. After all, your purpose for entering the crisis site is to locate and stop the assailant's deadly behavior. So, you should move through the crisis site with your head up and your weapon ready, all the while EXPECTING to find the assailant!

Physiological Responses

Communication, teamwork and a positive mindset will help facilitate each officer's ability to remain flexible and maintain necessary fluidity and continuous movement throughout the crisis site. To achieve a positive mindset, it is important to understand that each individual officer will experience stress and/or anxiety in one form or another. The extent of one's anxiety can range from mild concern to debilitating fear.

Regardless of their level of anxiety, officers should also be aware that this stress causes a physiological reaction within the body. This is often referred to as the "flight or fight" syndrome. When this happens, the muscles often become tense, heart rate increases and breathing becomes more rapid. Additionally, physiological reactions such as "binocular reduction," also known as "tunnel vision," may occur. "Auditory exclusion," where sounds are muted, and the sensation of events unfolding in slow motion can also be experienced. People may also find their bodies reposition in a way that can be described as a "boxer's stance." When this occurs, the hips and shoulders are facing forward toward the threat, the knees are slightly flexed and the hands are held in front of the body for defense and/or readiness to strike.

All of these are defense mechanisms that help people survive when the threat of harm is anticipated. The body and mind are made ready for battle in this way. Therefore, understanding that these automatic reactions may occur during an immediate action/rapid deployment situation, and exploiting these natural defense mechanisms, should be considered a positive tool for officer survival.

Communications

After entry into the crisis site has been made, contact and rescue teams must establish communications, both amongst themselves and with the command post (CP). To begin, the team leader should determine the method used to communicate through the crisis site based upon the situation that is encountered within the structure. The condition of the crisis site and the activity of the assailant will dictate the type of communication techniques used. If audible alarms or other noise factors hinder the communication process, loud and clear voice commands would be appropriate. Loud and clear voice commands would also be appropriate if the assailant's deadly behavior is ongoing and detectable. However, if the crisis site is quiet or activity has ceased and the assailant's whereabouts are unknown, quiet voice commands or hand signals may be appropriate. Once the method of com-

munication has been determined, the assistant team leader (rear guard) is responsible for broadcasting the location of the team, victims, the suspect and any other pertinent information. The information should also be communicated to the command post. If a tactical frequency is being used, a radio telephone operator should be requested to staff the frequency to record any information that is transmitted. This is especially important at the onset of the incident when the command post is not fully staffed and the incident is the most chaotic.

The Low-Ready Position

To begin, when dealing with an immediate action/rapid deployment scenario, you should exploit available weaponry. In other words, if you have the opportunity to arm yourself with a shoulder weapon, do so.

No matter the weapon you are deploying, it is important to discuss how officers should handle their weapons in order to maximize safety and effectiveness as they move throughout the crisis site. Officers should consider themselves as "searching" as they move throughout the structure. Consequently, weapons should be at the "Low-Ready" position to help facilitate that process. Most law enforcement personnel are familiar with the term "Low-Ready."

Although a familiar term, there are apparently different interpretations as to what is considered a Low-Ready position and when its use is appropriate. If we dissect the term "Low-Ready," it would seem to offer the reader an obvious definition. But does it? The term might suggest to one that the weapon is "low" and "ready," but to another it suggests that the weapon is "low" and the operator is "ready." I offer this simple explanation: the "Low-Ready" position is the position of a firearm held by the officer with both hands, muzzle down and forward, with the officer's head up, thus ready.

A more in-depth definition of this position might include: muzzle positioned down toward an imaginary point half the distance between the operator and the target or threat area; the operator's primary hand trigger finger is alongside the receiver or frame; the operator's head is upright and focus is forward and, thereby, "ready." The "Low-Ready" can further be explained as the position that is generally used when searching or covering. The weapon is carried in such a way as to support that need.

Additionally, it is important to consider that most use-of-force policies require an officer to justify why their weapon has been presented or retrieved from a carrying device (holster or gun rack) and exhibited. When adequate justifications exist to present the weapon, the weapon should be carried in an efficient and ready position. The "Low-Ready" position is appropriate when an officer has reasonable cause to believe there is substantial risk that the situation may escalate to the point where deadly force may be justified. An immediate action/rapid deployment situation is certainly such a case.

The Alternative Force Method

Over the years, I have witnessed several variations of the "Low-Ready" position. One such variation is the "Alternative Force" position. The term "Alternative Force" is intended to give the user the flexibility to deliver both lethal and non-lethal force by positioning the firearm close to the primary side (gun side) with the support hand positioned in front of the torso in a pre-strike position. Those who support the use of this technique often argue that most contacts are non-lethal in nature. So, they explain, when an officer using this technique enters a structure, they are in a pre-staged position to use the support hand to strike, push, control, etc., a non-compliant contact.

I will agree that most contacts are non-lethal, however, it is my opinion that the Alternative Force position favors the non-lethal contact and forces the user to adjust to a lethal threat. If there is *sufficient* reason to exhibit the weapon, the user of that weapon should be poised and ready to immediately react to a lethal threat. Due to the seriousness of a lethal encounter, common sense dictates that if an adjustment must take place, the adjustment should be from a lethal ready position to a non-lethal ready position. The best ready position for a lethal contact is the aforementioned Low-Ready position. Remember, you have armed yourself in anticipation that deadly force may be appropriate. You should prepare yourself for that scenario by moving

forward with the proper mindset and the proper tactics.

The series of diagrams which follow detail the procedures for making entry and clearing a room by a contact team. Diagrams 2 through 4 depict entry methods when the assailant's location is unknown or there is no ongoing activity. When the assailant's whereabouts are unknown, two officers clear the room. Diagrams 5 through 7 portray entry techniques if the searching officers believe the assailant is in a specific location. When the assailant's whereabouts are known, three officers will enter, with the designated cover officer (DCO) as one of the first to enter, to take advantage of the DCO's superior firepower. When viewing the diagrams, the positions of assistant team leader and general purpose officer are interchangeable in regard to positioning and order of entry.

Basic Room-Clearing Techniques

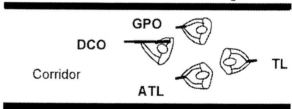

Diagram 1.

The basic formation used by contact and rescue teams is a diamond formation (Diagram 1). The team leader will designate the search team. The designated cover officer (DCO) is in the point position and should be armed with an Urban Police Rifle (UPR) or shotgun with rifled slug ammunition. There are officers on both flanks and a rear guard, to ensure 360-degree coverage. The assistant team leader (ATL) and general purpose officer (GPO) should be the flanks, and the team leader (TL) the rear guard. This allows the team leader to monitor the room being searched and the corridor at the same time. The team should move in formation to ensure complete coverage. Each team member has specific responsibilities, which are detailed in the diagrams.

This photo illustrates the diamond formation moving aggressively toward the entrance of the crisis site where activity is ongoing and detectable. The team leader is positioned on the left flank for control during aggressive movement.

Prior to entering a room, officers will stage outside the doorway. The position of the officers depends upon whether the door is open or closed, and which way the closed door opens. When entering, the officer positioned next to the hinge is usually the first to enter an uncleared room. However, when a closed door opens out, the officer positioned next to the doorknob will likely be the first to see the interior of the room. Therefore, it may be appropriate for the officer positioned on the doorknob side to enter the room first, regardless of the condition of the door. Officers should be aware that *in schools, classroom doors generally open out* into the corridors. When the officers make entry into a room, they will follow their respective wall, while

clearing their area of responsibility (AOR). The officers making entry must avoid overpenetration while visually clearing their AORs, since this can lead to exposure to hiding areas, additional doorways and deep corners of the room. After common living/working areas have been searched, it may be appropriate to search "hiding" areas. Ultimately, it is up to the team leader to determine how detailed the search will be, based on the information known at the time of the search. The initial clear is given if there is no immediate contact with the suspect.

When a team is conducting a search of potential hiding places, one officer will communicate, *Searching,* while the other officer communicates, *Covering.* This will prevent a situation where both officers are searching, leaving them uncovered. The officer will conduct a quick but adequate search of potential hiding places. After the search is completed, the searching officer will communicate, *Room Clear.* If contact is made, the officer will take appropriate action to control the occupants of the room. If no contact is made, both officers exit the room and continue to the next area to be searched. The officer nearest the door will then announce, *Coming Out,* and exit the room. When large search teams are used, the last officer will announce, *Last Out,* and exit the room.

No Activity

If activity is no longer detectable within the crisis site, and the whereabouts of the assailant(s) are unknown, the team will slow its momentum and conduct a systematic search, clearing room by room. Officers should not become complacent while conducting the search, since the assailants may present themselves without warning. Diagrams 2 through 4 detail the methods used to enter an uncleared room when searching for an active shooter and the shooter's location is unknown.

This photo shows the contact team in a search mode after activity is no longer detectable. The team leader has now taken the rear cover position in the back of the diamond for better control during a systematic search.

Open Door (Diagram 2a)

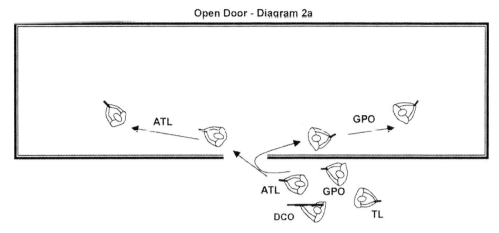

Diagram 2a.

- ATL stops short of the open doorway, briefly assesses, then communicates to GPO when ready to enter.
- GPO acknowledges the communication by squeezing the back of the ATL's leg or knee to signal entry can be made.
- ATL will step through the doorway, follow their respective wall and visually clear AOR.
- GPO will stop through the doorway, buttonhook and follow the wall, visually clearing the AOR.
- When their respective AOR is clear, each officer will quietly communicate, "CLEAR."

Open Door–Alternate Method (Diagram 2b)

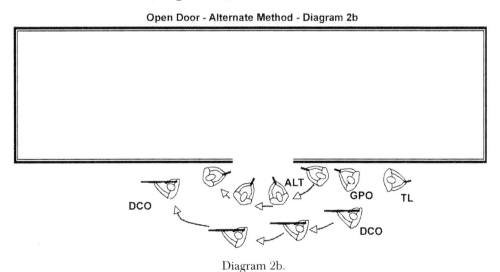

Diagram 2b.

- ATL will quickly assess to determine if there is any activity in the room.
- ATL will quickly cross the doorway, muzzle toward opening and stage for entry.
- DCO will also cross the doorway at the same time as the ATL.

- GPO and ATL are now staged for a crossover entry into the room, then will make eye contact (or verbalize if necessary) and smoothly enter the room.

- TL can assume a position next to the open doorway and monitor the search, while maintaining rearward cover.

Door Opens In (Diagram 3)

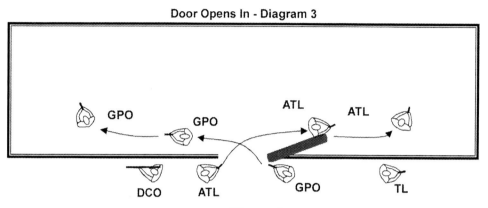

Diagram 3.

- DCO crosses the closed doorway to provide forward cover.
- ATL crosses the doorway, turns inward and takes a position facing the GPO.
- TL maintains rearward cover.
- GPO (staged next to the hinge) will be the first officer into the room.
- ATL will make eye contact with the GPO and open the door.
- GPO and ATL will crisscross through the doorway, then both clear their AOR, as previously described.

Door Opens Out (Diagram 4a)

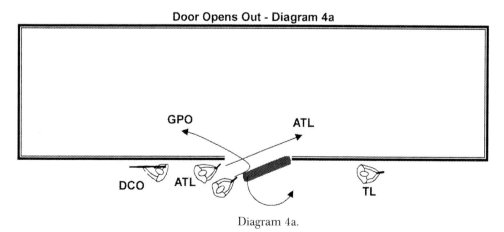

Diagram 4a.

- DCO crosses the closed doorway and provides forward cover, while the TL provides rearward cover.

- ATL crosses the doorway, turns inward and faces the door.
- ATL (staged next to the doorknob) will be the

first officer into the room.
- GPO takes a position behind the first officer (same side of the door).
- GPO will reach around the ATL and open the door, which allows the ATL to provide cover for the GPO as the door is being opened.

- Immediately after opening the door, the GPO steps behind the ATL.
- GPO will crossover through the doorway, followed by the ATL, who buttonhooks, then both clear their AOR.

Door Opens Out (Diagram 4b)

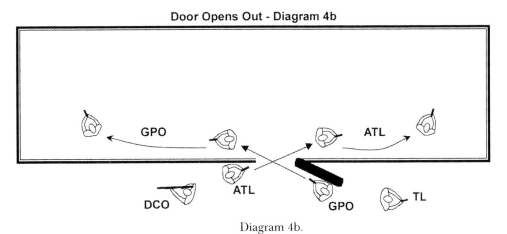

Diagram 4b.

- DCO crosses the closed doorway to provide forward cover.
- ATL crosses the doorway, turns inward and takes a position facing the GPO.
- TL maintains rearward cover.
- ATL (staged next to the knob) will be the first officer into the room.
- ATL makes eye contact with the GPO, who will lean across and open the door.
- GPO and ATL will crisscross through the doorway, then both clear their AOR, as previously described.

Aggressive, Deadly Behavior

When an assailant's location is known and the aggressive, deadly behavior is ongoing, the contact team must move with determination and aggressiveness to stop the assailant's behavior. Officers must be mentally prepared to engage the assailant with innocent persons in close proximity. When contact with the assailant is imminent, officers should exploit available cover, when appropriate. When entry into a room is necessary to contact the assailant, movement should be fluid and aggressive. Under these conditions, three officers from the contact team will enter the room. Diagrams 5 through 7 display room entry and clearing techniques when the assailant's presence is known.

If contact is made, officers will take appropriate action to take the assailant into custody or stop the deadly threat posed by the suspect. After an assailant has been taken into custody, the incident commander will ensure that the crisis site is thoroughly searched for additional assailants and victims before the area is considered "CLEAR." If an officer-involved-shooting (OIS) occurs, those officers involved will stay with the assailant and notify the incident commander.

Open Door (Diagram 5)

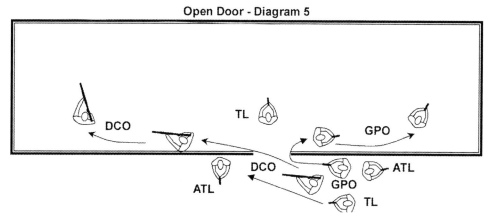

Diagram 5.

- DCO stops short of the open doorway to prepare to enter the room.
- TL will provide forward cover, while the ATL maintains rearward cover.
- GPO squeezes the back of the DCO's leg or knee to signal entry can be made.
- DCO will then step through the doorway following their momentum toward the near corner.

- GPO will step into the doorway, buttonhook to the opposite corner, and follow the wall while clearing from the near corner to the center of the room.
- TL will enter and move to the center of the room not to exceed the position of the DCO and GPO.
- ATL will move to the edge of the open doorway and monitor the corridor.

Door Opens In (Diagram 6)

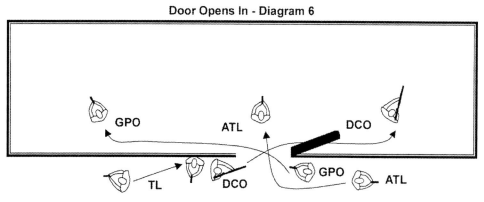

Diagram 6.

- DCO crosses the closed doorway, turns inward and facing the GPO.
- TL crosses the doorway and establishes forward cover, while the ATL provides cover rearward.

- DCO (near doorknob) will make eye contact with the other searching officer and open the door.
- GPO (near hinge) will be first into the room, followed by the DCO, in a crisscross pattern.

- GPO and DCO will follow their respective walls, clearing their AOR.
- ATL will collapse rear cover responsibility and enter as the third officer in the room.

- TL will move to the edge of the open doorway and monitor the corridor.
- Follow procedures previously described when contacting the assailant.

Door Opens Out (Diagram 7)

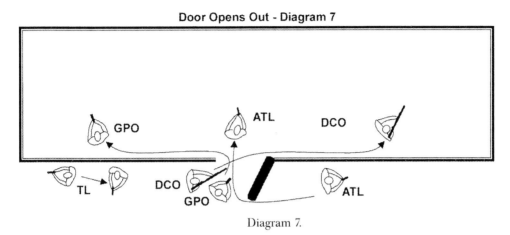

Diagram 7.

- DCO crosses the closed doorway, turns inward and prepares to enter the room.
- TL crosses the doorway and establishes forward cover, while the ATL provides rear cover.
- GPO takes a position behind the DCO and will reach around the DCO to open the door.
- DCO will crossover through the doorway.
- GPO immediately enters the doorway after the DCO and buttonhooks.
- GPO and DCO will follow their respective walls, clearing their AOR.
- ATL collapses rear cover responsibility and enters as a third officer.
- TL will move to the edge of the open doorway and monitor the corridor.
- Follow procedures previously described when contacting the assailant.

When SWAT Arrives

When tactical team personnel arrive on scene, they are generally better equipped and trained to resolve tactical situations. However, continued assistance by initial responders is critical. Under the direction of SWAT, officers may aid with contain-ment responsibilities and assist rescue teams. Contact teams are to advise SWAT of the last known location of the assailant, report location of explosives and provide any pertinent information (assailant description, weaponry, etc.).

CONCLUSION

Occasionally, there will be scenarios that require immediate action/rapid deployment from first responders. The goals of immediate action/rapid deployment are to stop deadly behavior, isolate, contain, bring order to chaos and save lives. Officer safety is always important; however, the issue of self-preservation is secondary to the responder's responsibility to move forward and intervene against assailants bent on aggressive, deadly behavior. Failure to do so can have catastrophic consequences.

As recently as January 2003, Los Angeles police officers responded to an incident in the North Hollywood area of Los Angeles which necessitated the use of immediate action/rapid deployment tactics. There, a hidden, lone gunman shot two of his neighbors. The two victims had simply been standing in their driveway. With the whereabouts of the gunman unknown and his deadly threat still menacing the neighborhood, members of the Special Weapons and Tactics (SWAT) team immediately moved into the field of fire. Within seconds, the two wounded victims and a third victim from inside the home were rescued. Although one of the victims succumbed to his wounds, the other victims were rescued and survived the terrible ordeal. Then, transitioning to the more conventional tactics utilized in a barricaded suspect scenario, members of the SWAT team ultimately took the gunman into custody several hours later.

As this illustrates, circumstances, even those that are not as dramatic as a nationally televised school or workplace shooting, will occasionally arise which require the implementation of immediate action/rapid deployment tactics. Though many officers will never face such a threat, it is essential that all officers be mentally and tactically prepared for the possibility. Since the infamous Columbine tragedy, many law enforcement personnel have chosen to utilize immediate deployment and/or intervention tactics in order to successfully thwart the efforts of assailants. As a result, the lives of numerous innocent people have been saved. In an active-shooter situation, time is of the essence. For this reason, the immediate and swift implementation of contact and rescue teams should be an essential element of law enforcement's response.

MICHAEL DE CAPUA

Michael De Capua is a retired director of public safety and municipal police chief, former emergency manager, and former SWAT commander with 29 years of public safety experience. He currently serves as the Homeland Security Manager for King County Metro Transit in Seattle, as well as a volunteer firefighter and county fire commissioner. Mr. De Capua is a state-certified HazMat Incident Commander, and has served as incident commander and media spokesperson at a variety of incidents ranging from terrorist attacks and school violence incidents to HazMat and major crime scenes. He serves as NTOA's WMD Advisor and course instructor.

Following a 27-year active duty and reserve military career, Mr. De Capua retired as a Lieutenant Colonel from the Air Force Reserve, where he served as a Special Operations pilot and Security Police officer. He holds a Bachelor of Science degree from St. Louis University and a Master's degree in Administration of Justice from Webster University. He is also a graduate of the 140th Session of the FBI National Academy.

Chapter 14

UNIFIED COMMAND:
FROM PLANNING TO RESPONSE

Michael De Capua

BACKGROUND

Following the tragic events of 9/11, the Fire Department of New York (FDNY) commissioned the McKinsey Group to study the Department's planning, training and communications in order to avoid the problems encountered in responding to the unprecedented tragedy. While the report describes the issues associated with the FDNY response, all the findings transfer directly into law enforcement planning. A complete copy of the McKinsey Report can be found at http://www.nyc.gov/html/fdny/html/mck_report/index.shtml.

Among the findings in the report were a lack of joint planning, joint training, joint communications, outdated and irrelevant plans and lack of command staff attention to tactical planning. As a result of the problems encountered by responding agencies, including federal agencies, in trying to coordinate, manage and control resources, the Department of Homeland Security developed Homeland Security Presidential Directive 5 (HSPD5), which President Bush signed on February 27, 2003. HSPD 5 requires any agency receiving federal assistance grant funds to adopt and comply with the new National Response Plan (NRP), National Incident Management System (NIMS), and incident command system for response to all hazards events, ranging from national conventions to natural disasters and WMD attacks.

This chapter will describe a joint (police, fire, EMS, SWAT, HazMat, and health) tactical planning process which can be used to implement the National Incident Management System and Incident Command System (ICS) required by Homeland Security Presidential Directive 5.

Strategy and Tactics

The NRP represents a strategic plan in that it describes what the federal government will do in response to Presidential declarations of disaster or national emergency. The NRP won't tell the FBI, for example, how to respond at the tactical level, it will simply indicate that the FBI respond and assume control of investigations at suspected terrorist events.

At the local level, most emergency management plans are strategic plans, in that they tell first responders what to do, such as "conduct evacuations." The next step is for first responders to develop tactical plans that address how to do evacuations. For example, unified command evaluates and decides evacuations are required, activates shelters, activates traffic control, stations medical along evacuation routes, etc. No federal and state plans will approach this level of detail, nor will most local

HazMat or emergency management plans.

Until a tactical all-hazards response plan is developed, an incident commander (whether fire or law enforcement) and planning staff cannot conduct pre-incident planning, determine equipment requirements, or determine training needs. In addition, law enforcement planning staffs must include fire, HazMat, EMS, public health and emergency management in the planning mix, as no one agency or discipline has the expertise and resources.

To date, DHS grant funding has been based on strategic plans, from which training and equipment requirements cannot be accurately gauged. For the most part, this federal linkage to strategy rather than tactics is based on the demographics of the Department of Homeland Security, i.e., very few DHS policy-makers have street law enforcement or fire experience. In April 2005, the General Accounting Office asked the NTOA's WMD advisor to provide recommendations on how DHS grant funding could be more effectively used. One of the recommendations made centered on DHS buy-in for tactical planning, not strategic planning, to form the basis for equipment and training needs.

Tactical Planning for All-Hazards Incident/Events

Law enforcement and fire response to any major incident, ranging from mass gatherings at conventions to mass casualty terrorist attacks, involves the five Cs: Command, Communication, Control, Coordination and Consolidation. A joint tactical plan should address these areas for each target or event.

Note: Life Safety is not just a fire term, public safety is accomplished through close partnership between police and fire.

Command and Communication

The first arriving unit (police or fire) assumes incident command responsibilities based on the tasks at hand and conducts a size-up or assessment that includes relaying information on:

- **Scene Security**
  Do not rush into any scene. Look for indicators, such as placards on vehicles, types of casualties (burns, nervous disorders, etc.), odors, fires, and note unusual color (bright white, for example), dead animals, and witnesses. Note wind direction and approach the scene from the upwind (wind at your back) side. If no wind, approach from the uphill side. Use the Department of Transportation Emergency Response Guide to determine vehicle placard symbols, initial containment and evacuation distances, and type of personal protective equipment (PPE) needed. A good rule of thumb is to remain at least 1,000 feet from the "hot zone" (scene) until sufficient responders and appropriate equipment is on scene. For first responders within that distance, evacuate to 1,000 feet while awaiting other units, if possible. Broadcast in plain language what you see. The 10-series may sound good on TV, but with multiple agencies responding, not everyone uses or knows each agency's codes.

- **Suspect/Weapons/Devices**
  Be aware that secondary devices and ambushes are likely. Do not approach the scene directly. All witnesses are potential suspects unless you have determined otherwise through pat-downs and interviews. Turn on a pocket recorder as soon as you arrive on scene, and leave it on. Ask about backpacks, weapons, explosions, any remaining suspects, suspects with luggage or packages, suspect descriptions and vehicle information. Look for blast indicators, such as pieces of vehicles and craters in pavement. If the event is radiological, use time, distance and shielding. Broadcast the information you have. Responder safety takes precedence over all actions.

- **Casualties**
  Most fire agencies consider five or more casualties as a Mass Casualty Incident (MCI), and need to know the approximate number and types of casualties. If you are unsure of the extent of injuries and numbers, broadcast your observations and what the victims relate to you. If the scene is not secure, broadcast for fire to stage. Some casualties may be suspects, so fire will need security as they begin to triage after arriving.

- **CBRNE/HazMat/Fire**
  Advise incoming responders of active fires and

fires with unusual color, such as brilliant white light. Advise if any vehicle with a placard is involved and the placard number. Also advise if any obvious HazMat (oil tanks, propane plant, aircraft crash, etc.) is involved. If the incident is terrorism-related, advise, if known, the type of Chemical, Biological, Radiological, Nuclear, or Explosive (CBRNE) agent. If odor is present or an obvious vapor cloud, evacuate immediately upwind and broadcast observations.

- **Access Routes/Safe Routes**
  Broadcast a safe route into the scene staging area. Make sure the route is upwind of the event. If no route is safe, advise responders to stage upwind at least 1,000 feet. Try to keep safe and access routes separate from evacuation routes to avoid congestion, accidents and chaos associated with the event.

- **Initial Incident Command**
  Establish the initial incident command post (ICP) at least 1,000 feet away and upwind from the hot zone. Use cover, remembering the "One-Plus Rule" (there is always another gun, suspect and device aimed at you and the other responders until you know otherwise). Broadcast the location of the ICP, safe routes to the ICP and the location of the staging area. Call only for units you need (SWAT, HazMat, etc.). Advise all others to assemble at the staging area to eliminate confusion at the ICP. Form unified command with fire and EMS initially. Internet incident command courses will not substitute for

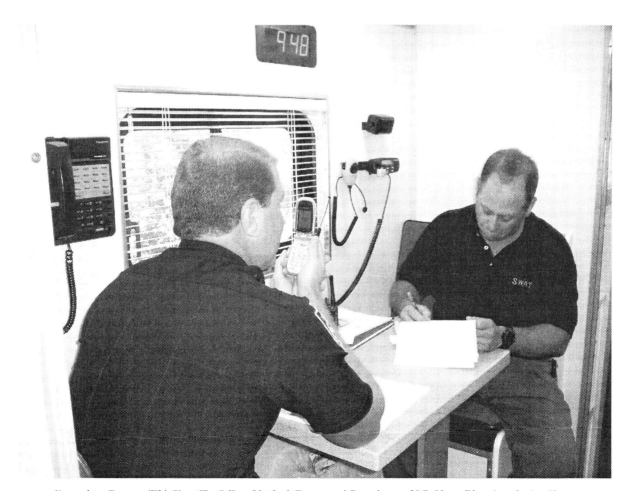

Escambia County (FL) Sheriff's Office Unified Command Post during U.S. Navy Blue Angels Air Show.

field training and exercises with fire, EMS, HazMat, and medical.

- **Initial Incident Action Plan**

  Until the HazMat or CBRNE threat is known, the initial incident commanders must isolate the area, deny entry and identify the threats. These principles constitute the initial action plan for first responders. Arriving units must not rush into the hot zone/kill zone without first identifying the hazards they face. Arriving units should never enter a warm or hot zone until donning the appropriate level of PPE, as determined by the incident commander.

- **Establish Unified Command to Include a Safety Officer and PIO**

  Unified command refers to incident commanders from the responsible jurisdictions acting together to develop incident strategy and set incident objectives. Each incident commander retains command of their respective resources and responders. Unified command identifies a safety officer who is knowledgeable with the

emergency operations underway, and has authority to stop any activity. Safety officers will rotate as the tasks change. For example, during fire fighting operations, fire will appoint a qualified safety officer. If SWAT operations are underway, the law enforcement safety officer will take over. Unified command also appoints Public Information Officers (PIOs), who will work in the Joint Information Center (JIC). All media releases are approved by unified command prior to release. For a terrorist event, the FBI has lead criminal investigations responsibilities and will assign agents to the Operation and Planning Sections. The FBI may be represented in unified command, but will not take over unified command duties. Initial incident commanders typically become part of the Operations Section once command is transferred to more qualified individuals.

- **Identify Continuing/New Threats**

  The threat faced initially by first responders may continue throughout the event. For example, a

An exercise Chemical Dispersal Device.

persistent nerve agent attack will contaminate hot zones and victims until the area is decontaminated or the agent dissipates. Continual air and sample monitoring by HazMat or other qualified teams extends throughout the incident until the responsible incident commander (usually fire) determines the threat no longer poses a danger to life and health. Other threats may surface as the incident progresses. Ambushes of first responders, improvised explosive devices (IEDs), health problems, diversionary attacks to draw response from primary scenes and panic pose problems that unified command tasks the Planning Section to identify and develop plans to address.

- **If Incident is Terrorism-Related, Notify FBI JTTF and Request Activation of the National Response Plan**
  The National Response Plan provides the means by which local incident commanders request federal resources. There are two methods to request federal assistance through activation of the National Response Plan: (1) Requests for these resources come from the incident commander through the Emergency Operations Center (EOC) responsible for incident support. This EOC either locates the resources or requests the state EOC to locate them. If the resources are not available at the state level, the governor requests the President to declare the incident an Incident of National Significance under the Stafford Act. Federal agencies are then mobilized by the Department of Homeland Security to provide the requested support, or (2) the local incident commander may contact the local FBI Joint Terrorism Task Force (JTTF) and request activation of the National Response Plan through the FBI chain of command to the Department of Homeland Security and the President.

- **Establish Unified Command Post (UCP)**
  Position UCPs at least 1,000 feet away from the hot zone (there is no need for the UCP to be within sight of the hot zone), uphill, upwind and upstream from the hot zone. Task the Planning Section to provide plans for rapid relocation of the UCP if the event situation or weather changes.

- **Establish Staging Area(s)**

The rule of thumb for staging area location is at least 2,500 feet from the hot zone, or three minutes driving time away, and within the cold zone. Staging area managers track and document: units and personnel arriving, task units deployed at the scene as directed by the Operations Section, and liaise with the Logistics Section for food, fuel and other supplies. Law enforcement will be tasked to provide security of staging areas.

- **Establish Incident PPE Requirements**
  Based on the threat to life posed by the incident, unified command will order the appropriate personal protective equipment (PPE) level for responders in the hot and warm zones. OSHA and EPA requirements are mandatory. Level "A" PPE is required for vapor protection and level "B" is required for splash protection. Level "C" protection affords little protection, and may only be used once unified command has evaluated situation parameters and determined level "C" is appropriate. Level "C" protection is never used during initial response into a hot or warm zone in which the threat has not been identified, or levels of contaminates determined through monitoring equipment used by qualified personnel.

- **Establish Communications Plan**
  Determine before an incident how the responding agencies intend to communicate during a major emergency. On-scene, confirm that the plan will work, or modify as needed. Do not use codes during multi-agency, multi-jurisdictional responses. Make sure backup communications needs are identified, and do not rely on technology backups, such as Internet, WI-FI, cell phones or trunked radio systems. Consider CB and HAM radio and satellite phones.

- **Identify Additional Resource Needs**
  Request capabilities, not team names, as these often change. For example, request radiological monitoring teams, not HazMat specialists or technicians, or the NEST team, unless you know these are what you need. Be specific in numbers. Don't ask for "some" or a "few." If you need 14 additional officers for traffic and perimeter control, make that request and indicate this team should be staged until called for by the Operations Section. If resources are not available, the EOC, not unified command, is respon-

sible for finding the capabilities unified command needs.

- **Develop Incident Action Plan (IAP)**
Unified command will task the Planning Section with developing the Incident Action Plan (incident objectives), task the Operations Section with developing the tactics to achieve the incident objectives, and expect regular updates. The IAP sets priorities and describes objectives to achieve the priorities for an operational period (usually 12 hours). Incident priorities may change if the incident situation changes.
- **Direct Planning Section to Develop Survive-To-Operate Plan (STOP)**
Unified or area command at the outset of an incident will direct the Planning Section to prepare a plan on how command will function until federal assistance arrives, using a 72-hour window in which to function until assistance arrives.

Control

Once the threats are identified, unified command must establish or determine the following:
- **Establish and Secure Gross Decontamination (Decon)**
Prior to sending a joint assessment or entry team into the hot zone, fire will establish gross decontamination for the team. The decon set-up may be as simple as two engines with hoses and small retaining pools.
- **Joint Assessment or Entry Team (JAT/JET)**

Field decon setup.

Unified command should deploy a predesignated and trained team, in proper PPE, into the hot zone to provide real-time intelligence and information. The JAT/JET should include law enforcement for team safety and threat neutralization, qualified HazMat technicians and tactical EMS for team safety and triage reconnaissance.

- **Establish and Secure Technical Decon**
  Separate decon for victims and responders and secure both lines. Detectives in appropriate PPE can be used to gather intelligence from victims and teams in decon lines.

- **Evacuation or Shelter-in-Place**
  Unified command will assess and decide based on monitoring, threat analysis, and JAT/JET observations, if evacuation or sheltering a population in place is appropriate. Evacuations often pose greater risks to the population and deplete law enforcement staffing. Sheltering-in-place should be used if a time-critical threat is present. Incident action plans will be updated accordingly.

- **Establish Responder Rehabilitation**
  Unified command will provide a secure environment for deconned responders to rest, rehydrate and receive medical attention, if needed.

- **Conduct Regular Situation Briefings**
  Major incidents generate tremendous amounts of information. Communication of this information leads to the success or failure of incident management. Successful incident commanders routinely establish hourly update briefings for all

Contaminated hostages.

section chiefs to ensure that everyone is operating with the same information. During these briefings, the Operations Section briefs the status of ongoing tactical operations and progress toward achieving IAP objectives. The Planning Section updates the IAP and intelligence information with the command staff and sections during the briefing. Logistics briefs any equipment or supply issues.

- **Update Incident Action Plan**
  No incident response is pre-canned and static. Planning must be an ongoing process using the latest and best intelligence.

Coordination

As the incident evolves, the involvement of other agencies will become crucial to successful mitigation. Unified command will:

- **Identify and Request Additional Support**

Through the EOC
EOCs may make strategic decisions as to competing incident resource requests if multiple incidents are involved.

- **Implement Area Command**
  If more than one incident occurs, the unified commands involved may elect to create an area command that manages joint planning, joint logistics and joint administration for all the events. Once area command is established (usually co-located at one of the responsible EOCs), unified command at each incident continues to manage operations at those sites. Area command may also be involved during an incident or event that is large scale without defined incident scenes, such as a bioterrorism attack or major earthquake with widespread damage.
- **Use Media Coverage**
  Unified or area command will form a Joint Information Center (JIC) to coordinate media

SWAT containment of a downtown Seattle transit tunnel during a full-scale exercise

releases and develop an overall strategy on the effective use of the media during the event. Once the FBI arrives at unified command and has established its Joint Field Office, the FBI incident commander will assume control of all media releases by forming a JIC to coordinate all releases. This JIC will ensure the investigations and intelligence functions are not compromised by uncoordinated media releases.

Consolidation

This phase of the event or incident involves the ability to sustain the response, safety of the scene and follow-on investigation for extended periods of time. Unified command will:

- **Identify Debriefing of Off-Going Personnel for Intelligence**
  Each agency will debrief its personnel going off duty and provide results to the Planning Section as the focal point for information and intelligence gathering.
- **Identify Critical Incident Stress Management Needs**
  At the scene, and at follow-on meetings, the EOC will arrange and provide religious and peer debriefing sessions for responders and communications personnel.
- **Develop Crime Scene Investigation Plan**
  If the event is terrorism related, crime scene processing could take weeks or months, as in the case of 9/11. As the lead investigation agency, the FBI may request continuing perimeter, medical and law enforcement support that will impact public safety agency staffing. Unified command will coordinate these requests and assess the impact on continuing operations.
- **Develop Demobilization Plan**
  Unified command will direct the Planning Section to prepare a demobilization plan that addresses continuing incident requirements and return-to-normal operations for response agencies. Demobilization plans provide for an orderly return to normal operations, while sustaining

any long-term incident management functions.
- **Incident Critique**
  Unified command or another designated group will conduct a no-fault incident critique to identify what areas went well and where additional planning, operations and logistics improvements can be made to existing plans.

Incident Command Tips

1. The incident commander cannot manage an incident when they are deeply involved in the operations of the incident. SWAT commanders and HazMat team leaders should not be incident commanders. These critical individuals should be assigned to the Operations Section.
2. Don't manage the chaos, manage the incident. At every emergency or major event, there will be chaos and confusion. Implement the incident command system and use checklists, and the chaos will disappear.
3. Delegate. The incident commander leads by observing and directing the actions of the Section Chiefs, not by counting how many rungs on the ladder the SWAT team needs to board the cruise ship that has been hijacked.
4. Institutionalize incident command. Use incident command for all major day-to-day response (armed robberies, major vehicle fatalities, large conventions, etc.).
5. Work closely with the fire department and HazMat teams. They have the expertise in HazMat response and containment, and will look to law enforcement for life safety. Remember, a WMD event is HazMat with bad guys!
6. Plan now. Once the sirens start, it is too late to find out that no one has interoperable communications.
7. Plan the joint tactical plan, train the plan, exercise the tactical plan, and then fix the plan. Remember, strategy tells us what to do—tactics tells us how to do it.

RICHARD CARMONA

Richard Carmona, M.D., was a full-time deputy sheriff, SWAT team leader, and instructor with the Pima County (AZ) Sheriff's Department for 21 years. He has extensive experience and background in military and police special operations, including service in the United States Army Special Forces in Vietnam and other areas. He is also a trauma surgeon, and has been published extensively in many areas of special operations, including tactics and Tactical Emergency Medical Support (TEMS), a concept he helped originate. He is the recipient of the Sheriff's Department's Medal of Valor and numerous commendations, among them the NTOA Award for Excellence. In 2002, former deputy Carmona became Vice Admiral Carmona, the United States Surgeon General.

Chapter 15

FIRST RESPONDER TO WEAPONS OF MASS DESTRUCTION INCIDENTS

Richard Carmona

"First Responders" is a collective term that refers to any public safety personnel who routinely respond to incidents in order to protect the health, safety and welfare of our citizens and communities. Typically, these personnel assets include law enforcement, firefighters, emergency medical service providers at all levels of proficiency and, more recently, the military. In addition, some communities utilize specially trained civilian volunteers, such as Civilian Emergency Response Teams, (CERT). In most cases the initial response and actions to a particular incident will be very similar for all first responders.

First responders have become quite expert at responding to and managing a variety of natural and man-made/caused threats. These would include, but not be limited to, automobile accidents, fires, hazardous materials exposures, explosions, storms, floods, hurricanes, earthquakes and multicasualty (disaster) incidents secondary to many other causes. More recently, our first responders have been faced with man-made threats intentionally utilized to create harm and/or provide leverage for various extremist groups domestically and abroad. These group members are collectively termed terrorists, and the tools of their trade are weapons of mass destruction (WMD). Weapons of mass destruction consist of conventional and specialized weapons that have the ability to cause widespread harm and damage.

Therefore, the awareness and initial responses of first responders in a potential weapons of mass destruction environment will have a significant impact on the public, themselves, and the overall outcome of the incident. Use of, or threatening to use, weapons of mass destruction constitutes a crime and, therefore, the area becomes a crime scene. Non-law enforcement first responders must therefore be aware that almost anything may be evidence, and that their actions within the crime scene should be carefully thought out in order to preserve evidence and operate safely and efficiently in this high-risk environment.

The advent of weapons of mass destruction domestically requires that our existing strong and proven response infrastructure and personnel incorporate new and essential information into their daily practices.

The comments in this chapter will be directed to law enforcement first responders.

Recent Events

For many years, Americans watched at a distance as other countries suffered through the ravages of terrorism and weapons of mass destruction. However, this past decade brought these atrocities to our home front. Beginning in 1993 with the bombing of the World Trade Center in New York City, and most recently culminating in the events of "9/11" in New York City and Washington, D.C., our individual first responders, communities, and the nation were challenged to respond as never before. This response not only included the consequence management of the aircraft devastation of national symbols, but also the subsequent bioterrorist (Anthrax) events and threats in several cities.

For many, whose daily work involved preparedness and consequence management, these events were no surprise, since it was always a question of when and how it would occur, and not if it would happen.

These events have magnified our individual and collective response system deficiencies and provided the impetus for local, state and federal leadership to strengthen and create "seamless" response systems.

The Threats

Weapons of mass destruction can be divided into conventional weapons of mass destruction (CWMD) and specialized weapons of mass destruction (SWMD). Conventional weapons of mass destruction include such entities as explosives, bullets and fire. Specialized weapons of mass destruction include nuclear, biologic and chemical agents. The reader will sometimes encounter different weapons of mass destruction description or categorization methods in some publications. For example, "B-NICE" refers to biologic, nuclear, incendiary, chemical and explosive agents.

Although not of a terrorist origin, our first responders have a considerable amount of training and expertise in responding to natural and manmade events involving personnel and property damage. Also, our communication, EMS and care systems have evolved significantly since their inception in the early 1970s. Therefore, a new area of concern as it relates to conventional weapons of mass destruction utilized by a terrorist is how and if these new threats should change the established practices of our law enforcement first responders.

In the threat area of specialized weapons of mass destruction the issues are far more complex. First, most first responders have knowledge and/or expertise in the response to and management of chemical events, albeit not from a terrorist source. Most are the result of accidental chemical spills that nevertheless can cause the same devastation as

those events that are terrorist induced. In fact, a subspecialty of fire and EMS has emerged over the past two decades that specifically addresses these events. Hazardous materials, or "HazMat," response is a well-recognized discipline that we have come to rely on when a chemical event occurs. Even though this is a highly specialized area, all first responders are at a minimum trained to recognize such events, request HazMat response and, in the interim, begin processes to limit further injury to personnel and damage to property, while not becoming a casualty themselves. The nuclear and biologic components of specialized weapons of mass destruction are the most problematic, since most first responders (and medical professionals) have had very little, if any, formal training in the recognition and response to these type of incidents.

In addition, both are unique in that responders may, in fact, be responding to an event that occurred days or weeks earlier in another location, but only now are persons succumbing to the threat. For example, a biologic agent, such as Smallpox, if intentionally spread today, would not be manifest as illness for a week or more due to the incubation or latency period. Once symptomatic, personnel unknowingly exposed can act as vectors and spread the disease to others. In another example, a source of radiation that was not associated with an overt explosion but rather covertly used could cause radiation harm (usually delayed) to many but may go undetected for some time. Although the amount of radiation would generally be small and the sequelae possibly not appreciated for years, the psychological effects could be devastating.

In both cases, this would be confounding for first responders to a "person down" call, since there may be no apparent source or cause at the scene. Another variation on the nuclear threat would be the so-called "dirty bomb," or improvised explosive device attached to a radiation source. First responders would be responding to an explosion and the property and personnel injuries expected. Unless tested for, the radiation component may go undetected until persons manifest radiation sickness, either acutely or some time later, depending on the type and the dose of radiation. These are all possible scenarios of many that will force us to change some of our practices and heighten our suspicions to any seemingly "straightforward" event.

The Location

The terrorist uses weapons of mass destruction against a superior adversary to create disruption, paranoia, fear and intimidation. The location of a terrorist event may, therefore, be carefully planned for maximal psychological and physical advantage. This may include targets of opportunity, such as the World Trade Center, the Pentagon or, possibly, large gatherings, such as athletic events to name a few. It should be noted that often the mere threat of a weapons of mass destruction event at a given location could have catastrophic consequences that first responders may have difficulty discerning from an actual event due to the panic, chaos and psychological effects of the worried.

Personnel Readiness And Awareness

The desired state of readiness is first and foremost dependent on the first responder's ability to recognize that a given event may, in fact, be terrorist induced. This heightened "awareness" is achieved through education and training.

In general, when responding to any call, especially those involving multiple casualties, the first responders must ask themselves, "Is there a logical explanation for this event?" Often, it may not be apparent that the event is terrorist caused unless there is an early claim by the perpetrators or the event is extremely unusual, such as planes crashing sequentially into buildings. Shortly after 9/11 there was a large explosion in a midtown New York City building which, because of heightened sensitivity, was feared to be another terrorist event. A short time after, it was determined that it was a faulty boiler that exploded accidentally.

A heightened index of suspicion based on the type of call, location, intelligence and history will assist the first responder in determining the probability that a given event may be terrorist induced. Unfortunately, there is no error-free methodology available to determine true accidents versus terrorist-caused events.

First responders should also be aware of the gen-

eral classes of agents that could be used, as well as possible methods of dispersion.

Nerve Agents

Nerve agents can be inhaled, absorbed or ingested. Nerve agents block nerve function and therefore can cause weakness, twitching or paralysis. Examples (and abbreviations) include Tabun (GA), Soman (GD), Sarin (GB) and VX. These agents can spread from person to person by cross-contamination. Therefore, decontamination procedures are very important.

Blister Agents

Blister agents damage tissue they come in contact with. This may be skin, eyes or the respiratory system. They usually cause pain and discomfort, but can sometimes be lethal, depending on the type, dose and health of those affected. Examples (and abbreviations) include Mustard (H), Phosgene Oxime (CX) and Lewisite (L). These agents can spread from person to person by cross-contamination.

Blood Agents

Various Cyanide compounds that are usually inhaled and block oxygen metabolism can be encountered. Depending on the compound of Cyanide used, the vapors may be lighter or heavier than air and therefore disperse quickly or stay in the air longer. These compounds can be rapidly fatal in higher doses. These agents are not contagious.

Choking Agents

These agents cause irritation in the respiratory tract and copious secretions. Persons feel as if they are drowning. Examples are Phosgene (GL) and Chlorine (CL).

These categories are one method of expressing the types of chemical agents that may be encountered. Although the agents are the same, there are also other methods of categorization that the reader may encounter in the literature.

Biologic Agents

Unlike chemical agents, whose effects generally are noted immediately and may be appreciated by one's senses, biologic agents are not obvious or apparent at a scene. In addition, biologic agents generally have no immediate effect, but rather cause symptoms days or weeks later. These agents can't penetrate unbroken skin and are usually inhaled or ingested. They are particularly sensitive to light, heat, humidity and temperature. In general, there are three types of biologic agents, bacteria, viruses and toxins. Rickettsia are another type of organism that have characteristics of both viruses and bacteria. Examples of bacteria are those causing anthrax, plague and cholera. Some biologic agents are contagious and therefore may cause epidemics, such as Smallpox. Anthrax is generally not contagious. Examples of viruses include Smallpox and some types of encephalitis. Toxins are poison-like substances that are derived from microorganisms, such as from botulism, or plants, such as ricin from the castor bean. Toxins can affect the nervous system or cells directly. Toxins are not contagious.

Nuclear Agents

Radiation is the transfer of energy through space. Radiation consists of high- and low-energy particles that may be harmful (or deadly) to tissue. The damage is dependent on the source and type of radiation, as well as the distance from the source over time. First responders, as well as most licensed medical professionals, have had little, if any, training or experience in dealing with radiation injury. This is due to the fact that there have been relatively few purposeful or accidental (much more common) radiation releases in our collective world history. In addition, the accidental releases generally cause little or no acute harm (a few exceptions, such as Chernobyl, are noted), and only occasionally, long-term illness and very infrequently, death. Sources of radiation vary from that naturally occurring in the environment to X-ray machines and nuclear devices or bombs meant to harm. Terrorist sources of radiation may be any or all of the aforementioned, plus others, such as nuclear reactors/power plants and so-called "dirty bombs,"

i.e., a conventional explosive attached to a radiation source.

It is difficult to comprehend the potential devastation of a nuclear bomb. A one-megaton device detonated 8,000 feet above the earth would level all buildings within a mile of ground zero and cause damage, death and injury twelve miles away. The ground and air would be contaminated, and many that didn't die from the initial blast would suffer the acute and long-term effects of radiation poisoning. The psychological impact would be equally devastating. Radiation injury may be overt or covert, and may or may not be accompanied by trauma or burns.

An initial first responder to a radiation event may not be aware, and may not have radiation detection equipment immediately available to determine exposure. In addition, radiation exposure may be external, from a source outside the body, through the skin, or internal from absorbed, inhaled or ingested radioactive materials. Externally radiated patients are not contaminated. Patients with radioactive materials on their skin and/or clothes are contaminated, as are some patients with internal contamination. These cases are often difficult to evaluate for first responders, as well as licensed medical professionals.

For external contamination, follow the usual decontamination procedures utilizing universal precautions. For internal contamination, a radiation safety officer or nuclear medicine physician should be contacted. If patients have concomitant life-threatening injuries, treat first then decontaminate. If the injuries are non-life threatening, decontaminate first and treat after. This is one area that requires a great deal of forethought, training and planning for agencies deploying first responders. Numerous resources are available in print and Web-based via military and civilian government agencies, such as the Army and the Department of Energy.

The Response

First responders to an event who are aware of the possible causes (including terrorism) through education and training stand a much better chance of successfully surviving, as well as mounting an effective response that will maximally reduce morbidity and mortality for all involved.

The response to a terrorist event that involves conventional weapons of mass destruction is generally no different than any other catastrophic event other than one must be concerned about secondary events, such as explosions or booby traps and securing the crime scene. Scene safety, evacuation, triage, stabilization and transfer proceed as usual, commensurate with available resources.

The response to an event involving specialized weapons of mass destruction (if known or suspected) will be different and dependent on the possible cause of the event. Nuclear events have been previously discussed. Chemical events are usually obvious, and we have over two decades of experience with HazMat responses, whether terrorist induced or just the usual accident. The first responder to a chemical event from any cause may see and/or smell a toxic substance and/or see persons immediately affected. Those affected may have respiratory problems, such as coughing and excess mucous production, as well as skin irritation or blistering, depending on the agent they are exposed to. Other agents that can affect the nervous system can cause twitching, weakness and paralysis. Irrespective of the agent causing the symptoms, the first responder needs to be aware and not become a casualty. Put on whatever personal protective equipment (PPE) you have, and request HazMat early. Cover all exposed skin and use a facemask with filter, if available. Stay upwind from the apparent location. Set up a perimeter widely around where most casualties appear to be. Do not enter the perimeter. Instead, verbally direct all walking wounded to a safe area (upwind) and begin having them disrobe and start basic decontamination, if water is available. Try to keep everyone together, and don't allow anyone to leave. Request wide evacuation of the area or consider "sheltering in place," depending on the threat and location. Those that are "down" in the affected area (hot zone) will have to remain there until properly equipped rescuers arrive. Begin thinking about ingress, egress and staging for all responding units. Implement an incident command system (ICS), and establish early triage, treatment and transportation areas. Gather as much intelligence and history as possible, and transmit the information to all responding units so they may prepare en route. Once HazMat units arrive, make sure you are evaluated and decontaminated, if necessary.

SUMMARY

Recent events have challenged our first responders to augment and strengthen our personal, personnel and system readiness to engage weapons of mass destruction events. Heightened awareness through education and training is essential. Personal and personnel readiness must be individually assessed, as well as assessed as part of a team and system. Scenario-based community testing is necessary to test the individual, agency and system responses to given threats. Deficiencies appreciated may then be corrected.

The first responder to a WMD event is the initial key to unlocking a multidisciplinary team response coordinated via an incident command system.

The appropriately aware and trained first responder has the ability to ensure a timely and cost-effective utilization of resources that will maximize efficiency while decreasing morbidity and mortality.

BIBLIOGRAPHY AND RESOURCE GUIDE

1. S. Drielak and T. Brandon. (2000). *Weapons of mass destruction, response and investigation.* Springfield, IL: Charles C Thomas, Publisher.
2. Federal Emergency Management Agency (FEMA).
3. Federal Bureau of Investigation (FBI).
4. Department of Health and Human Services (HHS).
5. Centers for Disease Control (CDC).
6. U. S. Environmental Protection Agency (EPA).
7. U. S. Department of Energy (DOE).
8. Department of Defense (DOD).
9. State Health Departments.
10. Professional organizations, such as the American College of Emergency Physicians, American College of Surgeons, the American College of Pediatrics and the American Public Health Association.

References 2–10 all have Web sites and links to various WMD-related information.

Part 5

LEGAL ASPECTS

RONALD M. McCARTHY

Ron McCarthy retired from the Los Angeles Police Department as a Sergeant after 25 years of service. During 14 years with "D" Platoon (SWAT) as a Squad Leader and Senior Supervisor, he was involved in several hundred SWAT operations. Mr. McCarthy continues to lecture extensively throughout the United States and a number of foreign countries on subjects ranging from SWAT operations and crowd and riot control, to use of force and counterterrorism.

Following retirement from the Los Angeles Police Department, Mr. McCarthy became the Chief of Tactical Operations for the U.S. Department of Energy Central Training Academy in Albuquerque, New Mexico. Subsequently, he accepted an offer to become the Manager of the Center For Advancing Police Studies for the International Association of Chiefs of Police. In 1990, he was appointed to the New York City Police Department Firearms Review Committee, and in 1993 was selected to participate in the evaluation of the F.B.I. operation at the Branch Davidian Compound near Waco, Texas. He testified before the U.S. Congress regarding this operation. Mr. McCarthy now operates a consulting firm, R.M. McCarthy & Associates, with offices in California and Arizona.

Ron is the co-author of *The Management of Police Specialized Tactical Units,* and the author of numerous law enforcement articles. He is a court-qualified expert witness on use of force/deadly force, SWAT, crowd and riot control, and police/private security practice. Mr. McCarthy is the recipient of the Los Angeles Police Department Medal of Valor, the Police Star and two Unit Citations, as well as numerous commendations. He is also the recipient of the National Tactical Officers Association (N.T.O.A.) Award of Excellence, the N.T.O.A. Lifetime Achievement Award, and the "All American Hero Award."

Chapter 16

LITIGATION AND SURVIVING LAWSUITS AND PROSECUTION

Ronald M. McCarthy

Although officers must be prepared to intelligently explain what occurred after a use-of-force incident, they are rarely trained in the verbal skills and tactics necessary to describe a variety of important topics. These are areas where plaintiffs' lawyers will try to "beat up" an officer. The example which follows describes a plaintiff's lawyer questioning an officer in a deposition concerning the officer's actions during a foot pursuit. The officer knew he had been following a felony suspect. When the suspect jumped from the vehicle he was driving and began to flee on foot, the officer naturally began to chase the suspect. The officer had only run about fifty feet when the suspect turned and displayed a handgun. The suspect then fired at the officer. Unfortunately, one of the rounds traveled almost one hundred yards, striking and killing a little girl. In the deposition, take note of the plaintiff's lawyer's questions, and how the lawyer manipulates the young officer.

Q. So do you think what you're telling us is—and you certainly believe you acted reasonably, don't you?

A. I believe so.

Q. You think that when you're acting reasonably, and you have a suspect in a stolen—with stolen plates or a stolen vehicle, you said that you have to assume the worst. And that's rea-sonable, isn't it?

A. To me that is reasonable.

Q. And it's also reasonable, therefore, to assume the suspect has a gun? That's reasonable, isn't it?

A. To me?

Q. Yes, sir.

A. That's reasonable to me.

Q. And it's reasonable, therefore, to assume that if you set out on foot in chase of this suspect and yell that you are the police—it's reasonable to assume that he may use that gun, isn't it?

A. I can't think of the mindset of a suspect, but I don't believe a reasonable person would shoot at the police.

Q. So you don't think it's reasonable to think that a suspect who is running on foot from a police officer who you assume has a gun—it's not reasonable to assume that he would use that gun, is that what you're telling us?

A. I don't know the suspect has a gun.

Q. You said earlier that you assume the worst, and therefore you assume the suspect had a gun. Isn't it also true that it's therefore reasonable to assume the suspect would use the gun?

A. No.

Q. It's not? All right. So when you are on the street and you are dealing with a fleeing felon who has a gun, you don't assume that he will use that gun?

A. First, I wouldn't know specifically that he had a gun.

Q. Let me make sure you understand my question because that's not what I was asking. What I intended to ask was, if you have a suspect that you believe–or, assume has a gun, and he's running from you, and he's got–running from a vehicle with stolen plates that's run stop signs and gone through residential neighborhoods at high rates of speed, you're saying it's not reasonable to assume the suspect might not use that gun? Is that what you're telling us?

A. First of all, I'm not going to agree. Is this a hypothetical that we're talking?

Q. Sure. You bet.

A. I don't necessarily think it's reasonable, no. Personally, I have chased many suspects on foot who have been armed and have not used the gun. I don't think a reasonable person–I don't think a reasonable suspect would be in the mindset to shoot at the police.

Q. You always assume that the suspects you're chasing are going to act reasonably?

A. I don't assume anything. I've just told you what I've experienced.

Q. Have you ever been taught in any of your classes or seen in any of your operations manuals that you should assume that someone who is fleeing with a gun might use that gun; that you should at least anticipate they might use the gun?

A. I don't believe you have to anticipate that a suspect fleeing is necessarily going to shoot at the police.

Q. In other words, you think it's reasonable to act as if the suspect will not use the gun?

A. Again, the suspect's action is based on a case-by-case scenario.

Q. Let me ask it this way. In a situation where a suspect pulls into an apartment complex with children riding bikes and walking along the sidewalks, and gets out–exits the vehicle and starts running, you know that if you assume the worst–you assume he has a gun–and you know if he uses that gun, you are certainly endangering the public, isn't that true?

A. You can't assume what a suspect is going to do.

Q. If the suspect uses that gun, the public is in danger?

A. If anyone uses a gun, anybody's in danger.

Q. So if this suspect in the scenario, as you have drawn it, where Officer Cox pulled up behind the suspect–if that suspect uses his gun, he's putting those individuals in the apartment complex in danger, don't you agree with that?

A. I said if a suspect shoots a gun, the lives of everyone in that area are endangered.

Q. And so as an officer–as you put it, one of your primary responsibilities is to protect the public–what you want to do is take actions that would tend to keep the suspect from using the gun rather than actions that would cause the suspect to use the gun, do you think that's reasonable?

A. Yes. Our responsibility is to protect the public and our actions don't control necessarily, the actions of a suspect.

Q. No. But don't you agree that there are times that your actions, as a police officer, could either tend to cause a suspect who has a gun to use it, and then there are times when your actions could tend to cause the suspect not to use a gun?

A. I wouldn't know how to measure how many times something has prevented something, if it hasn't happened.

Q. Maybe I'm not making myself clear. Obviously not. You don't think there are times when you, as a police officer, and you're dealing with a suspect who has a gun–you don't think there are times when your actions could diffuse the situation and not cause the suspect to use the gun, and then in that same situation, other actions that you take could cause the suspect to use the gun?

Q. You can't think of those kinds of scenarios?

A. Each scenario is based differently on the tactical situation, and the chief objective is to preserve the public life.

It is apparent that several factors are critical to understand here. The glaring fact is that a sincere young officer was doing his professional and level best to apprehend a felony suspect in the tradition of good law enforcement, and as he was trained to do. It is also apparent that the officer is no match for the lawyer, who has practiced law for decades, is credentialed and has an advantage that is unfair–playing the "word game." It is the belief of many in law enforcement that the "system" has become just that–"a game of words"–an unfair, structured and slanted process that attorneys use, with right and wrong, truth, courage, integrity and fairness taking a back seat.

It is unfortunate that there is little or no training provided by most police academies to prepare a police officer for a deposition. Depositions are totally adversarial. The attorney for the police officer can only object to the questions, but the questions must be answered by the officer. Later, in the trial, the plaintiff's lawyer reads from the transcript of the deposition and forces the officer into a "yes" or "no" response to the questions. "Officer, in your deposition, didn't you testify under oath that you should have anticipated that the suspect was armed, could possibly shoot at you, and therefore, could miss you and hit a citizen?" Following this logic, when foot pursuits of suspects running from burglaries, robberies, rapes, stolen vehicles and narcotics arrests occur, it would be an unreasonable action on the part of officers, and an unreasonable endangerment to the public, if the officer attempted to pursue. Unfortunately, some police departments are starting to create foot pursuit policies similar to vehicle pursuit policies.

Poorly Written Policy

The largest sheriff's department in the United States has a foot pursuit policy that is five full pages in length, and details every possible aspect of a foot pursuit. This document, as written, should be a lesson plan for training, not a policy. Policies are rules, and as such should be brief, easy to understand, and an asset to the young professional officer. Words such as "reasonable" should be used in place of "necessary." The word "generally" should be used in policies to allow for those incidents that confront officers wherein they are forced to think and react in a "reasonable" manner. For example, no deadly force policy covers those rare incidents when officers run over suspects who are trying to kill them (the police officer is using the police vehicle as a weapon). Such incidents are rare, but they have happened. In Missoula, Montana, a male Caucasian suspect fired at an officer while the officer was patrolling his beat. The suspect was standing in the street. The officer was struck by a round fired by the suspect. The bullet penetrated the windshield of the police vehicle and struck the officer in the chest. The officer was wearing body armor and the round was stopped by his vest. The officer deliberately ran the suspect down with his police vehicle. (The officer had been correctly trained to do exactly that in a training program only weeks prior to this event.)

Officers are put at great risk if policies are poorly written. If an officer is at risk civilly, and possibly criminally, because a policy is poorly worded, then, so too, is the department and the city, county, or state the officer serves.

There are several areas of concern that can create a use-of-force incident crisis when, in fact, the use of force was appropriate. Poorly written policy is only one of those areas.

Community Attitude

The general feelings that members of a community have about the law enforcement agency that serves them are critical to the potential of defending a use-of-force situation, even when the force was reasonable and ethical. Perception on the part of a significant number of people that the police department is unfair, or is using force unreasonably, can create doubt and distrust that are pervasive. This distrust, fueled by special interest groups and the media, can convince the community at large that a problem of excessive force exists when there is none. Therefore, it is every officer's obligation to be professional and ethical when using force. This is not to say that officers should be reluctant to use force, or to fire rounds, in response to a threat that is real, or reasonably appears to be real. All too often, an officer will respond to what appears to be a real threat, and after the event, investigation discloses that the suspect had a toy gun or an empty gun. Critics then opine that the use of deadly force was not necessary. In hindsight, it was not necessary, but it certainly was reasonable. If the law enforcement agency has the confidence of the community, the agency's explanation of such an event will be accepted.

Use-of-Force and Deadly Force Investigation

It is not easy to identify the biggest pitfall for law enforcement regarding the investigation of deadly force and use of-force incidents. In all probability, it

is the structure of the investigation that an agency adopts. This unfortunately occurs when an agency adopts a process that is designed more toward trying to satisfy critics within and outside the community. As a result, the officer is often treated like a suspect. It is no mystery then that many officers today ask for an attorney before answering questions about a shooting in which they were involved.

Although incidents of shootings and use of force have dropped dramatically over the last twenty-five years, complaints of brutality and wrongful death have increased. Where police departments have overreacted to community and media pressure, and initiated unreasonable procedures and unfair discipline, crime has gone up as morale and productivity have gone down. Officers leave the department looking for better working conditions at police agencies which have continued to maintain professionalism, organizational pride and high morale.

The law enforcement agency is obligated to do truthful and professional investigations, and inform the public about their findings in a reasonable time frame. The officer is entitled to be treated fairly, and should be confident that the investigators who conduct the investigation are not only of the highest quality, but specially trained to investigate officer shootings and use of force. There have been instances wherein officers have been disciplined and/or fired, and following a full review and appeal, it is determined the officer was not at fault. The police chief, sheriff or prosecutor reacted to community and media pressure before all available information was obtained and fired and/or prosecuted the officer.

All too often, the scene of the incident is not handled professionally, or evidence is lost or mishandled. It is important that officers have some knowledge of what constitutes a professional investigation, and know how to take steps to ensure they are advised of, and given, the rights to which they are entitled.

First, it is strongly recommended that officers carry an audiotape recorder, and use it at the beginning of every contact, no matter how routine the contact appears to be at the outset. Well over 60 percent of all officer-involved shootings are total surprises to the officer. Therefore, as the officer can never be certain where a police contact will go, the audiotape recorder should be turned on at the beginning of every stop, radio call, or citizen approach. It is now apparent that audiotapes and in-car cameras have exonerated officers time and time again. There are some states, such as Oregon and Washington, which have state constitutional restrictions against audiotaping. However, the United States Constitution and most states allow this procedure. It is an unfortunate fact that officers often must prove they are not guilty, as opposed to the general standard of being presumed innocent, and the burden of proving guilt placed upon the prosecution.

Where agencies have issued audiotape recorders, false complaints were positively identified in more than 90 percent of all complaints received by those agencies. It would be impossible otherwise to prove this fact to critics of the police or the media. Most police chiefs and police supervisors are shocked to learn that the false complaint percentage is so high. Significantly, the A.C.L.U. has never come out in favor of officers carrying and using audiotape recorders.

Why then is the audiotape recorder often ignored as a standard-issue item to field law enforcement officers? Law enforcement changes very slowly. Semiautomatic pistols were available in multiple choices of design and function from the mid-1930s. It took forty years for the often absurd reasons for not going to semiautos to finally evaporate. The issue of audiotape recorders is much the same.

Investigating Police Use of Force and Deadly Force

It has been the practice of law enforcement agencies to investigate police use of force through an internal affairs structure, with the emphasis placed on department policy, rules and regulations. Did the officer violate policy or rules? In deadly force cases, agencies often utilize homicide detectives to determine if the officer committed a crime. The research tells us that rarely is an officer who uses deadly force guilty of a crime. And, almost always, the officer does not violate agency policy or rules. Plaintiffs' attorneys will often focus on far more ambiguous issues, such as failure to supervise, failure to properly train, negative retention, the use of one force option rather than another, failure to use proper containment or verbalization that was less than perfect. Plaintiffs will also dig into an officer's private life, contacting ex-wives or ex-husbands, to attempt to elicit negative commentary about the officer from an angry ex-spouse.

Understanding that litigation will often go well beyond law and policy, investigating detectives must have special knowledge that is broad based to cover all the issues that *may* arise in a civil suit three or four years later. The author has worked as an expert witness on cases that are a decade old, and still ongoing. Detectives must know what training and equipment the department provides, why and how the training and equipment are relevant to the case, and what other methods or procedures are available in contemporary law enforcement. Some traditional functions or procedures are followed out of the "That is what we have always done" rationale. Some of these long-held procedures may be in need of review.

It is usually not advisable to take custody of or handle the officer's gun. Any trace evidence on the gun, such as a tiny piece of the suspect's skin on the front sight, may be lost in handling it. The suspect may have grabbed the officer's pistol in an effort to disarm them. An educated field supervisor will leave the gun untouched and secured in the officer's holster, monitoring the officer until the investigative detectives arrive to take control of the evidence, including the officer's pistol. The fact is, a large number of officer-involved shootings have been viewed with doubt or skepticism because too many people handled evidence, and eventually it was mishandled, lost or made unuseable.

It is difficult to predict what piece of evidence will be the most important or significant. Frequently, it is clothing, and often this is the suspect's shirt. The suspect's shirt is also a piece of evidence that is frequently lost or mishandled. It is often bloody, and remains in the emergency room and thrown away by hospital staff. The shirt can often reveal distance, trajectory and positions of the suspect and officer at the time of the shooting. It may also contain microscopic physical evidence. If the shirt is lost, the plaintiff will assert that this was deliberate on the part of the department in an effort to cover up a bad shooting.

Preparation by the Officer

The single most important consideration in any litigation, either civil or criminal, is that the officer tells the truth. Any honest error or action on the part of the officer can be understood by a jury. Any departure from the truth is disastrous. In preparing for a lawsuit or criminal prosecution, the issue of truth is followed closely by the officer developing a controlled attitude and an aggressive mindset. Look upon the lawsuit or prosecution as another tactical environment within which you must survive. The same factors that create survival in the field are relevant in litigation.

1. Officers must never quit (will to survive).
2. Officers must be in excellent mental condition.
3. Officers must be in excellent physical condition.
4. Officers must be tactically sound.
5. Officers must avoid complacency.
6. Officers must control their fear.

To fully understand how litigation compares to survival on the street, let's take each category and examine it carefully.

1. **Officers must never quit (will to survive).** Civil litigation, as well as prosecution, will weigh heavily on police officers' minds. There have been occasions where officers have been abandoned by their department when the incident in question involved politics or special interest groups or so-called "community leaders." The officer must remain steadfast and resolute in the face of tremendous pressure, for several reasons:
   a. If the officer allows the situation to impact too heavily upon them, it will have a devastating impact on the officer's family. Wives, children, husbands, mothers and fathers will all suffer the anxiety and pain of the situation. It is, therefore, the officer's responsibility to be strong and resolute and maintain a positive attitude around family

members and others who love them.
   b. The officer has an obligation to other officers who may be involved in the incident and could be impacted by the poor performance of a weak and less-than-professional officer.
   c. The agency has a right to expect the officer to be stable and competent, representing the agency well.
2. **Officers must be in excellent mental condition.** A lack of confidence and uncertainty can erode an officer's ability to respond properly in the field or in court. The officer can lose confidence and be filled with doubt and anxiety if they have failed to be truthful regarding the smallest detail. The officer can gain confidence if they have good legal counsel—someone the officer trusts. The officer should listen to the advice and direction their lawyer provides, and should not hesitate to make suggestions to them.

   The officer will also gain confidence when their lawyer spends time advising and preparing them for depositions, trial testimony and all aspects of the case, both in and out of court. A competent expert witness should be consulted and involved early in the process. Prior to the officer being deposed, an expert witness should be involved in a tactical analysis of the incident, which should include all of the primary officers.

   Psychologists who are well trained for law enforcement are an excellent asset for the department and the officer. Post-traumatic stress disorder is real, and can have a severe impact on the agency, the officer and the officer's family. Psychological services providers who are knowledgeable, experienced and dedicated can resolve emotional issues and support the agency's goals of responding to a critical incident aftermath with a professional approach that serves the public, the department and the officer. A police psychologist can also be a resource for the officer's family.
3. **Officers must be in excellent physical condition.** The officer may be in excellent physical condition at the time of the incident, but stress and anxiety of the lawsuit or unfair

prosecution will be so influential that the officer may stop working out and begin to gain weight. (Officers have gained as much as fifty or sixty pounds, in some cases, from the time of the incident until the litigation is complete.) This weight gain will cause the officer to feel both physically and mentally poor, and this will build upon the insecurity and uncertainty the officer is already experiencing. It is important that officers look their best in and out of court. Sloppy and poor appearance on the part of the officer does not help the situation. Opinions are formed and judgments made on the basis of appearance.

4. **Officers must be tactically sound**. Preparation for a deposition, court testimony, interviews conducted by the Department of Justice Federal Civil Rights Unit, or the local prosecutor, is no different than training and practicing for a felony vehicle stop. The officer must prepare for every potentially dangerous confrontation on the street. The events that follow, such as internal investigations, political inquisitions, lawsuits and unfair, unethical prosecutions are no less a threat to the officer's life.

If an officer is unfairly charged civilly with violation of civil rights, excessive force, abuse of authority, etc., and the result is that the officer is placed in a two- to eight-year stress-filled accusatory situation, the stress upon the officer and the officer's family is extremely damaging. If the result of the unfair accusations is a punitive judgment against the officer, it can ruin the officer financially. Very few families and marriages can withstand this kind of abuse.

If the officer is unfairly and unethically charged with a crime, the entire situation is devastating to the officer, their entire family, the department and law enforcement in the region. Certainly, the Rodney King incident had a ripple effect nationwide. The King incident ruined the lives of all the officers involved, even those who did nothing wrong. It devastated the police department. No one would suggest that the Los Angeles Police Department is a better police department

today than it was in 1991. Meanwhile, lawyers made millions of dollars, and Rodney King also became a millionaire. His multiple run-ins with law enforcement, other than the LAPD, since then, tell us how wise the entire system is in handling situations of this kind. In the King incident, police tactics and performance were less than exemplary. One could argue forever as to how the criminal, Rodney King, should have been handled. Most would agree that too many baton strikes were used. Most would agree that the suspect should have been "swarmed" by the officers. What was also apparent was that the single most excessive act was the stomp on the neck of Rodney King by an officer who did nothing other than that one illegal act. Note that he was the officer who testified against the other involved officers. Sometimes, the most guilty officer is the one who testifies against others.

Officers who are brutal are not candidates for support from their law enforcement agency, or their city, county or state. It is the responsibility of the agency to identify this misconduct when it occurs and to tell the community what the agency is doing to respond appropriately. If officers are brutal, prosecution and removal are the expected steps the agency should take.

Rarely are use-of-force events acts of brutality. Often, the perception on the part of witnesses is that they are witnessing brutality, when in fact it is not brutality at all. It may be excessive force, but not brutality. It may be reasonable force that is perceived as brutality or excessive force by parties who do not understand police use of force or see only part of the incident.

5. **Officers must avoid complacency**. As mentioned previously, officers who are the subject of a lawsuit usually have not violated any law or agency policy. Since the officer knows this, they will sometimes consider the entire process to be unfair and a waste of their time and energy to respond. The officer believes that because they were "right" in what they did, the jury will also see it that way. Nothing could be farther from the truth.

The officer will discover what many have experienced in the past: juries will fail to come to the right verdict because of complacency on the part of the agency, the attorney defending the case, the officer, or all three. When any part of the process fails, all three fail, and usually each of the three blames the other two parts of the equation. Just as the officer must prepare for confrontation in the field, they must be fundamentally sound in preparing to deal with a federal civil rights action or other lawsuit. The fundamentals are: (1) honesty, (2) accurate reports of the incident, (3) professional investigation by the department, (4) a good defense lawyer, and (5) close cooperation with case preparation throughout the lawsuit. If any one of these fundamentals is missing, failure can result. Because these situations can be protracted, and weeks and months may separate case activity, there may be a tendency to relax and think the case is "going away," or there may be failure to stay up-to-date with reports, depositions and issues.

Once the case goes to trial, the officer must be aware that parties connected to the case will evaluate them every time they see them. Being truthful is certainly the most important factor. Being professional and respectful of all parties involved, at all times, is also critical. Often, friends and family members are in the courtroom, the hallways of the courthouse, the restrooms or restaurants nearby. They may not have seen the plaintiff as the officer saw them. Family members of the plaintiff may honestly believe the suspect was not capable of what the officer said they (plaintiff) did. If people see the officer acting in any way the observer thinks is inappropriate, it may have a very negative impact on the case. Officers may say something that can be misconstrued, or laugh at a joke. The laughter may be taken as being related to the case, when there is no connection.

Again, appearance and neatness are issues the officer must consider. Often, a very neat dress uniform is the right choice. When that may not be the case, business attire is a must. "Cowboy" belt buckles and casual sport clothes are out! Bumper stickers announcing political leanings, or other strongly held opinions attached to an officer's vehicle, are also not appropriate. Shoes should be shined, and jewelry worn in other than a mainstream manner is not advisable. If the officer has been working undercover and looks like a suspect, the officer should "clean up" for trial. Sloppy appearance, loud or careless behavior is not acceptable, and should be reason for department discipline if it occurs.

6. **Officers must control their fear**. Some federal civil rights suits, lawsuits, and *all* criminal trials where the officer is the defendant, will create a level of uncertainty and concern that can elevate to real fear under certain circumstances. Certainly, some cases involve massive media coverage that is often inflammatory. Hundreds, and sometimes even thousands, of people may demonstrate and/or riot. Hate-filled speeches accusing officers of being "killers," and vile accusations on the part of "community activists," will inflame a community against the officers when the officer(s) have done nothing wrong. Officers have experienced going to court and finding hundreds of angry demonstrators in the hallway outside the courtroom. The officer's family and other people connected to the defense side of the case, including witnesses, are yelled at and harassed going into and out of the courtroom. Under some circumstances, phone calls threatening the officers' lives and families will occur.

Unfortunately, this is also part of the job. All of these occurrences are meant to make the lives of the officer and their family miserable. Knowing this, and understanding that being miserable is exactly what those who are attacking the officer want, will hopefully empower the officer to resist being threatened or intimidated.

Any threats to the officer and their family must immediately be reported to the officer's department and the department where the officer's family resides. Security steps that are appropriate should be taken. The media should be notified that the officer's family has been threatened. This should not be kept a secret. The department, or departments, involved should call a news conference and announce that security steps have been taken, and law violators will be arrested and prosecuted.

Sad to say, but police officer's children have been attacked at school and beaten because of inflammatory news coverage and outrageous commentary by community activists. *A Los Angeles Police Department detective was murdered by a narcotics dealer whom the detective had identified as murdering an eyewitness to the dealer's previous murder. The dealer was out on bail when he shot the detective to death in front of the detective's eight-year-old son at the child's elementary school.* Rarely, if ever, are cases of harassment, intimidation and assault of an officer's family made public. The law enforcement "minority" is fair game for the kind of treatment that is identified as hate crimes when other minorities are victimized in a similar manner.

The agencies which are part of a situation where an officer is the focal point of anger or possible revenge on the part of a family or group, are often complacent. Rather than anticipate, the agency will often not react with the application of security, even after threatening phone calls occur. The issue of officers being the target for harassment is much greater in small towns and rural counties. Because law enforcement agencies there are small in size, the community may have a few restaurants, one movie theater and one high school. As a result, the officer and those suspects they arrest will cross paths on a frequent basis. The officer's children will often come in contact with an arrestee's family and children or friends of the arrestee. Often, the children related to the arrestee are undisciplined, have few ethics, no rules and love to victimize others, especially cops' kids. Schools should be alerted to the potential for an officer's children being targeted because of the hatred of the officer on the part of those connected with an arrestee. It has been the author's experience that schools often do not take the potential for

violence seriously, and assume any threats are just childish bravado. *This may be changing because of past major failures on the part of schools to react appropriately to violence on campus.*

Fear is a complex human reaction to stress. There are thousands of stressors that impact upon human beings and, therefore, there are a variety of fears. Most fear situations that officers think about are field-related. Officers certainly are well served to contemplate situations in the field that could be life-threatening. An officer's academy tactics training relates to the officer being well prepared and competent. Much of the training, in some form, mentions the issue of fear and how it can be a source of failure on the part of the officer, or a resource that can enhance reaction if the fear is controlled.

Fear is also intrusive to an officer's performance in litigation when the officer is the accused. Obviously, the fear factor is different from the fear an officer experiences when they are assaulted in the field. There is no fear of physical harm in a deposition, courtroom, or an interrogation by investigators. The fear surrounding a use-of-force incident comes from the officer being undereducated and underprepared once the investigation begins. Almost all officers know they have a right to an attorney, but the officer is often afraid that if they exercise that right, the department may resent it. The officer's exercise of their right to an attorney does, in fact, cause resentment on the part of some police agency brass. This should not be the case, but it does sometimes happen.

Also, officers are frequently intimidated by the form and structure of the investigation of a use-of-force incident. This is especially true for officer-involved shootings.

After the officer has fired shots that either wound or kill a suspect, the officer is often whisked away from the shooting scene and taken to the station. Once at the station, the officer may be isolated in a small interrogation room, sometimes for hours. Because so much has to be done by so few officers, the shooting officer can sometimes be left alone without anyone providing a restroom opportunity, a drink of water or an opportunity to call home. The officer begins to become fearful of what is happening, and apprehensive about the process that is taking place.

CONCLUSION

It is important for agency management to understand that very little, if any, training is given to young officers concerning the details of the process of investigating a use of force or shooting by an officer. The officers usually learn from experience, and too frequently this experience is "bitter."

Fear and uncertainty of the process may not be the best circumstance for an investigator to elicit the

most accurate information from an officer. Officers should believe their agency will do a fair and honest investigation, and that the investigators are professional and well trained. While this is not always the case, through the cooperative efforts of department management and concerned officers, improvement is always possible.

Unfortunately, responding and reacting to litigation has become commonplace within contemporary law enforcement. However, officers who prepare themselves through education, training and experience, in combination with flexible and reasonable policies and investigative procedures, can considerably reduce the likelihood of the department and/or its officers being found criminally or civilly liable.

JEFF GABOR

Officer Jeff Gabor is a 9-year veteran of the Hudson, Illinois, Police Department, where he currently serves as a part-time officer. Officer Gabor works full-time for the Illinois Department of Corrections, and is a member of the Special Operations Response Team (SORT). He is a guest speaker on behalf of the Knox County state's attorney's office and speaks to new officers about the shooting incident described in this chapter.

Chapter 17

THEY ARRESTED ME FOR FIRST DEGREE MURDER: A STREET COP'S STORY

JEFF GABOR

INTRODUCTION

My name is Jeff Gabor, and I am a police officer for the Hudson, Illinois, Police Department. I was born in Bloomington, Illinois, and am 25 years old. I have a son who is 3 years old and am engaged to be married to his mother. I have a wonderful mother and stepdad, as well as a brother and sister and six other half-brothers and sisters. I also have about two dozen nieces and nephews.

As I was growing up, I always knew I wanted to help people. My father was a police officer and my mother was a park ranger for a while. I have two uncles who were police officers and one who was a fireman. Growing up I was very interested in police work. When I enrolled in junior high school, I learned about a police Explorer Program for young adults interested in law enforcement. I joined the program when I was 14 years old, and stayed with it until I was hired by a police department. When I was in high school, while most kids were on the football or basketball teams, or in jail, I was training in police practices and learning from the officers I idolized. As Explorers, we helped our local police agencies direct traffic at major events and any other situation where they needed us. After six years in the program and graduating from high school, I learned of a part-time police officer position that had opened up in the small town of Hudson, just north of where I lived. My dream had finally come true. I was a police officer.

After completing the State of Illinois mandatory 400-hour part-time training and 40-hour firearms class, I took the state test and passed. In December 1996, I was sworn in as a policeman. I have been with the department for five years, and have a perfect work record, with no citizen complaints. I have also worked for two other police departments and our county coroner's office.

I was very happy with my life. I had a career and a wonderful family and, like everyone else, was working to have the American dream. I never realized the fulfillment of my dream would lead to the biggest nightmare I would ever know. Just 23 years old and on the job for three years, I was involved in a shooting that left the suspect dead and me booked on first-degree murder charges.

This is My Story

Monday, July 24, 2000, started out like any other day for me. I was to report for duty at 6 p.m. I do not recall my activities that day prior to going to work, but I do remember that just before starting my shift, I kissed my son and fiancée goodbye and went to get my squad car. At 6 p.m., I prepared the squad car for duty, notified my dispatcher that I was 10-41 (on duty) and started my patrol duties.

Everything was normal, just like it was hundreds of other times I started a shift. This time would be different. This time would change many lives forever.

Around 6:10 p.m., I heard radio traffic reporting a vehicle pursuit in the Chenoa, Illinois, area. Officer Dennis Carter of the Chenoa Police Department advised he was in pursuit of a vehicle and that the suspect was heading south out of his town toward the town of Lexington, Illinois. As Carter continued south, he radioed for assistance. Lexington Police Officer Jason Edmunds and I responded. A short time passed, and Officer Edmunds advised that he had caught up to Carter and was now in pursuit. At this time, I was still driving toward the town of Towanda, Illinois, which is the next town south of Lexington. The Hudson Police Department has a contract with the town of Towanda, and that made it part of my area. The pursuit went through Lexington and headed toward Interstate 55. I reached Towanda when Carter stated that the suspect was now on I-55, southbound toward Towanda. As I entered Towanda, I saw a police officer from the town of Normal, Illinois, traveling Code 3 through the town. I followed that officer to the southbound exit ramp of I-55. The officer from Normal was there to help, and had a spike-strip in his car. I pulled in behind him, assisted him in putting the strip down, and then worked at stopping traffic from entering the Interstate.

As the Normal officer and I were putting the strip in the road, I heard Carter advise they were one mile north of us, and that the suspect was heading in our direction. As we were waiting, we could see the emergency lights and hear the sirens of the two pursuing squad cars. Carter then advised that the suspect vehicle was taking the southbound exit ramp to Towanda. I believe the suspect saw the Normal officer and me and took the exit ramp to avoid running over the spike-strip. The suspect had the presence of mind to realize that if he continued to travel south, his tires would have been flattened. Carter then advised that the vehicle was going east into Towanda. I returned to my squad car and drove across the median. Carter advised that the suspect was going to take the northbound entrance ramp and get back onto I-55. At this point, I did not know who the suspect was or what he was wanted for. Neither Carter nor my dispatcher gave me this

information. I knew the suspect was fleeing and eluding, but I did not know why. As I drove up the entrance ramp, I saw the suspect vehicle for the first time, a 1988 four-door Cadillac. The suspect was in the first car, Carter was the primary unit and Edmunds was in the second unit. I was following Edmunds to prevent traffic from overtaking the pursuit.

In Pursuit

As the pursuit went down the entrance ramp, I hung back a little in order to keep the public from catching up to, or trying to pass, the pursuit. When all the cars cleared the entrance ramp, Edmunds swung out to the left, passed the suspect's car and was able to get in front of the suspect. As we continued north, we ran into a construction zone that was reduced to one lane. I then asked Carter how many people were in the vehicle, because I had not heard anything over the radio about occupants. Carter stated that there was one male in the car. While in the construction zone just before the stop, Carter called over the radio, "He is doing a lot of reaching with his right hand. I have no idea what his problem is. We had him earlier on a theft case and that is what we have him for now." Hearing this statement from Carter made me think the suspect could be armed, or was trying to get something on the seat. This was also the first time anything was said about why this person was being chased.

Seconds later, we approached a bridge that was under construction. As we approached, I said over my radio, "Get 'm here," meaning stop the vehicle on the bridge. Officer Edmunds brought his squad car to a stop. That action forced the suspect to stop his car (after being chased through three towns and more than 20 miles). Officer Carter pulled his squad car in behind the suspect and I pulled in behind Carter. Officer Edmunds was driving a marked, full-sized Chevy Tahoe. All of our police vehicles were marked and had emergency lights on and operating.

All vehicles were now stopped on the bridge. Concrete dividers were on the left side of the bridge blocking the work lane. There were construction workers and machinery present. On the right side of the bridge there was a metal guardrail erected next to the creek area, as well as another concrete barrier on the right to keep cars from driving off the bridge into the water. This setting was a good spot, because it made it possible to keep the suspect contained in the area. However, it was also a very confined spot. There was only one lane for traffic.

As I exited my car, I was going to stop traffic and keep the public away. Then I saw Officer Carter with his gun out. I knew something was wrong, and turned my attention to the stop itself. This stop appeared to be a high-risk felony stop. I started to approach the suspect vehicle and took out my gun. At the time of this stop, I was carrying a Smith & Wesson .45-caliber semiautomatic pistol. I could hear Carter and Edmunds yelling, "Get out of the car with your hands up." That is when I also noticed Edmunds had his gun out. I then started yelling as well. We were now standing at the suspect vehicle with our guns out and pointed at the driver, yelling verbal commands to "Get out of the car." The suspect never responded. I then kicked the car twice in order to cause a distraction to get the suspect's attention. Again, no response. When the suspect reached over to the right side of the car around the floor area, I feared he was trying to reach for a weapon. Officer Carter stated that the suspect was doing a lot of reaching around in the car just prior to the stop. I then pulled out my ASP baton, and Officer Edmunds did too. We struck the driver's side window several times to gain access to the suspect to effect his arrest. As soon as the glass broke, the suspect placed the car into reverse and appeared to make a sweeping motion around the steering wheel, as if he was turning it toward me. I was at the left rear of the car by the wheel area. Officer Carter was near the middle of the car, around the driver's side door. Officer Edmunds was to the front left of the car by the engine area. That is when things started getting out of control, due to the suspect and his actions toward us.

The Suspect Turns Violent

The suspect rapidly accelerated in reverse, crashing into the front of the Chenoa squad truck, pushing it about 10 feet backward. As this was going on, Officer Carter had both of his arms inside the suspect's vehicle as the car went back. I then grabbed my baton, as I had set it on the trunk lid of the suspect's car after breaking the window. The suspect then dropped the gear into forward, and floored the gas. Again, Officer Carter had his arms inside the window, and again the suspect made a sweeping motion to the left. Officer Carter was in front of me at that time and was blocking my line of sight to Officer Edmunds. However, I knew Edmunds was in front of the car. When the suspect's car surged forward, I heard a shot fired. I had no idea where the shot had come from. I could no longer see the suspect or his hands. I knew Edmunds was in front of the suspect's car, and feared that he might have been shot, or was in danger of being run over by the suspect.

There was no place for us to go on the narrow bridge. I held my pistol in both hands in front of my face. I saw my front sight. After hearing the shot, I was totally focused on the suspect. I stepped out from Officer Carter's side and began to fire at the suspect. I fired three shots into the driver's side area of the car. The suspect's car then crashed into the back of the Lexington Police Tahoe and began pushing it forward about 25 feet. The tires of both cars were screaming, and the engine of the suspect's Cadillac was roaring. It sounded like it was going to explode. I stepped over to the rear of the suspect's car and fired four more shots. The first shot went into the back window of the car and diced the window to the point that you could only see a silhouette of the driver. As I fired the four shots, nothing changed. The car was still rapidly accelerating, the suspect was still moving around, and the Cadillac was still pushing the full-sized Tahoe. I then fired one more shot into the back window toward the suspect. When the final shot was fired, the suspect stopped moving, the car was still running, but no longer accelerating, and the car was no longer pushing the Tahoe. I then felt the threat to our safety was over.

I fired a total of eight shots. The suspect was hit five times (in the shoulder, back, and cheek), and died at the scene. I still had one live round in my weapon. I did not fire the last round because I thought the threat had stopped. I was very scared, and thought that not only was I going to die, but that my fellow officers were in danger of being killed. After the last shot was fired, I immediately called out, "Shots fired," to my dispatcher and requested an ambulance. Officer Edmunds stated over his radio, "Shots fired, tried to run me down." After the shooting, Edmunds and I shook hands, and he said to me, "Thank you, Jeff. You just saved my life." I don't know why we shook hands. It just happened.

Following Procedures

In the rural areas of Illinois, the State Police respond to investigate officer-involved shootings. When the State Police detectives arrived, Edmunds, Carter and I were separated and assigned a trooper to watch us. We could not talk to each other or speak with anyone. I started to go into shock and could not breathe. My stomach was severely upset. I started to vomit, but it hit the back of my throat and would not come out. The EMTs gave me oxygen and water, and monitored my blood pressure. They advised me that I should go to the hospital, as I had extreme stress. As that was being discussed, a state trooper told me I was not free to go unless it was so bad I could not handle being there. I was to stay put.

I was very concerned about the suspect and how he was doing; no one would provide me with any information. A state trooper then approached me and asked for my duty weapon. I knew this to be policy when a situation involves the discharge of a firearm by a policeman. I was at the scene for a couple of hours. I was scared, and did not know what to expect. Groups of officers were starting to form. They were standing about 30 feet away talking and pointing at me. I did not understand what was going on. Just a few seconds earlier a couple of officers stated to me that this was justified, and not to worry. Several field troopers questioned me, and I cooperated fully with each of them. I was also told that this suspect had been chased earlier at approximately 4:40 p.m. I was never given this information at any time during the incident. A short time later, my chief arrived and comforted me. I told him I had feared I was going to die, and also feared for the lives of the other officers. My chief has always been supportive of my actions, and I will always be grateful for that support.

At some point, I was called to a meeting involv-ing several investigators at the scene. I was told what to expect and what was going to take place next. I was then transferred to the local sheriff's office to meet with the investigating internal affairs people. I was introduced to two detectives from the State Police. I was asked if I would be willing to talk to them about what had taken place a couple of hours earlier. When I said "Yes," I was escorted to an interview room, where I spent an hour and 10 minutes answering questions and providing infor-mation to them. I also advised them that I had an in-car camera in my squad car that had been on and recording during the incident. I also told them that the Chenoa Police unit had a video camera, and that I believed it had been on and recording as well. The tapes from both cars were taken from the scene and watched by the detectives before we were ques-tioned. I knew Edmunds and Carter were also being questioned. The detectives told me they had watched both videotapes. After the interview, I was thanked for my cooperation and both detectives shook my hand and told me to, "Hang in there." The detectives treated me very well. I told them I never wanted to hurt anyone, and that I was very sad and upset by what had happened. I was not advised to have an attorney, but I also stated to them that I did not feel I needed an attorney. I was not given any Miranda warning or told to be con-cerned about anything. The detectives told me that if they needed anything else, they would call me. I was told I was free to go. I then met with two criti-cal incident counselors who offered to talk to Edmunds and me. After talking to them, we were able to go home. I called my dispatcher and told him that I was ending my tour of duty.

Arriving Home

When I got home, my mother and stepdad were in shock. I had called them from the scene to let them know I was okay, but that I was very upset. I could tell this was a very stressful thing my mother was going through. I told her not to worry, and that I was going to be okay, but I needed to be by myself for a while to collect my thoughts. I could not sleep, and was still numb and struggling to remember what had just happened. I saw the incident in my mind over and over. I understood that a man had died and I had shot him. The entire thing was like a cloud, or haze, hanging over me. The next day the nightmare would begin.

After having been involved in the most tragic event of my life, I had to sit down and try to remember everything I could about the incident. I was under pressure to write a report and get it filed as soon as possible. Because of this pressure, combined with the shock I was in, I did not put every single thing in the report, simply because I could not remember. I now know this is normal after a high-stress incident. I was forced to make split-second decisions under a tense, uncertain, and rapidly evolving situation. I do know that this incident lasted about 35 seconds. This was used against me later on. After struggling several hours to complete the report, I finally had it together to present to the State's Attorney.

The next several days were packed with media and news reports. Three construction workers witnessed the incident. The press and news stations interviewed them, and by the fourth day after the shooting, some people had described the shooting as a "cold-blooded murder." I had refused, and continued to refuse, to talk to anyone in the media. By the fifth day, the media was starting to report that the suspect had mental disabilities. At this time, I still did not know who the suspect was. I was told his name at the scene, but it did not help, because I had never met or dealt with the man. The media reported the suspect had had several contacts with the police for different violations. I was later informed the suspect was out on bond for six disorderly conduct charges and a felony charge of obstructing justice for lying to police on a traffic stop by giving a false name. I also heard the suspect became disabled at the hands of his father when he was three years old. Allegedly, he was thrown head first into a car, and his skull was fractured. I did not know how accurate this information was. However, at the time of the shooting, the suspect was 27 years old and had a driver's license that had been suspended several times for traffic offenses. He graduated from high school and was attending college. His mother stated that he worked very well with computers. The suspect's family reported that this 27-year-old man was harmless, and so disabled he was afraid of the police. The suspect had been

stopped several times, and was ticketed a number of times. Having interaction with the police was nothing new to him. In the past, he had stopped every time, but on this day he chose not to, and placed many lives in danger.

Time Passes

After a week had gone by, I heard that the State Police were going to send a preliminary report to the prosecutor for a review of charges. There was a public outcry now, and some people were putting pressure on the prosecutor. The story was that a 27-year-old mentally disabled man was killed because he had stolen gas from a service station. The media was also reporting that the Illinois State Police had chased this same suspect earlier in the day for the same thing. This was the second time that day he had stolen gas and was chased by the police. I was not aware of the first chase until after the shooting.

At this point, I thought I would need to seek legal advice about the media and their reporting. I was also concerned about the information they were reporting about reviewing the charges. I contacted Bloomington attorney Paul Welch. I met with him at his office and asked his opinion. Paul was a former prosecutor for my county, so I thought he would know both sides. He had not heard anything, and we needed to wait to see what, if anything, would happen. It was the longest wait of my life. Little did I know the damage had already been done.

Warrants Issued

On August 3, 2000, I received a phone call at my home. I was not at home at the time, so my answering machine picked it up. It was one of the detectives from the State Police. He stated that he just wanted to know how I was doing, and that he had a few questions regarding my training. I got home a short while later and listened to the message. I could tell by the tone in the voice of the detective that something was very wrong. I did not feel right. I then called Paul Welch at his office and advised him of the message. Paul told me to stay home and he would make a call and get back to me. About fifteen minutes later, Paul called. He told me he had talked to the assistant prosecutor. He also told me that I needed to come down to his office right away, and that things were not good. I then called my mother and picked her up at her home. I asked that she go with me. When we got to Paul's office, he told me there was no easy way to tell me what he had to say. I took a deep breath and grabbed my mom's hand. What was said next forever changed my life: "They have issued two murder warrants for your arrest." I went into shock, as did my mother. I could not believe what I was hearing. It was like a nightmare, and I would wake soon. It wasn't.

I asked what I was supposed to do. Paul had made arrangements for me to voluntarily surrender and cooperate fully. I called to tell my fiancée, but she had already left for work. Paul then drove my mother and me to the Sheriff's Office. I was swarmed by the same guys who I worked with. I saw a good friend of mine from the Normal Police Department in the parking lot and asked him to walk in with me. He was lighting a cigarette when I told him why I was there. His cigarette fell out of his mouth, and I started crying. Paul, my mom and my friend walked me in. I was led to an interview room–the same room I had been in just 11 days prior. I hugged my mom goodbye and told her that I loved her. I also thanked my friend and Paul.

Taken to Jail

I was taken to the jail after talking with the investigator who had called me. I was handcuffed and escorted to the jail by four deputies. I felt betrayed and dirty. These were guys I worked with, and they treated me like the Unabomber. I was booked for first and second degree murder. I felt that the very job I was sworn to had turned its back on me. I wondered how I could go from policeman to criminal in 35 seconds in the line of duty. I knew this had to be a mistake. My arrest was the most painful experience of my life. I was humiliated, and felt like a criminal. I was then fingerprinted and had my photograph taken. The jail staff seemed as shocked as I. They treated me well. One jailer had tears in her eyes.

I was then taken to a judge, who read the charges and set bond at $500,000. I was taken back to jail and made to wear a green jumpsuit like any other prisoner. I wanted to call my mom, but I was told I did not have time. I asked what that meant. They told me I was being moved out of the county for my safety. I was then taken to another county. When I arrived there, I had to be booked all over again. I was fingerprinted, had another picture taken and was given a different color jumpsuit to wear. This one was orange. I was then able to call home. I wanted to get out of that "hell-hole" that night. I cried when I talked to my family. What would my 2-year-old son think when I was not coming home? It tore everyone in half. I knew I had to stay strong. I knew being released on bond was impossible. My family are working people, and do not have that kind of money. But something was going on at my house and at my parent's house. They were angry. They were going to hire the best lawyer and get me out. But how? My family spent night and day trying to raise money for my defense and bond. I needed $25,000 for a retainer, and $500,000 for bond. My family did everything they could to get me home. My first night in the jail cell was pure hell. I could not eat or sleep. I just lay on the inch-thick mattress on a cold concrete slab and closed my eyes. I wanted to know why I was there and what I had done wrong. I could not understand what I could have possibly done to end up in this house of pain.

The next day I talked again to my family. God had answered our prayers. The community was there for me. I was sent hundreds of cards and letters of support. Local businesses were donating money and merchandise to help me. Several family friends had donated money, and my family gave everything they had. I was going nuts. I could not imagine how my mom and dad were going to get by doing all they were doing for me. My fiancée and her family donated money. By the time nightfall came on the second day, I called home as I did every night. I spent my 24th birthday locked up in jail.

My family raised $25,000 in less than 24 hours. I now had Paul Welch as lead man in my defense. The next several days were getting better for me. My mom told me that the goal now was to get me out on bond. I now had hope. I was in a cell by myself this whole time. It was called protective custody. I still could not eat or sleep, and was losing weight fast. About a week went by and Paul came to see me. My family and fiancée also came to visit me every time I was allowed visitors. Paul told me that the bond rule was that I needed to post 10 percent of the bail in order to get out. That meant that I needed $50,000. That was so much better than $500,000, but still way beyond our resources. I had already given my entire life savings to my defense. Paul then told me he would file a motion to reduce my bond, and hearing was set in a few days. I was glad to hear that, but did not know what to expect.

I spent hours reading my Bible and praying. My prayers were answered. Finally, 13 days after I was arrested, we had a hearing. The hearing lasted about 30 minutes. The judge listened to my attorney. I had strong family ties in my community. I had no money. I was not a flight risk, and although the charges were very serious, they were charges that arose from a situation in which I was a police officer in the line of duty and used deadly force against a suspect who used deadly force against me and two other officers. The judge gave careful thought to the situation. I was surprised when the prosecutor strongly opposed any bail reduction. The judge agreed with my attorney and reduced my bond to $20,000. About an hour later, I was bonded out by my grandmother, who was gracious enough to help me. I also learned that the suspect's father was out putting up pictures of my booking photo with the words "killer" and "murderer" on it.

About 30 friends and family members greeted me. I was so happy to be home, but I knew I had work to do. I was suspended from four part-time jobs as a result of this incident. Part of the conditions of my bond was that I could not possess a weapon. If it were not for that restriction, I would have been able to return to work. The next several days were spent having a fundraiser and getting support from anyone who would help. I was still sick from all of this. I sat up many nights wondering if my mom and stepdad could afford to eat, because they sacrificed almost all of their life's savings to pay for my defense. My brother, sister and fiancée did the same. My stepbrothers and sisters also sacrificed a lot for me.

A few days after coming home, I was served with a federal lawsuit. The charges were for civil rights violations, excessive force and wrongful death. I was also informed by the media that I was indicted by a grand jury on two counts of murder. I was arraigned a month after my release. I pled not guilty. The next several months involved many hours of meetings and discussions with my attorney. I also went to a doctor to get treated for stress-related symptoms. I continued to see a doctor, and was diagnosed with post-traumatic stress disorder. I was given medication and therapy until the trial.

Paul filed a motion for discovery, which means the prosecutor, by law, has to turn over all evidence they intend to use. The most important pieces of evidence were the videotapes from the squad cars. I had not seen them. I was told the reason I was charged was based on the videotape from the Chenoa car. On September 14, 2000, I was contacted by Paul and he showed me the tape for the first time. I was very upset seeing it. The only thing I saw that was different from what I told the detectives was how many times the suspect hit the police vehicles. I thought he hit them three times. I was wrong according to the tape. The police cars were struck twice. When you encounter a life-threatening situation, you have seconds to identify the threat and respond. Again, this incident lasted about 35 seconds, so it is impossible to remember accurately every single second of the incident when you are fighting to live. Perhaps the most comforting part of the tape was that Paul saw nothing in it that would bring first-degree murder charges against me. I also did not see anything I did that was a criminal act of any kind.

Experts Provide Much-Needed Support

A few days went by, and Paul and I decided we needed a use-of-force expert to review this incident and all the information that went along with it (the actual facts and circumstances we were in, and the information we had at the time of the incident). Paul contacted a friend of his in California and asked if he knew anyone who was a use-of-force expert. His friend did know of someone. That someone was the first person—outside of my family, friends, and attorney—who actually said that this shooting was justified. He was also the first one to give me the hope I needed that would get me to the end. He is one of my best friends today, and will be for the rest of my life. That someone was Ron McCarthy. I had never met Ron before this incident. Paul sent Ron all of the materials, including an over 500-page State Police report and the videotape. Paul talked to Ron by phone, asked that he review everything, and then asked if he would be interested in being an expert for my defense.

After a couple of weeks had gone by, Ron called Paul back with his findings–justified. Paul was making arrangements with Ron about coming out to Illinois to meet with us and go over everything. Paul then called to tell me of Ron's opinion. I was in tears. It was the first time the pressure in my chest released a little. What also made me feel good about Ron was that he was a retired sergeant from the Los Angeles Police Department with 24 years on the department. I also learned that he was a Director-at-Large with the National Tactical Officers Association (NTOA). The next couple of months were spent going over things with Paul and finding a time to meet Ron. I talked to Ron on the phone prior to him coming to see us. I was amazed at the things Ron said to me. He told me things I was going through I had never told anyone, not even my family. Ron knew exactly how I felt and exactly what I was struggling with, and yet I never told him, he told me. I thought the only way Ron could tell me these things, without me telling him, was that he must have gone through it himself. He had. I knew then that the struggle in trying to explain actions and feelings would be easier, because Ron knew the words that I did not. Now it was time to go to work. I was no longer hopeless. I knew now what I had to do.

In February 2001, Ron came out for the first time. Ron spent three days going over everything. My family and I were very impressed with Ron. We had a good three days, and got a lot accomplished. By now, the case was rolling through the court. The prosecutor, however, was a very determined individual. The prosecution blocked every motion we filed. The next six months were packed with status hearings, discovery problems with the prosecutor and debates over the video. We also discovered another expert who had been involved in a shooting, David Klinger. David, like Ron, was outstanding. David had also trained officers in Illinois, and is a member of NTOA. David came up to meet us and spent a lot of time with me. I liked David and

could relate to him. I was fortunate enough to have seen a series of seminars David did on officer-involved shootings. It was like he was talking to me from the video I was watching. Just like Ron, David gave me hope and strength. David and Ron were helping me in ways no one else could, not even the doctor. David and I spent time going over the scene, and he helped me understand what I was going through. David, as well as Ron, helped me to remember things by going to the scene. We also had an accident reconstructionist who could testify about the amount of force used by the vehicle the suspect was driving and what kind of damage the suspect could have done with his vehicle. We also had an eye doctor who could testify about tunnel vision. All of these experts were disclosed to the prosecutor and the court. This posed a threat to the prosecutor. We now had a very good defense team. We also brought on another defense attorney and former judge, Bill Caisley, who worked with Paul. More than 80 days after the incident and my arrest, the prosecutor filed misdemeanor charges against Edmunds for shooting at the tires of the suspect's car. Was this to intimidate Edmunds?

The judge allowed the prosecutor to be late turning over evidence to us. I believe the judge in this case was against us in every way. We were not late on any motions or turnover of any discovery items. In August 2001, we had another status hearing. Due to the prosecutor being late and waiting until the last second of the day to hand over evidence, we asked for a continuance to prepare. The judge denied it and set jury selection for September 10, 2001. We spent the next month getting everything ready and preparing for the trial. We also had all the research done regarding the experts and their right to testify. It was a long, tough road, but finally we were ready. On September 10, 2001, we had another motion hearing before jury selection. This was doomsday to my defense. Again, the tactics of the prosecutor hurt us. I was offered a plea agreement. If I pled guilty to second-degree murder, they would drop the first-degree murder charge. They, the prosecution, also recommended 16 years in prison, as opposed to a minimum of 45 years for first-degree, plus the penalty for second-degree murder. The answer was "No." I could not plead guilty to something I did not do.

On Monday, the motion hearing was held on our experts. The prosecutor gave her reasons as to why I should not have an expert, and we cited all the reasons why we should. After several bouts with the prosecutor and the judge, it was decided. All experts, Ron, David, and the other three, were barred from testifying. This basically shot down 75 percent of my defense. The judge then called for a recess. We went into a conference room, and I exploded. I could not believe what the judge just did to me. I felt like a convicted man, and there had not even been a trial yet. I asked Paul what we were to do now. Paul told me to calm down and get it together. I knew that I was probably going to be convicted based on the judge and the prosecutor. I felt this was a conspiracy from the start. I was not a very happy man. I said to Paul, "I'm done, right?" Paul had trouble answering me. He was just as much in shock as anyone.

We believed this was very unfair. The first reason the judge claimed to have barred my experts was because he did not know of any case in which an expert had testified for a police officer who had been charged with a crime such as I was, or any crime. We cited the Rodney King case and the Diallo case in New York. Both cases had use-of-force experts testify. We gave the judge the case numbers and dates of the cases. The judge said that those cases were not Illinois cases. Therefore, they did not apply to me. The judge then reversed his ruling, and said that if we could find Illinois cases, he would reconsider. This is exactly what we did. We found several cases involving police officers being charged in Illinois. Once again the judge told us that these cases were civil cases, and not criminal. Finally, the judge barred all of my experts from testifying in front of the jury. The judge then barred us from using the suspect's lengthy criminal record as a motive as to why he decided to flee. The suspect, as I mentioned before, was out on bond for six misdemeanor charges of disorderly conduct and one felony charge of obstructing justice. As if that was not enough, the judge further barred Officer Carter and Officer Edmunds from testifying that they felt that their lives were in danger. They were not allowed to say that they feared for their lives, although Officer Edmunds did say that in his testimony. The prosecutor won her argument by saying that it was not my actions that were in question, but rather my state of mind. Did I reasonably believe that I feared for my life based on the circumstances? You better believe it. I saw a motor vehicle violently ramming cars on a narrow bridge, and I saw the car aimed at Officer Edmunds. I thought it was reasonable to fear for my safety and the lives of my fellow officers. I strongly believed that one or more of us were going to be run over or crushed to death. The day concluded with almost every single motion we filed being denied. I was sick, and did not want to be around anyone after this injustice. It seemed like the criminal had all the rights and the officers were not being allowed to defend themselves.

A Tragedy Unfolds

The next day, September 11, a police officer's murder trial continued–day two of my trial. I remember waking up and still feeling as ill as the previous day, because of the judge and his rulings. The pressure was back in my chest. I was having problems keeping food down, and could not sleep well. As my family and I were preparing to go to the courthouse to begin another day of misery, another story started to break. A large aircraft had struck one of the World Trade Center towers. Initially, they said it could have been an accident. Then, the second aircraft sliced into the second tower; another hit the Pentagon. The last crash occurred in a field in Pennsylvania.

Jury selection was still to begin, and there was a nationwide ban on air travel. How would September 11 affect my trial? Several ways. Because of the air ban, Officer Carter, who was now a prosecution witness, had to fly to Illinois because he had moved away. With flights in limbo, we asked for a continuance, which, of course, was denied. This would also put Ron in a bad situation, because he would also have to fly. People were hearing the reports about the hundreds of cops and firemen who died trying to save innocent lives. The judge even refused to dismiss court early (Federal and state courts were taking security precautions).

On Wednesday, September 12, we spent more than eight hours selecting seven jurors. The prosecution still threatened to dismiss these jurors if Carter did not arrive by Friday. The way we were going, I did not think we would have a jury picked for the next year, let alone the end of the week. On Thursday, we spent another eight hours trying to pick a jury. Then on Friday, at last, a jury was picked for the case, after spending a week with delay after delay by the prosecution over whether or not Carter would be there. Six men, six women and three alternates were finally selected. The judge decided to keep this jury after the prosecution promised that Carter would arrive over the weekend. He had not been able to make it by the end of the day on Friday because his flight was canceled. Opening statements were expected to begin on Monday the 17th, if Carter arrived. We were notified over the weekend that he had arrived. The jury would weigh allegations of murder, against self-defense and justifiable use of force. We spent the weekend working with our experts and vigorously preparing for Monday. I felt good, but I was also scared by the way things were going. We were also told that all of our experts could testify on the record for appeal purposes. They were going to testify, but the jury would never hear them. After everything that had happened to me, I was ready to get it over with.

A Day in Court

On Monday, Carter was called after the opening statements were read. The prosecution said that I executed a simple-minded man who made a few small mistakes. They also had Carter twist his testimony to go against me. That was a move we think made the prosecutor and Carter look bad. Under cross-examination, Paul was able to get Carter to admit that the car had struck him. Carter also admitted that he had his gun out and pointed at the suspect because it was a dangerous situation. Carter denied that he felt threatened, even though he was the first officer to have his gun out. Carter testified as to who shot first. Carter said that I shot first, but in his statement to the detectives, he said Edmunds shot first. When asked about his statement, Carter said that the transcript was wrong. Also testifying was Carter's boss and an Illinois state trooper, who were involved in the first pursuit. The trooper testified that he told the suspect more than 20 times to get out of the car, and that he was under arrest, but

the suspect took off in his vehicle. The trooper gave chase, and the Chenoa Assistant Chief also joined in as a back-up. The trooper testified that the suspect would not stop, and refused all orders to pull over. The suspect then began driving erratically through construction zones. The trooper testified that the suspect was becoming reckless. The jurors were also shown the videotape of the incident. I noticed the jury's reaction when they saw the video of the shooting. I believed they were taking this case seriously, and not letting the emotional outbursts by the suspect's family sway them. They also heard testimony from the suspect's mother. She was asked by the prosecutor, "Did your son have any disabilities?" She answered, "Do you mean on that day?" She was referring to the day of the shooting. She then stated that her son had "oddities." She really had to stop and think about some of the questions. We did not ask her anything. I think she helped us. The father of the suspect was not called by the prosecution. I was told he was a convicted felon, and had been very abusive to his son.

Over the next several days, the prosecution called witnesses and presented their case. They called the crime scene investigators, the forensic pathologist who did the autopsy and the firearms expert from the crime lab. They also called several witnesses who were at the scene. All the other witnesses were police and firemen. Most all of the witnesses who were at the scene immediately after the shooting testified that I was in shock. Other people stated that I was crying and visibly shaken. One trooper testified I was shaking so badly that he had to unload my gun. On Thursday, the state rested its case and it was now our turn.

Witnesses Testify

Our first witness was Officer Edmunds. He testified that he feared for his life and that he fired first. He fired at the tires. Edmunds also stated that he shook my hand and thanked me for saving his life. The jurors paid close attention to his testimony. Edmunds also explained to the jury his observations during the chase. He stated that the suspect was forcing innocent motorists into closed construction zones and endangering their lives by attempting to hit police vehicles during the chase. After lengthy testimony, Edmunds was excused. We then called a couple of character witnesses to testify for me. I was called to the stand and answered about 20 minutes of questions. The remainder of the afternoon was spent listening to the barred experts testify for the record. Ron was called to testify that day. He went through the tape step by step to show what was going on, explained why I did what I did, and why it was justified. Ron testified that he reviewed all of my training (he spent a long time with me, going over my training, and David Klinger did, also). Based on the facts and circumstances, and after reviewing all of my training and applicable state law, Ron testified that he did not see anything that violated policy, ethics or training. He told the court that my actions were appropriate, and that I had followed the use-of-force continuum. He also testified that the suspect was a threat, and that officers' lives were in danger. Also, based on the level of force the suspect used, the level of force Edmunds and I used was justified. Ron was the last witness to testify that day.

I felt really good hearing Ron, even though the people who needed to hear him—the jury—did not hear his testimony. We went home and waited for a few days. At this point of the trial, I felt we were in good shape, despite having our defense crippled. The next day, Friday, I took the stand again. I went through the video step by step with Paul. It was a very hard thing to do. I was very upset when it came to the actual shooting. I testified that I feared for my life, which I did. I also testified that I thought the suspect was going to run over Edmunds. When I heard the first shot fired, I did not see where it had come from. I thought it might have come from inside the car, but I did not know. I thought the suspect might have shot at Edmunds and he was returning fire. I testified that the comment Carter made about the suspect reaching around inside the vehicle made me concerned, and that it was a danger sign. Carter had also initiated the pursuit. Therefore, he was the officer in charge. I followed his lead once the car was stopped. I saw Carter exit with his gun in hand, and that changed this to a high-risk stop. I testified about the use-of-force continuum, and the levels of force I was trained to follow. The prosecutor's questions were formed to criticize my use of force, suggesting that state law pro-

hibits police pursuits unless it is for a forcible felony. Her questions also suggested that none of the officers was in danger, because we were not directly in front of the car or behind it. It was our contention that the suspect did commit a forcible felony when he used his car as a deadly weapon to assault and try to run over officers while resisting arrest and attempting to escape. I also testified that the engine was roaring while I was shooting. When the last shot had been fired, I believed the threat had stopped.

I followed my training and proper police procedures the entire time. I also testified about the fear I had when the car was crashing into the squad cars. I was questioned by the prosecutor as to why I did not use pepper spray against a man who had his window rolled up and was crashing into cars. I told the prosecutor that the window was rolled up until we broke it. Once the glass broke, Carter reached into the car and his body filled up the driver's side window. Carter is a very large man. I could not have sprayed the suspect because Carter was in the way. I also explained to the prosecutor that I have been trained in the use of pepper spray, but not on spraying suspects in moving cars. The way the prosecutor treated me was even more important to the jury. She called me a cowboy, and said that all I wanted was a piece of the action. After five long, hard hours of testimony, the prosecutor ran out of questions. I was excused, and the judge called a recess.

After the recess, David Klinger was called to testify. He impressed everyone on my side, just as Ron had. He was very articulate. David testified about the stress to the body when going through a stressful life-threatening experience, such as mine. David also talked about how the body changes, and how stress affects vision—causing tunnel vision. He discussed how fear can change perception and have a bearing on your hearing. David also told the court about a female officer who was killed around the same time my trial was starting. As David explained how the officer was killed by a motor vehicle, the judge interrupted him and made him stop telling the story. The judge stated that the death of an officer by a car in another state had nothing to do with my case. David did an outstanding job relating his knowledge about the trauma an officer goes through during a stressful incident.

A Stressful Wait

David Klinger's testimony concluded the week. The trial was to start again the following Monday. Two weeks of trial had now gone by, and it was really taking its toll on me mentally, as well as on my family. The weekend was very stressful. I knew the trial was close to ending. The media reported that I gained some public support since some of the facts had come out. I was very nervous, and could not eat or sleep. I spent a lot of time with my family and friends. Together, we spent several hours praying. I had so much hope, thanks to Ron, David and Paul. My family kept me together, as well.

On Monday, September 24, we started week three of the trial. We spent the morning gathering the rest of the witnesses for my defense. Another emergency medical technician testified that she gave me oxygen, and that I was in shock. She also testified that my blood pressure ten minutes after the shooting was 154/110, and she was concerned because it was so high. I also had several friends who are police officers testify that I am a peaceful person, and have an excellent reputation in my community. My training instructor testified about the stress I had gone through. The doctor was barred from testifying, and the jury did not hear that he had treated me for post-traumatic stress disorder. I also had several supervisors testify on my behalf. They said I was a good police officer and known as a peaceful, law-abiding policeman, who did my job professionally.

After all my witnesses testified, I felt good again. The jury was hearing about me as a person, and not about a killer cop who lost control. I felt like they understood me and what I was saying. I believe they saw I was a victim, as well as a police officer. I was a victim because of the suspect and his actions. After my witnesses were finished, we took another recess to regroup. Closing arguments were next, and we were prepared. I was able to thank Ron and David before they left. I know they were both worried for me, and very interested in the outcome. The prosecution gave its closing arguments. Again, they called me names and urged the jury to have the courage to convict a police officer.

They finally rested. Next, it was Paul's turn. The jury liked Paul. They liked the way he conducted himself. While we did get shot down several times, Paul never lost his cool. Paul started his closing argument by saying that a tragedy had occurred. He explained again why the shooting was justified. He also asked the jury to understand what I was going through, and to see the situation as I experienced it. He argued against the prosecutor, and the way she tried to portray me. He went through every detail again. Paul asked the jury if they would consider their wife, husband or child free from danger if they were in my situation, in a very confined area with a car crashing around. Paul also mentioned the World Trade Center attack and pointed out that even a civilian aircraft can be used as a weapon. Motor vehicles are routinely used as weapons against police officers. Paul also told the jury that I cooperated 100 percent and that I had nothing to hide. I had been asked a number of hindsight questions. My training was not challenged by anyone from the state. Paul told the jury that I acted reasonably, under the situation. He said I had control over myself as I was firing because I knew when to stop firing, and did not unload my gun on the suspect. Paul reminded the jury that the prosecutor had not proven her case beyond a reasonable doubt, and that I had proved myself innocent by the evidence and testimony. The prosecutor was then allowed the last rebuttal on closing arguments. Again, the prosecutor said almost the same things.

After the prosecution finished, the judge began reading jury instructions. The judge told the jury to carefully consider the evidence and testimony. He explained to jury members that they could find me guilty or not guilty of the offenses of murder. The case went to the jury on Tuesday afternoon.

On Tuesday night, the jury wanted a copy of my statement to the investigators. They also wanted to see the videotape again. The judge ruled that the jury could be dismissed for the night, and the information they wanted would be given to them on Wednesday morning. The hardest part of the jury deliberation was when we were sent home. If the jury had a question, we were called at home by the lawyers and had to drive back to the courthouse. Every time the phone rang, we did not know if the jury just had another question, or if it had reached a verdict. This happened several times.

On Wednesday morning, jury members were given the materials they had requested. We were in court for about thirty minutes on Wednesday. The jury was now in its second day of deliberations. On the front page of our local newspaper, my story was printed. The paper also had a story on the front page under mine about a Cincinnati police officer who was found not guilty of murder after shooting a man to death. The media were saying that all police officers would be found innocent of killing people. We waited all day and nothing took place. We were happy in one regard. It seemed that members of the jury were really looking at this case and going through all the evidence. They were not in a hurry to get it over with. I think they wanted to make sure that what they were doing was right. We were called to go back to court later in the day and told the jury had not yet reached a verdict. The anxiety was picking up, and I was miserable. I had twelve people deciding whether or not I was going to live my life in peace, or if I was going to be sent to prison for doing my job. That night was extremely difficult. I felt the jury would have a verdict the next day. I spent several hours praying for the ability to cope. I had many friends and family around to comfort me. It was a blessing to have so many people supporting and believing in me. The next day would be the best day of my life. I did not know that then, but it was.

On Thursday morning, we had to go to the courthouse again to check in and wait for the jury members to come back. They were still undecided, and the judge told them to continue deliberations. We were then allowed to go home. A short time after going home, the phone rang. I was taking a nap, as I was mentally exhausted. I heard the phone ring and thought, "This is it." It was not the verdict, but we did have to go back, as the jury had another request. The jury wanted to see the videotape again in the deliberation room with no outside people involved. The judge granted their request. Again, we went home and waited. A few hours later, at 1:30 p.m., the phone rang again. This was it. The jury had reached a verdict. We needed to go right away. The ride to the courthouse was tense. The radio stations reported the verdict was in. Traffic seemed heavy, and it seemed like it was taking for-

ever to get there. I did not want to go. I wanted to stay home and be with my family. I was breaking down, and was scared to death. My mother and family embraced me, and kept me together. I told my mother that no matter what happened, I would be okay. We finally arrived.

The Verdict

We went into the courtroom and sat down. Members of the jury entered the courtroom, and the judge asked if they had reached a verdict. The foreperson told him that they had. The judge then asked for the verdict sheet. The judge read the verdict to himself and seemed shocked. The judge then told everyone in the courtroom that he would not tolerate any emotional outbursts, and advised them to stay seated until the verdict was read. The suspect's mom and dad then left the courtroom. They were not there when the verdict was read. After things calmed down, the verdict was read, "We the jury, find the defendant, Jeff Gabor, not guilty." My head fell to the table and I started to cry. I could breathe again. All of the pressure was gone, and I felt good. It was a huge weight off my shoulders. I hugged Paul and Bill. They did a great job, and it paid off. I was then escorted into a room, where we waited for the suspect's family to leave. The media were in full force to interview me. I declined.

We drove to a secret location and stayed there for a while until most of the news was over. I then went home. It was the greatest feeling on earth. I called Ron and David as soon as I could. It was great talking to them. They did so much for me. I do not think I could have gotten through this without them. God bless them. A couple of days after the verdict, I received dozens of cards from people I did not know. They congratulated me and wished me luck. The father of the suspect told the media that the court never would find a cop guilty of murder. It was the father who had lobbied so hard to have me charged with murder.

Back to Work

In December 2001, I was reinstated by the Hudson Police Department. Since my return, I have had no problems with anyone except the suspect's father. I am also going through the federal court system on civil rights charges, excessive force and wrongful death charges. I am thankful I survived this tragic incident, and am sorry that a young man died. I only wish it could have been different.

I hope and pray that by sharing this story with you, it will make you aware of what can happen if you have to make a split-second decision under stress. As I have learned, people will judge you and form opinions on what you should or should not have done. They have the comfort and security of their own home to make these conclusions, yet not one of them was there. I would like to share some things I learned from this horrible situation, and hope it will help you with your day-to-day encounters.

Do not always rely on your dispatcher to give you critical information during a pursuit, or any incident. It may not be their fault. They have a very important job to do as well. They get flooded with calls and have to deal with a number of things at once. Due to the nature of their job, it is not always possible for them to give accurate information about the offense the suspect is wanted for, or who the individual is. I was not informed that the suspect was mentally disabled, and all I knew was a 27-year veteran police officer was chasing someone and needed help. I do not fault our dispatchers for what took place that day.

If you are involved in a shooting, cooperate with the investigators. They have a difficult job. Ask them questions. As I mentioned before, no one would talk to me or tell me what was going on. I was afraid, and wondered why no one would communicate with me. I did not know what would come next, as I had never been involved in a situation like this. I did question whether or not I should have a lawyer present. It was not because I felt I had done something wrong. No one would tell me what was going to happen. At the trial, a state trooper did testify that I asked him if I should get a lawyer.

There were about ten detectives assigned to the case, and they treated me well, once we talked. We were split up and interviewed at different times. I was never read my rights. I did not think I was in trouble. I felt I had done the right thing by being 100 percent cooperative and answering questions while I was in shock. Again, the incident happened

so fast, and these guys wanted answers immediately. I was afraid, because I could not remember every detail, and concerned that any answer I gave would be wrong. I felt isolated and trapped. They were just doing their jobs, and I understood that. Cooperate fully, but if you want legal advice, seek it. That is your right. Do not lose your cool, and do not be angry with them. Remember, they are there because of the incident. Keep your comments about the incident to yourself. I made comments about little things that were not related to my situation. I made these comments to fellow officers. They want to know what happened. Do not tell them until you have talked to the investigator about the case. I talked to these people in what I thought was confidence. You might think you are talking to friends, but when their name shows up on a prosecution witness list, guess again. Almost everything I said to other officers was put into a report. I thought I was being helpful, and trying to assist in their efforts, but I was wrong.

If you are involved, try to keep your emotions under control. This may be the hardest thing you ever have to do. Focus on what happened. I was so distressed by what went on in my situation I could not remember every detail. This was caused by stress. The fact that my incident lasted 35 seconds also prohibited me from recalling accurately every detail. You are a human being. You are the one who has to recall exactly how it went down. Unfortunately for us, we only have split seconds to make a judgment that could haunt us forever. Whether you are right or wrong, you will be under fire.

As Ron correctly pointed out to me, do not take your emotions out on your family. They love you and will support you. They will be the ones there for you, your family and your friends. Your family will never know what it was like for you. You can talk to them and explain it, but they will never know what it was like as you experienced it. It is not their fault. They did not ask you to become a police officer. You know why you are there and the reason for it. I took my emotions out on my family. When we do this, we hurt the only people on our side. I am lucky that my fiancée did not leave me. She had every reason in the world to do so because of what I put her through. Get help. Talk to your friends, or find someone who has been through it.

Stay away from alcohol. This incident put undue pressure on my family, due to my job and situation. Again, do not blame your family. Be aware that not everyone will be in your corner. Do not expect people to be on your side. People who do not know you will blast you for whatever you did. I avoided places I used to go to because I feared what people thought of me. I did not want to face the people I worked with out of concern that they thought I did something wrong. That was not true with most of the people around me. I did not realize how much support I had, because I was too afraid to look.

It is important to realize that if you make a decision to shoot a suspect, you need to be aware of what can happen to you as a result of doing your job, or fearing for your life. There will be an investigation of some sort to determine if your actions were justified. A report will probably be sent to the prosecutor, and a grand jury may even return an indictment.

Another Trial

Absolutely count on being sued by the family of the suspect. This is happening to me right now. I have a whole new trial that is coming up. So, not only can you be criminally charged and go through state court, you can also be federally charged. In addition, you may face a civil lawsuit in a federal court, depending on the nature of the charges. You will most likely lose your entire life savings, as I have. I lost two other jobs, face mounting legal fees, and my reputation is under attack by the media. All of this happened because of a person who was breaking the law and endangering lives. The long-term agony of living with this is far worse than death. You do not have time to think about all of this when someone is trying to kill you. So, as you read this, do not let it scare you. You have the time now to think about it. Do not let it cause you to hesitate to save your life.

I chose to continue police work, even after everything that has or will happen to me. I had to ask myself a question that only I could answer. If it happens again, could I protect the public, or myself, or would I fail to act because of fear of prosecution? If you fear being prosecuted, which could happen, then you may not do the right thing, and could be killed as a result. If you think that you would hesitate, you need to find another job.

The most important thing you can do is educate yourself, and train as much as you can. Training will help more than you know. In training, you are in a controlled environment where you can make mistakes and learn from them. On the street, it is not controlled, and if you make a mistake or let your guard down, it could cost you your life. I always had the belief that it would never happen to me. I thought that incidents like what happened to me only took place in big towns. Do not think that way. When you least expect something to happen, it will.

The most important question that is asked of me is, "How did you survive the whole situation?" I survived this incident because of my faith in God and my family. It is important to have support groups. I think your church is a good place to start. I also survived because of my strong legal defense. Paul and Bill worked very hard to ensure I would be acquitted. My outstanding experts were a big support to me. They taught me not to second-guess myself, and to believe in myself. Ron and David are true professionals, and good friends. I believe I was given a chance to tell this story because of my will to live. By surviving this incident, I can help other police officers by sharing what I went through. I would like to assist in any way possible to keep officers safe. If my story can save one officer's life, it was worth it to me. Hopefully, it will help officers learn from my experience, and be aware of the consequences. Stay safe, wear your body armor and be aware. God bless all of you.

Update

The civil trial is over. The suspect's family settled the case out of court for $657,000. I was not punished in any way by the settlement. In other words, I was not sanctioned.

Secondly, in the spring of 2003, I received a letter from the Department of Justice, which had launched a criminal civil rights investigation into the shooting. The letter reported that there was insufficient evidence, and that federal charges would not be filed. The Department of Justice was finished with the case.

I am completely out of the woods at this point. Life is somewhat back in order, and while it may take many years to recover fully from this, it is getting better.

Acknowledgments

I would like to thank the following for their help and support, and especially for believing in me. My mother and stepfather, my fiancée and her family, my son, my brothers and sisters, my grandmothers and the rest of my huge family. Also, Ron McCarthy, David Klinger, Larry Glick, R.K. Miller, Paul Welch, Bill Caisley, the National Tactical Officers Association, the Hudson Police Department and the Normal Police Department.

EUGENE P. RAMIREZ

Eugene P. Ramirez, a founding member of Manning & Marder, Kass, Ellrod, Ramirez, Attorneys at Law, graduated from Whittier College School of Law in Southern California (J.D., 1987). He received his undergraduate degree in Political Science from California State University, Long Beach (B.A., 1983), where he minored in Criminal Justice and Public Policy.

Before joining the firm, Gene worked as a deputy district attorney for the Los Angeles County District Attorney's Office, where he conducted numerous misdemeanor and felony jury trials, including murder trials. Mr. Ramirez also has worked for the Long Beach Naval Legal Services Office and as a reserve police officer for the Whittier Police Department and the Monterey Park Police Department.

As a supervising member of the police civil liability team, he combines his civil experience with his former law enforcement background. He serves as an advisor to several public entities on the issues of use of force, policies and procedures, and on employment issues. Mr. Ramirez has acquired significant expertise on civil liability arising out of the use of police dogs in law enforcement, and has lectured widely on the subject to police departments nationwide. He is General Counsel for the United States Police Canine Association and has authored several articles for the USPCA's *Canine Courier.* He was recently retained as a consultant to the United States Secret Service Canine Unit.

Mr. Ramirez is also experienced in defending SWAT teams in civil liability cases, and is an instructor on liability issues for the Los Angeles County Sheriff's Department, the California Association of Tactical Officers (CATO) and the National Tactical Officers Association (NTOA). He was profiled in the April 2003 *California Lawyer* Magazine for Southern California. This award is only given to the top five percent of attorneys in the Los Angeles/Orange County Bar Association. He is also an adjunct professor of Trial Advocacy at Whittier College School of Law. Mr. Ramirez appears regularly on television as a legal commentator, and was a commentator for K-CAL, Channel 9 News during the "O.J. Simpson Trial."

Chapter 18

UNDERSTANDING THE LEGAL PROCESS

Eugene P. Ramirez

INTRODUCTION

Law enforcement officers have a dangerous job. Officers certainly face the risk of personal injury every day they pin on that badge. There are very few jobs where people face the risk of not coming home at night simply by showing up for work. Officers also have to deal with media, which fails to forgive even the slightest errors by peace officers in their efforts to achieve ratings and profits. The media's skewed views often leave law enforcement professionals frustrated. Officers also are increasingly facing the risk of criminal liability when they are compelled to use force. All officers certainly know about the risk of administrative discipline for the decisions they make in the field. What most officers do not fully understand, however, is the risk of civil liability. When an incident happens, your personal assets are suddenly on the line.

The civil liability system can often be confusing, uncomfortable, and as dangerous, at times, as an armed suspect in a dark alley. Officers need help understanding what can often seem to be a never-ending maze. They need practical advice for combating this very real danger. Most importantly, they need to understand the legal concepts that govern the use of force.

Knowledge of the two primary legal defenses available will assist officers in performing their duties with confidence. No one can prevent the filing of a lawsuit and civil litigants and their lawyers are well-armed with persuasive arguments and often twisted versions of the facts. Yet, thorough reporting by officers, along with an officer's comprehension of civil rights law and adequate preparation during litigation, will go a long way toward the successful defense of that lawsuit. Remember also that lawsuits may result in positive change to policy and training. Yes, lawsuits can sometimes benefit law enforcement and should be taken as a challenge as you strive to improve your agency and your own abilities.

First, a caveat. Many attorneys are not experts on the actual use of force. Yet, they are well-trained in the art of civil litigation and constitutional law. They understand the ramifications of failing to follow training and policy–an understanding developed through many years of litigation experience. Understand that your prior training and department's policy control your application of force and the reporting of that force. Knowledge about civil rights law will help you as you apply the training you have received and as you critically analyze the department policies that govern your conduct.

There are a few concepts that an officer must be conversant with in order to survive a civil lawsuit. First, you must know the gist of the Fourth Amendment: Every person has the right to be free from an unreasonable search and seizure. Second, you must know the definition of "objective reasonableness": An officer is judged not by what they think, but by what another officer would do if placed in the same or similar circumstance.

Civil Rights Lawsuits and the Civil Rights Statute

What follows is a brief review of the information you need to know in order to defeat the one adversary you do not train for: the civil litigant.

Most excessive force allegations are brought by plaintiffs alleging civil rights violations. These lawsuits are brought usually pursuant to Title 42 of the United States Code, section 1983 (42 U.S.C. §1983). One of the most dangerous aspects of a lawsuit brought under this statute, is the attorneys' fees provision, pursuant to the 42 U.S.C. §1988. Plaintiffs who win are entitled to collect the attorneys' fees incurred by their lawyers–amounts that can be in the hundreds of thousands of dollars. Of course, plaintiffs often do not get to keep these attorneys' fees because they are often kept by their counsel who supposedly have their best interests at heart.

Most of these civil rights lawsuits are litigated in federal court, often at the request of defense attorneys, because of the more restrictive rules of procedure. These lawsuits, however, can be litigated in state courts. Most of them are accompanied by state "tort" allegations, such as assault, battery and false arrest. The elements of these "tort" allegations are very similar to the elements of the Penal Code sections you enforce.

42 U.S.C. §1983 reads as follows:

> Every person who, under color of any statute, ordinance, regulation, custom or usage, of any State or Territory or the District of Columbia, subjects, or causes to be subjected, any citizen of the United States or other person within the jurisdiction thereof to the deprivation of any rights, privileges, or immunities secured by the Constitution and laws, shall be liable to the party injured in an action at law, suit in equity, or other proper proceeding for redress.

The Reasons Individual Officers Get Sued

Officers often question why they are being per-

sonally sued when a lawsuit has been filed. After all, were they not just doing their jobs? They may also ask why they are being sued in addition to their employing agency. There are a number of reasons why an officer will be individually sued. One reason is economic. A government entity cannot be held liable for punitive damages–those damages meant to punish or meant to set an example for other officers. An individual officer, however, *can* be personally liable for punitive damages. California is one of the few jurisdictions that allow municipalities the *option* of paying a punitive damage award against an officer if the city council or county board of supervisors finds that the officer was acting in the scope of employment, acted within policy, cooperated with their lawyers, and the payment is in the best interest of the municipality. *Most jurisdictions may not even provide this option.* In the unfortunate situation where a jury awards punitive damages against an officer, a municipality is not required and *may not even be able* to pay the damage award. An officer's personal assets, therefore, are always on the line.

Another reason individual officers get sued is personal. The opposing litigant or their attorney may want to exact some type of revenge against the involved officers and may want the officer to suffer discomfort in their personal and professional life. Officers may need to testify in front of a jury about their personal assets, debts, income, and property value if a plaintiff first establishes malice or gross negligence. This is, obviously, embarrassing and uncomfortable, and an officer's personal information becomes a matter of public record. Opposing attorneys will also name individual officers as defendants to make cases bigger and more complicated. They do this to accrue more attorneys' fees, so that if their clients win even a nominal amount, they can collect hundreds of thousands of dollars in attorneys' fees billing rates.

The Standards Governing the Use of Force

Every time an officer uses force, a judge may look at those actions and determine whether they were objectively reasonable under the circumstances. This legal standard applies to more than just the application of deadly force by a firearm. Every use of a baton, police service dog, Taser, O.C. spray or other type of implement must be objectively reasonable under the circumstances. The United States Supreme Court set forth this legal standard in the seminal case *Graham v. Connor*, 490 U.S. 386 (1989). This case requires lower courts to examine excessive force claims brought by plaintiffs under the Fourth Amendment (via 42 U.S.C. §1983) by determining whether the force used was reasonable.

Dethorne Graham was a diabetic who asked his friend to drive him to a local store to purchase orange juice to counteract the onset of an insulin reaction. Upon entering the store and seeing the number of people ahead of him, Graham hurried out and asked his friend to instead drive him to another friend's house. Officer Connor, a local police officer, became suspicious after seeing Graham hastily enter and then leave the store. He followed the car, made an investigatory stop, and ordered the two occupants to wait until he determined what had happened at the store. Graham, however, decided to be uncooperative. He got out of the car, ran around it twice, and finally sat down on the curb, where he passed out briefly. Graham's friend told the officer that Graham was simply suffering from a "sugar reaction." Back-up officers arrived and one of the officers rolled Graham over on the sidewalk and cuffed his hands tightly behind his back, ignoring the friend's pleas to get him some sugar.

One of the officers stated, "I have seen a lot of people with sugar diabetes that never acted like this. Ain't nothing wrong with the M.F. but drunk. Lock the S.B. up." Several officers then lifted Graham up from behind, carried him over to the friend's car and placed him face down on its hood. When he regained consciousness, Graham asked the officers to check his wallet for a diabetic decal that he carried. One of the officers, however, told him to "shut up" and shoved his face down against the hood of the car. Four officers then grabbed Graham and threw him head first into the police car. A friend of Graham's brought some orange juice to the car, but the officers refused to let him have any of the juice. Finally, Officer Connor received a report that Graham had done nothing wrong at the conven-

ience store. The officers drove Graham home and released him.

Dethorne Graham filed a lawsuit, pursuant to 42 U.S.C. §1983, against the individual officers alleging they had used excessive force during this investigatory stop, and, therefore, violated his rights guaranteed to him by the Fourth and Fourteenth Amendments to the United States Constitution. Graham claimed the officers had broken his foot, bruised his forehead and injured his shoulder. He also claimed that he had cuts on his wrists as a result of the incident and that he had developed a loud ringing in his right ear. The lower court eventually ruled in the officer's favor and Mr. Graham appealed this ruling to the United States Supreme Court.

The United States Supreme Court reversed the lower court's ruling and remanded the case for a new trial finding that the lower court had used the wrong standard for assessing excessive force claims. The Supreme Court in this case defined the standard that controls use of force law today, finding that judges must determine whether the officer's actions were "objectively reasonable" in light of the facts and circumstances confronting them. Essentially, courts must determine whether an officer of similar experience would employ the same type of force in a similar circumstance. The officer's subjective motives are not at issue. Evil intentions will not make a Fourth Amendment violation out of an objectively reasonable use of force. Of course, an officer's good intentions will, likewise, not make an objectively unreasonable use of force constitutional.

The objective reasonableness standard requires a careful analysis of the facts presented to the Court. Of course, each set of facts is different. To assist, the Supreme Court gave some guidelines to help lower courts determine whether the force was "objectively reasonable." Courts must consider the severity of the crime at issue, whether the suspect posed an immediate threat to the safety of officers or others and whether the suspect was actively resisting arrest or attempting to evade arrest by flight. Patrol officers must understand that the best place to get the facts to support a finding of objective reasonableness is in the original use-of-force report.

The authors of this Supreme Court opinion really seemed to understand the dangers law enforcement officers can face on a daily basis. The Court found that "officers are often forced to make split-second judgment—in circumstances that are tense, uncertain, and rapidly evolving. . . ." The Court essentially prohibited second guessing from the proverbial "ivory tower" by requiring the lower courts to judge reasonableness from the perspective of a "reasonable officer on the scene, rather than with the 20/20 vision of hindsight." Lower courts are required to stand in the boots of an officer on the scene when determining whether the force used was reasonable. The Supreme Court cautioned lower courts to recognize that "not every push or shove, even if it may later seem unnecessary in the peace of a judge's chambers, violates the Fourth Amendment." No "Monday morning quarterbacking" allowed.

The Primary Defenses: Reasonable Use of Force and Qualified Immunity

Even with lower courts being prohibited from analyzing "with the 20/20 vision of hindsight," the reality is that juries, if given the opportunity, may second guess your actions based on their own understanding of what you do for a living. Typically, judges make decisions of law and juries decide the facts. Though the inquiry on whether force was reasonable is a very fact-intensive issue, the United States Supreme Court, in the *Graham v. Connor* decision, left that analysis to be handled by the judge. It is one of the few situations where the judge is enabled to decide both law and fact. Police defense attorneys, therefore, often bring a motion for summary judgment on behalf of their law enforcement clients. This is the motion that, if successful, will eliminate the case without a need for a jury trial. Attorneys argue two alternative theories in excessive force cases: The use of force was reasonable under the law and/or the individual officers are entitled to qualified immunity.

Understanding these two defenses will enable officers to perform their jobs with confidence. While anyone may bring a lawsuit, these defenses are very helpful in stopping those lawsuits in their tracks. The courts recognize society's vested interest in the job you do every day. The public needs pro-

tection, and when officers act consistently with their training and their department's policy, those courts may be inclined to rule in law enforcement's favor. Nothing can protect an officer who engages in blatant misconduct. Officers, however, who use reasonable force or make reasonable mistakes, have these defenses which serve as a shield.

The reasonable use of force defense allowed by *Graham v. Connor* is simply a factual argument that, in light of the circumstances, the officer's actions were acceptable and reasonable. We often employ experienced police officers as expert witnesses to provide an analysis about the tactics used and offer this analysis in the form of declarations to the court. The best way, however, to get the description of the events before the court is through a detailed police report. Paint a picture for the court of all the factors you faced, being as descriptive as possible. If you include the necessary information, your police defense attorney will be able to make the argument that the force was reasonable under the circumstances.

Outline in your report the number of officers present and how many suspects you were dealing with. It is important to note if you were facing more than one suspect, whether you were alone, and the amount of time it would take or did take for your back-up to arrive. What was the environment like? Were you in a high crime rate area? Was it raining and were you standing on a slippery surface? What was your frame of mind at the time you employed the force? Did you see that the suspect had access to weapons? Were you in a kitchen where the suspect had access to knives and other weapons? Were you in a bedroom where your experience tells you that people often keep handguns? Were there any loose objects that the suspect could have used to inflict blunt force trauma upon you or someone else? And do not forget that there is always a weapon present at every incident scene—yours. How easy would it be for a suspect to gain access to your service weapon? Describe this fact in your report if it is an issue.

Identify in your report the age, gender and physical condition or relative strength of both the officers and the suspects. It is difficult for anyone to admit weakness, but if the suspect has a weightlifter's build and you do not, it is a factor that can be discussed in the initial use-of-force report that helps paint the picture. Were you in a fight where you were experiencing fatigue? Is your suspect a known gang member or dressed in gang attire? Describe his visible tattoos if this affected the level of caution you took. What were you wearing? A full uniform with all of the necessary equipment, or were you working undercover in casual attire? Did you have a radio to call for back-up. Even if you did, did the suspect give you the opportunity to use that radio?

Have you had prior contacts with the suspect or know of other contacts that officers have had with him in the past? If you knew about them at the time you used force, how did they impact your decisions? Was the suspect showing signs of mental illness or drug intoxication? Specify with particularity each symptom you observed. Was the suspect showing an unusual tolerance to pain or acting unexpectedly to the force you were using? The officers at a highly publicized use-of-force incident later described the suspect's bizarre behavior which suggested PCP intoxication, but their use-of-force report was absolutely silent about the symptoms they observed. Have you had specialized training or developed particular skills that help you recognize a specific threat? All of these factors need to come into play in your initial report, and this list is not meant to be exhaustive. Every situation is unique and a conscientious attempt to give a complete, accurate account will go a long way in helping to argue that the force was reasonable under the circumstances.

The other primary defense is qualified immunity. Officers are entitled to qualified immunity if "their conduct does not violate clearly established statutory or constitutional rights of which a reasonable person would have known." *Harlow v. Fitzgerald,* 457 U.S. 800 (1982). Qualified immunity "is an immunity from suit rather than a mere defense to liability." *Hunter v. Bryant,* 502 U.S. 224 (1991). The United States Supreme Court recently clarified the qualified immunity test in a case entitled *Saucier v. Katz,* 533 U.S. 194 (2001). This opinion requires lower courts to first ask whether the facts alleged show the officer's conduct violated a constitutional right.

In *Saucier,* plaintiff was attempting to hang a banner to protest experiments on animals at an event attended by Vice President Gore. Two military police officers dragged plaintiff away from the area to the extent that his feet were "barely touching the ground." Plaintiff was wearing a knee brace at the time. The police officer, however, did not remember seeing the brace. While there was a dispute over whether plaintiff was resisting the arrest, he "was shoved or thrown" into a van. "The reason for the shove remains unclear." In any event, plaintiff was not injured.

Plaintiff brought a lawsuit alleging that the military police officers violated his Fourth Amendment rights by using excessive force. The United States Supreme Court ruled that the officers were entitled to qualified immunity. "[T]he right to make an arrest or investigatory stop necessarily carries with it the right to use some degree of physical coercion or threat thereof to effect it." According to the Supreme Court, an officer may be entitled to use more force than was needed if he acted reasonably but mistakenly. Realizing that police officers have a difficult job given the "limitless factual circumstances" they encounter, the Court went on to say that an officer might correctly perceive all the relevant facts but have a mistaken understanding as to whether a particular amount of force is legal in those circumstances. If the officer's mistake as to what the law requires is reasonable, however, the officer is entitled to the immunity defense.

Police defense attorneys raise this defense in a motion at the earliest opportunity, because the defense is designed to absolve an officer from the lawsuit in its entirety–or at least from the civil rights violation allegation, which is the most serious an officer can face. Just as only individual officers are exposed to punitive damages liability, only individual officers enjoy this defense. Government entities are not entitled to qualified immunity. Though malice or bad motive is irrelevant in determining whether an actual application of force was objectively reasonable, the issue of your "good faith" will come up in a qualified immunity analysis. The critical question asked in this analysis is whether the officer could have *reasonably* believed that their actions were lawful in light of *clearly established law* based on the information the officer had at the time of the incident. The "good faith" inquiry will be focused on whether you *should have known* your conduct was unconstitutional.

A good example of well-established unconstitutional conduct that all officers know about can be derived from *Tennessee v. Garner,* 471 U.S. 1 (1985). This well-known United States Supreme Court case defines when officers may use deadly force. On October 3, 1974, at approximately 10:45 p.m., Memphis police officers Hymon and Wright were dispatched to answer a "prowler inside call." Upon arriving at the scene, they saw a woman standing on her porch gesturing toward an adjacent house. She told them that she had heard glass breaking and that she believed someone was breaking into the house next door. Officer Hymon went behind the house. He heard a door slam and saw a man, later identified as Edward Garner, run across the back yard and stop at a six-foot-high chain link fence at the edge of the yard. With the aid of a flashlight, Officer Hymon was able to see Garner facing him. He saw no sign of a weapon and, although not certain, was "reasonably sure," and "figured" that Garner was unarmed.

Officer Hymon believed Garner to be only 17 or 18 years old and about 5'5" or 5'7". While Garner was crouched at the base of the fence, Officer Hymon called out "police" and took a few steps toward Garner. Garner then began to climb over the fence. Officer Hymon was convinced that if Garner made it over the fence he would elude capture. Hymon then shot the suspect. Garner was taken by ambulance to a hospital where he died after being shot in the back of the head. Ten dollars and a purse taken from the house were found on his body. In using deadly force to prevent Garner's escape, Officer Hymon was acting under the authority of a Tennessee statute and pursuant to Memphis Police Department policy.

On the night of this shooting, Officer Hymon was entitled to rely in good faith upon the Tennessee statute and his own department policy, which allowed him to use deadly force to prevent escape. The United States Supreme Court eventually ruled that an officer's use of deadly force is reasonable only if "the officer has probable cause to believe that the suspect poses a significant threat of death or serious physical injury to the officer or others." This is the famous "*Garner* Fleeing Felon

Rule," where officers cannot use deadly force solely to prevent escape. Every officer now knows that, before using deadly force, they must have probable cause to believe that the suspect poses a threat of *serious physical harm* to the officer or others, or has committed a crime involving the infliction or threatened infliction of serious physical harm. An officer who violates this "Fleeing Felon Rule" today would be acting in direct contradiction to *clearly established law,* and a defense attorney would be hard-pressed to argue that the officer was unaware of the "Fleeing Felon Rule."

The bottom line on qualified immunity is that officers can have "a reasonable, but mistaken belief about the facts or what the law requires in any given situation and still be entitled to qualified immunity." *Romero v. Kitsap County,* 931 F.2d 624 (9th Cir. 1991). The qualified immunity defense "provides ample protection to all but the plainly incompetent or those who knowingly violate the law." *Estate of Ford v. Ramirez-Palmer,* 301 F.3d 1043 (9th Cir. 2002).

Other Factors to Consider When Writing a Police Report

In addition to the factors discussed above, it is important to be descriptive about other factual elements as well. Remember, if a piece of information is to the officer's benefit, and it is not in the original police report, then assume it did not happen. Courts are entitled to assess an officer's credibility by not only what is contained in a report, but also by what is not included in the relevant police report. More litigation has been caused by bad police reports than was ever caused by bad police work. Officers need to describe each action of resistance by the suspect. Did the suspect take a fighting stance or pull away from the officer? An officer should describe each tool used and also describe each time that tool was deployed. Do not just state you struck the suspect with your baton multiple times. Instead, identify each blow, identify the part of the suspect's body you struck, and, most importantly, describe the suspect's reaction to each blow. Remember, it is the suspect's actions which determine the officer's response. Keep this in mind when you document the actions you took to overcome the suspect's resistance so that you could take the suspect into custody. It is critical to document every application of force.

Make sure you lay out in detail the reasons for your preliminary contact with the suspect. Were you responding to a radio call? Did you observe the suspect on a sidewalk and stop to make contact with him? What justified the stop? Did you have reasonable suspicion of potential criminal activity? Was it a consensual encounter? Were you flagged down by a citizen? Also describe in detail the specific orders or commands that you gave to the suspect and each of the suspect's responses. Use the suspect's exact statements if possible. Make sure you also describe the aftermath after you used force. Did you render medical treatment or apply first aid? Did you double lock the suspect's handcuffs to prevent injuries to his wrists? What was the condition of your uniform at the end of the encounter? Was it ripped or damaged in some way? Were you physically injured? Your injuries, no matter how slight, must be described in the police report—even if it is just soreness or a complaint of pain. Did you call a supervisor to the scene? Is there an audiotape or videotaped recording of the incident? If so, make sure your descriptions are consistent with that recording, especially if it is a law enforcement controlled recording device.

It is critical that you not rely on others to write this report for you. Remember that you are not writing for your supervisor or your training officer. You are writing for your own future. Expect to be sued if you use force. And then take the preemptive strike by accurately describing as much as possible in as much detail as possible. Remember that whatever you write in that report is discoverable in a civil lawsuit. The suspect's attorney is going to go over your report with a microscope. The most important piece of advice is to be accurate and, above all, be truthful.

CONCLUSION

Civil rights lawsuits are dangerous, but know that you have attorneys who are absolutely on your side. I have been fortunate to work with hundreds of law enforcement officers. You defend the public daily, and I treat my defense of you as a true privilege. There are ways to protect yourself from the inevitable lawsuit: Conscientious action, comprehension of use-of-force law, and detailed police reports. Taking these preventive measures will assist you in successfully defending yourself from an excessive force lawsuit. This is one aspect of your life where "winning is everything."

ABOUT THE EDITOR

John Kolman retired from the Los Angeles County, California, Sheriff's Department as a Captain after 26¹/₂ years of service, almost nine of which were spent with the Department's tactical unit as a SWAT Team Leader and SWAT Commander. Mr. Kolman was the Chairman of the Inter-Agency In-Transit Security Subcommittee for the 1984 Summer Olympic Games in Los Angeles, and a security consultant for the 1987 Pan American Games in Indianapolis, Indiana.

Founder and former Director of the National Tactical Officers Association (NTOA), Mr. Kolman has lectured extensively on tactically-related subjects throughout the United States and several foreign countries. He is a court-qualified expert witness on the use of force and SWAT operations, and the author of *A Guide To the Development of Special Weapons and Tactics Teams,* Charles C Thomas, Publisher (1982), and *The Trials and Tribulations of Becoming a SWAT Commander,* Charles C Thomas, Publisher (2004). He has also authored numerous articles in the field of tactical operations. In May, 1993, he was selected by the U.S. Department of the Treasury to participate in the investigation and evaluation of the B.A.T.F. operation against the Branch Davidians near Waco, Texas. He testified on three separate occasions before the U.S. Congress regarding this operation. In March, 1998, Mr. Kolman was selected by a government agency to assess the capabilities of the police in Bosnia and Herzegovina to manage civil unrest. Following the assessment, he developed and implemented a one-month training program for both management and operational personnel from throughout this war-torn country. Mr. Kolman received both Bachelor of Science and Master of Arts degrees from California State University at Los Angeles, and is a graduate of the 140th Session of the F.B.I. National Academy.

Mr. Kolman is the recipient of the Sheriff's Department's Exemplary Service Medal and the Distinguished Service Medal, as well as numerous commendations from federal, state and local agencies. He is also the recipient of the NTOA Lifetime Achievement

Award, as well as the Uniformed Services University of the Health Sciences, Department of Military Medicine 1996 Achievement Award, and the International Tactical Emergency Medical Support Association (ITEMS) Lifetime Achievement Award.

Charles C Thomas
PUBLISHER • LTD.

P.O. Box 19265
Springfield, IL 62794-9265

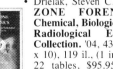
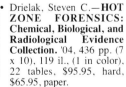
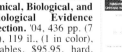
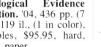

5 easy ways to order!

 PHONE: 1-800-258-8980 or (217) 789-8980

 FAX: (217) 789-9130

 EMAIL: books@ccthomas.com
Web: www.ccthomas.com

 MAIL: Charles C Thomas • Publisher, Ltd. P.O. Box 19265 Springfield, IL 62794-9265